This book is dedicated to my Mummy and Daddy, Joa Frost, an angel still by my side, and Michael Frost. Thank you for all your unconditional love and support. I feel truly blessed to have you both as my parents. Matthew, you will always be my 'little Mattsu'.

Love always,
Me xxxxx

CONTENTS

Introduction

One day not so long ago, when I was nanny to two little girls, we all went out to the park. It was a hot day and the girls were wearing bandannas to keep the sun off their heads. After we had been playing for a while, a woman came over to me. 'How did you manage to do that?' she asked in amazement. 'How did you get them to keep their bandannas on?' I looked at her and lowered my voice to a whisper. '*Superglue*. Just a little line across the forehead.' Judging by her horrified expression, I think she believed me for a fraction of a second. Then she realized I was joking!*

Needless to say, you won't find any techniques involving superglue in this book. You won't find anything that will harm children in any way – physically, mentally or emotionally. What you will find are common-sense ways of dealing with the type of ordinary challenges and problems most parents of children under five face most days of the week. I didn't invent the techniques. I suspect no one single person could put their hand on their heart and claim to have invented them out of the blue. By and large I've simply followed my instincts and observed parents and kids to see what worked and what didn't work. What I've called the 'Involvement Technique', for example, is just what many parents have done instinctively over the years when they have needed to get on with a household chore. The 'Naughty Step Technique' – a way of enforcing a rule by getting a child to think about their behaviour – has probably been around as long as stairs have had steps and rooms have had corners.

I didn't wake up one morning and decide to be a nanny, it just happened. But if I stop and think about it, my first ever Saturday job was in a maternity shop, so it's not surprising I've ended up working with children!

I love meeting different people and I love children. My parents would always joke that I was a real chatterbox when I was a child – and it seems nothing's changed! Mummy and Daddy were always being introduced to new people when we were on holiday because I made friends with their kids first. When I got older, I did a lot of baby-sitting and a bit of part-time nannying. I got my first permanent job after answering an advert posted up on a noticeboard in a bookshop.

Fifteen years later and I've had a lot of hands-on experience. I've been a permanent nanny, a temporary nanny and a trouble-shooting nanny. I've gone on holidays with families, moved home with them and even moved continents with them. I've looked after children ranging in ages from a few hours old to fourteen. I've answered countless calls from worried parents at 2 a.m., and from worried friends of those families I've worked for. Since the first series of the television programme *Supernanny*, I've been overwhelmed with letters from people I've never met who have tried the techniques featured on the programme and wanted to tell me how things have turned around for them. It's just wonderful to hear from them and get that positive feedback.

Some of those letters point out that I'm not a parent. That's true. I'm not a paediatrician, either, or a child psychologist. I've had no formal training to do what I do. Which puts me in much the same position as most parents, without the intense emotional attachment (although us nannies have feelings too!).

The big difference is that I've had many years of experience looking after all sorts of children at all stages and I'm not meeting these challenges for the first time. I've seen children through weaning and toilet training, teething, tantrums and the first day at school. Along the way I've observed behaviour, listened to other people talking about childcare issues and, most importantly, I've listened to my own gut instincts.

Quite early on, I worked out that nannying isn't just about looking after kids and nursery duties. In some ways, you are the bridge between the child and the parent. It puts you in the unique position of observing how families work. It's a dynamic that constantly fascinates me – the way everything is linked and related. You can see this clearly if you're in an objective position, without the tug on the heartstrings. The trouble is that when many parents find themselves in difficulties they're too emotionally involved to see the bigger picture.

This book is a way of helping parents step back and see the bigger picture. It's what I do on *Supernanny* when I'm working with individual families who've become troubled – simply because they've unknowingly allowed themselves to get trapped in a pattern that is sending them round in the same old negative circles. I don't think there's such a thing as a 'bad' child. I believe that every child has the potential to behave as expected. By that I don't mean Goody Two Shoes. I mean happy, relaxed children who have their own individual characters but who know where the limits are.

Everything I've seen and experienced convinces me that children need boundaries. And to keep those boundaries in place there needs to be discipline. Discipline is not about harsh punishment. A key part of it, in fact, is praise. But it does mean setting rules and backing up the rules with firm and fair control.

A lot of parents find it hard to discipline their kids. It could be that they fear their children won't love them any more. The result is that they let their kids take charge when they're not equipped to do that. And when you're a child, being in charge is a confusing and unhappy place to be.

Imagine walking into a bank to pay in a cheque and you're asked to step into the manager's shoes. Without the training, without working your way to the top, you wouldn't have the first idea what to do. It's the same with kids. Kids who find themselves in charge are in a situation that they mentally just cannot handle.

I had a secure, loving upbringing. I was blessed with parents who gave me self-belief and told me the world was my oyster. Neither of them ever broke a promise to me. My mother was an inspiration. She taught me so much without me even realizing I was being taught. My father made me feel safe – the world couldn't touch me. If I was worried about something, we would talk it through and he would reassure me. At the same time, though, my parents insisted on standards, on showing respect and on manners, in the way we all behaved both to each other and to other people. But I was still a child. I could get mucky, dirty and have fun like all kids, without the worries of the world resting on my shoulders.

Parenting is hard these days. Our society has changed. When I was a child I could go to the park with my brother Matthew without my parents over-worrying. People didn't even lock their doors where we lived. Now parents worry all the time. Every day there are scare stories in the media about what's dangerous or harmful for children; the next week those same reports are contradicted. It makes it difficult to know where you stand. At the same time, it seems being a parent has become so competitive. It's hard to relax and trust your instincts when other parents are constantly telling you how advanced and well-behaved their kids are.

In the past, there were often grandparents and other family members nearby who could lend a hand and give support and advice. Many parents today find that they have none of these traditional support systems in place. When both parents work, that means more stress and isolation. When there's just one parent coping with kids on their own, it's even harder. In a recent survey of British families for the charity Parent Talk one-third of all parents who took part considered themselves to be failures. That's a real pity.

Some people naturally take to parenting like ducks to water. Some don't. It's just something else that has to be learned, understood and practised. The more you know, the more you read and talk to people, the more you will trust yourself, find your own feet and make your own choices. Be confident. How you bring up your kids is your choice – it's up to you.

Raising your children is the most important role you will ever have. You are literally giving them strong foundations for life. But it doesn't have to be a slog. Parenting can and should be a joy.

When the opportunity came along to get involved in *Supernanny* (another advert, this time in a magazine) I saw it as a chance to put across some ideas and messages that I felt strongly about. We made the pilot, which involved showing a single parent how to get to grips with her four children. Together we worked through techniques on discipline, management and praise. These techniques worked. The result was one contented mum, four happy manageable kids and two weeks later I found myself with a television series.

For me, *Supernanny* has been and continues to be a wonderful chance to share the experience and lessons I've learned from working with families. It has also been a chance for me to give that something back.

Enjoy your children.

---

* ...So how *do* you get a child to keep her hat on? It's easy.
When she takes it off, you tell her to put it back on. She takes it off.
You tell her to put it back on. She takes it off. You tell her to put it back on.
She takes it off. You tell her to put it back on. She takes it off.
You tell her to put it back on. She takes it off. You tell her to put it back on ...

MY TOP TEN RULES

IF I COULD SUM UP MY APPROACH TO CARING FOR CHILDREN, THESE WOULD BE MY TOP TEN RULES. THEY'RE BASED ON OBSERVATION, NOT ON THEORY. THEY APPLY TO MOST SITUATIONS YOU'RE GOING TO FACE AND YOU'LL FIND THEM SUMMARIZED AT THE END OF EACH CHAPTER IN THE SECTION ON TROUBLE-SHOOTING, WHERE I'LL BE MORE SPECIFIC ABOUT HOW THEY APPLY IN DIFFERENT CASES.

1. PRAISE AND REWARDS

The best rewards are attention, praise and love. Sweets, treats and toys are not necessary as rewards. A star chart or a special outing can back up a pattern of good behaviour.

2. CONSISTENCY

Once you have made a rule, don't change it for the sake of a quiet life or because you're embarrassed. Make sure that everyone – which includes carers and your partner – keeps to the same rules as well. A rule is a rule is a rule.

3. ROUTINE

Keep your home in basic order and maintain a routine. Set times for waking, meals, bath and bed are the cornerstones of family life. Once a routine is in place, you can be a little flexible, if you're on holiday, for example. It's a framework, but it doesn't have to be rigid.

4. BOUNDARIES

Children need to know there are limits to their behaviour – which means what is acceptable and what is not. You need to set rules and tell them what you expect.

5. DISCIPLINE

You can only keep the boundaries in place by discipline. This means firm and fair control. It may just take an authoritative voice and a warning to get the message across. Otherwise, there are other techniques you can use, none of which involve punishment.

6 WARNINGS

There are two kinds of warning. One tells a child what's coming next –
you're the Speaking Clock telling her that bathtime is coming up soon,
or that you're getting near to putting her lunch on the table. The other
is a warning for bad behaviour. That gives her the chance to correct her
behaviour without any further discipline.

7 EXPLANATIONS

A small child can't understand how you want him to behave unless you
tell him. Show and tell to get the message across. Don't reason or make
it too complicated – just state the obvious. When you are disciplining
a child, explain why in a way that is appropriate for his age. Ask him
if he understands the reason why he has been disciplined so that the
message hits home.

8. RESTRAINT

Keep cool. You're the parent and you're in charge. Don't answer a
tantrum by a display of anger or respond to shouting by shouting back.
You're the adult here. Don't let them wind you up.

9. RESPONSIBILITY

Childhood is all about growing up. Let them. Allow them to do small,
achievable things to boost their self-confidence and learn the necessary
life and social skills. Get them involved in family life. But make sure
your expectations are reasonable. Don't set them up for failure.

10. RELAXATION

Quality time is important for everyone, including yourself. Let your
child unwind at bedtime with a story and cuddles. Make sure you, your
partner and your other kids have quality time for individual attention.

Ages and stages

The first five years of childhood are a time of rapid change on all fronts – physically, mentally and emotionally. The physical milestones are easy to spot. In what seems like the blink of an eye, the beautiful little bundle you brought home from the maternity ward sits up, crawls, then takes his first tottering steps. Before long, he's mountaineering over the side of his cot and getting into everything.

What's going on inside your child's head is every bit as dramatic, though far less obvious. Between birth and five years old she will make huge advances in the way she understands the world and relates to those around her.

'Isn't Jemima walking yet? Molly walked at nine months.'

There's enough competitiveness attached to parenting these days without me adding to it. The point of this chapter is not to burden you with anxiety if your child is not meeting a particular 'target' or to suggest you give yourself a pat on the back if he is streets ahead. It's simply to show what you can realistically expect from each stage. Or, more importantly, what you shouldn't expect.

Knowing what makes your child tick will help you adjust your parenting skills to suit her stage of development. Time after time in my work I've seen parents trying to 'reason' with a child who is simply too young to follow a logical conversation. I've seen toddlers asked to choose between a huge range of options when they have next to no means of making those kinds of decisions.

Once a child starts to talk, it's surprising how quickly parents seem to forget that they are not dealing with a pint-sized, wayward adult but someone whose take on the world is still very basic. Just as you wouldn't expect a six-week-old baby to pull herself to standing, you shouldn't expect a two-year-old toddler to have the social and mental skills of a child twice her age.

All this has a direct bearing on how you look after your kids. Understanding how children change and grow – inwardly as well as outwardly – helps every parent meet their child's needs in the right way and in their own time.

The new baby: birth to six months

A newborn baby has no idea what a person is. He doesn't yet know that the person who is holding him is his mother, or that the person holding him is separate from him at all. But he is tuned right in to the sight of your face, the feeling of being held, the sound of your voice. That's because deep down he knows his survival is going to depend on getting his needs regularly met by someone else. Which means you.

Studies have shown that babies can hear in the womb and it is thought that they may even recognize their mother's voice from birth. For mothers, on the other hand, it takes a while to recognize their child's cry and even longer to work out what that cry means. Hunger? Wind? Tiredness? What no mother would deny is that crying works. That's because it's supposed to.

The early months are a steep learning curve. If it's your first baby, you're going to feel a bit like you're on a rollercoaster – high as a kite one minute, all at sea emotionally the next, pretty tired most of the time. What's most important about this stage is not how expertly you can change a nappy but that you keep on responding to your baby's needs, and that you get your own needs met, too.

You cannot spoil a baby. Contrary to what your mother or grandmother may tell you, your baby is too young to be 'wrapping you round her little finger' – that delightful stage is yet to come! By responding to your baby when she cries, you are not 'giving in' to her, you are giving her tender loving care. Each time you do, she learns to trust that her needs will be met in the future.

Leaving a young baby to cry for long periods in the first four months of life doesn't teach him to wait a bit longer for a feed, until the time is more convenient for you. It doesn't teach him that he doesn't need another cuddle. It doesn't teach him to go back to sleep. It teaches him that there is no one out there who cares and that there's nothing he can do about it.

In the same way, discipline has no role at all in the early months. That is not to say that babies do not benefit from the reassurance of routine. The early weeks may show very little consistency when it comes to eating and sleeping patterns. By three to six weeks you'll probably find things have become much more predictable.

You can't force a two-month-old baby into a routine when it comes to sleeping, but you can ease her into a feeding routine. Start by observing how much milk your baby takes. If she cries after a feed, she might be a hungrier than average baby and need more. Between three to six weeks, as babies take more milk, most fall into a pattern of wanting a feed every two to four hours.

Now you've got a choice here. You can go with the flow, or you can use that pattern to develop a routine. It's up to you. But remember, as a parent, you have more control over the situation than you think. If your baby seems to be wanting a feed at the same times each day, but those times mean you are woken often during the night, you can shift things along by feeding her slightly earlier than usual, until the intervals are easier for you to cope with. Sometimes if you give a breastfed baby a bottle at 11 p.m., she can hold out until 4 a.m. before she needs another feed.

Babies need a lot of physical care from the word go – feeding, changing, bathing, soothing. But they also need stimulation. They can't talk yet, but they love to hear your voice and watch your face. Keep communicating and before very long you'll be rewarded with the first smile. A short while after that will come the first babbling sounds as your baby 'talks' back, imitating the sounds you have made to her.

NEW BABIES REALLY ENJOY:

- Loads of kisses

- Close physical contact – cuddling, carrying, back-rubbing and massaging

- Watching faces – in the early weeks, the human face is the best toy of all

- Rocking and rhythmic jiggling

- Music and the sound of your voice

- Colourful patterned objects at a fairly close range, particularly those that move

COPING STRATEGIES:

- Take every chance you can to rest. Sleep while the baby's sleeping.

- Keep things ticking over, but don't expect to achieve domestic perfection.

- Enlist help from your partner, friends, mother – anyone who can share the load of cooking, shopping, and so on.

- Set aside at least some time for your significant others – your partner and other children – to nip any feeling of resentment or jealousy in the bud.

- Share baby duties – bathing, winding, nappy changes.

- Feel human again. Pamper yourself. Get your hair done.

The older baby: six months to 18 months

Enormous changes have taken place in the first six months.
Your helpless infant has become a baby who can hold his head
up, roll, grab a toy, smile, laugh, babble and recognize Mum,
Dad, brothers and sisters, and other familiar faces. He will have
started on his first solid food; he may be taking drinks from a
cup. The second half of the first year, your baby really begins
to explore the world.

During this stage, physical development is pushing forward
to that first tottering step, which often occurs some time around
or before the first birthday, and nearly always by 18 months.
Increasing mobility, by rolling and crawling, means your baby
no longer has to wait for the world to be brought to her; she can go
and look for it herself. And when she finds it, she usually puts it
in her mouth. If you haven't done so already, now's most definitely
the time to think about child-proofing your home and being extra
careful with hygiene – see Action Stations, page 42.

Every day your baby will seem more like a little person, with
his own likes and dislikes and with his own individual character.
Feeding and sleeping should be much easier; if not, there are
strategies you can adopt that are featured elsewhere in this book.
But what you should bear in mind is that until your child is at least
a year old he is still a baby. When he cries, he's letting you know
he needs something or that something has upset him – maybe it's
just that you've told him 'no'. You can't 'spoil' him at this stage
any more than you can spoil a newborn.

Babies of this age sometimes get into things they shouldn't.
A baby pulls a cup off a shelf because a) he can and b) no one
stopped him. He doesn't pull a cup off a shelf to annoy you or defy
you or because he is naughty. It's just where his mission to explore
has taken him that day. 'Look! A smooth blue thing! Let's put it
in my mouth and see what it is. Oops. Too heavy! Where's it gone?'

You can't use discipline on a ten-month-old baby, but you can
and should warn her not to do something. Use a firm, low voice
to say 'No' or to warn her not to touch. You can also explain why.
'That's hot.' She won't understand the words, but she'll respond

to your tone and it will get you in the habit of explaining, which will become much more important later.

In many ways, this is a delightful age; in other ways, it can be pretty testing. You have to keep a step ahead of the game; eyes in the back of the head come in handy. You'll be able to get less done while your baby is awake because she's more mobile – and she'll be awake for longer. During this time, you'll also notice that your baby needs increasing attention from you in the form of play. She can't yet do much by herself, but she's old enough to get bored when she isn't getting enough stimulation. Putting her in a playpen with plenty of toys and something to look at can help to ease the strain for short periods. But don't dump the baby in a playpen or cot when you're angry or fed up or when she's crying – she'll come to associate it with bad feelings.

TEETHING

If boredom is a new reason for crying at this age, so is teething. Just when you congratulated yourself on getting into some kind of routine, here comes the tooth monster to upset the apple cart. The first tooth, which appears around six months, usually comes as much as a surprise to the parents as it does to the baby. After you've got through the first bout of teething, you'll know how to spot the signs the next time. And the time after that.

Once the first tooth is cut, the key is knowing when a child is teething, when she's sick and when she's just having an off-day. If her temperature is very raised or she has other signs of illness, you need to take her to the doctor without delay. If she's just fretful and shows no other signs, she's probably not teething.

SIGNS OF TEETHING:

- Red cheeks. I call this 'noughts and crosses' cheeks, because the redness often shows up as fine red criss-cross lines.

- Drooling

- Biting down hard on everything

- Small white clear bubbles on the gums

- A slight temperature, raised by no more than a degree. If the temperature goes up, seek medical attention.

- Smellier nappies than usual – the smell is unmistakable

- Sometimes a nappy rash

- Fretful crying and waking in the night – it hurts!

- Slight loss of appetite

REMEDIES:

- Hard teething rings. Some can be frozen for extra relief.

- Herbal teething powders

- Mild sedatives to take away the pain

- Plenty of comfort and empathy

SEPARATION ANXIETY

Another feature of this stage is that the baby will generally show signs of becoming even more attached to his mother, preferring Mum above everyone else. This often takes the form of protest or distress when Mum leaves the room or even when she moves towards the door. As long as your baby can see you, he's happy, but as soon as he can't, he begins to cry. Children vary as to how clingy they are and how long this stage lasts, but it generally peaks at about nine months and tails off gradually afterwards, reappearing again at 18 months. It's often called 'separation anxiety' and it's thought to be a sign that the baby is now old enough to remember and compare. He knows you're leaving and he knows he's not going to like it when you go, because he didn't like it the last time.

When you can't even go for a pee without triggering a bout of wailing, you may find your patience becomes as strained as your bladder. If you have arranged to go back to work during this period, you may find your plans at odds with this particular stage of development.

EASING SEPARATION ANXIETY:

* Make sure your child is not ill or under emotional stress. Children can also get clingy for those reasons.

* Accept that it's a stage and it will pass. The worst time for separation anxiety will be before the first birthday.

* Don't allow yourself to get angry or feel trapped. Take a deep breath when you start to feel overwhelmed or stressed.

* If you have to leave the room quickly for a short period, keep chatting to your baby to let her know you're still around.

* Don't vanish when she's not looking.

* If you need to leave your child with a carer during this period, make sure she gets to know that new person well first. It will help her to settle in.

* Reassure your partner that he hasn't done anything wrong and the baby is not taking sides! Dads can feel left out when separation anxiety is at its worst. They also need to know that this will pass and that there are other ways they can help.

* I like to play peekaboo games with young children. It helps to teach them that what they can't see is still there. I might pull a sheet over my head or get on the bed and cover my whole body with the duvet. With older children, I'll turn myself into Paul Daniels and make balls disappear under cups. If you can make it fun and make them laugh, they learn much more quickly.

The toddler: 18 months to three years

After a child has taken his first step, things will have started to get even more interesting. He will have been launched like a NASA probe into a whole new stage of mobility. All sorts of things will have become much more fun to play with, not to mention to take to bits. Full speech will still be some way off, but by 18 months he may be saying a few recognizable words. One of which will almost certainly be 'no'.

Which brings us to the really interesting part. From now until around three years old, your child is officially a 'toddler'. She's no longer a baby, but she doesn't have anything like the skills, physical, mental or social, that she'll have by her first day at school. Like the teenager, she's somewhere in between. And sometimes that's a nice place to be and sometimes it isn't – for you and for her. That gives us another first. The First Tantrum.

Unlike the previous stage, when the world was a wonderful, surprising thing to explore, the toddler rapidly discovers that the world – and that includes you – often exists simply to prevent him getting what he wants when he wants it: which is NOW. He has new physical freedoms he's just itching to try out. For the first time, he's getting an idea of what it's like to be a little individual with a will of his own. The problem is that he's not yet equipped to be one. For a very good reason: the part of the brain that will eventually give him self-control is not yet fully developed. Although he's striving for independence, he's still very dependent on you.

Even if your toddler is talking nineteen to the dozen and seems to be understanding what you say, his mind works very differently from yours. Up until two and a half at the earliest, there are a number of key things that he just can't do or understand.

Toddlerhood, which used to be called the 'Terrible Twos', has stages of its own. When it begins, generally before two, your child will have next to no control over her impulses and will often be frustrated by her own inabilities or by the world around her. As it comes to an end, around about three or slightly later, she will have matured to the point that you can expect some self-control. Not much, but some.

Toddlerhood is challenging. But it doesn't even have to be a bad time if you approach it with sensible expectations. Toddlers can be stroppy, illogical, exhausting and unpredictable. But they can also be funny, loving, enthusiastic and full of life. Enjoy this time while you can.

WHAT MAKES TODDLERS TICK:

★ Patience is not a toddler virtue. Some toddlers can hang on for a bit but many can't wait – not even for a minute.

★ He can't plan ahead. If he has an impulse, he'll act on it and he won't have the first idea where that's going to take him or what he'll feel like when he gets there.

★ He can't control himself.

★ He has no sense of danger.

★ His memory is limited. That means you're going to have to repeat yourself. Over and over.

★ He doesn't understand what a promise is until it's delivered. When he wants something, he wants it right away. His mind will be set on one thing. That means you can't bargain with him. Or you can try, but you'll lose.

★ He can't cope with too many choices. He simply doesn't understand what 'either…or' is all about. A lot of things he'll say he wants will be contradictory. He'll want his shoes on and he'll want his shoes off – at the same time.

★ He can't understand that his actions may affect other people's feelings. He doesn't want to take turns. If you say, 'Let Susie have the toy for a little while', he'll think the toy has gone for good. Cue explosion.

★ He wants more attention than it is humanly possible to give and he wants it for longer than there are hours in the day.

COPING STRATEGIES

Reasoning, pleading, bargaining, threatening – none of these work with this age group. For these strategies to work your child would need mental powers she just does not yet have.

Setting boundaries, firm and fair control and routine do work. As soon as toddlerhood sets in, your child will do everything in her power to rule the roost and get her own way. At times it might seem to you like she is forever having a mad moment – usually after she's pushed another toddler over at playgroup and you're dying of embarrassment. But she isn't being malicious and she isn't being aggressive on purpose. She is resorting to physical behaviour because she can't resolve what she's feeling verbally.

That doesn't mean you should give in or turn a blind eye. Nor does it mean you should try to turn back the clock and stamp on all attempts at independence, however messy and time-consuming they are. At this stage it doesn't matter if your child covers his face, the table and the floor with dinner in his attempt to feed himself. It does matter if he's using the full range of toddler weapons – screaming, kicking, throwing tantrums – to turn the household upside down and impose his will. What he needs now are clear boundaries and the sense that there's something bigger out there that he cannot control – which is you.

Consistency starts to become a real issue at this time. Before, if your child noticed any differences in the care she received, she wouldn't have known how to turn that to her advantage. Now, however, she will sense that there is much mileage to be gained by 'divide and rule'. Divide and rule is one of the first manipulation strategies that young children master. They learn this one fast. If you don't present a united front, or if you change your tune according to how strong you're feeling on any given day, your toddler will find that chink in your armour like a heat-seeking missile.

TANTRUMS

Your child is very unlikely to get through toddlerhood without erupting in one of those spectacular floor shows that is also known as a tantrum. Some children are more prone to tantrums than others; they seem to have a shorter fuse. Perhaps it's just something in their makeup.

The tantrum is where the toddler comes up bang against the world and the world doesn't budge. It can be triggered by many different things but the root cause is always some form of frustration. Either your child has found she can't do something that she wants to do because she doesn't yet have the necessary skills to do it, or something hasn't turned out the way she expected, or you have stopped her from doing something she wants to do, or tried to make her do something she doesn't want to do – or she has simply got to the end of her emotional tether. Whatever the reason, the fuse is lit and everything blows.

It's bad enough when the tantrum happens on the living room floor. But it can just as easily happen at the supermarket, in the car, at a friend's house, in front of your parents … or any other place where it's going to be a million times more excruciating.

You can minimize the frustration your child encounters at this age but you can't get rid of it completely: it's built into the learning process and your child is at the stage where he is wired to learn. Involvement techniques and similar strategies outlined in the chapter Setting Boundaries (page 58) can sometimes head a tantrum off at the pass. But not always.

What you mustn't do once the tantrum has started is give in. Giving in to a tantrum is the best way of ensuring that there will be plenty more where that one came from. You've just proved it worked.

Once a child is in the throes of a full-blown tantrum, it's pretty terrifying – for you and for her. She has literally 'lost it' and is absolutely flooded with feelings of rage. Some children run around screaming, some fall on the floor kicking and yelling, some will headbutt the furniture or even you.

Here's how to deal with a tantrum:

- The first thing to do is to make sure she can't hurt herself, hurt other people or damage things.

- Try to stay calm. Anger will only inflame the situation. If you can't guarantee you'll keep your temper, leave the room. The worst thing you can do is have a tantrum back.

- Forget about trying to reason with her. She can't hear you (and doesn't want to).

- Some children come out of a tantrum quicker if they are held securely. With others, that makes it worse.

- Remove yourself from the room – if you can – once you are sure she's not going to hurt herself or damage anything. If the tantrum is semi-deliberate, as it can be when an older toddler wants her way, removing attention completely can do the trick.

CLINGINESS

The drive to independence is a powerful process that pushes the toddler forward. At the same time, he can be surprisingly clingy. This is not a time when he will separate easily from you. He's unlikely to wail every time you leave the room, unlike the nine-month-old, but he'll be keen to know that you're around and won't like being left with someone else he doesn't know or trust very well.

Although your child won't necessarily cry when you leave the room, she may well cry, scream and generally kick up a fuss when you go out and leave her with a babysitter. Some children react so badly and get so hysterical that parents abandon a social life altogether rather than go through the experience again. Sometimes the child's anxiety seems to transfer itself to the parents, so they become unusually worried that something will happen when they are out of the house.

Here's how to cope:

* Use a sitter that your child knows and likes. Don't spring a stranger on him.

* Ask the sitter to come early so that your child can get stuck into a fun activity before you leave.

* Explain calmly that you're going out and that you'll be back.

* Give him a kiss and a cuddle and say, 'See you later'.

* Leave promptly.

* Remind yourself that the tears will probably be over by the time you've turned the corner.

* Repeat this during the daytime, too, at a crèche or at a friend's house, so your child can see the pattern.

TOILET TRAINING

Timing is everything when it comes to toilet
training. It's a big mistake to start too early –
it always leads to problems later on. There's
a very good reason why you shouldn't even
think about toilet training before two or
two and a half. Before 18 months, a child is
physically incapable of controlling his bowels
or bladder. It takes longer for him to
understand cause and effect. When a child is
ready, both physically and mentally – which
may not be until the age of two or three –
toilet training can often be easy and quick.

See Toilet Training, page 104.

The pre-schooler: three to five

Toddler behaviour doesn't magically go away at three; in fact, many experts consider children as old as four still technically to be toddlers. Self-control comes gradually and tantrums may lessen because a child can reason better, but they won't disappear completely. The maturing process can also be upset by the arrival of a new brother or sister. Suddenly that sensible little four-year-old vanishes and you've got your bolshy toddler back again.

But somewhere between three and five, toddlerhood begins to wane. The brain is now more developed. There's an increase in self-control and less acting on impulse. Your child is learning to think and beginning to play with other kids rather than simply alongside them. He can wait (a little). Altogether he's less wrapped up in his own little world and beginning to realize that other people live in it too.

This is the age of constant questions. Speech development varies, but by the age of three, many kids can express themselves pretty clearly. If the two-year-old's favourite word was 'No!', the three-year-old's is 'Why?' Kids at this stage not only ask a lot of questions, they love to challenge you and get involved in conversations. But a full grasp of reasoning is still some way off. Don't expect them to follow a logical argument or a detailed explanation. When a three-year-old wants her way, 'Why?' is just a more sophisticated version of 'No!' This becomes obvious when you've given her an explanation and it promptly leads to another 'Why?'

A young child's powers of reasoning being what they are, many find it difficult to separate truth from fiction, or fact from fantasy. Whatever pops into his head somehow becomes true. Around the age of four an 'imaginary friend' can appear out of the blue and hang around for a while. Often that imaginary friend will have similar likes and dislikes: 'Binky doesn't like peas either.' Sometimes 'Binky' will be blamed when the child has done something wrong.

Make-believe, tall tales and imaginary friends don't mean your child is developing into a liar; it's just a normal stage of development and a sign of an imagination in overdrive. Without directly challenging the child or denying his very real feelings, you can start to introduce him gently to the difference between what is true and what isn't. Teach him that it's good to tell the truth and take responsibility for what he does, and not blame others – even imaginary others – all the time.

MAKING FRIENDS

One of the main ways in which this age group differs from toddlers is that they start to be able to play with other kids. When a toddler plays, she's entirely absorbed in her own world. She might play contentedly alongside another child for a little while, and she might watch the other child playing, but she won't play with her.

Sharing does not come any more naturally to three-year-olds but at this age they start to enjoy playing with other children, which gives you something to build on. By four, kids are slightly better at understanding that other people have feelings just like they do. This eventually matures into a much more developed form of shared play.

At five, your child will have come an incredibly long way from the newborn baby who had no idea that he was a separate being from you. At five, your child not only knows there are other people out there, he is able to show concern about their feelings, too.

I'm a firm believer in the benefits of routine for young children. A routine provides a clear structure for daily life. It also allows you to arrange things so that everyone gets some quality time for themselves.

Small children function best when things are predictable and when more or less the same things happen at the same time each day. There are good reasons for this. If you don't have a set time when your child goes to bed, for example, sometimes you will be trying to put her to bed when she's not tired and at other times you'll be trying to put her to bed when she's overtired. You will think she's playing up when what she really needs is sleep. A child's bedtime is too important a part of their day and has too much of a knock-on effect on everyone else in the household to be left to such a hit-and-miss approach. In the same way, many parents don't realize that moving mealtimes around drastically or leaving too long a gap between them can play havoc with their child's blood sugar levels, leading to mood swings and unnecessary tiredness.

A routine will help you meet your child's physical needs at the right time – food when she's hungry, bed when she's tired. Set times for key activities are essential. Going through the same stages every day also means a child knows what to expect. Without a clear routine, when basically anything be handled in a very different way from an infant. She will be desperate to try things out for herself and hugely resistant if you persist in babying her by not allowing her to attempt simple tasks such as feeding herself. She'll be too little to do that neatly, but you'll save yourself unnecessary conflict if you let her express her independence in ways that don't harm anyone. She needs to learn. Don't suppress that.

Don't expect perfection. Work with what you've got. Get real and you won't be setting your child up for failure.

BE CONSISTENT

Many parents make up the rules as they go along. That's okay – in some circumstances you have to. The problem comes when parents don't consult each other about the rules they set. The result is often inconsistency. It's worth making some time to sit down together and discuss a common approach. What type of behaviour do you both consider unacceptable? What are you prepared to be more relaxed about? Where do you differ? It is essential to reach an agreement so that you have one set of house rules that everyone can follow. If Mum and Dad don't present a united front, children very quickly learn to play one off against the other emotionally.

When you and your partner have very different ideas about how you expect your kids to behave, it will quickly become impossible to enforce any rules at all – good, bad or indifferent. Talking things over can help to air what lies behind your different approaches. It may be that you were brought up in a stricter household than your partner, or vice versa. That might never have mattered until now. But the arrival of a child can reveal differences between you and your partner that you were not aware of before. Whatever your individual expectations, now's the time to sort them out and come up with a shared approach.

The parent who is with the child most of the time may have a better idea of what that child is capable of understanding and therefore which rules are most appropriate for that particular age group. At the same time, that parent may be too worn out by the ceaseless demands of a bolshy toddler to see the wood for the trees and spot how that child is walking all over them. Open the lines of communication and keep them open, so you not only deal with the current situation but are also able to anticipate the changes to come.

UNACCEPTABLE BEHAVIOUR

There are certain types of behaviour that are always beyond the pale. Your child may yet be too young to understand the reasons why, but she needs to be shown, clearly and firmly, that there are some things she is not allowed to do. The 'strictly forbidden' category includes behaviour that hurts other people – hitting, biting, punching, pushing, name-calling – and behaviour that could endanger the child herself – such as unbuckling her seat belt or not holding your hand when crossing a road. When a child is very young, such behaviour is largely thoughtless and impulsive, but as soon as she shows signs of doing it on purpose, firm and fair control and enforcement of the rules are required. If you don't teach your child not to hit you or her brothers and sisters, she will think she can hit strangers or other children outside the home. It's a moral issue.

LESS IS MORE

When it comes to household rules for young children, a few clear rules are better than too many. If you have a rule about simply everything, you'll spend more time policing your kids than parenting. A small child can't tell the difference between an important rule – 'hitting people is wrong' – and a petty one – 'keep your mouth closed when you're chewing'. When he's very small, forget about minor misbehaviour and focus on the big stuff. Constantly bringing your kids up short takes all the fun out of family life and heightens tension. Toddlers get frustrated enough in the daily course of events; don't pile on the opportunities for more frustration or you'll have a real battle on your hands.

As children get older, you can develop a new level of rules once they have mastered the one before. Move with your child as he develops.

Working with other carers

Clear guidelines – a daily routine and agreed house rules – help a great deal when you are sharing the care of your children with others. Not only do Mum and Dad have to work together and follow more or less the same agenda, so should grandparents, childminders, babysitters, au pairs and nannies.

Before you leave your children in the care of other people, spend some time explaining what should happen when and what sort of behaviour you do and don't allow. Kids get confused when they are exposed to different ways of doing things all the time. Grandma may be much stricter than you and a stickler for manners, or she might be much more lenient, happily indulging her grandchildren in a way she would never have done when you yourself were small. You need to explain how you do things so your child stands a chance of staying on an even keel.

At the same time, allow each person to develop their own special relationship with your child, as long as what they do doesn't undermine your efforts. A grandparent often enjoys the role of being a softie and few can resist slipping their grandchildren a few treats. Don't rob them of that – they've earned it, after all.

Leaving your child for a short while in the care of other people is one thing, but if you need to return to work and the arrangement is more permanent, a shared understanding of the basic rules and routines is essential. Parents, particularly working mothers, often experience strong feelings of guilt when they leave their children in the care of others. Sometimes that results in a relaxation of the rules on the part of the parent when they come home from work. But you aren't doing your child any favours if you indulge him in an attempt to overcome your own guilty feelings. He needs quality time with you when you come home, but he doesn't need to have the rulebook thrown out of the window. He will feel much happier and much more secure if he senses that everyone who looks after him does so in the same way. When a parent relaxes the rules, it's also unfair on the carer, who will have to pick up the pieces the next day. Make sure you allow enough time to have a chat about what happened during the day.

Coping with disruption

No matter how organized you are and how smooth your daily routine is, there will be times when things are less predictable. Some types of disruption are unavoidable – illness and bouts of teething fall into this category. Other types of disruption are either avoidable or you can take steps to lessen their impact.

Routines don't have to be set in stone. It's fine to relax the routine a little at the weekend and allow your children to stay up a bit later on Saturday night. Just be prepared to be strong on Sunday.

Avoid scheduling potentially disruptive events when they could have a knock-on effect on your child's routine. For example, don't invite guests over at a time that might interrupt kids' meals or bedtimes. Small children find it difficult to separate from their parents or to forego their attention and some are very shy of people they haven't met before or don't know very well. If something out of the ordinary is coming up, take the time to explain to your child what's likely to happen.

Routines often go out of the window on holidays. A fortnight away is not a huge break when you're an adult, but for a small child it might as well be a lifetime. If you abandon a routine completely on holiday, you're going to have your work cut out when you get home. Going on holiday can throw your child's sleeping habits out of kilter or even introduce a sleeping problem when none existed before. The solution is not to stay at home but to plan in advance how you can stick to the routine. Mealtimes and naptimes should be kept to as far as possible.

AWAY FROM HOME:

⚠ Recognize that if you choose a far-flung holiday destination you are going to have to deal with the disruption that comes from long periods in transit, as well as jet lag if there's a major shift of time zone. Young children suffer from jet lag just like adults. They will need a few days to adjust.

⚠ Keep to the key times in your routine as far as possible – waking, meals, bath and bedtime are the cornerstones of the schedule. Activities and location are inevitably going to be different and that's enough change for most kids to cope with.

⚠ If it's hot, expect your child to want to eat less. Don't make an issue of it, and remember to offer her plenty of water.

⚠ Take comforters, toys and reminders of home to help your child settle in a different bed. If there's something she really likes to eat, you might consider taking a supply of it with you. Always take medication, basic remedies and formula milk with you in case you can't get it at your destination.

Setting
boundaries

Routines and household rules are important for small children. Making sure that basic structure is kept in place means discipline.

From how much telly should be allowed, to questions of diet and nutrition, almost any issue remotely connected with kids and their care has a tendency to spark off a heated debate in the media. But discipline is one area of family life that is absolutely guaranteed to arouse controversy.

What's too strict? What's not strict enough? I could sit and debate the issues all day long. But I do know one thing. Parents lose their authority when they bend over backwards to try and become their kid's best mate. Discipline is about finding that balance where you are warm with your children, but you're firm when you need to be. That means there has to be respect on both sides.

If you're too tough on your kids, you'll run the risk of breaking their spirit. But if you don't set any limits at all, you'll end up with kids who don't know how to control themselves. Sooner or later – generally at school – those children will face a situation outside the home where that lack of self-control is going to result in an even bigger problem. It might affect the child's ability to learn; it might make it hard for her to make friends.

You might think that a child who is allowed to do exactly what he wants, when he wants, would be happy

and carefree. But that's not the case. A child who gets away with everything thinks that he's in charge. When you're a toddler, that's a confusing idea. Too much freedom doesn't tell a child that you love him so much you want him to have anything and everything, it tells him that you are not bothering to show him where the limits are. Children who go undisciplined are often frightened, insecure, angry, confused and unhappy. They have no idea whatsoever where they're going and that upsets them. When they get what they want, or what they think they want, they are still not content, but keep on pushing at the boundaries to see if there's anything at all you're prepared to stop them from doing or having.

In the first series of *Supernanny*, I visited a family where the head of the household was two and a half years old. Charlie was literally ruling the roost. If Charlie made the whole family – Mum, Dad and his two older siblings – sit in the dark with the TV off and the fire off, that's what the family did. Charlie was getting his way all the time, every day, but that didn't make him happy. The more his parents gave in to him, the more he screamed and yelled. After we introduced a few basic techniques of discipline, along with a new routine, an agreed set of household rules, and plenty of praise and encouragement, Charlie was a changed child. Instead of the angry little boy who hadn't the first idea what to do with the freedom he had been given, he was relaxed, happy and secure, knowing he could participate in family life without running the show.

You wouldn't give your car keys to your toddler and expect her to drive to the shops. But you are doing something rather similar if in the course of everyday life you let her dictate who does what, when, where and how. Just as she's some years away from taking her driving test, she doesn't yet have the reasoning powers or the common sense to run her own life – not to mention yours.

In my experience, many parents who start out imposing no rules at all often wind up changing their minds somewhere down the line when things are getting really out of hand. Then they find they don't have many techniques at their disposal. Once a pattern of bad behaviour has been established, it takes effort to change it. But, surprisingly, it can be done without too much grief. Then it's not just the Charlies of this world who become happier and more relaxed. Everyone else in the family benefits, too.

Finding the right approach

All children have their own characters that are obvious from the word go. There are the lively ones, who don't sleep much and who are tuned into everything that's happening around them. There are the laid-back ones, who go with the flow, and the ones who are more strong-willed. You can't predict what sort of child you will have, but you can adapt your methods to deal with the new person who has arrived in your life. Some won't need as much firmness as others. But please remember that discipline is not about stamping on your child's personality, breaking her spirit or trying to turn her into someone she's not. The whole point is to allow kids to be themselves within the limits of acceptable behaviour.

You stand a better chance of success if you are comfortable with the style of discipline you adopt. But if you're one of those parents who find it hard to take charge at all, this is not to say that you should forget about discipline altogether! There are a number of different techniques outlined in this chapter and you might find some of them work better for you than others. Don't give up if a technique feels a bit unnatural at first. Parenting sometimes means you're called upon to play a role. With practice, you'll get the hang of it.

LOVE AND RESPECT

One thing that it is important to understand is that disciplining your child won't make her love you any less. People who think discipline is the same as harsh punishment are getting the wrong end of the stick. Discipline means teaching your child how to behave and giving him boundaries and limits. It means praise and encouragement as much as firm and fair control.

Even in the most chaotic families I've visited, there's always been plenty of love around. But sometimes there hasn't been much respect. If a child doesn't respect her parents or her siblings, she's going to carry the same attitude into other situations – when she meets other children or when she starts at nursery or school – with potentially explosive results. In a good parent–child relationship there's love and respect on both sides.

Talking to your child

You've had a bad morning. Your toddler has been up to all his usual tricks and is now running riot in the living room. 'Stop it', you say. He pays no attention 'Stop it right now! NO! Don't touch that!' Your words fall on deaf ears. 'Did you hear what I said? Stop it RIGHT NOW!'

Stop it! Stop it! Stop it! Don't touch! Don't touch! Don't touch! Shouting at your child in this kind of relentless way only communicates one thing: the fact that you're really wound up. If your child has been trying to get your attention by behaving naughtily, at this point he'll know he's succeeded.

Constantly shouting or screaming at your child is not going to change his behaviour for the better. It's far more upsetting for both you and your child than disciplining him sensibly and it raises the emotional temperature to boiling point. Who's lost control now?

Let's look at the other extreme. Say you pride yourself on not being the type of parent who loses their cool. You wouldn't ever dream of shouting or screaming. Instead you say something like: 'Please don't do that. Oh, come on now, please don't do that.' You smile.

And still nothing happens.

The first step in learning how to discipline your child is learning how to talk to her.

GO LARGE

When you're talking to children, they don't just focus on what you're saying. In fact, it might sail right over their heads if you use long words or make it too complicated. Instead, kids take in the whole package: your tone of voice, your body language, whether you're unsure, worried or anxious. They have powerful antennae. Sometimes I think they've got a sixth sense us adults have forgotten all about.

Go large when you communicate with them. Exaggerate your expressions. It's a bit like role play. Many parents do this instinctively, but some don't because it makes them feel self-conscious or silly. Let your inhibitions go – be confident and playful when you talk to your child and when you respond to what he's saying. If you refer to yourself in the third person, it can take the heat out of the battle of wills sometimes. 'Mum's going to wash your hands now.'

HOW TO TALK TO YOUR CHILD:

- Don't scream and shout. Use the Voice of Authority for bad behaviour.

- Praise your child when he's behaving well.

- Try to talk to your child in a positive way as much as possible. Instead of always telling him what you don't want him to do, try putting it in a different way. Instead of saying, 'Don't put your dirty hands all over the sofa', say, 'Let's wash your hands now. They're dirty. Then you can come on the sofa and I'll read you a story.'

- Don't be abrupt or bark out commands. You'll get instant resistance.

- Never use hurtful words or label your child. Make it clear it's the bad behaviour you don't like, not your child.

- Be courteous.

- If your child shouts back at you, don't rise to the bait. A screaming match does no one any good. Tell your child not to speak to you in that manner.

- Don't compare your child unfavourably with his brothers and sisters and never, ever talk about him to a third party within earshot. He might not look like he's listening, but he'll have caught every word.

- Don't offer too many choices to a small child.

- Don't bargain with her when she's having a tantrum.

- Go large. Let her read your body language. Be playful in the way you talk to your child.

Avoidance strategies

Avoidance strategies play an important role in controlling children's behaviour. Very young children, who are just coming into toddlerhood, are at a stage when they are most impulsive and reckless. Involvement techniques and similar strategies work well at this age. If you can see it coming, and you can head it off, you'll save yourself unnecessary and exhausting conflicts.

★ Make sure your home is safe, secure and free of temptations. Why waste time and energy trying to keep precious objects out of a toddler's hands, when you could simply remove them from the scene altogether? See Action Stations, page 42.

★ Get to know which times of the day are most fractious and see if you can't improve matters by altering your routine. Bringing a mealtime forward by half an hour is much better than having to face half an hour of whining brought on by low blood sugar every day.

★ Work out which activities are causing the most upset. If your attempts to wash your child's hair lead to regular explosive outbursts at bathtime and wreck the bedtime routine, set aside another time in the day to get out the shampoo. It'll still be a problem, but some problems you can choose when to tackle.

★ Don't expect your child to wind down immediately after a period of boisterous play. She's not going to come indoors after chasing around the park and settle right down.

★ Don't rush a child from one activity to the next. Give him clear warnings at regular intervals about what's coming next so that he has time to prepare himself.

★ If there's a particular toy or game that always leads to a dispute, put it away for the time being. Don't let it become a bone of contention day after day

★ Don't go looking for perfection or have unreasonably high expectations of your child's behaviour. Know what to expect at each stage of the game.

★ If you can see trouble heading your way, try a distraction or diversion. Point out something interesting that's happening outside. 'Do you see that little bird in the garden? What do you think he's doing?' Or invite your child to help you with a household chore. Take advantage of her short attention span to steer her away from trouble.

The involvement technique

The Involvement Technique is one of my favourites. It works really well with small children. The technique can be a big help when it comes to dealing with jealousy. It can even turn round that typical toddler flashpoint, the supermarket shop (see page 170).

Small children need attention. When they don't get it, they play up. The trouble is that there simply aren't enough hours in the day for you to give your toddler the attention he wants and deal with everything else as well. When you have two or more kids, short of cloning yourself you have to think of ways round the problem.

You can't always expect a small child to play contentedly while you get on with sorting the laundry, washing the dishes or feeding his little brother. This might work once or twice if your child is in the right mood to get stuck into play. But chances are it won't work all the time, particularly if your child already resents the attention you're paying to a younger sibling.

The answer is to get the child involved with what you're doing. Small children don't find tasks like cleaning, sorting, fetching and carrying as boring as their older brothers and sisters sometimes do. Small children love to help. Helping makes them feel responsible and gives them confidence. They see it as a challenge they are succeeding in.

Of course, you have to give your child a job that suits what he can do, otherwise you'll just be adding to the long list of toddler frustrations, not to mention asking for mayhem and breakage. It's very important that you don't set him up for failure. But while you wouldn't expect him to be able to stack a dishwasher or run the hoover over the living room carpet, there are plenty of ways he can join in. When you're changing a duvet cover, he can hold a corner for you. When you're washing the car, you can wrap him up in a cagoule and give him his own sponge and bucket of water. When you're washing vegetables, you can stand him beside you on a chair and let him wash a potato or two. Toy appliances are also a great idea. Little kids love mini dustpans and brushes. Chores may take a little bit longer and things might get a little messier, but you'll get the chore done and your child will get the benefit of your attention.

Most importantly, when you've got to attend to younger siblings, you can nip jealousy in the bud by involving your older child in the same activity. Asking her to fetch a toy or a flannel at bathtime or to help spoonfeed the baby means you can pay her attention at the same time as you pay attention to her younger sibling. That way, you kill two birds with the same stone.

The Involvement Technique allows you to keep paying attention to your child by talking about whatever you're doing at the time. And an important part of it is praise. Thank your child for her efforts, tell her what a good job she's doing and how it has helped you.

How to discipline your child

When your child does something really unacceptable – and you can see he's done it on purpose – or if he has settled into a pattern of naughty behaviour, you have to take further steps and back up your rules with firm and fair control. The techniques outlined in the following sections are appropriate for children over the age of two and a half. Unless your child is very advanced for his age, that is the youngest you can start using these methods and expect results. Below then, a child's reasoning is not developed enough to understand what you're trying to teach him.

The main reason for bad behaviour in kids between the ages of two and five is attention-seeking to get a reaction. The number two reason is jealousy, which, in a funny sort of way, amounts to the same thing. Small children will do almost anything to keep the spotlight trained on themselves. With the arrival of a new sibling, there's suddenly serious competition for your attention.

There are two important things to remember about using any method of discipline:

- Be consistent. Stick to your guns. Don't change the rules. Both parents must follow through the same way and back each other up. A child who's being disciplined by one parent will naturally go to the other to see if there's any mileage to be gained by that. Good cop, bad cop may work in television police dramas but inconsistency in parenting makes disciplining impossible.

- Act immediately. Don't put off taking action. Toddlers don't remember things for very long. They won't associate the discipline with the bad behaviour if there's too big a gap between the two.

WHEN NOT TO DISCIPLINE:

● When a child is ill or recovering from illness. Some parents find that a sure sign of illness is when their boisterous toddler suddenly becomes much easier to deal with. Other children will have a shorter fuse when they're ill or teething. A sick child needs the right treatment and plenty of TLC.

● When there is considerable doubt about who did what to whom. Most small children are pretty transparent and you'll be able to tell who was the guilty party in a dispute that happened behind your back. But if a child gets repeatedly disciplined for things he hasn't done, he'll have every right to feel persecuted and will start to lie.

● When the bad behaviour has given her a real shock and she's genuinely sorry. She may have broken a vase she's been repeatedly warned not to touch and the accident has shocked her into floods of tears. She's already learned the hard way and chances are she won't do that again. (You've learned the hard way, too, for not putting the vase out of reach.) Accept the accident and talk to her about why it happened. Remind her of the rules and leave it at that. Discipline when a child is already upset and sorry for what she's done is giving her the wrong message.

● When there's maximum disruption. Expect your child's behaviour to go downhill if his world has been turned upside down by moving house, the birth of a new baby, family illness, or similar. Don't worry about discipline too much until the tension dies down. You have to make leeway for the emotional upset.

● When he's already been disciplined. Don't discipline a child twice for the same offence. If he's been disciplined already by your partner or another carer, the incident is over.

The naughty step technique

The basic idea behind this technique is to remove the child from the scene for a few minutes and allow her time to cool down, think about what she's done and get ready to apologize. The point is to teach her that a particular type of unacceptable behaviour will result in this consequence. This not only shows your child very clearly and effectively that she has crossed a line and broken an important rule, it also serves to take the tension out of the situation. You need that breathing space as much as she does.

The naughty step doesn't have to be a step. It can be a corner or a room. I like to use a step because it's away from the rest of the household but not so far removed that you have to keep running up and down the stairs all the time. If you don't have stairs, you could put your child in the corner of the room, or even put her in another room altogether.

If you do use a room, use one that offers the child no distraction or stimulation. Putting your child in a roomful of toys or where there's a TV defeats the point of the exercise. She needs to be somewhere where she's going to be bored, where she's got time to think about things. In the first programme of the American series of *Supernanny* I visited a family where the two children, aged six and two, were sent to their bedrooms when they behaved badly. The trouble with this arrangement is that it gave the children a mixed message. You want your child to feel comfortable and secure in his own bedroom, not to associate it with a place of discipline.

The Naughty Step Technique is the same as what many childcare experts call 'Time Out'. Personally, I don't think it does children any harm to know that when they've been naughty, they have to sit on the 'naughty' step. But if a different name makes it easier for you to use the technique, it really doesn't matter.

Your jealous four-year-old has pushed his little sister and thrown a toy at her. She's fallen over and has started to wail. It's all going pear-shaped. You'll be furious; you might be worried and panicky, too. Check first that your daughter is okay, resist the adrenalin surge that makes you want to yell at the top of your lungs and put the Naughty Step Technique into practice.

HOW IT WORKS

This technique can break the cycle of bad behaviour very quickly. But remember that you and your partner have to be consistent. And don't leave out a stage. The Warnings and the Explanations are essential. If in the heat of the moment you go straight to C, bypassing A and B, the method won't work.

THE WARNING Go to your son, come down to his level and look him straight in the eye. Use the Voice of Authority to give him a verbal warning. Say, 'That behaviour is unacceptable. We don't push people or throw things at them. It's wrong. Please don't do it again.' The Warning is a key stage in the technique. It gives your child the chance to correct his own behaviour. If you leave out the Warning, you've given him nowhere to go.

THE ULTIMATUM Five minutes later, your child does the same thing again. This time, using the same low, firm tone and confident body language, you issue an Ultimatum. Say, 'I told you not to push your sister or throw things at her. That was very naughty. We don't push people. The next time you do it, you're going to the Naughty Step.'

THE NAUGHTY STEP As soon as the bad behaviour is repeated, take your child straight to the step. Sit him down and tell him to stay there. How long you should make him stay there will depend on his age. A couple of minutes is long enough for a two-and-a-half-year-old. Five minutes is about right for four-year-olds and over.

THE EXPLANATION Like the Warning, this is another key stage. Before you leave your child, explain why he's been put on the step. Say, 'We don't push people or throw things at them. It's unacceptable behaviour. People will get hurt. You're going to sit here for five minutes and think about what you've done. When five minutes is over, I will come and get you and I want you to apologize, please. Now stay there.'

she really wants may have nothing to do with clothes at all: it's simply to get her own way. Another way parents often respond to this kind of situation is by trying to dress their child as if he were still a baby who couldn't even put his own arm into a sleeve. If you try to force a child to get dressed you'll soon come up against a physical limit – yours. Toddlers aren't helpless babies. They can kick, wriggle, squirm, run off – and they will. To cap it all, they'll have a tantrum. And all you wanted to do was put his shoes on.

Dressing often becomes an issue because it's rushed. To a parent, dressing or undressing their child is something that has to be done – quickly, quickly! – before something else can happen – going on an outing, picking older children up from school, getting ready for bed. You've got your eye on the clock. You want to hurry things along. At the slightest hint she's being rushed, your toddler will dig in her heels. That's how getting your child dressed can end up taking all day.

This kind of problem can be turned around very quickly using a combination of techniques. The first is to be clear about what you would like your child to wear and cut down on the choices you put in front of him. The second is to involve him in what you're doing and encourage him to learn to dress himself. And the third is to back up repeated struggles with firm and fair control.

What are we going to wear today?

'What are we going to wear today?' is not a question you should be asking a young child. If you ask that question, you might think to yourself that you're being kind by inviting your child to have a say in what he wears, or that you're sidestepping a potential explosion by getting him to choose. Your toddler will immediately think that a) you don't know the answer – otherwise why are you asking him? – and b) dressing is optional. All that choices offer young children is uncertainty. Someone has to be in charge: that means it's down to him to take over. And he will.

If you offer full choice to an older child who's more capable of having an opinion on what she would like to wear but still doesn't know how to make choices appropriately, don't be surprised if she picks a spangly summer top for an outing to the park in midwinter. It's only fair to offer an older child some say in what she wears. But instead of allowing her to pick anything from her wardrobe, offer her a choice between two or three things, all of which are suitable for the occasion and the weather. Or you can sidestep the problem by putting summer clothes away in the winter and vice versa, just like you might rotate your own wardrobe.

Do listen to a child if she repeatedly refuses to wear a particular item of clothing on the grounds of discomfort. Pay attention to her if she says a top is too tight every time she wears it. Some children hate the feeling of wool next to the skin and say it feels too 'itchy'. Too bad if the jumper was lovingly handknitted by your auntie – if it feels like a hair shirt to your child, don't make her wear it.

One way you can take the heat out of dressing disputes and also relieve some of the time pressure is to lay clothes out the night before. Pick out the clothes and explain to your child that he's going to be wearing those jeans and that top tomorrow and then you'll be going round to his friend's house. Then getting dressed isn't an issue in itself, it's part of something to look forward to, which includes an outing.

Encouraging your child to dress

If you think about it from a child's point of view, being dressed by someone else must be a bit alarming at times. One second your arms are shoved down sleeves, then your legs are forced into tights and before you know it, a skirt comes down over your head and you can't see or breathe properly.

If you dress a child in a hurry, chances are you won't be as gentle as you should be or take the time to prepare her for what's coming next. You wouldn't like it if someone more than twice your size threw a jersey over your head without warning or yanked your arms to force them down sleeves or did up a zip in such a hurry that it pinched your skin.

Even when a child is quite young, you can start encouraging her to dress herself. The first stage is to involve her in the process so she doesn't feel rushed from pillar to post. Keep talking and telling her what you're doing and what you're going to do next.

'Now let's put on your top. Can you put your arm in the sleeve, please? Well done. Now you try the other arm.' Lots of praise makes it go smoothly.

The second stage is to encourage more active involvement. Make it easy for your child to learn to dress himself by choosing clothes that don't have complicated fastenings. He's not going to be able to tie his own shoelaces or do up fiddly buttons, but he can pull up a zip or tug at a strap. Shoes that fasten with Velcro are better for young children than those with laces or buckles.

Play is another way of encouraging a child to dress herself. What else is dressing and undressing dollies all about? Or you might buy her one of those educational toys designed to help teach children basic dressing skills such as doing up buttons or tying shoelaces.

While she's learning how to dress, things are still going to be frustrating and frustration can turn into a tantrum in the blink of an eye. Don't set her up for failure. Don't just decide one day that she's perfectly capable of doing it herself, then leave her to it and stand back ready to correct her when she gets it wrong. Show her and involve her. Put on one of her shoes, then ask her to put on the other one. Explain how to do it. 'Put the strap through the buckle – that's it! Now pull it through.'

PROBLEM:
REFUSING TO GET DRESSED/ UNDRESSED

Small children often prolong or avoid dressing as a way of delaying bedtime. It's not the clothes that are the issue. Having exactly the right pair of trainers with exactly the right label in exactly the right colour won't be a problem until later. And, although many toddlers love to remove all or part of their clothes and run around stark naked, they aren't particularly anti-clothes as such. They're just delighting in a new skill – the undoing (or undressing) always comes before the doing.

Children who turn dressing and undressing into repeated episodes of screaming and kicking need firm and fair control. It might seem like a petty issue, but if you don't tackle it, you're heading off down the path where dressing can turn into a day-long struggle.

SOLUTION:
AVOIDANCE/THE NAUGHTY STEP TECHNIQUE

★ Allow plenty of time in your daily routine for getting your child dressed. You can throw on your clothes in seconds, and might barely consider dressing an activity at all, but your child needs much longer.

★ Lay out clothes the night before and don't offer a toddler too much choice over what he wears. Two choices are enough for a toddler. He hasn't the sense to make a choice on grounds of suitability and style is completely irrelevant to him. Left to his own devices, he might be happy going to the supermarket in the nude or wearing his pants on his head.

★ For a three-year-old child, you can increase the choices to three, based round clothes that are suitable for the occasion and the weather.

★ Involve your child and encourage her to dress herself by giving her small achievable tasks.

★ Keep up a running commentary that is positive and involving. Give plenty of praise. Make it fun – even make it silly.

★ If dressing becomes a real issue – if it leads to defiance, aggression and other forms of bad behaviour – use the Naughty Step Technique (see page 80). Remember to include the Warning and Explanation.

PROBLEM:
THE FADDY DRESSER

It doesn't have to be Halloween for you to see a fair number of fairy princesses or action heroes doing the shopping with their parents on Saturday morning. In fact, I've walked Spiderman down the street before. If your child is reasonably cooperative about getting dressed most of the time and hasn't turned the whole issue into a battle of wills, it does her no harm at all to wear the fairy dress to the supermarket or put on the tights that make an eye-watering clash with the skirt. Parents need to learn to chill out. Fancy dressers aren't always faddy dressers. Let kids be kids and dress up. It's part of their play.

When it does start to matter is when your child develops a fad for a particular colour or piece of clothing that means he won't wear anything else but green, or the T-shirt with the dinosaur on the front. If you give into this, it can go on for months.

SOLUTION:
AVOIDANCE

★ Be on the look-out for signs of faddy dressing. It's far easier to nip this in the bud than it is to get the child out of a pattern of behaviour that has been going on for ages.

★ You may need to go back a step if your child shows signs of faddy dressing. Instead of offering limited choice, offer none at all. Lay out the clothes the night before and remove the outfit that she is becoming obsessed with. Tell her that it's in the wash – it'll need it by now!

★ Give plenty of positive reinforcement for those occasions when she gets dressed without turning it into a huge exercise. A star chart can be a good way of showing your approval.

Washing

Washing – bathing, brushing the teeth, washing and
de-tangling the hair, washing hands and face, cutting
fingernails and toenails – are activities that are closely
associated with dressing and undressing in the daily
routine. Most small children enjoy water and don't
need too much encouragement to make a splash in
the sink or the bath.

What they will need, as well as plenty of hands-on
help and supervision, are constant reminders to follow
through with the routine. A toddler won't skip
brushing his teeth or washing his hands because he
hates the idea of clean teeth or clean hands – it'll just
have gone straight out of his head.

6. WARNINGS

Remind your kids repeatedly when it's time to get dressed or washed, or when it's time get in or out of the bath. Don't spring sudden changes of activity on them. Let them know what's happening next.

7. EXPLANATIONS

Show and tell your child how to dress and wash and brush her teeth. Explain why it's important to be clean and what the different products are for. Keep up a running commentary in a fun way.

8. RESTRAINT

Don't shout and bark out commands to your child. Use a calm, authoritative voice. Don't rush your child or let her know that you are pressed for time. Don't try to force her into her clothes.

9. RESPONSIBILITY

Encourage your child to dress himself. Make it easy for him to learn by making sure his clothes don't have complicated fastenings. Use the Involvement Technique when you need to occupy yourself with your other kids.

10. RELAXATION

Make bathtime fun with games of 'let's pretend'. It's a good chance to unwind, relax and be silly before calming down for the night. The same kind of playful approach also works well with dressing.

Toilet training

A lot of parents are obsessed by getting their child out of nappies. Let me say that any child who is toilet-trained by two years old is doing incredibly well – and that's not meant to sound like a target you should be aiming for. Toilet training is far more likely to happen some time between two and a half and three, at which time it will happen much more quickly. If you get the timing right, you can toilet-train your child in a week or two. If you start to train her before she is ready, or if you stop and start the training according to when it's convenient for you, expect it to go on for ages – even months.

Of course, getting a child out of nappies is a welcome stage for parents. But bear in mind that these days, with disposable nappies, you aren't saying goodbye to hours of laundering and soaking stinking terrycloth in pails of disinfectant and bleach, you're just crossing another item off your weekly shop and removing a rather messy, smelly chore from your routine.

Although you shouldn't start training too early, what you can do is prepare your child for this stage when it does come by being relaxed and comfortable about natural bodily

ACCIDENTS

All kids have accidents, wet their pants and even soil themselves once or twice. These kinds of accidents often happen when a child has got over-excited or too distracted to pick up what his body is trying to tell him. When that happens, your child will be upset. Don't make a big deal out of it. Excessive attention or comfort might eventually give a toddler the idea that accidents can have their uses. Simply treat the episode in a calm, matter-of-fact way. Tell him that these things happen and forget about it.

You can help prevent accidents by having reasonable expectations. When a child says he wants to go, he wants to go. Take him seriously and don't expect him to be able to wait for very long.

Sometimes a child will have an accident because she's too lazy to take herself to the toilet or because she thinks she's going to miss out on something that's much more interesting. Let her know that this is not acceptable. If she's using an accident as a stalling tactic – holding on until it's at its most inconvenient – take that burden away from her. Take the initiative and suggest she goes to the toilet now. Before you get in the car.

Bedwetting is often a sign that you've left off the night-time nappies too soon. You need to see several dry ones in a row before you can leave off a nappy at night. But bedwetting can also indicate some kind of emotional upset. A strange bed is enough to set some kids off. It stands to reason that the arrival of a new baby brother or sister, a move or a bad nightmare may also lead to the same result. These are emotional issues and need to be addressed delicately and with no blame attached. Bedwetting also goes along with periods of illness.

If bedwetting is associated with a fear of the dark and the child's reluctance to make the trip to the toilet in the middle of the night, keep the potty in the bedroom at night-time and add a night light.

PROBLEM:
PERSISTENT BEDWETTING

Persistent bedwetting in an older child is far from rare. It's upsetting for the child and it makes work for you. There are many reasons why this might be happening. Stress and emotional problems are often to blame. Sometimes a child may have developed a urinary infection. If you've ruled out the obvious causes and the accidents keep happening with depressing regularity, it may well be the case that she is using them as a means of getting attention.

If your child regularly wets the bed at night, don't be tempted to bring her into your own bed. Obviously, you don't want to discipline a child for bedwetting. But you shouldn't reward her, either.

SOLUTION:
BREAK THE PATTERN

Whatever the reason behind the bedwetting, the important thing is to break the pattern. The most effective way is to lift your child out of bed, sit him on the potty or the toilet and try to get him to have a wee last thing at night just before you go to bed. If he's normally a good sleeper, you can usually do this with a minimum of fuss and he will fall straight back to sleep. It also makes sense to limit his fluid intake after supper. A child who drains a huge glass of milk or juice just before going to bed will find it harder to stay dry.

PROBLEM:
SOILING

This is a tricky one. Soiling often coincides with illness, times when your child is preoccupied, scared or distracted, or periods of family disruption. Always give your child the benefit of the doubt and keep on with the training. If you rush in and discipline for soiling, you can set the clock back on toilet training by months.

Some kids find bowel control much harder than bladder control. Others find bowel movements a real cause of anxiety. They may be scared of the motion itself or of seeing the result. For that reason, they try and hold on until nature takes over and they have a distressing accident. It's important to be sensitive, but don't over-pacify them. Say, 'That's because you held it' in a light tone. 'Never mind.' Explain why they had the accident. One episode like this is usually upsetting enough to change things.

SOLUTION:
KEEP IT LOW-KEY

If accidents keep on happening, allow enough time in your routine for changing him out of his clothes and pack fresh pants, wet wipes and clean trousers as a matter of course. Don't rush him on the potty. Don't give him the first idea that time is ticking past or that you are anxious about that fact. Each time he has an accident, clean him up but don't give him extra attention. As soon as he stops soiling himself, give him lots of praise.

Sometimes anxiety over bowel movements can lead to constipation. I always put children who are constipated for whatever reason into a warm bath. That helps the muscles to relax. If constipation is a regular problem, make sure there's enough fresh fruit and vegetables in the diet and your child is getting plenty of fluids.

MY TOP TEN RULES

TO SUM UP, HERE'S HOW MY TOP TEN RULES APPLY TO TOILET TRAINING:

1. PRAISE AND REWARDS

Give plenty of praise and encouragement every step of the way. Motif pants are a great incentive.

2. CONSISTENCY

Once you start toilet training, don't stop for any reason. Keep it up, even if it's going to cause you inconvenience. Don't use pull-ups as a halfway stage – it confuses the issue.

3. ROUTINE

Don't rush things. Allow time for kids to go to the toilet before you go out and remind them at every opportunity.

4. BOUNDARIES

Have realistic expectations of toilet training. Don't be tempted to start too early or the whole process will drag on for months. Learn to spot the signs of readiness. Keep potties in the bathroom where they belong. Don't leave off the night-time nappy too soon.

5. DISCIPLINE

Positive reinforcement is the key to toilet training. Never discipline a child for accidents. Limit the chances of bedwetting by putting your child on the potty or the toilet last thing at night before you go to bed.

6. WARNINGS

During the toilet-training period, keep asking your child over and over again if she needs to go to the toilet. Even after she's trained, keep asking her at key times of the day. Small children can't wait very long when they need to go.

7. EXPLANATIONS

Teach your child what it feels like to need to go. Show and tell her what happens in the bathroom – let her watch you go to the toilet and wash your hands afterwards. Take the opportunity to teach her about hygiene.

8. RESTRAINT

Don't make a big deal of accidents or occasional bedwetting. Allow children their privacy if they ask for it.

9. RESPONSIBILITY

Encourage your child to wash her hands and wipe herself correctly as soon as she is able.

10. RELAXATION

Approach toilet training in an open and relaxed way. It's a natural part of life.

Eating

Feeding your child should be simple. There's no shortage of advice available on what makes a good balanced diet, and these days we don't have to hunt, gather or grow our food, we just have to go to the shops. You ought to be able to put a bowl or plate of nourishing food down in front of your child at breakfast, lunch and dinner and let hunger do the rest. If only it was that simple.

All too often mealtimes are battles fought on a number of fronts. First, there's that good nourishing food you've bought, prepared and cooked but your child has decided tastes like poison. Then, there's the whole sitting-at-table issue, which has somehow become an optional extra as far as she is concerned. And, last but not least, there's what your child would *really* like to eat: snacks, crisps, chocolate, sweets and sugary drinks. You've lost track of the number of times in the day when your child has demanded a biscuit, but you certainly haven't heard her screaming for broccoli.

Like many other areas of daily life, eating is an activity where young children very soon start exercising their desire for independence. It doesn't take long for them to work out the obvious: *you can't make them eat.* Soon after they've worked that one out, they pick up on the fact that food is one of the things that their parents worry about the most.

It's understandable that parents worry about feeding their kids. From that first hungry newborn cry, you'll know that getting food into your child at regular intervals is vital for his development and growth. And you won't just know it, you'll feel it.

In the early weeks and months, feeding is a time of special closeness. It's often when the emotional bonds between parent and child are deepened and strengthened. Later on, if your child acts up at mealtimes or rejects the food you have given her, you're bound to find it difficult to be patient and objective. Feeding children is an emotional issue right from the start.

By setting routines, rules and boundaries you can begin to take the emotional heat out of the situation so that mealtimes become something to enjoy again. When children are small and for some long while after, it's up to you to show them how to eat, just as much as it's your job to put the right sort of food in front of them. After all, no parent ever handed their child a biscuit by accident!

Give your children a proper nutritional diet right from the start. Make it a way of life. Children aren't born craving sugar. If they're only given good, nutritional food, they won't know any different – a chopped up peach will be as much of a treat for them as a bowl of ice cream might be for another child.

Introducing solid food

Four to five months is the right sort of time to start your baby on solid food. You'll know it's the right time if he is demanding more and more feeds or if his weight gain has slowed for no reason. Don't expect an overnight switch from milk to solid food: at the beginning, you're just offering tastes to get him used to the idea. He'll still be getting most of his food intake from milk.

There's nothing like the expression that crosses a baby's face the first time she tastes her first solid food. It's not just the taste, it's the texture and consistency that come as such a surprise. She may take to it at once or she may not like it at all. Spitting out a mouthful of food doesn't necessarily mean she doesn't like it; it just means she doesn't know what to do with it yet. But if she shows a lot of resistance, wait a week or so and then try her on something else.

Foods should be introduced gradually. One at a time is best. That way you can see if any food is particularly disliked or if it causes a bad reaction. Begin by offering fairly bland, semi-solid food such as baby rice or baby cereal mixed with milk or cooled boiled water. Pureed fruit and vegetables such as cooked carrot, potato, apple and pear, along with mashed-up banana and avocado are also good early foods.

NEW TASTES:

★ Introduce solid food at a specific set time. It can be breakfast or lunch.

★ Use a plastic spoon to feed your baby and give him a spoon to hold, too. He won't be able to use it yet but it may help to make the experience more fun for him.

★ At the beginning don't expect him to manage more than a couple of spoonfuls at a time once a day. At the beginning more of it will be on his bib or on the floor than in his mouth. He'll take time to get used to the idea. He isn't really spitting out the food, what he's doing is exploring it by pushing his tongue in and out of his mouth. That tends to make the food watery.

★ Be extra careful with hygiene.

★ If he turns his head away, either he's had enough or he doesn't like it. Don't force him to eat. Watch out for facial expressions.

★ Always test the temperature of the food to make sure it isn't too hot. You can buy spoons these days that indicate when food is too hot by turning a different colour.

★ Mince, puree, grate, mash or strain food so there are no hard lumps that could cause choking.

★ At any signs of allergic reaction, do not hesitate to take your child immediately to the hospital.

WHAT TO AVOID

Introduce vegetables and fruit first, protein second. Separating the food groups allows you to keep an eye out for any allergic reactions. You should delay giving a baby certain types of food for longer. Allergies can result if a baby is introduced to food such as nuts, cow's milk and eggs too early. Signs to look out for include patches of reddened itching skin and sudden bouts of diarrhoea or vomiting.

Watch out for these foods:

SALT Don't add salt to food or offer salty foods. This puts a strain on a young child's kidneys.

SUGAR Babies and young children don't need sugary foods or additional sugar. The natural sugars found in fruit and vegetables are enough.

NUTS These are a no-no. They can provoke allergies and are also choking hazards.

COW'S MILK Delay the introduction of cow's milk until one year. Never give young children skimmed milk – they need the calories that the fat in whole milk provides.

EGGS Wait until after one year before introducing whole eggs. The same goes for products that contain eggs.

SHELLFISH It's best not to give shellfish until your child is two years old.

CITRUS FRUITS These can upset a baby's tummy. Always deseed fruit.

SEEDS AND RAW FOOD Avoid food that might cause choking, such as seeds or hard pieces of food. No raw food whatsoever.

Weaning

After your baby has got used to a small meal of a dozen spoonfuls once a day, you can start offering him food at other times as well. If you began by giving him food at lunchtime, you can now introduce breakfast.

Offer regular drinks of diluted baby juice or cooled boiled water, both with mealtimes and at other times of the day. You can use either a bottle or a plastic baby cup. With your baby's nutritional needs increasingly met by solid food and his thirst quenched with water or diluted juice, his demands for a milk feed, breast or bottle, may start to tail off naturally until you are down to a feed first thing in the morning and last thing at night.

Some babies abruptly wean themselves and start to show little interest in breast or bottle once solid food is well established. If you're bottle-feeding, that's no problem, but if you're breastfeeding and your milk supply has not decreased, this can leave you with painfully engorged breasts for a few days. Expressing milk is not the answer, as it will only serve to stimulate the supply in the way the baby's sucking does. Wearing a well-fitting nursing bra night and day can help, and so can aloe vera gels.

More often, a breastfed baby will continue to want a 'feed' even when your supply of milk is next to nothing. In this case, what she wants is the continued comfort of the breast, not the milk itself. Essentially what she's doing is using the nipple as a pacifier.

If you want to stop breastfeeding and your child has settled into eating solid food and is taking enough fluids from a cup or bottle, cut the feeds right down, to two if possible. Then look out for a time when she skips one of those feeds and don't offer her the breast again. For many mothers, this is a real emotional stepping stone. But there are gains to be made – your child is ready for a new stage and so are you.

After six to eight months, your baby needs more nutrients than bottle milk can give her. By carrying on feeding round the clock, you may be filling her up so much she doesn't have an appetite for the solid food you're introducing.

Some parents find weaning a bit of a juggling act. There's no hard and fast rule that can be applied to every child or parent – but if you have your mealtimes in place there's no reason why you won't get there in the end.

MY TOP TEN RULES

TO SUM UP, HERE'S HOW MY TOP TEN RULES APPLY TO EATING PROBLEMS:

1. PRAISE AND REWARDS

Praise and encouragement are the best rewards. Don't wait for exceptionally good behaviour – praise the good moments when they happen. Don't use snacks as bribes. Don't praise a child for eating a second helping.

2. CONSISTENCY

Stick to the same rules and follow them through. Make sure you and your partner are consistent. If you insist on 'three more spoonfuls', don't change your mind under pressure and reduce it to two, or one. Don't give a child a snack if he hasn't eaten his meal – that's a mixed message and a half!

3. ROUTINE

Don't shift mealtimes around drastically. Meals are a cornerstone of your routine. When children are older, you can be a little more flexible. Half an hour earlier or later won't hurt.

4. BOUNDARIES

A set mealtime is an important boundary. So are agreed rules for sitting at the table and basic behaviour. Boundaries help you to take the emotional heat out of mealtimes.

5. DISCIPLINE

Don't discipline a child for not eating. Do discipline for unacceptable behaviour at mealtimes, such as hitting, throwing food or refusing to sit at the table. Use the Naughty Step Technique.

6. WARNINGS

Give plenty of advance notice when a meal is coming up so your child has a chance to prepare for the change in activity. Don't expect her to settle down immediately at the table if she has been running round the garden. Allow a period for her to calm down first. Give an advance warning if she has been naughty, so she has the chance to correct her behaviour.

7. EXPLANATIONS

When your child has behaved badly at the table, explain that the behaviour is unacceptable and why. Don't, however, offer complex explanations to toddlers. The reasoning will just sail over their heads.

8. RESTRAINT

Ignore passing food fads. Fussy eating is about attention-seeking – ignore it. Keep offering variety and don't allow your kids to write their own menus. At the same time, don't make your dislikes their dislikes.

9. RESPONSIBILITY

Encourage your toddlers to feed themselves, even if it takes longer and makes a mess. Teach them to say 'Please' and 'Thank you'. Involve older kids in laying the table and other simple tasks.

10. RELAXATION

Mealtimes should be fun and sociable occasions. Try to eat together as a family as much as possible.

Social skills

One of the most important things a child needs to learn is how to get along with other people. Toddlers tend to see other people as annoying obstacles who keep standing in the way of what they want to do. It takes a while before any child can appreciate that other people have feelings, too, and that sharing, taking turns and being nice are good skills to have. In some ways, you can't rush things. But you can make it clear what the limits are and head your child in the right direction.

What you can do, at each and every stage, is join in and have fun with your child. Take the time to do that – forget about having a perfect house. Enjoy your child. Many parents just don't play with their kids enough, yet playing is how children learn all sorts of things, including how to get on with other people. I'd really like to encourage parents to forget about being embarrassed and to let their hair down and be silly with their children. Go into their world and let them lead the play.

Playing

Play is how kids have fun, but it's also how they learn. From the six-month-old baby exploring a rattle by putting it in her mouth, to the two-year-old trying to bang a round peg into the square hole of a shape-sorter, or the four-year-old lost in a world of make-believe, play has as much to do with finding out about the world and learning to get on with other people, as it does with entertainment.

A child who isn't given enough opportunities to play is going to be bored. When he's bored, he'll be cross and frustrated and then he'll start getting into trouble. At the same time, he won't be learning the things he could be learning from play, and I'm not just talking about the type of mental skills that 'educational' toys are meant to give him. Kicking a football around the garden isn't just an excuse for letting off steam. Your mini Beckham is also learning physical coordination and other motor skills at the same time. Puzzles and games where your child has to sit down and concentrate will help increase his attention span so that when he gets to nursery or school he won't be one of those children who can't sit still and listen. Role play, 'let's pretend' and dressing up feed the imagination. Drawing and painting are an outlet for creativity and help a child gain fine pincer control.

BABIES

It starts at a very early age. Babies need stimulation. It's just as important to meet that need for stimulation as it is to feed her when she's hungry or to change her when she's wet. A baby lacks both the coordination and the mobility to explore the world without help from you. For example, if you prop a toy where she can see it, she will gain some basic stimulation from the colour and shape. But if you leave it within her reach she will eventually bat it and make it move. The first time she does that, it will be by accident. But that accident will very quickly get repeated and turned into a game. And that game has taught her how to make something move with her hand, which is the beginning of coordination.

As soon as your child can walk, play turns into a fascinating game of exploration. Everything is up for grabs. Giving your child safe ways of experiencing the variety around him will feed that desire to learn. This is a great time for improvisation: wooden spoons and saucepans, plastic cups – basically anything safe you can pull out of the kitchen cupboards – will keep him just as happy and teach him just as much as a load of expensive toys.

TODDLERS

By the time your child is a toddler, play is as much an opportunity for frustration as it is for delight and discovery. She wants to post the shape into that box, she's seen you do it; she's seen her brother do it, but she can't manage to do it herself. The answer is not to remove all the things that might frustrate her – because she will never learn what she needs to learn that way – but you can divert her with another toy that she might be able to manage better. Or you can do what I do and place your hands over hers and help her post the shape into the box. That way she will learn, but she will still feel like she's doing it herself.

Don't expect her to concentrate on one thing for very long at this stage and don't expect to see her play with another child. She may play beside another child and hardly notice that he's there. If she does notice him, it will be to clock the fact that he's playing with a very interesting-looking toy that she wouldn't mind playing with herself. The next minute, she'll have snatched it off him.

SHARED PLAY

Before kids get to the stage where they can play with other children properly, sharing and cooperating, they need adults to help them play, and that's where problems can arise. You've got things you need to do and if your child is happily stuck into play, you'll see that as the ideal time to get on with your chores. Your child, on the other hand, will see playtime as the ideal time to have fun with you. And as soon as you start to get busy with the chores, he'll make it clear that he'd like your attention – by acting up if that's what it takes. You need to keep times for chores separate from playtime.

Young children don't really think about different activities as 'play' and 'work' the way their parents do. Everything has the potential to be fun, including helping you wash the car. So an ideal solution for this between-stage is to get them involved with what you're doing. I've explained the Involvement Technique in the chapter Setting Boundaries (page 76) and it's a really useful way of giving your child attention when you need to be occupied doing something else. When your child is standing on a chair beside you, 'helping' you wash the carrots, you're not being a slave-driver or making him do something he'll see as a chore. He'll be having the time of his life.

Kids need clear lessons in sharing and taking turns. Simple games where two or more can play help to teach them give and take. But don't just leave them to it. Sit down with them. Show them how the game works. Tell them what the rules are. They won't be able to play together properly unless you've taught them how. 'Now it's Arthur's turn.'

When they are playing nicely, leave them to it. Don't hover or breathe down their necks. They will develop their own relationship and sort out their own squabbles and bickering if you aren't constantly acting as a referee.

TOYS

Toys multiply – fast. It seems like only yesterday when you could fit all your baby's toys into a single basket or box. Now that a few birthdays and Christmases have come and gone, you know you've got a house somewhere if you could only find it under all that Lego.

Kids love toys and parents love giving toys to their children. But just like anything else, toys can end up becoming things that kids learn to bargain with, fight over, beg for, and refuse to tidy up. Toys can become an Issue.

Many parents at some stage or another have given their kids toys because they feel guilty about not spending more time with them. Others routinely hand out new treats as either a bribe or reward for halfway decent behaviour. None of this has much to do with playing or learning through play. It has a lot to do with your emotions. If you use toys in this way, you'll be setting up a situation where your child knows he can manipulate you.

TOY ROTATION

Small children need toys to play with, but they don't need expensive toys and they don't need every toy in the toyshop. It's not just a question of 'learning to appreciate what they've got'. Older kids do need to be taught to respect their belongings, but that's much too grown-up a notion for a two-year-old. When small children find themselves in the position where they're surrounded by hundreds of toys, all within reach, what they're facing is literally hundreds of choices in solid form. They may have lots of toys, but they don't all have to be out at the same time. Rotating toys in and out of view gives small

children, who can't choose between too many options, the chance to focus a little better on their play and develop their powers of concentration. They won't feel so overwhelmed by what's on offer. At a later date you can bring out the toys you have put away and they will greet them with as much excitement as if they were new. An added advantage of this strategy is that tidying up will be much easier.

TIDYING UP

When your home looks like a bomb-site two minutes after you've tidied up the temptation can be to leave it that way. Many parents, faced with the never-ending struggle to put things away or get their kids to tidy up after themselves, decide it's easier to live with chaos for the time being. The trouble is that the chaos sometimes lasts for years. It doesn't have to be that way – and it shouldn't be that way.

Some parents leave the mess because they don't want to spend time tidying up. What they forget is that mess itself is time-consuming and can even be expensive, if you're going to have to spend hours looking for missing pieces of jigsaws or fork out more money to buy new ones. A chaotic messy environment tells children that they don't have to respect their belongings. It also tells them that they don't have to respect yours.

When there are toys spread over every surface, your child will find it difficult to accept that there is anywhere in the home or anything in the home you might want to call your own. I've also noticed that mess makes discipline almost impossible to enforce. I'm not saying you should keep things pin-neat and rush round constantly plumping up the cushions. But basic order is essential – kids can't learn anything when they're surrounded by chaos.

You can't expect a toddler to be tidy or to clean up after herself. But you can get her to join in when you tidy up – another good use for the Involvement Technique. Plenty of praise works wonders. The toy doesn't have to be in the right box. All the toys don't have to be picked up. Simply making it fun and getting them to join in lays down a good foundation for later. Sort different types of toys or equipment into different coloured boxes – she'll find it easier to help that way. Make it a game: 'Who can tidy up the fastest?' Older kids need to know that you have rules about mess and that there are places in the home where you don't want toys underfoot all the time.

Here's how to cope:

* Make tidying up into a game. Involve your child and give him praise when he helps.

* Don't set unreasonably high standards.

* Save yourself extra work by not allowing every single toy to be out at once. Rotate toys in and out of view.

* Keep art materials, pens, markers and paints well out of reach. Supervise messy or creative play in an area where cleaning up is easy.

* Explain the rules about tidying up but don't expect perfection.

* You can leave toys out in a playroom all day, or even tidy up every other day. You can always close the door on the chaos. But don't leave the mess for months.

How much TV?

Far too much is the answer in many cases. In some homes, the telly is on all day, morning, noon and night. Kids who watch telly round the clock aren't getting healthy exercise, they aren't using their imaginations and they aren't interacting with each other. What they are getting is mindless stimulation that will wind them up, shorten their attention spans and give them all sorts of ideas that you would rather they didn't have. I'm not just talking about exposure to violence or bad language, I'm talking about the adverts that will whet their appetite for food you don't want them to eat or toys you can't afford.

It's almost as bad if the telly is on and no one's watching it. All it's doing is adding to the noise levels and general confusion.

Here's how to manage your kids' viewing:

- [ ] You need to be the boss of the remote control. Decide how long you are prepared to allow your kids to watch TV and decide which programmes are suitable. In the case of older children, you can involve them in the choice.

- [ ] Don't use the TV as a babysitter. It's not the answer to childcare or time management. But if you pop your child in front of Snow White on the video to get an extra half hour in bed on Saturday morning, don't beat yourself up about it. You're not the only one. And it's perfectly acceptable to put a video on for your little boy while you sit on the sofa and breastfeed his sister. Just use the TV wisely.

- [ ] Don't allow children to watch noisy cartoons or play computer games in the run-up to bed. It makes them over-excited and over-stimulated.

- [ ] Don't let your kids watch programmes that scare them. Even children's films and cartoons can be scary for some children. Keep an eye on what they're watching and how they react.

Tips for happy play

Variety is the spice of life. Keep activities varied and you stand a better chance of keeping your kids happy. Play doesn't just mean toys – it means outings and trips to the park, a kick-about in the garden, 'helping' Mum and Dad with a job, creative fun with paints and plasticine, games of 'let's pretend'. Games don't have to be loud and boisterous. Quiet times can be just as much fun.

Let your child choose what she wants to play.

Encourage your child to work things out for herself. Show her how, but let her do it. That's how she learns.

Let your hair down. Don't be serious about play. Be silly, join in and enjoy yourself. Let your child direct the play.

When rain stops outdoor play and you and your kids feel cooped up, improvise play. Make them a 'den' or a 'tent' using old sheets and blankets draped over a table or a sofa.

Let your child's imagination run riot. Dressing-up clothes are great for role play. Give her your old clothes to have fun with.

Don't push a child into playing with a toy that is too old for her. It won't speed up her development and it will only frustrate her. Toys and games come with recommended ages not just for reasons of safety.

Don't buy expensive breakable toys for children who are too young to be careful. You're just giving yourself something else to worry and nag about, and you'll only end up blaming your child when the toy does get broken. And that's not fair on the child. Expense means nothing to a small child. It certainly does not mean a better toy. Think of all the fun a two-year-old can have with wrapping paper and empty boxes.

Get outside whenever you can. Kids need room to breathe and space to run around and get rid of their excess energy. You need it too!

PROBLEM:
FIGHTING/AGGRESSIVE BEHAVIOUR

Play can sometimes bring out the worst in kids. One minute they're playing nicely and the next World War Three has just broken out in the living room.

Hostilities can erupt for all sorts of reasons. In toddlers, it's often unthinking. A young toddler will act on impulse unless he is diverted or prevented from doing so. He won't know that kicking someone will hurt. It just seemed like a good idea for the nanosecond it flashed through his head. Young kids sometimes lash out physically because they can't resolve things in words.

Older toddlers quickly learn that fighting, biting and other kinds of aggressive behaviour get them instant attention. It's negative attention, but it's better than none at all. Jealousy can also be to blame, as well as a shaky grasp of sharing and cooperation. Losing a game or refusing to hand over a toy can trigger an outburst of violent fury.

Bear in mind that there's a difference between the odd skirmish, quarrel or squabble and out-and-out fighting. Don't rush in at the first sign of an argument. Let them see if they can sort it out for themselves. Fighting and aggression is different.

It's important to understand the reasons that lie behind fighting and aggression but it's equally important to make it clear that you just won't tolerate it. Any child who gets away with aggressive behaviour in the home will get the idea that the same thing is acceptable at her friend's house, in the park and at nursery or school.

SOLUTION:
THE NAUGHTY STEP TECHNIQUE

Fighting and aggression in young toddlers should be nipped in the bud. As soon as your child shows that she is old enough to understand what she's doing, use the Naughty Step Technique (see page 80) to show her that this kind of behaviour is just not allowed. There's no two ways about it. Fighting means zero tolerance. Use the One-Strike-And-You're-Out Technique (page 84) in the case of an older child who really should know better.

When fighting is constantly happening at playtime, you need to make sure your child understands what shared play is all about. After the discipline is over, sit down and play with your kids and show them how to take turns.

PROBLEM:
DESTRUCTIVE
BEHAVIOUR

If you give a baby a book with paper pages,
the next time you look, some of those pages
might be chewed, scrumpled, torn, sucked or
otherwise investigated. That's not destructive
behaviour. If your young toddler has knocked
into a table and sent an ornament flying,
that's not destructive behaviour, either.
It's an accident (and an oversight on your
part). If your four-year-old is tearing the
wallpaper off his bedroom wall and scribbling
on the doors with felt tips; if he breaks a toy
ten minutes after he's been given it – that's
destructive behaviour.

SOLUTION:
TEACHING
RESPECT

Make sure your child understands the rules.
Explain that writing on the walls, ripping
wallpaper, breaking toys is just not allowed.
Use the Naughty Step Technique (see page
80) to back up your rules. In extreme cases,
you might want to use the Toy Confiscation
Technique (page 86) and limit his toys to ten
until he learns how to play nicely with them
and look after them.

At the same time, take a good hard look
at your home. If it's total chaos, your child
won't get the message that it's important to
respect his surroundings and his belongings.
To enforce discipline on this issue and on
most other issues, too, you don't need a show
home, but you do need a basic degree of order.

Other behavioural issues

Parenting throws up lots of grey areas. It's not a grey area when your child spits or throws food; it's not a grey area if he hurts another child. But what about whining and whingeing? What about shyness?

Children are little copycats and they pick things up fast. Before they set foot in a school playground for the first time, you can't very well blame bad language on other kids. They're most likely to have heard those naughty words coming from you – even worse, the first time they come out with them it's bound to be in front of someone you'd least like to hear them. Your parents, for example.

First, look at your own behaviour. You can't set standards for children in the abstract. You can't say one thing and do the other and expect them to do what you say. Positive reinforcement in the form of praise for good behaviour can go a long way to correcting these kind of 'grey area' issues.

PROBLEM:
WHINING

Kids pick up everything. If you spend a lot of time complaining, chances are your child is bound to pick up that whingeing tone and start to use it on you. That drip-drip-drip is designed to wear you down until you give up and give him what he wants.

SOLUTION:
DON'T GIVE IN

Don't give in to whining. Giving in teaches a child that whining is the sort of behaviour and tone of voice that will guarantee a result. If your child is whining for something you don't want her to have, explain that a) you aren't going to give her the biscuit because it's nearly lunchtime and b) that whining is not the way to ask for things.

If she is whining for something she can have, explain that she can have it as soon as she asks for it properly. Show and tell her how you want her to behave:

'Don't whine for juice.' Copy her whining face and tone. Every time I do that with children, they collapse in fits of giggles. It gets the message across.

Then tell her how to ask properly. 'You can have some juice when you ask for it politely. Say, "Please can I have some juice?" Now you say it.'

PROBLEM:
SHYNESS

Babies and toddlers are often shy of people they don't know. This is natural and it's a feature of that stage where a child is very attached to her mother or her prime carer and is anxious about any form of separation. It's not really shyness. Don't pay too much attention to it and try to resist the temptation to label your child as 'shy' or even worse to think that her behaviour is 'sweet'.

It's okay if your kid is a little shy. There's nothing wrong with it. Some children are naturally more outgoing than others. But extreme shyness in older children can cause difficulties when you invite people round or go round to your friends' houses. If you don't get to grips with it, it may end up causing problems when your child comes to settle at school.

Some children use shy behaviour as a way of getting attention or to get out of doing something they don't want to do. Those are the ones clinging to Mum's skirt while Mum makes desperate attempts to get them to say hello to someone they know perfectly well.

SOLUTION:
SHOW AND TELL

Don't make a fuss of shyness and give your child more attention than he would otherwise have got. Show and tell him how you expect him to behave with other people. Coax his confidence along in a light-hearted way. From a young age, expose your child to situations where he is surrounded by other people, especially other children.

Teach him that it's nice and polite to say 'Hello' to other people. Explain new situations before your child encounters them so he won't react by hanging back. Let him see you move confidently around other people – at the park, in your friend's home, at playgroup – and don't let him draw you into his own shy little corner.

PROBLEM:
FEARS

Small children are frightened by lots of things: nightmares, loud noises, water, dogs, witches and other products of their busy imaginations. Always take fears seriously. They're very serious to the child.

Some fears are associated with certain ages. Many children around a year to two years old hate the sound of the hoover and other domestic machines like food processors. When children get to four or thereabouts, they often become scared of dogs. Irrational fears are a feature of the stage when there's no clear line between fantasy and reality. That doesn't mean the fear is any less real.

A child may also have a nightmare if he's seen something scary on TV. Even cartoons and Disney films can scare some kids. Keep an eye on what's he watching and how he's reacting – and switch off if he seems to be getting upset.

SOLUTION:
EXPLANATION AND REASSURANCE

When your child is frightened, the first thing she needs is your reassurance and comfort. Explanations can go a long way. Fears like being scared of the hoover will usually pass by themselves. In the meantime you can help things along by gradually getting her used to the sound of a hoover or blender or whatever appliance is frightening her. Bring her into the room with you but keep her a good distance away from the appliance. Tell her you're going to use the hoover. Switch it on and off quickly a few times so she can hear the noise stop as well as start. Then use the appliance, but keep your distance from your child. It's being close to the sound that panics her.

Other fears – like fear of water or fear of dogs – need to be handled by introducing the child gradually and in a subtle way to what's scaring him so he can learn to relax and get over the fear. Try to put yourself in his shoes. Viewed from an adult height, a dog might not be particularly scary. A four-year-old is seeing a much bigger picture of the same animal, and it's right in his face. Once he has relaxed, instead of climbing on your shoulder to bury his face in your neck, he'll be on the floor and his own two feet.

Never doubt a child the first time she comes to wake you reporting a nightmare. She needs to feel she can talk to you about what's scaring her. You've got to keep the lines of communication open and not dismiss her fears.

If it's night time and your child has had a nightmare or has woken up and imagined something scary, take her back to bed and give her comfort and reassurance. She might have got frightened by the strange shape a toy made in the dark. Sit with her, with the lights off, and show her that the silhouette is just her favourite doll. Leave the door ajar and the hall light on. When she has settled down, tell her where you'll be and what you'll be doing: 'I'm just going to be downstairs if you need to talk to me. I'm going to have my supper and then I'm going to watch TV.' Tuck her in with her favourite cuddly toys and soothers.

Out and about

Kids really do choose their moments. They reserve some of their worst behaviour for situations where it's going to embarrass you the most, and that means in full public view. That's not surprising. Your child can read you like a book and will have picked up the signals that you're stressed, tense or anxious before you even leave the house. You might even have made it specially easy for him by telling him that you don't want him to act up. 'We're going to the supermarket and this time I want you to behave. Do you hear?'

If the embarrassment factor isn't bad enough, there's also the fear factor. Walking down the street or driving in the car with small children are potentially dangerous situations. Before a child is old enough to appreciate the importance of safety, a rule about a seat belt is just another restriction that she might decide to test to the limit.

PROBLEM:
THE SUPERMARKET SHOP

Small children misbehave in supermarkets. They whinge to get down from the trolley, they run off down the aisles, they pull things off shelves, they beg for treats and – when all else fails – they have a tantrum at the checkout.

Many parents live in absolute dread of the weekly supermarket shop. Or of any shopping expedition. Some dread it so much that they never take their kids with them.

It just isn't always practical to arrange your shopping expeditions around the times when your kids can be looked after by someone else. There are better ways to use those occasions – on quality time for yourself and your partner, for example.

SOLUTION:
THE INVOLVEMENT TECHNIQUE

You might find the weekly shop a chore, but you don't need to communicate that fact to your toddler. Children play up in supermarkets because they're bored, you're busy and distracted, and they know that gives them the perfect opportunity to misbehave.

The solution, which works wonders with toddlers and small children, is to involve your child in what you're doing. Make it exciting for him. Give him tasks to do.

When I take a child to the supermarket, I make her a little shopping list of her own. I have a big list and she has a mini list, with a few things on it that she is in charge of getting. These are proper adult things, like bread, milk, oranges and juice. While we're going up and down the aisles, I keep reminding her what's on her list and telling her to look out for them. 'Have you seen the milk yet?'

You can draw pictures instead of writing words on the mini list if you like, but I find that even small children can remember a short list of three or four things. Make sure you include something to find at the beginning of the shop, something from the middle aisles and something from the end so the game lasts the whole way round the supermarket.

On *Supernanny*, we tried this technique on Charlie, a two-and-a-half-year-old who had previously had plenty of experience terrorizing supermarkets. The sequence wasn't included in the final programme, but I can tell you the technique worked like a charm.

PROBLEM:
CAR JOURNEYS

SOLUTION:
DISTRACTION AND INVOLVEMENT

The lowest level of problem you'll get in the car is the 'Are we there yet?' variety, when your child makes it clear at ten-second intervals that the whole trip's taking far too long and he's fed up. He'll usually start on this refrain as soon as you turn out of your road.

If you've got more than one child in the back, boredom can lead to squabbling and bickering, fighting and kicking. In extreme cases, a child may try to escape from the car seat or unbuckle her seat belt.

Very occasionally, children will behave badly in the car because they're frightened of that particular situation. Sometimes, the problem may be down to carsickness. Before your child can communicate clearly to you that travelling in a car (or a train for that matter) makes her feel sick, the first indication you'll have (after the screaming and crying) is an ashen grey face, immediately before she actually is sick. Ask your doctor or pharmacist for motion sickness remedies if you suspect that carsickness is at the root of the problem. It can make children really miserable. Make sure your car is not too hot and stuffy. That can make children queasy. There are also strips you can buy that hang underneath the car from the axle and drag along the road. By grounding the car, these help prevent carsickness.

Try to pre-empt bad behaviour in the car by making journeys interesting and exciting in themselves, not just a means to an end. Get your child to choose a favourite toy to play with in the car. Play audio books and cassettes. Point out interesting things out of the window. You can get older kids to play simple spotting games – 'How many red cars can you see?' – and 'I spy with my little eye' is another good one.

If your child persists in acting up in the car or has managed to escape from his child seat or seat belt, pull over at the first safe opportunity. Unrestrained children are in real danger in cars, which is why it's illegal for them not to be belted in a childseat. Put him back in his seat, buckle him up, resisting the stiff legs, back arching and tantrum that might result, and wait until he is calm before setting off again. Explain very sternly how important it is that he stays in his seat.

RUNNING OFF

RULES AND EXPLANATIONS/REINS

For every clingy toddler, there's one who just loves to give you the slip – in the park, on the street, in the shop. One minute he's holding your hand and the next minute your heart is in your mouth. To him, it's an exciting game of chase, or hide and seek on a grand scale. To you, until you find him again unharmed, it's potentially the worst-case scenario.

Make it very clear that your child is to hold your hand at all times when you are crossing the road. Explain why. Teach her in a positive way and get her to rehearse the reasons each time you come to a crossing. 'Now what do we do? We hold hands. We look out for cars. We look both ways and when it's safe we cross the road.' You can't repeat it often enough. 'Look for the green man. Can you see the green man? When you see the green man, that means it's safe to cross the road.'

When you take your child to the park or somewhere similar, explain carefully how far he can go. 'Stay around the slide where I can see you.' Build up trust. If he runs off, bring him back and make him hold your hand, hold the pram, or sit in the buggy. It's like pulling on imaginary reins.

But if you've got a toddler on your hands who is determined to run off at every opportunity, rules and explanations won't work. If your anxiety has got the better of you, I don't see any reason why you shouldn't use real reins in this situation. It will make you feel better, at least. Until he gets to the age when he's got a bit of common sense and can control his impulse to run off, it's better to be safe than sorry.

MY TOP TEN RULES

**TO SUM UP, HERE'S HOW MY TOP TEN RULES APPLY
TO SOCIAL SKILLS AND BEHAVIOUR PROBLEMS:**

1. PRAISE AND REWARDS

Praise and positive reinforcement are important when it comes to
teaching social skills. Notice good behaviour. Don't use toys as treats
on a regular basis.

2. CONSISTENCY

Don't change or make up rules as you go along. Follow through and
make sure your partner backs you up. Constantly reinforce important
rules, like those about crossing the road safely.

3. ROUTINE

Build time into your schedule for play, indoors and out. Vary play
activities and have special treats or games up your sleeve for days
when rain stops play. Try to get outdoors as much as possible
to let children blow off steam.

4. BOUNDARIES

Be clear about your rules and what you expect in terms of behaviour.
Set limits on TV watching. Teach respect for possessions by keeping
chaos under control. Don't give into whining and whingeing.

5. DISCIPLINE

Use the Naughty Step Technique for unacceptable behaviour
like fighting and aggression.

6. WARNINGS

Give warnings about what's happening next so your child can prepare herself. Don't interrupt play suddenly and expect your child to move smoothly on to the next activity. Give warnings before disciplining so she can correct her behaviour herself.

7. EXPLANATIONS

Show and tell your child how you expect him to behave when it comes to 'grey areas'. Always talk over the reasons behind fears and give plenty of reassurance. Teach your children how to play games and how to play with toys.

8. RESTRAINT

Don't buy your child the entire contents of the toy shop. Improvised toys are just as much fun. Practise toy rotation so that everything's not out at once. Take control of the TV and monitor what your children are watching.

9. RESPONSIBILITY

Teach your child how to share and take turns. Don't always hover over your kids when they play. Use the Involvement Technique for supermarket shopping and at other times when you need to be busy.

10. RELAXATION

Enjoy your children. Get involved in their play and let them direct it. Cuddle up with them and read them a story.

Bedtime

Remember sleep? Remember getting into bed, snuggling down beside your partner *and sleeping through the night*? Remember waking up, refreshed and ready for the day? A good night's sleep is a distant memory for many parents of small children. But it doesn't have to be that way.

I think it's fair to say that sleeping problems send more parents in search of support and advice than any other childcare issue. That's not surprising. Of all the family battlegrounds and crisis points, difficulties at bedtime have the potential to cause the greatest distress. From the baby who cries off and on all night, to the boisterous toddler whose idea of a good game is to spin out bedtime until midnight, to the pre-schooler plagued with night terrors who creeps into your bed hours before dawn, sleep problems take many forms and can occur at any age.

If your child doesn't sleep, or sleeps poorly, if it takes the whole evening just to put your child to bed, everyone is going to suffer. Anyone can bounce back after the odd broken night, but weeks and weeks of lost evenings or disturbed rest amount to pure torture. When you're that exhausted, the simplest task becomes an uphill struggle. Without regular sleep, even the happiest, most easy-going person will be irritable, depressed, less able to concentrate and more likely to have accidents or fall ill. If that zombie-like state isn't bad enough, you'll also find it harder to cope with your child during the daytime, and you'll lose your patience, which will mean more clashes, more tantrums and frayed nerves all round.

And the effects ripple outwards. One wakeful little body and you'll not only have an exhausted Mum but a worn-out Dad and tetchy older children, too – in other words, an entire household running on empty. Last but not least, despite all appearances to the contrary, your sleepless child will also suffer. It may not seem that way, but the bright-eyed toddler bouncing off the walls at 4 a.m. is not getting the rest he needs. Unlike adults or older kids, a toddler or young child who gets to sleep late or wakes up for long periods during the night is not usually able to catch up that sleep.

The good news is that even the worst sleep problems can be turned round in a surprisingly short space of time. It may only take a few days. Once you've sorted out a proper sleep pattern for your child, you won't look back. I have used the techniques outlined in this chapter countless times with success. They work. And the benefits are immediate, for everyone in the household. You'll be amazed to find your child not only sleeping through the night, but taking regular daytime naps, too. You'll probably notice that her appetite also improves. Daytimes will be calmer and you'll begin to enjoy your child much more.

As with any rule or technique, you have to stick with it. At the end of the day, when you're tired, or in the middle of the night, when you've just stumbled from a warm bed, it's easy to let things slide. All parents are programmed to respond to crying, but there is a difference between genuine distress and the type of crying whose purpose is to wear you down so that you give in. Remember: you're not being mean. You are simply teaching your child how to get what all kids need, which is a good night's sleep. He doesn't know he needs to sleep, but you do. And you know best.

PROBLEM:
REFUSING TO GO TO BED

SOLUTION:
THE BEDTIME ROUTINE

The child who refuses to go to bed is depriving himself of much-needed sleep and you of much-needed quality time that you could be spending on yourself, your partner or your other kids. This may not be as serious as the exhaustion that results from repeated waking in the night, but it is a major source of irritation and tension in many families. A milder version of the same problem is where the child asks for umpteen drinks of water, trips to the toilet and indulges in similar delaying tactics in an attempt to fend off the inevitable moment of separation.

Toddlers who have gained the upper hand in other areas of family life are particularly prone to this type of behaviour; for many kids, bedtimes can continue to be battlegrounds for years to come.

A bedtime routine has two important functions. It lets your child know that there is a consistent pattern to going to bed, which she is not going to be able to change or manipulate at will, and it prepares her for sleep in a calming sequence of events that are designed to help her relax.

A sensible bedtime

The first step is to set a time for going to bed. Whatever time young children are put to bed, they tend to wake up at the same time in the morning – generally fairly early, and sometimes as soon as it gets light. That means the later they go to bed, the more tired they will be the next day. The whole notion of a 'lie-in' is alien to under-fives.

In my experience, most kids of pre-school age benefit from a bedtime of 7.00 to 8.00 p.m. Once the bedtime routine has been put into practice, many parents who have previously reported that their child seems to need less sleep than others their age are often surprised to find their wakeful toddler happily going to bed much earlier than they expected and sleeping for longer.

However, at some point between the ages of two and four, the blissful interval of the afternoon nap will be outgrown. Parents of young children understandably treasure that brief window of sanity, when they can have a shower, a cup of tea or simply enjoy the sound of silence. But you can't reasonably expect this stage to last forever. If you start to find bedtimes getting difficult again and your child doesn't seem particularly sleepy despite all your soothing strategies, it may be time for the nap to become a thing of the past. Inevitably, there may be a period of transition, when your child is too wakeful at bedtime if she has a nap in the afternoon, but overtired and fractious if she doesn't have one. Trust me, it's short-lived.

A set bedtime gives small children the rest they need. It gives older siblings an extra hour or so when they can call on your attention – for a chat, for help with homework, or just to be with you. And it gives you and your partner your evenings back.

HOW TO SPOT A SLEEPY CHILD

If bedtimes in your household are war zones, you may be missing the signs that tell you your child is ready for bed, whatever they are saying to the contrary. A yawn is a dead giveaway, of course, but other signs include whining and fractious behaviour (the whole 'tears before bedtime' scenario) as well as rubbing eyes, thumb sucking and flopping on the floor. If your child shows such signs much earlier than the bedtime you have set, you can move your schedule forward; if the signs are delayed, you can move it back by small steps each day.

Countdown to bed

You've set a bedtime. It's posted up there on the wall as part of your family timetable. Now you have to put it into practice.

The key to an effective bedtime routine is to allow just enough time for each stage so the child does not feel like he is being rushed into things, but not so much that he starts to get the idea that all of a sudden there is room for manoeuvre. About an hour from getting into bath to saying goodnight is about right.

Unless your child is very precocious, she's not going to have any idea what an hour feels like. Children have only very sketchy notions of time. It's your job to be the Speaking Clock:

'In five minutes, it's time to get into the bath.'

'In two minutes, it's time to get out of the bath.'

'After I read you this story, it's time to put out the light.'

Easing the child through the bedtime routine means giving regular notice about what's coming next so the child has time to prepare for each stage. In some ways, this works a little bit like the verbal warnings you give for bad behaviour, except there's no disapproval attached.

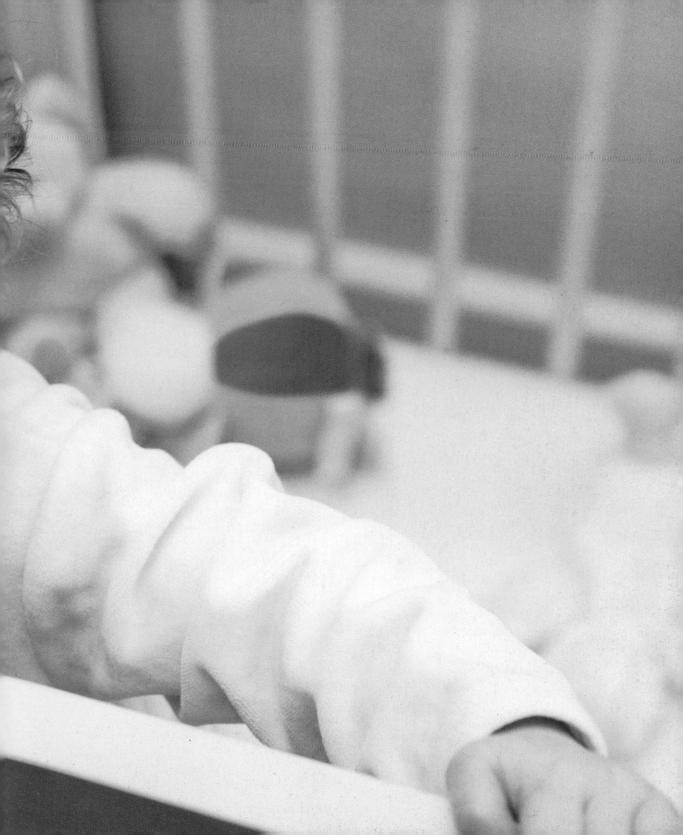

HOW TO PUT YOUR CHILD TO BED:

🧸 In the run-up to bedtime, keep things as calm as possible. This is not the time for noisy cartoons and videos, computer games or rough and tumble. An over-stimulated, over-excited child can't just switch off and go to sleep any more than an adult can. Winding down is important.

🧸 Give a clear indication that bedtime is approaching about ten minutes before you start the routine.

🧸 Begin with a bath. Warm water is a natural aid to relaxation. Give a warning before the bath begins and before it's about to finish.

🧸 Enlist the child's cooperation over simple tasks. It will help her feel involved. 'Now it's time to get out of the bath. Can you pull out the plug for me? Well done!'

🧸 Praise the child when each stage is completed smoothly.

🧸 Read your child a bedtime story. Let her choose one from a small selection. Don't offer too much choice or you might get locked into a battle of wills, but if she has a favourite story by all means read that (and be prepared to read it the next night, and the night after that, and the night after that …) Ask her questions about the pictures to engage her attention. 'Can you see the rabbit? What's the rabbit doing?'

🧸 You may find that after the story he wants to talk for a little while. This is a good time for reassurance, praise and for singling out good moments. 'You were a very good boy at lunch today.' You might also want to tell him what's going to be happening tomorrow. 'We're going to the park with Rose and then we're going to Izzie's for tea.'

🧸 A few comforters or soft toys can all help ease the separation of bedtime but don't turn the cot into a playpen. When you sneak back to check on her later, you can put a few toys at the bottom of the cot in case she wakes up early and wants to play.

🧸 As the time for 'lights out' approaches, give a few minutes' notice.

🧸 Don't get into the habit of waiting with your child until she falls asleep. If she's tired and you've been through the routine step by step, she should be fairly drowsy by now and will drift off easily.

🧸 Lights out! No child can learn how to get to sleep with the light on.

🧸 Don't be tempted to take a shortcut and rush the routine. If you leave out a stage, your child will notice and you'll lose his cooperation. That way, it will probably end up taking even longer.

🧸 If you're taking turns with your partner to put your child to bed, make sure you both follow the same rules and stages. Be consistent and present a united front.

🧸 Don't let your child fall asleep on the sofa and then move him into bed. He'll wake up in a panic wondering how he got there.

Managing multiple bedtimes

Older kids can manage many of the bedtime stages with minimal supervision. But if you have more than one child under five, bedtime is still very much a hands-on affair. The more kids you have, the more hands you're going to need.

The answer is to split or stagger the bedtimes so that the younger goes to bed first, shortly followed by the older child. If at all possible, divide your efforts so that one parent is reponsible for one child, while the other parent looks after the other one. Bedtime works best when each child gets some degree of individual attention. Make sure you swap things round the next night so that each child has a chance to have a special time with Mum and Dad.

Where multiple bedtimes can usefully overlap is bathtime. You can enlist the help of your older child when it comes to bathing her younger sibling. Simple tasks like fetching the soap or flannel, and getting a towel or toy, can boost a child's confidence and willingness to cooperate. This type of involvement often has a knock-on effect, making her much better behaved when it comes to her own bedtime routine.

Disrupted routines

There are two types of disruption that can play havoc with routines: those that are avoidable and those that are not. By all means allow your children to stay up a little later on Saturday, provided you're prepared to stand your corner and enforce regular bedtime on Sunday night. But don't allow yourself to be talked into allowing a child to stay up to watch a television programme. That's what the video is for.

However, there are times when a routine goes out of the window. When a child is ill or teething, physical discomfort will inevitably overrule any soothing strategy. Once the crisis has past, get back to the routine as soon as possible. Don't allow the interruption to become an excuse to relax the rules.

Children identify very strongly with their own beds and derive great security from familiar surroundings, which often makes it difficult to settle them when you are away from home. Reminders of their own bed and bedroom can be useful comforters in a strange setting – take favourite toys and blankets. Try to stick to a similar routine when you're away as far as possible so that you don't have to reinvent the wheel when you get home.

PROBLEM:
NOT BEING ABLE TO GET TO SLEEP ALONE

If you've always waited until your child has fallen asleep before you leave the room, your presence will be built into her notion of bedtime and she's going to find the moment of separation particularly difficult. And you're going to find large chunks of your evening are vanishing without trace.

Children who can only get to sleep with a parent in the room need to learn how to fall asleep by themselves. What might start as a little extra comfort when the child is very little can turn into an issue of control as the child learns how to put off the moment of separation longer and longer to keep you by their side.

SOLUTION:
THE SLEEP SEPARATION TECHNIQUE

This technique is a means of gradually breaking the cycle of dependency, so your child learns that he can get to sleep without you being in the room.

★ When you put your child to bed, don't get into bed with him. Don't sit on the bed. Say goodnight, give him a cuddle and tell him it's time to go to sleep. Then sit very close to the bed on the floor.

★ Turn the child so he's facing away from you. If he keeps eye contact with you, he will try to start a conversation. Tell him to close his eyes and that it's time to go to sleep.

★ Make sure the light is off and the door is open.

★ Sit in silence, not looking at the child, until the child goes to sleep. Each time he tries to talk to you, just tell him, 'Sleep'.

★ The next night, repeat the same stages, sitting a little further away from the bed. Over the coming nights, move further and further towards the door until you are sitting outside the open door.

★ The last stage is to go through the procedure sitting outside the door, with the door ajar. Naturally this technique is going to take quite a while but remember you're breaking a habit that could otherwise go on for years.

PROBLEM:
WAKING IN THE NIGHT

All children, and adults, too, have brief periods of wakefulness throughout the night. Every hour or so we come to the brink of consciousness, then turn over and drift back to sleep. That's part of a natural sleep pattern. What isn't natural is when that brief wakeful period leads to full consciousness and the inability to settle back into sleep.

Everyone has experienced nights like that. You may find yourself wide awake at 3 a.m. unable to switch off your anxieties over a looming deadline or an unforeseen expense. Or you may have woken to the sound of your neighbours throwing the party of a lifetime next door and find you can't tune out the noise and get back to sleep again. Fears, nightmares and things that go bump in the night can also wake children, as can the discomfort of teething or illness. But persistent waking, over days and weeks, accompanied by crying and/or getting out of bed is a different story altogether. If you respond to night-waking by offering food, comfort and entertainment on demand, you will only reinforce a bad habit and your child won't learn how to settle by herself.

BABIES

Very young babies, particularly those who are breastfed, will wake at regular intervals throughout the night chiefly because they are hungry or wet. An infant can only take in so much milk at one time; when that's digested, your baby will be ready for more and will soon let you know it.

When feeding is going on round the clock, interrupted sleep is inevitable, but there are various ways in which you can minimize the disruption to yourself and start to teach your baby the difference between day and night.

★ Use a nightlight.

★ In the very early days, keep the baby's cot or basket in your room so you can respond before a grizzle turns into a full-throated cry, waking everyone in the vicinity. However, I would suggest that you don't keep the baby in your room for too long. You may find yourself waking unnecessarily when she makes the slightest noise and it may well make separation an issue later on. Three months is a suitable age to move a baby into her own room.

★ When the baby wakes, feed her, but don't talk to her or stimulate her with play. Get across the message that night is different from day. Wind her, change her nappy and settle her down.

★ If your baby is sleeping, but you haven't gone to bed yet, don't tiptoe around the house trying to keep everything as quiet as possible. A sudden loud noise may wake a baby, but normal household sounds won't.

★ Share the load. If you are bottle-feeding, work out a rota so that your partner shares some of the night feeds. If you are breastfeeding, express some milk.

★ Once the baby is fed, he may well fall to sleep in your arms. If he doesn't, put him back into his cot and let him settle himself to sleep. If the grizzling carries on, try a gentle rub on the back or the tummy, but don't pick him up again unless he starts to cry in earnest. It may be wind that is bothering him, in which case, ease him over your shoulder and pat his back.

AFTER WEANING

After solid food is an established part of the diet, *there is no reason why a baby should not sleep through the night*. If he carries on waking several times a night, night after night, it's not through hunger, but for a different reason altogether and that's usually to seek comfort.

If it isn't bad enough getting up every hour to see to a crying child, many parents then find themselves locked into hours of pacing or rocking with a wide-awake child over their shoulder. After a while broken nights become the norm. A child who is picked up, fed and soothed every time she wakes and cries soon learns that there's more of the same where that came from. Let's face it, you don't want to be driving around the neighbourhood in your pyjamas, trying to get the child buckled in the car seat behind you to doze off.

★ If the night-waking is recent and has only lasted a few days, the cause may be teething. Sniffles and colds will also disrupt a baby's sleep. Rule out illness or teething first.

★ Bouts of wakefulness are sometimes caused when a child feels she has missed out on attention during the day, in which case it's a protest to let you know she feels short-changed. If you've been very busy or harried, think about ways you can spend more quality time with her during the day.

★ If the child is easily soothed by a reassuring back rub or a quick cuddle, you don't need to take further steps. The problem will sort itself out with time. Don't respond to every grizzle: give him a chance to learn how to settle himself.

★ If you want to carry on breastfeeding past the introduction of solid food, restrict feeds to the daytime, last thing at night and first thing in the morning. You don't stand a chance of getting a child to sleep through if you are still feeding her at night. It's much too great a comfort to miss out on!

SOLUTION:
THE CONTROLLED CRYING TECHNIQUE

If the wakefulness has settled into a regular pattern and is taking a severe toll on the family, you can try the Controlled Crying Technique. Versions of this technique are widely used by many sleep-trainers and family coaches and I have always found it highly effective. In many cases, the technique will do the trick in less than a week.

At the outset, it is important to state that 'controlled crying' is not the same as 'leaving a child to cry'. That old-fashioned remedy is not acceptable today; quite rightly, as it is both brutal and ineffective. 'Controlled crying' is completely different. Unlike leaving a child to cry for long periods unattended, which reinforces a sense of abandonment, 'controlled crying' demonstrates that you are still at hand, that you have not gone away, but that you are in charge and it's time to sleep.

I know that some parents don't want to leave their child crying for any length of time. While I wouldn't recommend the technique for every family, I do think it's one of the best ways of breaking a cycle of wakefulness.

The key to the technique is learning to distinguish between different types of cry. A high-pitched continuous cry or a low, groaning sound is the sign of a child in severe distress or pain. If your child is crying like that, it's time to act promptly and see what's the matter.

Crying for comfort or attention sounds different. It may begin with a grizzle or a wail, but it tends to break off at intervals while the child waits for results, and then it returns. It's like a wave pattern.

It's your job to observe and listen to your child's crying. Until you feel totally confident that you can recognize the different types of cry, don't start the technique.

This is how I use the technique:

★ The first time your child wakes, spend a few moments listening to the tone of the cry. Listen and observe. It's hard for any parent to have to listen to their child cry and not respond, but try to stay calm and don't allow yourself to be swamped by feelings of panic. If the crying does not indicate distress, wait a moment.

★ When there has been a sustained amount of crying, go to the child. Don't turn on the light. Don't make eye contact – look at the bridge of your child's nose or at his tummy. Don't talk or make conversation. Make a soothing noise – 'sh' or 'hush' – rub him on the back or the tummy, replace the covers and leave.

★ Accept the fact that your child will wake and cry again – it's a pattern you're dealing with. It might be an hour later, it might be five minutes later. When she cries again, wait for double the time before going into her and then repeat the same procedure.

★ On subsequent wakings, carry on doubling the intervals between going in to soothe him. This is the point when most parents find the going gets tough. Let me tell you the emotions you're going to be feeling. Responding to your child's cry is a natural instinct. When you're trying to resist that urge, you'll have a rush of adrenalin, your hands will get hot and clammy, your heart will pound and you'll feel like you're losing control. Understand that this is just your body's natural reaction and try to stay calm. Get support from your partner or ask a friend to stay with you overnight – someone who can give you comfort and strength when you're feeling like this.

★ Don't give up and don't let it slide. The message will get across, perhaps sooner than you think. You should begin to see substantial improvements within a week.

PROBLEM:
GETTING OUT OF BED

Between two and three years, perhaps younger, your child will discover she has a secret weapon at her disposal; she can get out of bed! Children who settle down to sleep at a reasonable time and then repeatedly get out of bed during the night are generally looking for attention. They may give a variety of reasons for their wakefulness – hunger, thirst, nightmare, too hot, too cold – some of which may be contradictory! The simple fact, whatever they tell you, is that the wakefulness has become a bad habit that they know they can get away with.

SOLUTION:
THE STAYING IN BED TECHNIQUE

First of all, eliminate all possible excuses for getting out of bed. Make sure there's a glass of water beside the bed if your child gets thirsty at night. Make sure she's had a wee before she gets into bed. Give her fewer and fewer things to get out of bed for.

If that doesn't work, use the Staying In Bed Technique. Results are generally very rapid with this technique. The key is not to allow yourself to debate the reasons for the wakefulness – the logic of the under-fives being what it is, you won't win.

★ The first time the child gets out of bed, escort him back and explain that it's bedtime. Give him a little cuddle. Then leave.

★ The second time, put him back to bed and say, 'It's bedtime, darling'. Give another cuddle and leave.

★ The third time, put him back to bed without saying a word.

★ Subsequent episodes should be treated in the same way. No talking, no conversation, no debate. You must get to grips with yourself and understand your emotions. You are not being mean, you are just teaching your child to stay in bed.

★ It is very important with this technique that the parent who put the child to bed in the first place is the one who takes him back to bed when he wakes up. Following through is essential. This lets the child know that he cannot play one parent off the other.

★ Use a star chart to reward your child for a trouble-free night. Let him know that once he has won a number of stars (no less than three, no more than five) he can have a reward for his behaviour. But please be sensible with your rewards! You don't want to make another rod for your back.

PROBLEM:
GETTING INTO YOUR BED

There's a huge difference of opinion on whether or not you should allow your kids to share your bed. For some, it's a natural, cosy part of family life. For others, it's their worst nightmare.

If your child is not well or is particularly insecure for some reason, then I don't see why she shouldn't have the comfort of your bed. Weekend mornings are good times for this type of closeness.

That's different from having your kids in bed with you every single night. At the risk of fanning the flames of controversy, I have to say I think that's a bad idea. Why?

★ You are unlikely to get a good night's sleep unless you, your partner and your child/children are all sound sleepers. Small children can occupy a disproportionate amount of bed space (often diagonally), and that's not even taking into account the wriggling and sudden desire for a chat at four in the morning. One minute, there'll be a sharp little elbow in your ribs, the next it's a little foot in your face. The squirming will carry on until you find yourself with 5% of the bed and 0% of the duvet. Then your kid will fall asleep and you won't dare move. It's true, you may get more sleep, but that doesn't mean it's the right solution to that particular problem.

★ Parents need a private space to call their own. At the very least, this should be their own bed. A child in your bed is the most effective contraceptive there is. Becoming a parent doesn't mean you should have to say goodbye to intimacy or a sex life.

★ From my experience, it's dads who get the rawest deal. When a child slips into the parental bed, Dad often has to retreat to the living room sofa, the child's vacated bed, or, in extreme circumstances, the floor, just to get a decent night's sleep. If this goes on too long, your marriage will begin to show signs of strain.

★ Allow one child to get into bed with you and you won't be able to say 'no' to her brothers and sisters. It's the thin end of the wedge. In the same way, mothers who relax the 'not in my bed' rule when their partners are away are storing up trouble for later.

★ Letting your child sleep with you is rarely a positive choice. In my experience, it's often a way of avoiding solving another problem.

SOLUTION:
THE CONTROLLED CRYING/STAYING IN BED TECHNIQUES

Which technique you choose will depend on the age of your child. If your toddler repeatedly wakes and cries in the night and you have been dealing with this problem by bringing him into bed with you, adopt the Controlled Crying Technique (see page 194). In the case of the persistent night-time intruder, the older child who has got himself up and slipped into your bed, the Staying In Bed Technique (see opposite) works wonders. If your child has been getting into your bed regularly for the past five years, you're not necessarily going to break this pattern overnight.

PROBLEM:
NIGHTMARES AND NIGHT FEARS

All children occasionally suffer from nightmares and some develop a short-lived fear of the dark. Bad dreams and bouts of childhood illness go hand in hand and nightmares can also be associated with periods of stress and anxiety: the arrival of a new sibling, for example, or the first days settling in at nursery. Often, however, there's no traceable cause. But there's a difference between the odd nightmare and the child who wakes up repeatedly night after night reporting a bad dream. In the latter case, it's probably a bad habit we're talking about.

SOLUTION:
SOOTHING/STAYING IN BED TECHNIQUE

In the case of a nightmare, go to the child or escort him back to his bed, soothe him and explain he has had a bad dream. Stay with him for a little while until the distress fades. Always take his fears seriously.

If a child develops a fear of the dark, nightlights in the bedroom and bathroom can be comforting. Leave the hall light on and the door ajar. Don't allow the child to persuade you to let her sleep with the light on. A favourite soft toy can be comforting.

Children who repeatedly use nightmares as an excuse for getting out of bed are probably trying to sneak round your defences. For them, use the Staying In Bed Technique (page 196).

PROBLEM:
EARLY WAKING

Nine times out of ten, young children are raring to go much earlier in the morning than their parents. Children who have a natural sleeping pattern and who are put to bed at a time when they are tired, rather than over-tired, often wake up, if not at first light, then fairly soon afterwards. You may be hoping to snatch another half-hour's sleep, but your child has other ideas and is bouncing on your bed letting you know all about them.

SOLUTION:
THE STAYING IN BED TECHNIQUE

As a parent of a young child, it is important to accept that long mornings in bed are a thing of the past for the time being. If your child is sleeping well, you should be getting adequate rest yourself and should be able to adjust your own schedule so that getting up earlier is not such a shock to the system. At the same time, there's early and there's the crack of dawn. If you have a real early bird on your hands, chances are you're not going to persuade her to go back to sleep. In this case, escort her back to bed, explain it is too early and tell her she can play quietly in bed or in her room until it is time for you to get up. This works a bit like the Staying In Bed Technique (page 196), in that you are limiting access to you at unacceptable times.

MY TOP TEN RULES

**TO SUM UP, HERE'S HOW MY TOP TEN RULES
APPLY TO SLEEPING PROBLEMS:**

1. PRAISE AND REWARDS

Praise each stage in the bedtime routine that is smoothly completed.
Praise children for their help and involvement. Single out something
to praise them for at the end of the day just before they go to sleep.

2. CONSISTENCY

Make sure that everyone involved in caring for your kids abides by the
same rules. Make sure that the parent who has put the child to bed is
the one who follows through if the child then wakes and gets up. It's
nice to let your kids snuggle up in bed with you on weekend mornings
but don't allow your kids to get into bed with you on other occasions.

3. ROUTINE

Stick to the bedtime routine. Don't allow times to slip and don't rush
things. Don't make exceptions to accommodate the TV schedule.

4. BOUNDARIES

A set bedtime and a set bedtime routine are clear boundaries that
tell your child that you are in charge. Making sure the child sleeps
through the night in her own bed spells out the same message.
These boundaries also make it clear that there are places and times
of the day reserved for you and your partner.

5. DISCIPLINE

Use the Sleep Separation Technique, the Controlled Crying Technique
and the Staying In Bed Technique to overcome sleep problems.

Part II   The Practice Arena

Part III   Legislation, Law, Reimbursement, and Policy

CONTENTS

A previous edition of this book was publsihed in 1986 as
Nurses, Nurse Practitioners: The Evolution of Primary Care by
Little, Brown and Company.

Cover and interior design by Holly Block

Springer Publishing Company, Inc.
536 Broadway
New York, NY 10012-3955

94 95 96 97 / 5 4 3

Nurses, nurse practitioners : evolution to advanced
   practice / Mathy D. Mezey, Diane O. McGivern,
   editors. — New ed.
      p.   cm. — (Springer series on advanced practice
         nursing)
   Includes bibliographical references and index.
   ISBN 0-8261-7770-0
   1. Nurse practitioners.   2. Primary care
(Medicine).   I. Mezey, Mathy Doval.   II. McGivern,
Diane O'Neill.   III. Series.
   [DNLM: 1. Nurse Practitioners.   2. Primary Health
Care.   WY 128 N9744 1993]
RT82.8.N884   1993
610.73′06′92—dc20
DNLM/DLC
for Library of Congress   93–13719
                                                      CIP

Printed in the United States of America

New Edition

Nurses, Nurse Practitioners

Evolution to Advanced Practice

Mathy D. Mezey, RN, EdD, FAAN
Diane O. McGivern, RN, PhD, FAAN
Editors

SPRINGER PUBLISHING COMPANY
New York

Mathy Doval Mezey, R.N., Ed.D., F.A.A.N., received her baccalaureate, master's, and doctoral degrees from Columbia University. She taught at Lehman College in New York City and in the School of Nursing at the University of Pennsylvania, where she was Director of the Geriatric Nurse Practitioner Program. She is the past Director of the Robert Wood Johnson Foundation Teaching Nursing Home Program. Currently, she is the Independence Foundation Professor of Nursing Education in the Division of Nursing at New York University.

Diane O'Neill McGivern, R.N., Ph.D., F.A.A.N., received her baccalaureate degree from St. John College, Cleveland, Ohio and her master's and doctorate from New York University. In addition to her clinical practice at Cleveland Clinic Hospital and Bellevue Hospital, she has held faculty positions at Lehman College and The University of Pennsylvania and is currently the Head of the Division of Nursing, New York University.

Springer Series on
Advanced Practice Nursing

Terry T. Fulmer, R.N., Ph.D., C., F.A.A.N., Series Editor
Anna C. Maxwell Professor of Nursing and
Associate Dean for Research
Columbia University School of Nursing
New York, New York

ADVISORY BOARD:

6. WARNINGS

Tell your child what comes next in the bedtime routine so he is mentally prepared for each stage. Set short time limits. Your aim is to be authoritative but not intimidating.

7. EXPLANATIONS

Keep explanations and debates to a minimum when settling children who have woken in the night. The first two times, explain that 'It's bedtime' and after that, say nothing.

8. RESTRAINT

Don't become so overwhelmed by the sound of your child crying that you rush in to comfort her every two minutes. Keep the emotional temperature down as far as possible.

9. RESPONSIBILITY

Get your kids involved in their own bedtime, by setting them small achievable tasks – undressing, pulling out the bath plug, fetching a toy for a sibling.

10. RELAXATION

Bedtime and the run-up to bedtime should be a period of calm. Baths and bedtime stories help a child unwind. And once you've got a good sleeping pattern established for your child, make the most of the rest of the evening and relax yourself!

Quality time

In an ideal world, every minute you spend with your family should be quality time. In the real world, it's not going to work out exactly like that. Bringing up kids is rewarding, but it's also hard work.

You need to take every opportunity you can to turn that work into fun. If you set boundaries in place and back them up, you'll start to enjoy your kids rather than see them as a chore to be dealt with. Enjoyment is important. This is a precious period, even if it doesn't always seem that way, and it will be over all too quickly.

Quality time also means that each person in the family should get what they need – Mum, Dad, older brothers and sisters, as well as young children. That takes a bit of juggling and planning so that everyone gets individual attention as well as time off.

When you're a parent and your mental, emotional and physical purse is empty, you won't be able to hand out loose change to anyone else. There's a fine line between doing the right thing and being a martyr. If you don't look after yourself and your relationship, everything else is going to suffer in the long run.

In our parents' or grandparents' day, it was rare for both parents to work and single-parent households were not that common. Today both types of family are on the increase. That's just a fact of life. Working mothers and single parents come in for a lot of stick in the media. Ignore it. Just as you shouldn't set your child up for failure, don't set yourself up for blame and guilt. Get the support you need, use it and relax.

Getting support

A lot of the stress associated with parenting comes from unrealistic expectations. There's no such thing as a perfect parent. And whatever any other mum or dad might tell you, there's no such thing as a perfect child. Some people are always boasting about their kids and what they can do and how early they did it. Don't let that make you feel inadequate. If those same parents were completely truthful, they'd let you in on the problems they're keeping to themselves.

In the old days, when people didn't move around as much as they do today, most families lived close to a natural support network of friends and relatives, people who they trusted and had known all their lives. Parents may not have relied on the paid services of childminders, babysitters or nannies but that doesn't mean Auntie Edith or Gran wasn't called upon from time to time to take up the slack.

You can't do it alone. Getting support is not a sign of failure, it's a sign of strength. Parenting is an enormous organizational job whether you're a working parent or not. Everyone needs to rely on other people from time to time for support.

You don't just need support at obvious crisis times – when you're going to be in hospital having a new baby, for example, or on moving day. You need it as a matter of course. Parents should not give up their identities and outside interests just because children have come along. Both parents need time to do things for themselves and time to be together as adults.

Find a babysitter you can trust and rely on. Set up a babysitting circle with other families who have small children. Ask your mum down for the weekend. We may not live in such close-knit communities these days but there are still plenty of ways to put a support group in place.

Look after yourself

In a paid job, you'd expect a bonus once in a while, maybe even a promotion. In the same way, you should give yourself a monthly treat – a massage, a haircut, a trip to the cinema, a shopping trip, a meal in a restaurant, an evening with friends. You have needs just like everyone else in the household and unless you look after them, you're going to be running on empty. Quality time is not an optional extra. It's a necessity.

The early months can be a particular time of adjustment, with plenty of highs and lows. Recognize that you need to look after yourself, as post-natal depression can creep up on you.

If you were an athlete, you'd expect to train for your event. You'd watch your diet. If you had an important meeting or presentation at work, you'd prepare ahead of time. Being a parent is an important role and you shouldn't neglect your physical, mental or emotional well-being. You shouldn't be putting up with sleep deprivation; you shouldn't allow yourself to become housebound and isolated. You shouldn't find it impossible to read the paper or curl up with a book. Although you will definitely make many sacrifices, parenting is not about martyrdom. It's about meeting needs, including your own.

If this is important for a parent who has given up work to look after children, it's doubly important for a single working mum or dad. Don't allow yourself to be so tortured with guilt about not staying home with the kids that you give up any idea of looking after yourself or having your own life. You've got a childminder, nanny or family member who's looking after the kids – or maybe they're in school – and they are getting what they need. You're spending quality time with them when you come home from work and at the weekends. But you also need time for yourself so you can keep on an even keel.

Individual attention

One of the key functions of a daily routine, aside from setting fixed times for meals and bed, is to juggle your schedule so that each child in your family has individual attention from both Mum and Dad. This can be done very easily by swapping over the bedtime routine. One night, it's Dad's turn to put the six-year-old to bed and Mum's turn to bath the toddler and settle her down. The next night, it's the other way round. At the weekend, you can also vary who does what. Mum takes the eleven-year-old out on a shopping trip while Dad and the four-year-old wash the car together. Think of ways of mixing it up so that you aren't always stuck in the same roles all the time.

Very demanding small children have a habit of stealing the limelight from their older brothers and sisters, who may not even complain. Don't mistake a lack of protest for acceptance. Older kids need your attention, too. They need help with homework, a chance to talk over what's happened at school, advice and support. They can tie their shoelaces and run their own baths, but they still need you in lots of ways. One-on-one attention from both parents is essential and it should be equal to the attention you pay to your younger kids.

Sibling rivalry

One of the great enemies of quality time is sibling rivalry. It happens in practically every family. A common age gap between children is two years. It's not up to me to tell you how to space your children, but it's important to be aware that the two-year gap can result in a more intense form of sibling rivalry than a gap of three or four years. At three or four, your older child will still be jealous but you will have a better chance of dealing with it because he will be able to understand more than a child who's in the throes of toddlerhood.

PREPARING FOR THE CHANGE

Your child may not know that your fast-disappearing waistline means a baby is on the way but she may well have picked up on subtle changes before you even tell her that she's going to have a new baby brother or sister. It might be simply that you're more tired than usual, or feeling sick.

If your child notices your expanding tummy and asks about it, use that as the opportunity to tell her the news so you can start to prepare her for the new addition to your family. Otherwise, let it go until you're about six months along. Time passes very slowly for little kids – three months is enough time to prepare her but not such a long time for her to wait.

Let your child feel your bump. Let him feel the baby kicking. Don't go overboard and build up the new arrival too much. Most small children would rather have you to themselves than share attention with a new baby brother or sister. Instead of telling him how much he's going to love his new sibling, let him know that he's going to be a big brother and a big help to you. Keep talking about what you're going to do together after the birth. It may sound strange, but many small children think that a new baby is a replacement, not an addition. When a child gets anxious about a new arrival, he's thinking: 'What's going to happen to me? Am I still going to live here?'

Your child may have lots of questions about the mechanics of birth. Don't give her more information than she can handle and don't tell her anything that might make her worry about you.

FAMILY FUN

Make time to have fun together as a family. It can be an outing, it can be a picnic in the garden. It can be a holiday at the seaside, or a wet Sunday afternoon playing a board game. Forget about the chores for once – they'll get done. When you look back in years to come you won't remember the fact that you didn't change the beds one week, you'll remember that special day flying kites in the park.

Enjoy your children!

MY TOP TEN RULES

TO SUM UP, HERE'S HOW MY TOP TEN RULES APPLY TO QUALITY TIME:

1. PRAISE AND REWARDS

Praise and attention are the best rewards. But do treat your child to a special present and card when a new brother or sister comes along. It will really help him feel involved.

2. CONSISTENCY

Parents are likely to find it easier to be consistent when they have enough time together as a couple. Make sure you get away for the odd weekend together and have regular nights off.

3. ROUTINE

Arrange your routine so that every child has one-on-one attention from each parent every day. Make these 'special' times. Work out a rota so that parents also share chores.

4. BOUNDARIES

Children must learn to respect the fact that you need quality time for yourself and as a couple. Clear rules about behaviour help to prevent excessive sibling rivalry.

5. DISCIPLINE

Back up your rules with discipline if necessary. Use the Naughty Step Technique for aggressive behaviour or constant fighting. Be prepared to separate warring toddlers.

6. WARNINGS

A verbal warning is an essential part of discipline. It allows the child the chance to correct her own behaviour. Don't rush to discipline a child for aggression or fighting without giving a warning first.

7. EXPLANATIONS

Prepare your child for the arrival of a new family member. Give her plenty of reassurance, but don't give her so much information she starts to worry.

8. RESTRAINT

Don't over-react to every skirmish. Let children sort some things out for themselves, providing they are at no risk of hurting themselves or each other.

9. RESPONSIBILITY

Use the Involvement Technique to ease jealousy. Give lots of praise. Allow older children to run games for the little ones.

10. RELAXATION

Don't allow yourself to get run-down or overloaded. Get support and look after yourself as a matter of course. Make time for family fun.

USEFUL CONTACTS

Association for Post Natal Illness
Tel. 020 7386 0868 / www.apni.org
Charity offering information and support for
postnatally depressed mothers, with helpline

Association of Breastfeeding Mothers
Tel: 0870 4017711 / www.abm.me.uk
Voluntary organization run by mothers offering
support and information. 24-hour helpline with
qualified breastfeeding counsellor

B4Ugo-Ga-Ga
www.b4ugo-ga-ga.co.uk
Check out my website! It's got information about
the type of work I do with families and children

Breastfeeding Network
Tel: 0870 900 8787
www.breastfeedingnetwork.org.uk
Breastfeeding information

British Au Pair Agencies Association
www.bapaa.org.uk
Non-commercial association of British
au pair agencies

Childcare Link
Tel: 0800 096 0296 / www.childcarelink.gov.uk
Government resource giving information on
national and local childcare and early education.
Helps you find what's available in your area

Cry-sis
Tel: 020 7404 5011 / www.cry-sis.com
Helpline and support for parents with crying
and sleepless children

Disabled Parents Network
Tel: 08702 410450
www.disabledparentsnetwork.org.uk
Organization for disabled people who are parents
or who hope to become parents, and their families

e-parents
www.e-parents.org
Information and advice from the National Family
and Parenting Institute, a charity campaigning
for a more family-friendly society

Early Learning Centre
www.elc.co.uk
Leading toy shop for children aged 0–6, with
branches all over the UK. Visit the website for
local branches or shop on-line

Enuresis Resource and Information Centre
Tel: 0117 960 3060 / www.enuresis.org.uk
Provides support, advice and information
for parents whose children are incontinent

Families Online
www.familiesonline.co.uk
Features and articles for families of young children

Family Nurturing Network (FNN)
Tel: 01865 791711 / www.fnn.org.uk
Group programmes for families with children
aged 2 to 12

Fathers Direct
www.fathersdirect.com
Information and support for fathers on all aspects
of parenting. Interactive website

Gingerbread
Tel: 0800 018 4318 / www.gingerbread.org.uk
Organization for single-parent families. Advice
line, national network of self-help groups

Grandparents' Association
Tel: 01279 444 964
www.grandparents-federation.org.uk
Provides an advice line for issues relating
to grandparenting

HomeDad
Tel: 07752 549085 / www.homedad.org.uk
Contact information putting stay-at-home dads
in touch with each other. Information and advice

Home-Start
Tel: 0800 068 6368 / www.home-start.org.uk
Support from parent volunteers for parents
of children under five

La Leche League
Tel: 0845 120 2918 / www.laleche.org.uk
Support helpline for breastfeeding mothers.
Advice and information

**National Association of Toy
and Leisure Libraries**
Tel: 020 7255 4600 / www.natll.org.uk
Charity running toy libraries, where good quality toys
are available on loan to parents with young children

National Childbirth Trust
Tel: 0870 444 8707
www.pregnancyandbabycare.com
Antenatal classes. Advice and information
on pregnancy, breastfeeding and looking
after babies. Network of local support groups.
Contact to find new parents in your area

**National Childminding Association
of England and Wales**
Tel: 0800 169 4486 / www.ncma.org.uk
Contact for advice on how to find a registered
childminder in your area

NSPCC
Tel: 0808 800 5000 / www.nspcc.org.uk
Charity devoted to child protection

One Parent Families
Tel: 0800 018 5026 / www.oneparentfamilies.org.uk
Information service for single-parent families. Offers
support to enable single parents to return to work

The Parent Centre
Tel: 0870 000 2288 / www.parentcentre.gov.uk
Government organization providing information
on children's education and helping children
to learn. Choosing childcare, help for single or
working parents

Parentline Plus
Tel: 0808 800 2222 / www.parentlineplus.org.uk
National free 24-hour helpline for parents and
carers. Parenting courses and information leaflets

Practical Parenting Advice
www.practicalparent.org.uk
Information on child behaviour and family
relationships. On-line parenting course

Raising Kids
www.raisingkids.co.uk
Website offering support and information
to anyone raising kids

SureStart
Tel: 0870 000 2288 / www.surestart.gov.uk
Government initiative to help families prepare
children for school, focusing on health and
well-being

Twins and Multiple Birth Association (TAMBA)
Tel: 0870 770 3305 / www.tamba.org.uk
Information and support networks for
multiple-birth families

Twins Club
www.twinsclub.co.uk
Multiple birth website

Working Families
Tel: 0800 013 0313 / www.workingfamilies.org.uk
Legal helpline. Help for parents to enable them to
balance work and home life. Factsheets on parental
leave and childcare

INDEX

SUPERNANNY INDEX

FOREWORD

The new Springer Series on Advanced Practice Nursing (APN) represents an exciting opportunity to provide state-of-the-art science on the topic of Advance Practice Nursing. The first volume in this series could not be more appropriate nor written by individuals more expert. *Nurses, Nurse Practitioners: Evolution to Advanced Practice* by Mezey and McGivern chronicles the evolution of primary care and professional nursing's dynamic and prominent role in the nation's health care delivery system. The 1990s promise to be a time when professional nursing will come into its own in terms of primary care and creative new activities that blend advanced practice, caring, and technology. Drs. Mezey and McGivern are closely identified with the nurse practitioner movement, and as visionary leaders are defining advanced practice nursing as it moves into the 21st century.

The APN Editorial Advisory Board is comprised of some of the finest advanced practice nurses in the country. The Board, which will expand over time, has been developed with the goal of reflecting areas where APNs are so central: oncology, cardiovascular, geriatrics, AIDS, and pediatrics. Nurses with additional specialties will be included in the future. We look forward to providing a stimulating forum for the discussion of Advanced Practice Nursing.

TERRY T. FULMER, R.N., Ph.D., C., F.A.A.N.
SERIES EDITOR
Summer 1993, New York City

ix

FOREWORD

For over a quarter of a century, the nurse practitioner model of advanced nursing practice has progressed from a deviant of yesteryear, to the norm of today, and the tradition of tomorrow (Ford, 1979). Since I began the first training program for nurse practitioners in 1965, countless research and descriptive articles and opinion pieces have been written on the effectiveness, efficiency, and economy of this new breed of nurse. Indeed, publications are scattered in the public press and professional literature throughout the world. In the early years, there were very few neutral reporters. Nurse practitioner watchers have made some interesting, if not always accurate, observations. That's why it is so refreshing to have a scholarly, comprehensive broadly conceived publication such as this one. It provides up-to-date information, conceptual designs, cameos of experience by experts in various specialties, and exploration of all the pertinent issues in advanced nursing practice, legislation and law, reimbursement, and health care politics and policies.

The book is organized into three parts and each is excellent. Part I brings the reader insights and understandings of the philosophical, historic, educational, and research perspectives on nurses and nurse practitioners. Part II of this book includes cameos by practitioners in a host of settings; impressive, thoughtful slices of life in the specialty practice of nurse practitioners. Particularly welcome in this section and the next are contributions from colleagues in medicine and law. From their expertise and experience, they offer viewpoints and insights about the health care environments and opportunities that are particularly important to nurse practitioners.

The third section completes this superb book. Issues of legislation and law, credentialling, reimbursement, and politics and policy are examined. All the pertinent, complex, and complicated challenges facing nursing and nurse practitioners are explored by authors whose sterling reputations as experts make this section a fascinating compendium that every nurse practitioner and others will find indispensable for learning about the past, present, and future of the field. As a matter of fact, the whole book brings together a resource that every student, practitioner, faculty member/scholar and policymaker will want to own as a reference book. The chapters are well documented, scholarly and interesting, and organized in a logical sequence, with pertinent content and in-depth examinations of major issues.

The nurse practitioner, no longer a deviant, is one of the modern versions of advanced nursing practice. But, as indicated by this comprehensive volume, in a state of dynamic evolution toward becoming the expert professional nurse for all settings.

LORETTA C. FORD, R.N., Ed.D., F.A.A.N.
Professor and Dean Emeritus
School of Nursing
University of Rochester
Rochester, NY

REFERENCE

Ford, L. C. (1979). A nurse for all settings: The nurse practitioner. *Nursing Outlook, 27*(8), 521.

PREFACE

In 1965 nursing and medicine collaborated on the preparation of a new primary health care provider, the nurse practitioner. Originally introduced to provide access to children who lacked basic primary care services, the use of nurse practitioners quickly expanded to encompass services to adults and the elderly.

Despite enthusiastic support by some nurses, physicians, and government agencies, nurse practitioners were not universally embraced. Professional nursing organizations worried that nurse practitioners would become "mini" doctors and operate outside of nursing. Physicians worried that nurses would usurp physician power and practice medicine without a license. Facilities were concerned with scope of practice and reimbursement for services. Yet, despite such concerns, in a short period of time nurse practitioners became indispensable and highly effective providers in inner-city clinics, rural ambulatory settings, and nursing homes.

In 1987 we undertook to chronicle the evolution of the nurse practitioner movement, in our book *Nurses, Nurse Practitioners: The Evolution of Primary Care*.

The past 5 years have seen an enormous change in our health care system. The shift in acute care services to ambulatory sites, burgeoning health care costs, and the continued selection of specialty practice by young physicians has created a vacuum as to who provides primary care services. And more and more, this vacuum is being filled by nurse practitioners.

A paradigm shift in which nurse practitioners are *the preferred provider* of primary care services is now openly debated. Twenty years of research as to their effectiveness supports such a paradigm. Anecdotes such as "if you need a primary care physician call a nurse" and "Marcus Welby is a nurse" have begun to circulate widely as practitioners and policymakers seek ways to provide affordable, humane primary care.

Changes in the site of care delivery are of major importance in this debate. Many people now receiving ambulatory care require a provider familiar with subacute and acute care. Similarly, hospitals increasingly need providers who can address patients' health care needs prior to and subsequent to hospitalization. In this new world, health care facilities need providers who can comfortably deliver traditional hands on, primary care and also provide education and liaison with patients, families, and a vast array of health care and community agencies.

Nursing has moved swiftly to address these new health care needs by blending the traditional primary care skills of nurse practitioners with those of hospital based clinical nurse specialists. The purpose of this new edition is to chronicle this paradigm shift and to describe the role of nurse practitioners in both traditional and new primary care settings as well as in acute care facilities.

MATHY D. MEZEY, R.N., Ed.D., F.A.A.N.

DIANE O. MCGIVERN, R.N., Ph.D, F.A.A.N.

CONTRIBUTORS

Ellen D. Baer, Ph.D., F.A.A.N., is an Associate Professor at the University of Pennsylvania School of Nursing where she holds the Hillman Term Professorship in nursing. Dr. Baer initiated and directs Penn's federally funded project for nursing students to care for children and adults with AIDS in all health care settings. She also is an award-winning researcher and writer in nursing history.

Henry L. Barnett, M.D., is a pediatrician and Medical Director of The Children's Aid Society. He is responsible for the agency's health services, which include foster care and adoption; Head Start and after school community programs; and a mobile medical van. Dr. Barnett was the founding Chair of the Department of Pediatrics of the Albert Einstein College of Medicine where he now serves as a Distinguished University Professor Emeritus.

Bonnie Bullough is a family nurse practicner and sociologist who has written extensively on legal issues. She is Dean Emeritus of the State University of New York, Buffalo, School of Nursing.

Jane Kummerer Butler has been a nurse practitioner in a continuing care retirement community since 1975. During the first thirteen years of her association with the community she was also the Director of Nursing. The life care community is comprised of independent and dependent living units for people over age 65 and guarantees access to a continuum of health care services.

Walter Thomas Eccard, Esq., is a partner in the Washington, D.C. office of Brown & Wood.

Claire M. Fagin is the former Dean of the University of Pennsylvania's School of Nursing and the Leadership Professor at the School. She has been a long-standing advocate for health care reform. Her work in psychiatric nursing, primary care, and the cost effectiveness of advanced practice nurses is widely recognized. She is currently Interim President at the University of Pennsylvania.

Bonnie J. Fields is a doctoral candidate in Nursing Administration at the University of Pennsylvania School of Nursing. She has had twelve years of clinical and administrative experience in maternal–child health nursing.

Cynthia M. Freund became a family nurse practioner in 1973 and worked in a rural satellite clinic and a medical clinic in North Carolina. She also helped establish three Family Nurse Practitioner programs in the State, and has studied the cost-effectiveness of nurse practitioners. She is currently Dean of the School of Nursing, University of North Carolina at Chapel Hill.

Edward E. Gainor, Esq., is a former newspaper and broadcast journalist and is now an attorney in the Washington, D.C. office of Brown & Wood.

William Kavesh, M.D., M.P.H., is the Medical Director of the Philadelphia Geriatric Center and the Chairman, Division of Geriatric Medicine, Albert Einstein Medical Center, Philadelphia, Pennsylvania. He is Associate Professor of Medicine at Temple University School of Medicine and Adjunct Assistant Professor of Medicine (Health Services) Boston University School of Medicine.

Joseph H. Kelly is a nurse methods analyst at an Army Medical center on the East Coast. He is a doctoral candidate in Nursing Administration at the University of Pennsylvania School of Nursing.

Elizabeth Kuehne is a pediatric nurse practitioner with a special interest in providing health care services to foster children in a variety of urban clinical settings. She also holds an appointment to a school of nursing where she teaches in the pediatric nurse practioner program.

Joan E. Lynaugh is a professor at the School of Nursing, University of Pennsylvania and Associate Dean and Director of Graduate Studies. She has been involved in the nurse practitioner movement since 1970; more recently her research and writing is focused on the history of health care and policy development in the United States.

Pamela Maraldo, Ph.D., R.N., F.A.A.N., is President of the Planned Parenthood Federation of America. She served as the Chief Executive Officer of the National League for Nursing from 1983 to 1993. During her tenure at NLN she led a programmatic and financial revitalization of the organization, which resulted in a quadrupling of its size. She is a nationally acclaimed speaker and contributor to the health care arena.

Barbara Medoff-Cooper is a pediatric nurse practitioner who currently practices with a pediatric group practice on the East Coast and maintains a university school of nursing appointment coordinating a practitioner program. She has completed her doctorate in child development, and a postdoctoral fellowship as a Robert Wood Johnson Clinical Nurse Scholar.

Pamela Mittelstadt, R.N., M.P.H., is Director of the Medical Affairs Department at the Group Health Association of America (GHAA) in Washington, D.C. where she is currently responsible for directing and developing the activities of GHAA's Medical Management Council that includes issues of quality assurance, outcome measurement and technology assessment. Ms. Mittelstadt has prior clinical experience in home health, reproductive health, and public health.

Madeline A. Naegle is a psychiatric nurse clinician who maintains a private practice in New York City. Past President of the New York State Nurses Association, she is currently Associate Professor at New York University in the Division of Nursing. She is nationally recognized for development and evaluation of substance abuse education for health professionals.

Ann L. O'Sullivan is a pediatric nurse practitioner currently holding a joint position where she provides primary care to adolescent families in a specialized practice and teaches at the University of Pennsylvania School of Nursing. Her doctorate is in educational anthropology and she was a Robert Wood Johnson Foundation Primary Care Nurse Faculty Fellow.

Geraldine Paier, Ph.D., R.N., C., has held a joint appointment in the School of Nursing, University of Pennsylvania, and Foulkeways, a continuing care retirement community near Philadelphia. Her research interest is functional status in the elderly and she has recently accepted a post-doctoral fellowship at the University of Arizona in Tucson.

Marianne Warguska Reilly holds joint positions as a pediatric nurse practitioner, in-patient newborn nursery, at Columbia Presbyterian Medical Center and as a member of the faculty of the pediatric nurse practitioner program, Columbia University in New York City. She is also the former Director of Health Services at the Children's Aid Society.

Jo Anne Staats is an adult nurse practioner who has worked with patients with HIV/AIDS for the past six years. She was the nurse practitioner at Bailey House, a group residence for persons with AIDS, and is currently a nurse practitioner with the AIDS Center at St. Vincents Hospital and Medical Center.

Neville E. Strumpf, Ph.D., R.N., C., F.A.A.N., is Doris Schwartz Term Professor and Director, Gerontological Nurse Practitioner Program, University of Pennsylvania. She is engaged in research concerning use of physical restraints with frail elders, quality of care outcomes for elders with cancer, and access to health care for elderly minority refugees.

Eileen M. Sullivan is an adult nurse practitioner who currently is Project Manager of a nurse-managed Geriatric Day Hospital. She is a doctoral candidate in gerontology at the University of Pennsylvania School of Nursing.

Joyce Beebe Thompson is a nurse midwife who has practiced in the United States, Africa, and South America. She is a Professor and Director of Nurse Midwifery at the University of Pennsylvania School of Nursing. She is also Director of the Malawi-Penn Women for Women's Health Program in Central Africa and a consultant in midwifery, public health, maternal child health, and ethics.

Ellen-Marie Whelan is a pediatric nurse practitioner who currently practices in an urban community center on the East Coast. She is a lecturer in pediatric nursing and doctoral student at the University of Pennsylvania School of Nursing.

PHILOSOPHICAL, HISTORICAL, EDUCATIONAL, AND RESEARCH PERSPECTIVES

Chapter 1

THE EVOLUTION TO ADVANCED NURSING PRACTICE

Diane O. McGivern

HISTORY

A LTHOUGH the political, social, and educational forces of the 1950s
and the early 1960s, which promoted the development of an expanded practice role for nurses have changed, the need for and value of the role remain confirmed (Kane et al., 1989; Kirkland & Tinsley, 1990; McGrath, 1990). Indeed, the current health care situation reinforces the need to provide accessible, cost-effective, and competent care, all of which are achievable through the advanced nursing practice model (Elder & Bullough, 1990).

Clinical specialization is not new in nursing. Hospital-based courses in anesthesia, operating room, and obstetrical nursing developed between 1900 and 1930 (Bullough, 1992). This led the way to the post-World War II development of the clinical nurse specialist (CNS) role through educational programs supported by the Nurse Training Act. The CNS role was seen as a way to provide expert patient care and consultation and offer role models for less expert staff, as well as facilitate clinical research. Those who focused on indirect care viewed this role as

3

nonresponsive to the need for more comprehensive health care delivery via mid-level providers (Elder & Bullough, 1990).

Functional preparation of nurses for teaching and administration became less a focus through the 1960s and 1970s as clinical training gained importance. Graduate programs increased in number and narrowness of specialization (Kitchens, Piazza, & Ellison, 1989) but were without consistency in content or competencies.

The development of the first nurse practitioner (NP) program in 1965 by Loretta Ford and Henry Silver was based on a "nursing model focused on the promotion of health in daily living, growth and development for children in families as well as the prevention of disease and disability" (Ford, 1982, 1986). Ford notes that societal needs and nursing's potential led to this development; the primary care physician shortage, which is described as a contributing factor in other parts of the country (Elder & Bullough, 1990; McGivern, 1986), is defined by Ford as the *opportunity*, and not the reason, for the new role (Ford, 1982).

Initial resistance to the nurse practitioner concept came from academia and some federal agencies, but the idea was born at a time of general concern for accessible, affordable, and humane care. The supportive environment of the 1960s and 1970s eventually created a role which served populations in many settings and became fully integrated into baccalaureate and master's education. Studies (Feldman, Ventura, & Crosby, 1987) exhaustively examined the quality, cost effectiveness, productivity, clinical decision-making skills, and job satisfaction of nurse practitioners, making this role the most completely analyzed in any other discipline (See Freund, Chapter 3).

Bullough (1992) believes these events have produced two models of specialization in nursing: the nursing model of the CNS, and the collaborative model of practitioners, midwives, and anesthetists. These models share the commitment to research and utilization of knowledge from other disciplines, but differ in their emphasis on nursing theory and medical content.

The evolution of preparatory programs, from physician- and nurse-taught nurse practitioner certificate programs to well-integrated knowledge and skills in baccalaureate and master's programs, was relatively rapid and consistent across the country. The consolidation of advanced practice skills and role expectations for master's (and certificate-program) prepared nurses has resulted in more diverse but well-developed roles defined by inpatient or outpatient practice sites, populations served, patients' levels of health/illness, and/or body system. The proliferation of master's degree programs preparing clinical nurse specialists, nurse clinicians, nurse practitioners, and nurse midwives reflects the endorsement of educators, administrators, practitioners, and, possibly, patients and clients. Government support for advanced practice has been contradictory and uneven; on the one hand, federal funds for advanced training programs have been available; on the other hand, legislation supporting advanced practice and reimbursement is limited according to state and practice site.

The proliferation of educational programs, exhaustive examination, and defense of these nurse provider roles, and the fluctuating receptiveness of the health care system, has set the stage for an analysis of advanced practice in nursing, and perhaps a mid-course correction (Hockenberry-Eaton & Powell, 1991). A conscious decision by the profession to fold together clinician and practitioner preparation and practice roles would give nursing the initiative and control that will be lost if developments are the product of inattention or other vested interests. The merger of advanced practice roles would simplify the concept for consumers and practice sites; take advantage of the demand in acute care settings; and enable practitioners to follow patients through various care settings.

DEFINITION

Advanced practice is defined by the National Council of State Boards of Nursing (NCSBN, 1992) as

> the advanced practice of nursing by nurse practitioners, nurse anesthetists, nurse midwives, and clinical nurse specialists, based on the following: knowledge and skills required in basic nursing education; licensure as a registered nurse; graduate degree and experience in the designated area of practice which includes advanced nursing theory; substantial knowledge of physical and psychosocial assessment; appropriate interventions and management of health care status.
>
> The skills and abilities essential for the advance practice role within an identified specialty area include: providing patient/client and community education; promoting stress prevention and management; encouraging self help; subscribing to caring; advocacy; accountability, accessibility; and collaboration with other health and community professionals.

The Council also notes that "each individual who practices nursing at an advanced level does so with substantial autonomy and independence resulting in a high level of accountability" (NCSBN, p. 4).

STATISTICS

The relatively small number of nurses currently in advanced practice roles who reflect all the requirements of this definition presents both opportunities for and difficulties in achieving better integration of these provider roles. Advanced practice nursing opportunities continue to increase in response to the demand for access to primary care for increasing numbers of uninsured and underinsured, to medicine's failure to convince physicians to enter primary care specialties, and to the emerging political leverage of nurses. Advanced practice role consolidation may be more easily achieved in view of the limited number of practitioners designated as nurse clinicians, clinical specialists, and practitioners. However, the relatively small numbers of advanced practitioners do not support the arguments for nurses to become physician substitutes or primary providers in an increasing number of settings.

The 1988 survey indicated that 123,637, or 6%, of 2,033,032 professional nurses have graduate preparation in education, administration, or clinical practice. These master's-prepared nurses are only a fraction of nurses designated as nurse practitioners, clinical specialists, or nurse clinicians, since the majority of individuals holding these titles are certificate program-prepared or designated by experience or position title (DHHS, Seventh Report to Congress 1988).

The number and percentage of master's prepared nurses will increase in light of the decline of nondegree granting programs, the retirement of diploma- and certificate-program-prepared practitioners, the recent growth of associate, baccalaureate, and master's programs and enrollment, (Nursing Data Review, 1991); and the recognized need for uniform credentials for reimbursement and practice privileges. Yet, despite the fact that 40% (83 of 212) of master's programs offer practitioner programs, and that the majority of enrollments are in clinical practice options, the demand for master's-prepared nurses is almost double the projected supply (DHHS, Seventh Report to Congress, 1988). In specific practice areas, while not specifying beginning or advanced preparation, there is a projected need of 26.3% more nurses in inpatient hospital practice, 57.4% in nursing homes, 115.7% in community health, and 50.1% in HMO, PPO, and fee-for-services settings, including physicians' offices (Harrington & Shea, 1991, Nursing Data Review, 1991, DHHS Seventh Report to Congress, 1988). However, these projected needs by clinical specialty area do not correspond to the enrollments in CNS/NP programs. For example, in contrast to the need for community health preparation nurses, this specialty ranks fourth in enrollment; gerontology, fifth. In contrast to the more limited 26.3% increased need in tertiary care facilities and 50.1% in HMO practices, medical-surgical nursing ranks first in enrollment (Nursing Data Review, 1991). The apparent discrepancy between clients' need for services and the nurse's choice of an educational program is a social, professional, educational, and economic issue.

Creating a common core of knowledge and skills in master's preparation would facilitate mobility in practice. Providing the common practice elements which the nurse would bring to any setting has been pursued by funding sources and educators, and would facilitate movement across areas of specialty and setting.

FACTORS SHAPING CURRENT PRACTICE

The tangible factors shaping advanced nursing practice are well described in the literature of health care economics, medicine and nursing. The popular media also covers many of the political and social considerations which determine the "who" and "what" of health care services.

Advanced nursing practice has been shaped in part by parallel educational program developments, the depressed economy and continued pressure for health care cost containment, slow recognition of nursing services as reimbursable, increasingly complex care problems necessitating provider collaboration, and the international call for accessible and affordable care for all (Koch, Pazaki, & Campbell, 1992). Adding to these influential factors are the increasing similarities between inpatient and outpatient care with respect to patient acuity, treatment regimens, and need for specialty care. Equally similar is the need in all settings for practitioners to bring a combination of clinical and administrative or management skills in order to arrive at the best clinical/resource decisions.

Educational Preparation and Practice

The effect of the proliferation of master's programs and their perceived diversity in titles, content, competencies, and degree of clinical specialization on graduates and curriculum is discussed by Mezey in Chapter 2.

Economy and Cost Containment

A consistent determinant of health care services, provider preparation, health manpower, and client eligibility is the depressed personal, national, and provider economy. The state of the economy influences citizens' willingness to support programs for general health and welfare, clients' access to services, providers' ability to compete, and the effect of competition on available services.

The state of the economy and lack of optimistic economic signals for recovery in the near future support continued pressure on institutional and individual providers to offer services at lower cost, that is, to provide fewer services, or provide lower cost interventions which limit the need for future services. In this environment, nursing departments and advanced practitioners are responding to the cost containment efforts in a variety of ways. Cost containment for institutionally based care has created significant pressure on nursing to maintain quality, improve productivity, and help produce prudent purchasing decisions. Nurses in advanced hospital-based practice have potential leverage because they participate in clinical decision making and determine how to improve the productivity and quality of care (Pointer & Pointer, 1989). However, the clinical nurse specialist role was not initially defined or defended along cost effectiveness or cost containment lines, but rather on the presumption of improved quality of care outcomes. It is only recently that advocates have pointed to the CNS role as a vehicle to achieve cost savings (Gravely & Littlefield, 1991), exhorting specialists to find additional ways to demonstrate their cost effectiveness (Brunk, 1982; Harrison, 1989) or indirectly promoting their cost effectiveness by documenting the impact of improved quality of care on institutional costs (Boyd et al., 1991; Papenhausen & Beecroft, 1990; Peglow et al., 1992).

In contrast, demonstrated cost effectiveness has been a major component of nurse practitioner evaluation since 1965, and has included examination of the specialty practice areas in occupational health (Scharon, Tsai, & Bernacki, 1987; Murphy, 1989), gerontology (Kane et al., 1989), midwifery, and pediatrics (see Freund, Chapter 3).

All advanced practice nurses, whatever their setting or specialty, will not only have to demonstrate both direct and indirect cost savings, but will also need to establish consumer and corporate support. Cost savings data alone without the political and consumer support can be disregarded.

Health Manpower

The strong growth in every health provider group has been the product of two to three decades of government support. In fact, the health services sector is seen as one of the few areas of economic growth for the near future. In the period between 1980 and 1986, the number of physicians grew 18.8%, dentists 13.3%, podiatrists 18%, and nurses 25.9%. At the same time, the allied health professions were experiencing a 20.9% growth (Clare, Sprately, Schwab, & Iglehart, 1987). While the increase in the number of professional nurses has been significant, the expansion of the master's prepared nurse population has been less so, and the number of full-time students readily available for advanced practice has been reduced (Nursing Data Review, 1991).

The number of nurses in advanced practice is determined by basic program enrollments; financial aid, scholarship, and tuition benefit support for graduate education; available practice opportunities, and adequate social and economic incentives. The 7% increase in baccalaureate program enrollment and close to 9% increase in all basic programs in 1989 provide the future candidates for master's programs. The increased number of master's programs and their improving enrollments is a positive sign. However, the most important determinant increasing the numbers of advanced practice nurses is improved funding for graduate education from federal, institutional, and private sources. Increased enrollments will also depend on a significantly more aggressive and comprehensive marketing campaign to inform potential nursing students and the general public about the various practice opportunities and the benefits to consumers.

The contrast between projected physician surplus and nurse shortage makes the proposition of advanced practice nurses as physician substitutes artificially problematic. The superficial imbalance hides the primary care physician shortage and the opportunity for nurses to provide primary care services. A variety of initiatives by the government and medical educators to enhance primary care, including dedication of medical schools to primary care training and an interdisciplinary team approach, have met with a striking lack of success. This is attributable to a continued physician disinterest in primary care and a continued physician surplus which equates surplus with consumer access. Politzer notes that between 1978 and 1998 the number of general internists is expected to increase by 77%, in contrast to a 205% increase in subspecialty selection (Politzer, Harris, Gaston, & Mullan, 1991).

The continued expansion of populations requiring a range of nursing services including more women and children at risk, the elderly, chronically ill, and worried well, combined with the expansion of the traditional demands for advanced practice nurses in acute care, home care, and long term care would seem to create unlimited opportunities and potentially greater public appreciation for nursing's contribution.

An analysis of over 1000 advertisements for nurse practitioners placed in one journal, *Nurse Practitioner*, between 1975 and 1986, compared demand by region, setting and responsibilities, clinical specialty, and preparation. Despite the conventional wisdom that the poor economy and physician oversupply were obstacles, the analysis indicated that the demand for nurse practitioners, particularly in primary care, had increased (Shanks-Meile, Shipley, Collins, & Tacker, 1989).

Primary care for nurses continues to be a major practice opportunity. Hayes (1985) urges practitioners to choose practice sites, specialties, and services that physicians will not. She suggests that competition for independent practice is less likely to be successful than the opportunities in HMOs and PPOs, where collegial relationships with other providers are possible.

A recurring theme has been the predicted negative effect of the physician surplus on the acceptance and utilization of nurses in advanced practice. However, several arguments mitigate against the simple surplus equation. First, despite the continued surplus projections, the "oversupply" has been countered by the elasticity of the medical specialties and subspecialties in accommodating more practitioners. Second, medical dominance of the marketplace has been eroded somewhat over the years, as a result of government controls on Medicare and Medicaid payments, which in turn has had a similar impact on other third party payers. Third, the increasing pressure of large businesses and insurers to reduce health care costs has imposed corporate controls on medicine. Finally, the change in younger physicians' expectations for balance between professional and personal life has resulted in a willingness to work as salaried providers to achieve such a lifestyle. In addition, there is a cautious willingness to examine ways to reduce physician production, including small reductions in medical school class size, which may produce opportunities for nurses in advanced practice.

Available manpower is also determined by the number of practitioners available to meet the needs of patients. It is estimated that 80% of nurse practitioners work with underserved populations. In a study of the different perspectives of nurses and physician assistants, Dross noted that while physician assistants emphasize problem-oriented, curative care and objectivity, nurses are sensitive to the "voice of the life-world," taking into account the patients, illness, or problems, as part of their personal subjective experiences (Dross, 1988, 167).

Financial and Professional Recognition

Recognition of practitioners and clinicians in the form of compensation, credentialing and admitting, and prescriptive privileges is part of nursing's legislative and policy agenda.

Reimbursement

Adequate compensation, in the form of salary or direct third party payment for services which recognize credentials as well as practice experience, has been a strong, continuous theme for organized professional nursing.

The sophisticated analysis of nurses' salaries and the study of the relationship of compensation to supply and demand (Aiken & Mullinix, 1987) was associated with a marketplace responsiveness producing improved starting salaries, particularly in urban areas. The compensation for nurses generally, and CNS and NPs in particular, is well documented, and reflects the same recent increases.

Despite the fact that most nurses, including those in advanced practice, are salaried and not directly dependent on third party payment, reimbursement remains a priority for organized nursing (LaBar, 1990). Efforts to ensure access to nursing services by making those services reimbursable have been advocated since 1948. There are a number of arguments raised in support of third party payment. Reimbursement is viewed as an indicator of professional status and as an important prerequisite for independent practice (Friedman, 1990; Hogue, 1989; LaBar, 1990; see Mittlestadt, 1993, Chapter 13; Sebastian, 1991). Third party payment also recognizes the documented euality and equality of nursing care as well as its cost-effectiveness. Finally, direct reimbursement for advanced practice services is already a clear trend in state and federal law, and is the practice of many identified health insurance companies, as well as the Civilian Health and Medical Program of the Uniformed Services (CHAMPUS) and the Federal Employees Health Benefit Plan (Scott & Harrison, 1990; Sullivan, 1992).

Currently, 26 states have legislation that authorizes reimbursement to nurse practitioners from private and commercial insurers; however, although state law supports reimbursement, compliance by insurers does not automatically follow (Scott & Harrison, 1990) and must often by negotiated (LaBar, 1990; Scott & Harrison, 1990). Thirty-eight states allow Medicaid reimbursement for nurse practitioners. In 1986 the Omnibus Budget Reconciliation Act [OBRA] provided for direct payment of certified nurse anesthetists, although fee schedule regulations were not immediately finalized. Medicare payment reform established through OBRA in 1989 provided for payment to nurse practitioners providing services to nursing home residents (Mittlestadt, 1990). It also allowed both nurse practitioners and clinical nurse specialists to certify and recertify medical necessity for skilled nursing services. Current law provides Medicare payment to nurse practitioners and clinical nurse spe cialists working in rural health clinics, for services provided incident to physician services, and in HMOs or competitive medical plans (CMPs) if those services would be covered if provided by a physician.

The level of payment issue necessarily follows the reimbursement question. Should nurses and others be paid at the same rate or at a lower rate? Should services, not providers, determine the level of payment? Harrington and Culbertson (1990) point out that physician assistants have already created a precedent for lower fees, since they receive 85% of physician payment in nursing homes, 75% in hospital, and 65% in surgery. They go on to argue, however, that nurses should receive the same payment as physicians. Because Congress recognizes that all physicians should receive payment regardless of specialty preparation, therefore, the same reasoning should apply to nurses acting as physician substitutes. Cost containment should be achieved by emphasis on primary care and preventive services, and not through a discounted fee schedule for nurse providers. Based on considerable evidence on quality and effectiveness, nurses should insist that their services should be reimbursed at the same level. However, the momentum for direct payment for nurses collides with the current view that fee-for-service arrangements for any provider drive up utilization and costs accordingly. The establishment and successful expansion of HMOs, PPOs, and CMPs, and the use of fee schedules and capitated payments are attempts to reverse the fee-for-service structure (Safriet, 1992).

In the absence of a clear federal plan for universal health coverage which emphasizes primary care or controls costs of technologically based care in a tertiary setting, nurses must pursue both third party payment and appropriate salaries to fully establish their place in whatever universal coverage plan prevails.

Regulation

In a draft position paper, the National Council of State Boards of Nursing noted the significantly increased demand for nurses practicing in advanced roles with greater autonomy. Regulations of advanced nursing practice have been spurred by federal regulations requiring statutory recognition for third party reimbursement (NCSBN, 1992). Certification and regulation have also been promoted by organized nursing as a way to insure professional recognition and clarification of the authority to practice. (NCSBN, 1992, 1–8)

Credentialing currently is a function of professional organizations through certification (see Bullough, Chapter 11). Voluntary certification is offered through the American Nurses Credentialing Center, as well as through specialty organizations. However, certification does not necessarily reflect comparable education or even advanced practice. To address the attendant confusion, the NCSBN is recommending that the credential for advanced practice be licensure, based on their observation that:

> The evolution of advanced nursing has produced an expanded scope of practice and a high level of autonomy based on advance knowledge, skills abilities. Safe and competent advanced nursing practice requires licensure as a method of regulation necessary to protect the public. (National Council of State Boards of Nursing, 1992, p. 8)

The NCSBN's Subcommittee to Study Regulation of Advanced Nursing Practice reported the 1991 survey of member boards. Fifty-four of the 56 boards which regulate registered nurses responded; 50 boards have language which addresses advanced practice, 43 have regulatory oversight, and 14 reported that medical boards have that responsibility. Licensure for at least one advanced practice role is already in place in 16 jurisdictions; state certificates are issued by 22 boards, and 19 boards issue other forms of recognition, including endorsements of licenses (Alabama) which allow advanced practice. On an international level, the World Health Organization Study Group on regulatory mechanisms supports regulation of education and practice in order to insure focus on primary health care (Smith, 1989).

Practice Privileges

Linked closely with credentialing and reimbursement are the issues of prescriptive authority and staff admitting privileges. Hospital and nursing home staff privileges are viewed as necessary in order to follow clients and patients through acute and chronic care episodes. This possibility was technically created in 1983, when the Joint Commission opened hospital staff membership to nonphysician providers (An Open Letter, 1992; Smithing, & Wiley, 1989). Hospital privileges are also a way to demonstrate to other providers and the general community both evaluation of credentials and the recognition of clinical competency. Establishment of credentials is also consistent with the role of advanced nursing practitioners as case managers who coordinate patients' care with other professionals and with the patient's family while maintaining a holistic perspective on the patient.

Prescriptive authority is a priority (An Open Letter, 1992) for nurses in advanced practice which is being addressed state by state. To date, 35 boards provide for prescriptive authority; 26 authorize one or more categories of advanced practice to prescribe, nine boards have other methods, such as in California, where nurses "furnish" medications, or whereby nurses prescribe as part of their delegated medical functions. However, this may present a picture of more limited practice than actually exists. In the 1989 survey of nurse practitioners (Towers, 1989) it was reported that they "managed" pharmacologic therapeutics in all fifty states: over 50% prescribed under their own name, fewer than 10% signed jointly with a physician, and the remainder either recommended medications or prescribed under a physician's name. Analgesics, antihistamines, antimicrobials, and anti-inflammatories, topicals, and vitamins are the most likely drug groups to be prescribed or recommended.

This seems to be confirmed by Pearson (1988), who asserted that NPs write prescriptions regardless of state legislation. Just as importantly, it is noted that practitioners are conservative prescribers and do influence formulary designations and prescriptive choices.

Thus, practice privileges are important, not only for their endorsement value, but to insure adequacy of therapeutic regimens and continuity of care between community-based and tertiary and/or long-term care institutions.

Nursing and Public Policy

International, national, and the profession's own policy papers are helping to shape practice through their combined emphasis on primary care, collaborative practice, and creation of facilitating legislation and regulation.

An early international mandate for primary care and health for all was the theme of the Declaration at Alma Ata (1978; International Conference Declaration, 1978). The idea that improved health care for everyone was possible was predicated in part on the belief that nurses are the key primary care providers. Health for the Year 2000 also emphasizes health promotion and primary care by outlining specific, attainable health improvement goals for populations at risk.

Nursing's Agenda for Health Care Reform (1991), devised and endorsed by many of the professional nursing organizations, calls for immediate health care reform which would emphasize community-based primary care, include a package of essential services, and target more vulnerable populations first. Consumers would have access to all qualified providers, including advanced practice nurses (Nursing's Agenda for Health Care, 1991).

Henderson (1989) concludes that all nurses need to function in all settings as they do in areas traditionally underserved by physicians. In order to meet the demands of such an international perspective and effect a universal primary care approach, Henderson suggests that elements of nursing's value system be addressed: an orientation toward inpatient medical-surgical nursing and the associated hierarchical orientation; a view of community nursing as peripheral; and an unwillingness to exercise legitimate power and move beyond dependency and passivity.

The 1987 recommendations of the WHO Study Group (Regulatory Mechanisms for Nursing Training and Practice, 1987; Smith, 1989) support the view that nursing education and practice have to change to meet the international goal of health for all. Generally, the Study Group recommended that legislative support is necessary to maximize nurses' contribution to the development and delivery of primary care services. Specific recommendations were: (1) that countries and regulatory bodies initiate support of educational programs that will advance primary care roles for all nurses, (2) that educational programs be designed to prepare primary care practitioners able to collaborate with professionals and community members, (3) that regulatory mechanisms that eliminate deterrents and ensure nurses full participation in primary care be put in place, (4) that regulation of education and practice be controlled by nursing boards, and (5) that national nursing organizations give priority to promoting facilitating legislation and regulation affecting education and practice.

Two facts have been established: primary care nursing is consistent with the basic nursing role for beginning and advanced practice, and primary care is not synonymous with nurse practitioners. Given the need for more primary care services by advanced practice nurses, the question becomes should primary care be an element in every advanced practice specialty, as well as continue as a recognized clinical specialty?

FUTURE CLINICAL PRACTICE

In light of these defining issues, what are the best strategies for nursing in order to solidify the profession's gains in advanced nursing practice, and position practitioners for future opportunities?

Three strategies seem to be both timely and natural extensions of advanced preparation and practice to date. They are: (1) to merge the roles of the nurse clinician, clinical nurse specialist, and nurse practitioner, (2) to advance the primary care role while balancing it with other practice opportunities, and (3) to facilitate collaborative practice with physicians and other providers.

Styles believes that "nursing destiny is being shaped—[in] the realm of advanced practice" and that "nurse practitioners represent the frontier in nursing" (Styles, 1990). If advanced practice is to shape nursing's destiny, what are the most effective strategies that best serve both patients and practitioners?

Merging Roles

Mezey (see Chapter 2) suggests that as practitioners and clinical specialists practice in the same setting, it becomes less useful to nurses and institutions to pursue the role differentiation. She proposes three possibilities for the future: continued role differentiation, eventual role fusion, or a role elimination.

Historical Perspective on Scope of Practice

Initially, nurse practitioners and clinical specialists defined their roles quite differently. The original linkage between primary care, the nurse practitioner role, and ambulatory settings determined early program content, which emphasized direct care of individual clients and families in hospital-based clinics and free-standing ambulatory care facilities. Nurse practitioners have traditionally defined their scope of practice primarily as the provision of a broad range of direct services to patients and families (American Nurse's Association [ANA], 1988b). They are the only group of nurses with graduate education who have remained exclusively involved in direct patient care services (Brown, 1983). Inherent in the nurse practitioner role is the ability to: adequately assess a wide range of actual or potential health problems; interpret data and formulate an informed opinion by contrasting individual patient characteristics with knowledge derived from physical, psychological, social, and cultural variables; initiate a comprehensive plan of care that includes health promotion, treatment, guidance and counseling, education, and referral; maintain contact with the patient and coordinate care; and be seen as a colleague by other collaborative professionals (Grey & Flint, 1989; Kane et al., 1989; Lynaugh, 1986; Rosenaur, 1984).

Although nurse practitioners recognize the importance of traditionally defined medical skills, such as physical examination, interpretation of laboratory results and the ability to initiate and monitor medical management, their greatest satisfaction with the NP role comes from their degree of autonomy, their ability to provide comprehensive services, and the respect of, and collaboration with, other health professionals (Grey & Flint, 1989; Kitzman, 1983; Lynaugh, 1983; Sultz, 1983b).

In contrast to nurse practitioners, clinical specialists have traditionally defined their role in terms of consultation to and education of patients, families, and staff, coupled with specialized knowledge of discrete clinical problems encountered in secondary and tertiary hospitals (Kitzman,

1983; ANA, 1988a; Beecroft, 1989). The original designation of clinical specialist was as an institutionally based practitioner whose major role was indirect care. The clinical nurse specialist programs are described as providing knowledge and skills for direct care, consultation, education, and research with an emphasis on role modeling and improving the patient care environment (Arena & Page, 1992; Kimmel, 1989; Reilly, 1989; Sparacino, 1990a). Descriptions of CNS practice emphasize the role components of practitioner, educator, scholar, and consultant without ever arriving at a completely integrated or balanced composite.

While the clinical specialist role traditionally encompasses responsibility for improvement of patient care, according to Brown, the inevitable happened: indirect care functions began to gobble up the lion's share of the clinical nurse specialist's time. So great are the needs of bedside nurses for support, guidance, and education and in clinical matters that many clinical specialists find that they have little time in which to render care to patients (Brown, 1987).

In the late 1970s and early 1980s, differentiation between the nurse practitioner and the clinical specialist was highly formalized. Several factors contributed to this role differentiation. One was the ambiguity and hostility of individual nurses, nurse educators, and nursing organizations to nurse practitioners (Rogers, 1975). Most nurse practitioners were highly sensitive to the criticism that they aspired to the medical model, or were functioning outside the scope of nursing practice.

Other nurses were concerned that the title *nurse practitioner*, while designating that they had primary care skills, failed to differentiate between educational levels of preparation. Furthermore, the true nature of the practice was ambiguous and open to wide interpretation, ranging from that of assistant to the physician to comprehensive nursing care. Therefore, despite the fact that other titles failed to connote the expanded functions of nurse practitioners, master's-prepared nurses were reluctant to use what was felt to be a restrictive title, and were more inclined to align themselves with nurse clinicians or clinical nurse specialists. In 1973, the term *nurse clinician* or *clinical specialist* was preferred by almost three-quarters of the graduate programs producing nurse practitioners (Sultz, 1983a). These initial fearful and angry responses have faded, and acceptance of nurse practitioners within nursing is now complete. Master's programs have begun to prepare graduates for certification as either nurse practitioners and clinical specialists.

Arguments for Blending Nurse Practitioner and Clinical Specialist Roles

There are a number of compelling arguments for the blending of these roles, including (1) the recognition, through legal and reimbursement mechanisms, of NPs' direct provider services, (2) the difficulty in maintaining support for the CNS' indirect care and other roles, (3) the similarities in educational preparation (see Mezey, Chapter 2), and (4) the similarities in clinical practice.

The event that did not take place in the 1950s—creation of an advanced practice role which met contemporary needs—may be ready to happen. The growing dialogue regarding role merger is thoughtful and nondefensive (Hanson & Martin, 1990; Hockenberry-Eaton & Powell, 1991; Reilly, 1989, Worley, Drago, & Hadley, 1990) and worthy of more immediate attention. It is proposed that even if the roles are not purposefully merged, a natural evolution will occur (Elder & Bullough, 1990).

The extraordinary examination by nurses, physicians, and others has produced solid documentation for reimbursement and continued practice opportunities. The quality, cost effectiveness, and acceptability of nurse practitioner services are well established, and could serve to promote the roles of the CNS as well as the NP, since educational preparation and practice settings for the two are similar. Elder and Bullough (1990) suggest that both groups bring strengths to a merger; the CNS role is strongly supported by nursing education, while the NP role is well recognized and valued for its tangible quality and cost savings. Combining the practitioners' (Edmunds, 1990) and specialists' roles would also produce a strengthened and cost-effective organizational power base, programmatic cost effectiveness, and increased job mobility for graduates (Forbes, Rafson, Spross, & Kozlowski, 1990). Because NPs have been easily able to document a unit of patient service, historically these nurses have had an advantage over clinical specialists in eligibility for third party reimbursement. The Omnibus Reconciliation Act of 1991 recognizes both nurse practitioners and clinical specialists as eligible for reimbursement under Medicare and Medicaid (Omnibus Budget Reconciliation Act, 1991). The prospect of second licensure as the credential for both clinical specialists and nurse practitioners would seem to advance the role merger.

In contrast, the clinical nurse specialist role is described by its components, frequently with shifting emphasis on one or another role, or a role is described in terms of what it might become in order to assure continued recognition of clinical specialists (Hamric, 1992; Storr, 1988). Various proponents suggest that while first-generation clinical specialists focused on patient care and consultation, second-generation CNS will have to focus on administration and/or systems as a way to demonstrate cost effectiveness (Wolf, 1990), convince non-nurses of CNS importance (Mills, 1989), or make the role more marketable (Elder & Bullough, 1990). Others insist that the clinical nurse specialist role has expanded beyond hospital-based practice and can now be described as client-based, focused on patient or client and family (Beecroft & Papenhausen, 1989; Hamric, 1992; Nelson-Conley, 1990; O'Rourke, 1989). The need to provide expert role models for nursing staff may be a less compelling reason for the CNS now than it was in the early 1950s, in light of the increase in baccalaureate and master's prepared staff.

Elder and Bullough (1990) conducted a survey of CNS and NP alumni in a 10-year cohort. While there were no significant demographic differences, the CNS group included had psychiatric nursing as a specialty and a greater percentage moved into education and administration. In 25 work activities associated with the clinical role, two-thirds were comparably reported. Both groups reported a high level of involvement in teaching patients and families, and initiating, managing, and evaluating treatment regimens. CNSs and NPs provided counseling and performed psychosocial assessments. Eight activities were rated differently by NPs and CNSs: clinical nurse specialists reported more indirect care, staff teaching, support group, and psychotherapy activities. NPs performed more physical examinations, ordered laboratory tests, medications, and treatments, and made referrals more often. Eighty-one percent of the NPs were prepared to choose their role again, versus 52% of the CNS group. Generally, the views of the two groups on professional issues were similar; in response to a specific question about the addition of NP preparation to the CNS program, two-thirds were positive. Elder and Bullough concluded that although members of the two groups carry out some different tasks, and although they tend to use different terms to describe their diagnostic practices, the large area of overlapping functions and opinions on professional issues is the most impressive finding of the study.

Forbes et al.'s (1990) study included student practice and graduate employment settings; student and graduate NPs worked in ambulatory settings, although clinical nurse specialists did also. Clinical nurse specialists practiced primarily in tertiary care settings, as did some NPs. In fact, the loss of distinction by setting was evident more than a decade ago, as nurse practitioners moved into inpatient practice, emergency rooms, and long-term care institutions (Jones, 1985). There are many examples of adult and pediatric nurse practitioners employed in hospital clinics, emergency rooms, and inpatient services, such as medical units and newborn nurseries of city hospitals (Grey & Flint, 1989; Levine, 1991). Likewise, clinical specialists work in private practices, community-based clinics, prisons, shelters for the homeless, and migrant work camps. Their roles include care of older people (Beyerman, 1989), health promotion, mental/emotional assessment and management

(Yoest, 1989), education, research, consultation, and, increasingly, middle management (DHHS, Seventh Report to Congress, 1990)

Primary Care and Other Practice Opportunities

The perennial consideration of provider competition and reimbursement questions serves as incentive to take advantage of every potential practice niche. More than a decade ago, a classic contributor to the dialogue about nurse practitioners (Lewis, 1982) suggested that practice opportunities occur under four circumstances: in service areas in which physicians cannot or will not participate; in situations where the patient care outcomes are improved to the point of reduced demand; concerning populations typically not served by physicians; or in truly complementary practice situations where economic competition does not exist.

Each of the opportunities originally identified by Lewis has expanded considerably since 1982. There is today almost no practice setting, or client or patient population, not served by advanced practice nurses in some location. In fact, master's preparation which blended NP and CNS knowledge and skills would enable providers to move more easily into different practice settings. The dilemma will be preparing a sufficient number of advanced practice nurses for the full range of specialty practices, including primary care (Mullan, Rivo, & Politzer, 1993).

The unlinking of nurse practitioners and primary care notwithstanding, primary care remains a major practice opportunity for advanced practice nurses. The drive to provide services in the least expensive setting, services which promote health and prevent more costly episodes of illness, and services to populations who continue to be underserved makes primary care an attractive practice option. Primary care is the heart of reform proposals, including Nursing's Agenda for Health Care Reform (1991) and practice models, such as HMOs.

The expanding number of primary care sites, including HMOs, community health centers, and group practices will absorb available primary care physicians, creating an even greater demand for nurses to provide primary care services in these as well as in other community settings. Plum (1989) points out that in order to predict the performance of the HMO model, it is necessary to assess two basic assumptions; one, that outpatient care can substitute for inpatient, and two, that other providers can substitute for physicians.

Populations not served by physicians cover a wide range of clients, patients, and families traditionally served by nurses, as well as the new underserved groups, including school children, recent immigrants, persons with HIV/AIDS, and substance abusers. Nurses have demonstrated a willingness to care for clients in all settings. The first-hand experiences described in Chapter 7 accurately depict the care nurse practitioners deliver to underserved populations. But for nurses to be the providers for these populations, public and private support for these services must be available in the form of salary, direct payment, or third party payment.

Direct economic competition between physicians and nurses may not be an obstacle in institutionally based practice situations, where both groups are salaried, or in settings where responsibilities are quite disparate.

Collaboration

The desire to establish practice and language as distinctly and separately within the realm of nursing was triggered and sustained by nursing theorists and strategists who equated survival with isolation from medicine. For reasons both developmental and practical, there is a need to examine advanced practice and nursing's roles in collaborative and interdisciplinary based health care (Fagin, 1992).

Collaboration was essential to the development of the nurse practitioner movement, beginning with the first program initiated by Ford and Silver. Since 1965 much has been written about collaborative practice (Dashiff, Griener, & Cannon, 1990; Stilwell, 1987) as nurses and physicians debated practice as complementary or overlapping. Nurse practitioners worked with physicians in interdisciplinary teams (Uribelarrea, 1987), group practice (Salisbury & Tettersell, 1988), and in back-up arrangements (Thompson, 1986). Clinical nurse specialists' primarily emphasized collaboration with other nurses, patients and families, and less directly that between nurse and physician.

Full collaboration, subscribed to by all providers, may eventually result from the complexity of patients' problems, institutionally based practice, and quality assurance activities, including published data on hospitals' morbidity and mortality, and regulatory language.

The goals of collaborative practice are quality care at lower costs (Kerfoot, 1989) and tangible patient outcomes, including decreased mortality (Knaus, Draper, Wagner, & Zimmerman, 1986). The basis of patient care, and the success of collaborative practice, is successful communication. In a study of provider communications, Campbell, Mauksch, Neikirk, and Hosokawa (1990) noted that joint practice may expand the scope of primary care by integrating nursing's focus on contextual care and medicine's perspective on illness. This has been demonstrated to be important in studies of physicians and nurse practitioners in routine practice, where nurse practitioners show similar effectiveness but demonstrate greater concern for psychosocial issues (Campbell et al., 1990). More than 20% of family practice patients present some form of functional somatic symptoms, including depression and anxiety (Connelly, Philbrick, Smith, Kaiser, & Wymer, 1989; Glenn, 1985; Martin and Davis, 1989). Glenn (1985) notes that nursing has considerable primary care experience in assisting families with a variety of health and illness problems. Patients with high levels of psychological distress use a disproportionate share of ambulatory services (Connelly, Philbrick, et al., 1989). Even patients who simply perceive themselves to be less well may use more health care services. In a study of 208 patients seen in a primary care practice and questioned about their use of services over a twelve-month period, five percent of all office visits were attributed solely to poor health perceptions; the patients with the lowest health perceptions were anxious, depressed, and incurred the most health care expenses (Connelly, Philbrick, et al., 1989).

Brody noted that patient satisfaction with medical visits relates to the use of nontechnical interventions, including education, stress counseling, and discussion—all traditional nursing activities (Brody et al., 1989). Quality assurance which acknowledges the importance of these elements also reveals that collaborative practice has been shown to improve patient outcomes, improve job satisfaction, and improve quality of care at lower costs (Kerfoot, 1989).

The convergence of advanced practice roles and collaborative practice is realized in the hospital nurse practitioner (Covington, Erwin, & Sellers, 1992; Silver & McAtee, 1988). As visualized by Silver & McAtee (1988), the advanced practice nurse would collaborate with physicians to admit patients, complete history and physical examinations, carry out diagnostic and therapeutic procedures, and prescribe medications. Silver concludes that studies done by him and others show that advanced practice nurses and physician assistants are comparable to first-year residents in clinical competence, quality of care, and productivity. Collaborative practice in the inpatient setting may be driven by the replacement of resident housestaff by nurses with advanced practice preparation (Gamble, 1989; Silver & McAtee, 1988). Decline in numbers of residents, particularly in oversubscribed specialty areas, will result from a desire to reduce graduate medical education cost and physician supply. The role of the advanced practice nurse, as described by Silver and McAtee, would include admission of patients in collaboration with the physician, comprehensive history taking and physical examination, ordering and carrying out of diagnostic and therapeutic procedures, prescribing of medications, and integration of care by other providers, while also providing health promotion and maintenance activities. Subspecialty skills would be added to this role for nurse associate residents.

The economic and regulatory pressure to reduce housestaff in teaching hospitals led to a time and motion study of residents in two urban hospital centers to determine how residents actually use their time and whether advanced practice nurses and others would be appropriate substitutes. A model of analysis in which a midlevel practitioner is coordinating care would mean that only 20% of residents' lost time would need to be replaced by other physicians. This model would require the midlevel practitioner to work closely with the physician to develop and implement the patient's plan of care and assume more of the data collection and documentation activities (Knickman, Lipkin, Finkler, Thompson, & Kiel, 1992). A critical question associated with this institutional practice development is what budgetary lines will be used to support these practitioners? If nursing department lines are used, it will reduce the number of professional nurses necessary for patient care; if medicine's lines are used, who will claim the revenue?

Gleeson et al. (1990) described one institutional model of advanced practice nursing in which the nurses collaborate with medical staff and primary nurses in patients' plan of care, complete histories and physical examinations, review diagnostic data, and work with patients and families. In this model, the nurse practices one day a week in the outpatient clinic. The advantages of this combined specialist/practitioner model include improved quality, continuity, and cost effectiveness of care, expanded professional development, coordinated management of patient care, and expanded health teaching and referral.

The acute care institution may continue to be the locus of both primary and acute care. Vladeck (1991) proposes that acute care hospitals be asked to take on the responsibility for the full spectrum of health services, including health promotion/public education, primary care, acute care, and long-term care. New York is an example of policy dictating a decrease of inpatient capacity, but failing to provide the noninstitutional capacity to provide health services. And although it may be less costly to provide community-based clinic services, outpatient departments are already operational. Therefore, it may be more appropriate for those acute care institutions that already have the regulatory and financial leverage to build the community-based primary care services (Vladeck, 1991).

State regulation requires nurses in advanced practice to work with physicians, although physician involvement varies from state to state. In one or more advanced practice roles, nurses function independently in 15 states, with physician supervision in 16 and collaboratively in 25 states. Collaborative practice will continue to be important, and will be the special responsibility of advanced practice nurses, since it has been shown to be successful for nurses with graduate preparation, who have observed faculty collaboration, and who had faculty as resources in clinical experience (Weiss, 1985).

Summary

If advanced practice nursing is nursing's destiny, it is important to recognize the factors that will influence its direction, and to take active steps to shape the scope, support, and future site of clinical practice. At issue is whether it is opportune for organized nursing to merge the advanced practice roles, and whether such a merger would facilitate nursing's movement into the mainstream of practice opportunities, reimbursement and revenue generation, and consumer choice.

REFERENCES

Aiken, L., & Mullinix, C. (1987). The nursing shortage. Myth or reality? *New England Journal of Medicine, 317*(10), 641–646.

American Nurses Association. (1988a). *The role of the clinical nurse specialist*. Washington, DC: Author.

American Nurses Association. (1988b). *The scope of practice of the primary health care nurse practitioner*. Washington, DC.

American Nurses Association. (1988c). *Standards of practice of the primary health care nurse practitioner*. Washington, DC.

An open letter on nurse midwifery. (1992). *Report*. The Official Newsletter of the New York State Nurses Association. *23*, 4.

Arena, D., & Page, N. (1992). The imposter phenomenon in the clinical nurse specialist role. *Image, Journal of Nursing Scholarship, 24*, 121–125.

Beecroft, P., & Papenhausen, J. (1989). Who is a clinical nurse specialist? *Clinical Nurse Specialist, 3*, 103–104.

Beyerman, K. (1989). Making a difference: The gerontological CNS. *Journal of Gerontological Nursing, 15*, 36–41.

Boyd, N., Stasiowski, S., Catoe, P., Wells, P., Stahl, B., Judson, E., Hartman, A., & Lander, J. (1991). The merit and significance of clinical nurse specialists. *Journal of Nursing Administration, 21*, 35–43.

Bradford, R. (1989). Obstacles to collaborative practice. *Nursing Management, 20*, 72I–72P.

Brody, D., Miller, S., Lerman, C., Smith, D., Lazaro, C., & Blum, M. (1989). The relationship between patients' satisfaction with their physicians and perspective about interventions they desired and received. *Medical Care, 27*, 1027–1035.

Brown, M., & Waybrant, K. (1987). Delineation of the nurse practitioner role: Influence of individual characteristics and practice setting on coordinational and health promotion activities. *Journal of Ambulatory Care Management, 10,* 8–19.

Brown, J. (1983). The clinical nurse specialist. *Nursing Administration Quarterly,* Fall, 36–46.

Brunk, D. (1992). The clinical nurse specialist as an external consultant: A framework for practice. *Clinical Nurse Specialist, 6,* 2–4.

Bullough, B. (1992). Alternative models for specialty nursing practice. *Nursing and Health Care, 13,* 254–259.

Campbell, J., Mauksch, H., Neikirk, H., & Hosokawa, M. (1990). Collaborative practice and provider styles of delivering health care. *Social Science and Medicine, 30,* 1359–1365.

Clare, F., Sprately, E., Schwab, P., & Iglehart, J. (1987). Trends in health personnel. *Health Affairs, 6,* 90–103.

Connelly, J., Philbrick, P., Smith, G., Kaiser, D., & Wymer, A. (1989). Health perceptions of primary care patients and the influence on health care utilization. *Medical Care, 27,* S99–109.

Covington, C., Erwin, T., & Sellers, F. (1992). Implementation of a nurse practitioner-staffed fast track. *Journal of Emergency Nursing, 18,* 124–131.

Dashiff, C., Griener, D., & Cannon, N. (1990). Physician and nurse collaboration in a medical clinic for indigent patients. *Family Systems Medicine, 8,* 57–69.

The declaration at Alma Ata: Primary health care for all by the year 2000. (1978). World Health Organization. Geneva, Switzerland.

Department of Health and Human Services. (1988). Seventh report to the President and Congress on the status of health personnel in the United States. Washington, DC: Bureau of Health Professions, Health Resources and Services Administration, DHHS.

Dross, K. (1988). Discourse and occupational perspective: A comparison of nurse practitioners and physician assistants. *Discourse Processes, 11,* 163–181.

Earnings of nursing and non-nursing personnel in the nation's private hospitals, United States and selected metropolitan areas. (1991). Division of Nursing, Bureau of Health Professions, Health Resources and Services Administration, DHHS.

Edmunds, M. (1990). National alliance of nurse practitioners: A five year progress report. *Nurse Practitioner, 15,* 44–46.

Elder, R., & Bullough, B. (1990). Nurse practitioners and clinical nurse specialists: Are the roles merging? *Clinical Nurse Specialist, 4,* 78–84.

Fagin, C. (1992). Collaboration between nurses and physicians: No longer a choice. *Nursing and Health Care, 13,* 354–363.

Faucher, M. (1992). Prescriptive authority for advanced nurse practitioners: A blue-print for action. *Journal of Pediatric Health Care, 6,* 25–31.

Feldman, M., Ventura, M., & Crosby, F. (1987). Studies of nurse practitioner effectiveness. *Nursing Research, 3,* 303–308.

Forbes, K., Rafson, J., Spross, J., & Kozlowski, D. (1990). The clinical nurse specialist and nurse practitioner: Core curriculum survey results. *Clinical Nurse Specialist, 4*, 63–66.

Ford, M. (1990). The nurse specialist: A cornerstone of quality patient care. *Journal of MAG, 79*, 101–103.

Ford, L. (1986). Nurses, nurse practitioners: The evolution of primary care: Review of Nurses, nurse practitioners: The evolution of primary care. *Image: Journal of Nursing Scholarship, 18*, 177–178.

Ford, L. C. (198?) Nurse practitioners: History of a new idea and predictions for the future (pp. 231–247). In L. H. Aiken & S. R. Gortner (Eds.), *Nursing in the 1980s: Crises, Opportunities, Challenges*. Philadelphia: Lippincott.

Friedman, E. (1990). Nursing: Breaking the bonds? *Journal of the American Medical Association, 264*, 3117–3122.

Gamble, S. (1989). Changing roles in the 90s: Will RNs manage MDs? *Hospitals, 63*, 42–44.

Gleeson, R., McIlwain-Simpson, G., Boos, M., Sweet, E., Trzcinski, K., Solberg, C., & Doughty, R. (1990). Advanced practice nursing: A model of collaborative care. *Maternal Child Nursing, 15*, 9–12.

Glenn, M. (1985). Toward collaborative family-oriented health care. *Family Systems Medicine, 3*, 466–475.

Graveley, E., & Littlefield, J. (1992). A cost-effectiveness analysis of three staffing models for the delivery of low-risk prenatal care. *American Journal of Public Health, 82*, 180–184.

Grey, M., & Flint, S. (1989). NAPNAP membership survey: Characteristics of members' practice. *Journal of Pediatric Health Care, 3*, 336–341.

Hamric, A. (1992). Creating our future: Challenges and opportunities for the clinical nurse specialist. *Oncology Nursing Forum, 19*, 11–15.

Hanson, C., & Martin, L. (1990). The nurse practitioner and clinical nurse specialist: Should the roles be merged? *Journal of the American Academy of Nurse Practitioners, 2*, 2–9.

Harrington, C., & Culbertson, R. (1990). Nurses left out of health care reimbursement reform. *Nursing Outlook, 38*, 156–158.

Harrington, C., & Shea, S. (1991). Effects of nursing reimbursement rates on access to care for Medicare beneficiaries, particularly those who are underserved. San Francisco: University of California School of Nursing, Institute for Health and Aging.

Harrison, E. (1989). Product evaluation and the clinical nurse specialist: An opportunity for role development. *Clinical Nurse Specialist, 3*, 85–89.

Hayes, E. (1985). The nurse practitioners: History, current conflicts and future survival. *Journal of the Association of College Health, 34*, 144–147.

Henderson, V. (1989). Countdown to 2000: A major international conference for the primary health care team. *Journal of Advanced Nursing, 14*, 81–85.

Hilderley, L. (1991). Nurse-physician collaborative practice: The clinical nurse specialist in radiation oncology private practice. *Oncology Nursing Forum, 18*, 585–591.

Hockenberry-Eaton, M., & Powell, M. (1991). Merging advanced practice roles: The NP and CNS. *Journal of Pediatric Health Care, 5,* 158–159.

Hogue, E. (1989). Opportunities for nurses seeking third party reimbursement using existing mechanisms. *Pediatric Nursing, 15,* 279–280.

Holt, F. (1990). Managed care and the clinical nurse specialist. *Clinical Nurse Specialist, 4,* 27.

Hupcey, J. (1990). The socialization process of master-level nurse practitioner students. *Journal of Nursing Education, 29,* 196–201.

Jacox, A. (1982). Role restructuring in hospital nursing. In L. Aiken (Ed.), *Nursing in the 1980s: Crises, opportunities, challenges* (pp. 75–99). Philadelphia: Lippincott.

Jones, L. (1985). In-patient nurse practitioners. *Nurse Practitioner, 10,* 48–50.

Kane, R., Garrard, J., Skay, C., Radosevich, D., Buchanan, J., McDermott, S., Arnold, S., & Kepferle, L. (1989). Effects of a geriatric nurse practitioner on process and outcome of nursing home care. *American Journal of Public Health, 79,* 1271–1277.

Kerfoot, K. (1989). Nursing management considerations. *Nursing Economics, 7,* 335–338.

Kimmel, L. (1989). Guiding the way: Acting as a preceptor for graduate students. *Journal of Psychosocial Nursing, 27,* 14–21.

King, E., & Sagan, P. (1989). Nurse practitioner liability and authority. *Nursing Administration Quarterly, 13,* 57–60.

Kirkland, S., & Tinsley, D. (1990). CNS: Special skills really contain costs! *Nursing Management, 21,* 97–98.

Kitchens, E., Piazza, D., & Ellison, K. (1989). Specialization in adult health/medical surgical nursing: What does it mean? *Journal of Nursing Education, 28,* 221–226.

Kitzman, H. (1983). The clinical nurse specialist and the nurse practitioner. In A. Hamric & S. Spross (Eds.), *The clinical nurse specialist in theory and practice* (pp. 275–290). New York: Grune and Stratton.

Knaus, W., Draper, E., Wagner, D., & Zimmerman, J. (1986). An evaluation of outcome from intensive care in major medical centers. *Annals of Internal Medicine, 104,* 410–418.

Knickman, J., Lipkin, M., Finkler, S., Thompson, W., & Kiel, J. (1992). The potential for using non-physicians to compensate for the reduced availability of residents. *Academic Medicine, 67,* 429–438.

Koch, L., Pazaki, S., & Campbell. (1992). The first 20 years of nurse practitioner literature: An evolution of joint practice issues. *Nurse Practitioner, 17,* 64–66.

LeBar, C. (1990). The issue of third party reimbursement: Advice for nurse practitioners from a national expert. *Nurse Practitioner, 15,* 46–47.

Levine, S. (1991). The development of nurse practitioners. *Nursing.* Bronx, NY: Bronx Municipal Hospital Center. p. 3.

Lewis, C. (1982). Nurse practitioner and the physician surplus. In L. Aiken (Ed.), *Nursing in the 1980s: Crises, opportunities, challenges* (pp. 249–266). Philadelphia: Lippincott.

Lynaugh, J. E., Gerritty, P. L., & Hagopian, L. (1985). Patterns of practice: Master's prepared nurse practitioners. *Journal of Nursing Education, 24*(7), 241–250.

Lynaugh, J. (1986). The nurse practitioner: Issues in practice. In M. Mezey and D. McGivern (Eds.), *Nurses, nurse practitioners*. Philadelphia: Little, Brown, pp. 137–145.

McGivern, D. (1986). The evolution of primary care nursing. In M. Mezey & D. McGivern (Eds.), *Nurses, nurse practitioners: The evolution of primary care* (pp. 3–14). Boston: Little, Brown.

McGrath, S. (1990). The cost effectiveness of nurse practitioner. *Nurse Practitioners, 15*, 40–42.

Martin, A., & Davis, L. (1989). Mental health problems in primary care: A study of nurse practitioners' practice. *Nurse Practitioner, 14*, 46–56.

Mezey, M. (1986). Issues in graduate education. In M. Mezey & D. McGivern (Eds.), *Nurses, nurse practitioners: The evolution of primary care* (pp. 101–119). Boston: Little, Brown.

Mittelstadt, P. (1990). Reimbursement extended to NPs. *American Nurse, 22*, 2, 10.

Mills, M. (1989). Clinical nurse specialist organizational value and role support. *Clinical Nurse Specialist, 3*, 186–187.

Mullan, F., Rivo, M.L., & Politzer, R.M. (1993). Doctors dollars and determination: Making physician work-force policy. *Health Affairs, 12*, 138–151.

Murphy, D. (1989). The primary care role in occupational health. *American Association of Occupational Health Journal, 37*, 470–474.

National Council of State Boards of Nursing. (1992). Position paper on the licensure of advanced practice nursing. Unpublished manuscript, pp. 1–8.

Nelson-Conley, C. (1990). Role development of the clinical nurse specialist within the Indian Health Service. *Clinical Nurse Specialist, 4*, 142–146.

Nursing's Agenda for Health Care Reform. (1991). Washington, DC: American Nurses Association.

Nursing Data Review, 1991. (1991). New York: National League for Nursing Press.

O'Rourke, M. (1989). Generic professional behaviors: Implications for the clinical nurse specialist role. *Clinical Nurse Specialist, 3*, 128–132.

Papenhausen, J., & Beecroft, P. (1990). Communicating clinical nurse specialist effectiveness. *Clinical Nurse Specialist, 4*, 1–2.

Pearson, L. (1988). Let's capitalize on our successes. *Nurse Practitioner, 13*, 6–7.

Peglow, D., Klatt, E., Stelton, S., Cutillo, T., Howard, J., & Wolff, P. (1992). Evaluation of clinical nurse specialist practice. *Clinical Nurse Specialist, 6*, 28–35.

Pointer, D., & Pointer, T. (1989). Case based prospective price reimbursement. *Nursing Management, 20*, 30–34.

Politzer, R., Harris, D., Gaston, M., & Mullan, F. (1991). Primary care physician supply and the medically underserved. *Journal of the American Medical Association, 266*, 104–113.

Plum, K. (1989). Analysis of a capitation plan for the chronically mentally ill. *Nursing Economics, 7*, 250–256.

Radke, K., McArt, E., Schmitt, M., & Walker, E. (1990). Administrative preparation of clinical nurse specialists. *Journal of Professional Nursing, 6,* 221–228.

Regulation of advanced nursing practice update. (1992). *Issues. 13,* 1 and 6.

Regulatory mechanisms for nursing training and practice: Meeting primary health care needs: Conclusions and recommendations of the WHO Study Group. (1987). *International Nursing Review, 34,* 52–54.

Reilly, C. (1989). The consultative role of the gerontological nurse specialist in hospitals. *Nursing Clinics of North America, 24,* 733–740.

Rogers, B., Sweeting, S., & Davis, B. (1989). Employment and salary characteristics of nurse practitioners. *Nurse Practitioners, 14,* 56–66.

Rogers, M. (1975). Nursing is coming of age through the practitioner movement: Con. *American Journal of Nursing, 75,* 1844–1847.

Rosenaur, J., Stanford, D., Morgan, W., & Curtin, B. (1984). Prescribing behavior of primary care nurse practitioners. *American Journal of Public Health, 74*(1), 110–113.

Safriet, B. (1992). Health care dollars and regulatory sense: The role of advanced practice nursing. *Yale Journal on Regulation, 9,* 472–488.

Salisbury, C., & Tettersell, M. (1988). Comparison of the work of a nurse practitioner with that of a general practitioner. *Journal of the Royal College of General Practitioners, 3,* 314–316.

Scharon, G., Tsai, S., & Bernacki, E. (1987). Nurse practitioners. *American Association of Occupational Health Nursing Journal, 35,* 280–284.

Schickler, J., & Johnston, L. (1987). Contributions by nurse practitioners in primary care to prevention and management of illness. *Nursing Administration Quarterly, XX,* 18–22.

Scott, C., & Harrison, A. (1990). Direct reimbursement of nurse practitioners in health insurance plans of research universities. *Journal of Professional Nursing, 6,* 21–32.

Sebastian, L. (1991). Third party reimbursement for nurses in advanced practice. *Perspectives in Psychiatric Care, 27,* 5–10.

Shanks-Meile, S., Shipley, A., Collins, P., & Tacker, A. (1989). Changes in the advertised demand for nurse practitioners in the United States, 1975–1986. *Nurse Practitioner, 14,* 41–49.

Silver, H., & McAtee, P. (1988). Should nurses substitute for house staff. *American Journal of Nursing, 88,* 1671–1673.

Smith, J. (1989). Guidelines for regulatory changes in nursing education and practice to promote primary health care. *Journal of Advanced Nursing, 14,* 603–605.

Smithing, R., & Wiley, M. (1989). Hospital privileges: Who needs them? *Journal of the American Academy of Nurse Practitioners, 1,* 150–151.

Sparacino, P. (1990a). Clinical nurse specialist curriculum planning: A step toward development of a standard. *Clinical Nurse Specialist, 4,* 43–44.

Sparacino, P. (1990b). Strategies for implementing advanced practice. *Clinical Nurse Specialist, 4,* 151–152.

Sprague-McRae, J. (1988). Nurse practitioners and collaborative interdisciplinary research roles in an HMO. *Pediatric Nursing, 14,* 503–508.

Stilwell, B. (1987). How important is nursing in general practice? *The Practitioner,* 231, 978–979.

Storr, G. (1988). The clinical nurse specialist: From the outside looking in. *Journal of Advanced Nursing, 13,* 265–272.

Styles, M. (1990). Nurse practitioners creating new horizons for the 1990s. *Nurse Practitioner, 15,* 4–57.

Sullivan, E. (1992). Nurse practitioners and reimbursement: Care analysis. *Nursing and Health Care, 13,* 236–241.

Sultz, H. (1983a). A decade of change for nurse practitioners: Part I. *Nursing Outlook, 31,* 137–142.

Sultz, H. (1983b). Nurse practitioners: A decade of change: Part II. *Nursing Outlook, 31,* 216–219.

Thompson, J. (1986). Primary health care for women. In M. Mezey & D. McGivern (Eds.), *Nurses, nurse practitioners: The evolution of primary care* (pp. 173–200). Boston: Little, Brown.

Towers, J. (1989). Report of the National Survey of the American Academy of Nurse Practitioners: Part II: Pharmacologic management practices. *Journal of the American Academy of Nurse Practitioners, 1,* 137–142.

Uribellarea, M. (1986). Team practice. In M. Mezey & D. McGivern (Eds.), *Nurses, nurse practitioners: The evolution of primary care* (pp. 164–172). Boston: Little, Brown.

Vladeck, B. (1991). Paradigm lost: Health policy in New York State in the post-Axelrod era. United Hospital Fund President's Letter. September 1991, p. 1–6.

Weiss, S. (1985). The influence of discourse on collaboration among nurses, physicians, and consumers. *Research in Nursing and Health, 8,* 49–59.

Wolf, G. (1990). Clinical nurse specialists: The second generation. *Journal of Nursing Administration, 20,* 7–8.

Worley, N., Drago, L., & Hadley, T. (1990). Improving the physical health-mental health interface for the chronically mentally ill: Could nurse case managers make a difference? *Archives of Psychiatric Nursing, 4,* 108–113.

Wright, J. (1990). Joining forces for the good of our clients. *Clinical Nurse Specialist, 4,* 76–77.

Yoest, M. A. (1989). The clinical nurse specialist on the psychiatric team. *Journal of Psychosocial Nursing and Mental Health Services, 27*(3), 27–32.

_____ Chapter **2**

PREPARATION FOR ADVANCED PRACTICE

M. Mezey

W HEN the concept of nurse practitioners was first introduced in the mid-1960s, there was a general sense of uncertainty as to where and how educational preparation of these nurses could best be accomplished. Initial options as to site of preparation (i.e., master's programs, certificate programs offered both in universities and as continuing education programs, and generalist preparation in baccalaureate programs) reflected the political realities, geographical differences, and the relative lack of knowledge as to optimum curriculum development and expected outcomes.

The experience of the past 30 years has provided an increasing appreciation of the multiplicity of factors affecting the education of nurse practitioners. Certain societal factors—attention to chronicity, vertical integration of health care services, and the trend to expand nurse practitioner practice into acute, long-term, and home health care—have been discussed in Chapter 1. The purpose of this chapter is twofold. The first section discusses specific academic and professional issues that influence nurse practitioner preparation: academic programming, the changing characteristics of students entering nursing, faculty, linkages between education and practice, certification, and movement to unite the practitioner and clinical specialist roles. The second section summarizes anticipated changes in the preparation of nurse practitioners that will occur in response to societal and professional pressures, and outlines some curriculum issues responsive to anticipated future needs.

ACADEMIC AND PROFESSIONAL ISSUES INFLUENCING NURSE PRACTITIONER PREPARATION

Preparation of Nurse Practitioners: The Site and the Student

Although the evidence now clearly supports that nurse practitioners should be prepared at the master's level, initially, the appropriate education model was not at all clear. During the 1970s, primary care nurses were prepared in diverse educational settings: universities, hospitals and other service settings, medical schools, and continuing education programs (Bates, 1973; Bates & Lynaugh, 1975; NLN, 1979 Secretary's Committee to Study Extended Roles for Nurses, 1972). Although this somewhat disorganized approach created problems, it also yielded advantages that have contributed to the gradual acceptance and legitimization of nurse practitioner practice and of primary care as an accepted component of nursing practice.

Most early primary care providers were graduated from certificate programs offered both inside and outside of university settings (Sultz, 1983a; Sultz, 1983b; Sultz, 1983c; Sultz, 1984). While from 1970 to 1977 certificate programs increased more rapidly than did master's programs, this trend was sharply reversed beginning in 1977. By 1989, 85% of all federally funded nurse practitioner programs were at the master's level and only 15% were certificate programs (DHHS, Report to Congress on Study of Need for Nurse Advanced Trained Specialists, 1990). This movement toward master's preparation can be attributed to a variety of factors. Over the last two decades the need for educational credentialing in nursing has become increasingly apparent. Nurses recognize that credentials other than academic degrees are deficient in terms of transportability, longevity, and recognition by professional colleagues. Moreover, the increased number of master's programs has made access to graduate education less of an issue and nurses have taken advantage of the opportunity to gain advanced academic degrees.

Currently, of the 72,800 nurses with master's degrees, 65% are in clinical practice. Of these 29,000 hold the title of clinical nurse specialist (34% master's-prepared); 17,600 hold the title of nurse clinician (11%

master's-prepared); and approximately 23,500 hold the title of nurse practitioner and nurse midwife (34% master's-prepared) (Hill, 1989; 1990). As of 1988, there were 197 master's programs in nursing, an increase from 78 in 1978 (American Nurses Association [ANA], 1989). These programs offer many subspecializations in nursing practice. For example, the 108 programs which responded to a national survey offered over 350 graduate nurse practitioner and clinical nurse specialist options (Forbes, 1990; Forbes, Rafson, Spross, & Kozlowski, 1990). Graduations from these programs totalled 6,000 in 1987–1988, an increase of 39% from 1977–1978. Enrollment increased 75%. Perhaps most importantly, in 1988, 64% of all enrollees were in advanced clinical practice specialty options (nurse practitioner and clinical specialist).

By the year 2000, the total supply of nurses with advanced clinical preparation is expected to reach 87,500, twice the 1988 supply (1990). Yet, this number will fall markedly short of the estimated 259,000 needed (Hill, 1989).

Contribution of Certificate and Continuing Education Programs

While the preparation of nurse practitioners in certificate programs has decreased substantially, the contribution of such programs cannot be overemphasized. The success of graduates of continuing education programs helped validate that primary care practice builds on an existing nursing foundation; for if it were a completely new activity, it could not have been successfully taught in short continuing education or certificate programs to noninitiated students (Leinenger, 1972; Robert Wood Johnson Foundation, 1980). Continuing education programs also helped to create a "critical mass" of practitioners, facilitating evaluation of the overall worth of nurse practitioners. While some attempts have been made to differentiate practitioners by level of education, in effect the major evaluation studies have concentrated on the ability of all nurse practitioners to deliver comprehensive, effective, and safe primary care services (Hedrich, 1987; Nolan, Beaman, & Sullivan, 1988; Prescott & Driscoll, 1978). To this end the contribution of nurses prepared in continuing education programs has been invaluable.

Lastly, continuing education programs have consistently educated nurses who might be ineligible to enter master's programs and who work with underserved populations, including ethnic minorities, the elderly, and rural populations. It is unrealistic, even now, to expect that all nurses will obtain a master's degree in order to function as nurse practitioners. While master's education is clearly the predominant mode of preparation, in some areas of the country, and for some specific areas of practice, for the immediate future, certificate programs continue to be a source of preparation for nurse practitioners (Department of Health, Education, & Welfare, 1980; Yedidia, 1981).

Undergraduate Programs

As early as 1971, nursing programs experimented with the possibility of preparing nurse practitioners at the baccalaureate level (Fagin & Goodwin, 1972, McGivern, 1974). These innovations were responsible for the introduction of many of the skills used by nurse practitioners into undergraduate curricula, and demonstrated the logic of primary care as a conceptual framework for baccalaureate education (Diers, 1982; Diers & Molde, 1983; McGivern, Mezey, & Baer, 1976).

Nevertheless, there is now a general consensus within nursing that the role of nurse practitioner requires specialized knowledge, which is best acquired in a master's program (ANA, 1988b). Even though they possess many primary care concepts and skills, graduates of baccalaureate programs are beginning practitioners prepared to assume generalist nursing positions. The differentiation between baccalaureate and master's preparation and delineation as to the appropriate preparation for primary care providers is spelled out in the following National League for Nursing (NLN) definitions:

> Undergraduate programs are offered in senior colleges and universities and lead to the baccalaureate or first professional degree in nursing. Graduates of NLN accredited baccalaureate programs are prepared for beginning general practice of professional nursing in hospitals and community health nursing agencies and all other health care agencies where health care and nursing care are given.
>
> The purpose of master's education is to prepare professional nursing leaders. These are the clinical specialists (advanced nurse practitioners), teachers, supervisors, and administrators whose special knowledge and skills are required now and will continue to be required in the future.
>
> The National League for Nursing believes that the nurse practitioner should hold a master's degree in nursing in order to insure competence and quality care. Furthermore, the League believes that the nurse practitioner should be educated within nursing's formally recognized education structure where emphasis in graduate nursing study would be placed on an expanded specialized nursing function, rather than on the performance of certain medical tasks. . . . Since the nurse practitioner role has a high degree of autonomy in and out of institutions, the League believes it is essential that these practitioners have advanced education and training in graduate nursing education programs to prepare them for independent decision-making and provide them with a specialized, in-depth knowledge base. (NLN, 1990, p. 8)

Students

Little is written as to the characteristics of students entering nurse practitioner programs. Sultz, for example, only briefly discussed applicant characteristics in his four-part study (Sultz, 1983a; Sultz, 1983b; Sultz, 1983c; Sultz, 1984). Since 1973, nurse practitioner students have become increasingly younger and have fewer years of experience. Most students have previously worked in acute care settings. Their primary reasons for entering nurse practitioner programs (to provide better patient care, to have more interesting work, and for educational mobility) have remained unchanged. An increasing number of students cite greater independence as an additional factor in their decision to become practitioners (Sultz, 1984; Williamson, 1983). Lynaugh, Gerrity, & Hagopian (1985) report on a sample of 103 nurse practitioner graduates from one master's program. Approximately 41% were below the age of 29, and 50% of the sample has been employed in hospitals prior to entering the program, while 22% had practiced in community health. The two main reasons given for entering the master's program were a desire to influence patient care and increased independence (Lynaugh, 1985).

Over the past few years, an increasing number of applicants to generic baccalaureate programs hold a second, and at times, a third non-nursing degree (Rogers, Sweeting & Davis, 1989; Slavinsky, Diers, & Dixon, 1983). In recognition of this changing applicant pool, many universities have established programs in which students with a non-nursing degree who have completed all biological and behavioral science prerequisites can complete requirements for a bachelor of science in nursing (BSN) in one calendar year. These applicants differ from the more traditional student in that they are educationally advantaged, professionally motivated, and are willing to relocate in order to enter nursing programs they see as meeting their unique educational and lifestyle needs. Some select an area of specialized practice prior to entering a generic program. Many are attracted to the nurse practitioner role.

In light of the above change, the experience of the few schools that have programs preparing nurse practitioners with a master's as the first professional degree take on increasing significance. These schools, for example, at University of Pennsylvania, Pace University, Yale, and Massachusetts General Hospital, admit students holding bachelor's degrees in non-nursing majors. They offer an accelerated curriculum incorporating both traditional content and content necessary to function as a nurse practitioner. These specialty master's programs provide a model for bridging generalist and specialist preparation for second-degree students. Specifically, these programs: (1) confirm the existence of a cadre of second-degree students interested in nurse practitioner practice; (2)

demonstrate that these students successfully adapt to an accelerated curriculum that includes preparation for nurse practitioner functions; and (3) show that graduates of such programs are successful in finding positions and practice as primary care providers.

In summary, the status of education as of the early 1990s is such that although many concepts and skills inherent in the primary care role are now successfully infused into generalist undergraduate education, master's level specialization is the accepted means for preparing to practice as a nurse practitioner. Certificate programs have and will continue to make a contribution in the preparation of a decreasing percentage of overall providers. For an as yet small, but professionally significant, number of students entering nursing—for example, those with a second degree—the current differentiation between generalist and specialized preparation may be neither applicable or efficient. Existing programs that have demonstrated successful educational strategies for preparing such atypical students offer innovative approaches to bridge differences between baccalaureate and master's education.

The Development of Nurse Practitioner Faculty

When nurse practitioner programs first came into existence, faculty often consisted of nurse-physician teams as co-directors, with physicians delivering content on physical assessment and on common manifestations of disease. Clinical experiences followed a model similar to the one used in medical schools and residency training programs. It is rare to meet a nurse practitioner prepared before the mid-1970s who was taught primarily by nurses.

Preparation of nurse practitioner faculty has evolved through three stages of development: the acquisition of physical assessment skills by nursing faculty; the development of a cadre of faculty with primary care practice experience; and the incorporation of nurses who are primarily practitioners into the school of nursing faculty.

In understanding the first stage of development, it is important to remember that the introduction of primary care skills occurred at a time when academic nursing faculty were preoccupied with establishing legitimate positions within academic institutions. Faculty therefore were extremely suspicious of initiatives that would deflect their efforts and attention from the designated goals of academics: research and education. Nursing faculty whose interests were primarily clinical were seen as possibly "diluting" the curriculum's potential for teaching students the use of a scientific method. Moreover, practicing nurses were seen as suspect, "sullied" by their experience in the real world. Students were to be educated not to emulate the current systems, but to change it, and the status of nursing within it.

Nevertheless, a number of faculty were sufficiently forward-thinking to understand that preparation of nurses for expanded practice would contribute to the increasing stature of nursing both within the university and within the health care delivery system. Therefore, in those schools of nursing where interest in and preparation for primary care were established, the logical method for preparing faculty was to encourage existing faculty with established academic credentials to acquire additional primary care skills.

Initially, it was seen as sufficient to attain skill in history-taking, physical examination, and use of the problem-oriented method. The literature is replete with descriptions of activities used by nursing faculty to acquire physical assessment skills, including the incorporation of physicians in school of nursing faculties, attendance at summer workshops, preceptorships, and so forth (Bates & Lynaugh, 1973, 1975). Concurrent with the acquisition of primary care skills, nursing faculty engaged in an extensive exploration of how to incorporate these skills in such a way that they would be seen as nursing rather than medical activities, discussions not unknown within schools of nursing today!

The second phase in the preparation of nursing faculty to teach primary care developed as a response to such initiatives as the Robert Wood Johnson Nurse Faculty Fellows Program. This program provided an opportunity for existing faculty to gain experience in primary care practice beyond the simple acquisition of physical assessment skills, and to interact with other faculties and physicians in four centers throughout the country (Robert Wood Johnson Foundation, 1980). In 1978 when these faculty practitioners, 99 in number, began to filter back into the academic setting, they had two agendas. The first was to resume their academic careers, which in many instances included beginning or resuming doctoral study. Those who already held doctorates sought to resume their tenure track positions. The second agenda of these faculty members was to maintain their primary care skills. To this end, they began to negotiate with schools of nursing to incorporate clinical practice opportunities as legitimate faculty activities, thus bringing to the forefront issues of faculty practice and joint appointments. The results of such influences are now being felt, and are exemplified in some of the practitioner case reports in Chapter 6.

The third phase in the preparation of nursing faculty as primary care providers became apparent when a sufficient number of graduates of primary care master's programs had established themselves in practice settings. During the course of their master's programs, these graduates often developed close linkages with faculty. In many instances, as students, they not only had contact with faculty in the classroom, but also worked alongside them in comanaging patients. Similarly, faculty took both a professional and personal interest, a mentoring role if you will, in both the clinical and continuing professional activities of graduates. Many graduates saw themselves as both clinicians and teachers. They thus initiated and responded to requests by schools of nursing to precept students and to participate in teaching in primary care programs. By the mid 1980s a critical mass of clinically prepared nurses able to assume leadership in universities was assembled and prepared to contribute to advances in nursing practice as well as education and research.

The Role of Physician-Faculty

Nurses carry the major faculty responsibility in educational programs preparing nurse practitioners. Sultz documents a substantial decrease in reliance on physicians as well as on nurses who are not nurse practitioners in both certificate and master's programs (Sultz, 1983c). Nevertheless, physicians continue to make major contributions to the presentation of didactic content. Physicians continue to coteach content specifically related to presentation and management of disease, clinical decisionmaking, and models for establishing collaborative practice within service sites.

The major change in physician contribution to nurse practitioner programs has come in the area of precepted clinical experiences. All programs preparing nurse practitioners have clinical preceptorships. The increase in clinical preceptorships in master's programs is a positive response to earlier findings, which indicated that the graduates of master's programs believed that clinical preparation would be improved by more and longer preceptor experiences (Hupcey, 1990; Sultz, 1984). By 1980, the majority of master's programs provided joint nurse practitioner and/or physician preceptors, and the percentage of physician-only preceptors in master's programs had decreased from almost 17 percent in 1973 to only 1 percent (Sultz, 1984). This change reflects the fact that increasing numbers of nursing faculty have clinical practices as part of their ongoing academic responsibility. In many instances, nurse faculty practices are in interdisciplinary practice settings with physicians.

The continued involvement of physicians in presenting didactic content and as clinical preceptors is described as one of the strengths of programs preparing nurse practitioners. Such ongoing involvement also helps facilitate nurse practitioner entry into the work setting (Hupcey, 1990; Levine, 1991). Lynaugh (1985) and others (Grey & Flint, 1989; Kane, 1989) confirm that there is a high degree of consistency in physician consultation patterns of practitioner students and nurses practitioner graduates. Graduates report a high proportion of their activity devoted to assessments, interventions, and education of patients. Consultation with physicians occurs mainly in instances of medical ambiguity or life-threatening symptomatology (Kane, 1989; Lynaugh et al., 1985). It is therefore appropriate that physicians continue to address these issues within nurse practitioner programs.

The Significance of Efforts to Link Education and Practice

For both altruistic and financial reasons, universities have intensified their efforts to create joint relationships with service agencies. These renewed efforts to bring together nursing practice and university nursing education can be traced to the late 1960s, when nursing leaders at the University of Florida (Smith, 1965) and Case Western University (MacPhail, 1972) published accounts of their projects.

Many other collaborative practice and education projects have sprung up in recent years, culminating in new efforts to develop Community Nursing Centers (Arvino, 1989; NLN, 1991). In part these projects are a reassertion of belief in the centrality of clinical practice to the discipline of nursing. For many years university schools of nursing, such as the University of Rochester and Rush University, have been centrally involved in the delivery of nurse services in their affiliated teaching hospitals (Christman & Grace, 1981; Ford, 1981). We have also seen the proliferation of other affiliation models with nursing homes, home care agencies, and the development of model units within hospital settings.

The diminished interest of physicians in primary care specialty training (family practice, internal medicine, pediatrics) has created unanticipated opportunities for closer collaboration between schools of nursing and hospitals. Unable to recruit housestaff, hospitals are offering attractive student preceptorships as incentives to subsequent recruitment of nurse practitioners (Grey, 1989; Jones, 1985; Levine, 1991). This collaboration is beginning to yield benefits to patient care, as hospitals experience the benefits of nurse practitioners over physicians in health promotion and patient teaching.

Several examples outside of the acute care setting testify to the expansion and creativity of joint education and service ventures in university health care services (Shortridge & McLain, 1986), home care, and nursing homes. In one university-managed home health care agency, community health nursing students provide care to families from a variety of socioeconomic and racial backgrounds. Nursing faculty administer the agency and provide direct clinical services in addition to their teaching responsibilities. In this way students receive not only clinical experience, but also the unique model of community service provided by the university (Herman & Krall, 1983). In a collaborative relationship with a proprietary nursing home, the University of Washington is responsible for all of the nursing and health care delivered in the facility (Diamond, 1992).

The Teaching Nursing Home Program, cosponsored by the Robert Wood Johnson Foundation and the American Academy of Nursing, offers another example of a joint practice-education model that linked schools of nursing in affiliations with nursing homes for the purpose of pooling personnel, physical, and financial resources for the mutual benefit of both institutions and society. The anticipated outcomes of the Teaching Nursing Home Program were not simple mergers in which schools of nursing carried out education and research, while nursing homes continued clinical care of older people. Rather, the 11 projects in the program developed new activities and services: innovations in patient-resident health care; more and better education for health professionals; and new understanding of care needs through clinical research (Garrard, Kane, Ratner, & Buchanon, 1991; Mezey & Lynaugh, 1989). This project demonstrated that such collaborative relationships can both improve patient care and provide new clinical laboratory experiences for students (Mezey, 1992).

Expansion of efforts to link education and practice has major significance for the future preparation of nurse practitioners. Such efforts serve to redefine and broaden the faculty role. The presence of experienced and exemplary practitioners is essential if schools are to concern themselves with service. To be successful, however, ways must be found to assure that issues of practice have equal stature to teaching and research within academic schools of nursing. Many universities continue to struggle with mechanisms to legitimize the contributions of persons choosing to focus on practice issues, be it by altering conditions for achieving tenure, or creating new clinician faculty positions (Diers, 1992; Lowery, 1983; Mezey & Lynaugh, 1989; Siegel & Elsberg, 1979).

Commitment to practice on the part of university schools of nursing serves to attract to education nurses who want to retain a practice emphasis while participating in teaching and research. Nurse practitioners, by actively responding to efforts to link service and education, not only expand the pool of available providers, but also influence the style of practice in ambulatory, acute, and long term care settings. Furthermore, such linkages encourage both clinical and administrative advancement of nurse practitioners, affording nurses with clinical interests opportunity to attain stature in both the educational and service setting.

The Influence of Certification on Curriculum

Traditionally, in the United States, designating minimal level practice competency within professions is a function of the state, implemented through a process of professional licensure. Credentialing of competency in specialty or advanced practice has been left largely to the professions themselves and has taken a variety of forms. Credentialing serves a twofold function. It serves to protect the public by identifying practitioners who have successfully completed an approved course of study. It also provides a mechanism for federal, state, and private agencies and clients to identify providers who can appropriately be reimbursed for service.

The chapters in Part III of this text describe in detail the different mechanisms for credentialing of nurse practitioners that have evolved over the past 20 years. Among the varying approaches to credentialing are certification of individual practitioners and program certification. In the case of individual certification, practitioners who meet specific criteria apply as individuals to a credentialing body, and a certificate is conferred on review of eligibility and/or successful completion of an examination. Examples of such certification mechanisms include the American Nurses' Association (ANA) certification examination for primary care practice as adult, pediatric, and geriatric nurse practitioner (ANA, 1991), and specialty organization certification, such as National Association of Pediatric Nurse Associates and Practitioners (NAP-NAP). Some states and professional organizations certify educational programs following review of curricula and faculty credentials. Certification in such instances is automatically conferred on graduates who successfully complete the certified program. Examples of such mechanisms include certification for nurse practitioner practice by state boards of nursing and by the American College of Nurse Midwifery.

Certification for Nurse Midwives is described at length in Chapter 7. Because the American College of Nurse Midwifery maintains the dual function of both designating curriculum requirements and certification, such credentialing has served to create a standard minimum curriculum that assures comparability of preparation, and therefore mobility, for graduates throughout the United States. Likewise, such guidelines augment the faculty bargaining position within schools of nursing. For example, midwifery faculty are able to successfully make a case for low faculty student-ratios by using criteria set by the national organization, which threatens removal of certification if guidelines are not adhered to.

In contrast to the nurse midwifery example, the lack of certification comparability in most other practice areas has caused major dilemmas in curriculum development. There are no guidelines for the preparation of adult and geriatric nurse practitioners as to type or amount of didactic content, minimal number of clinically precepted hours, and types of precepted experiences. Directors of practitioner programs are quick to share stories of program graduates barred with no recourse from practicing in adjoining states. In some instances a Catch-22 situation is created. For example, a graduate of a practitioner program may be unable to gain practice privileges because a state requires evidence of graduation from a state-certified program and the state from which the degree was obtained has no such mechanism for program certification. Furthermore, some credentialing practices by state boards of nursing have caused ethical dilemmas for program faculty. In some states, Pennsylvania, for example, in order for a nurse practitioner program to gain state certification, a necessary requirement for functioning as a practitioner within the state, a program must demonstrate that it is preparing practitioners to practice beyond the Nurse Practice Act of the state and to assume responsibility for medical management of patients.

As of 1991, all but five states had some mechanism for credentialing nurse practitioners and/or nurse midwives (see Bullough, Chapter 11). However, the mechanisms for achieving certification vary by state and include national certification exam, state board of medicine and/or nursing approval, state examination, an academic degree, or some combination of the above. In response to this highly frustrating and diverse situation, most programs preparing nurse practitioners have attempted to establish curricula which allow for the greatest degree of flexibility. Programs are structured consistent with eligibility requirements for ANA certification examinations. In states where program certification is the accepted model, most nurse practitioner curricula comply with state regulations.

The impact of this current pattern of certification on nurse practitioner curricula is profound. In those instances where one certification mechanism is applied uniformly across all states, for example, in the case of nurse midwifery, certification has had a stabilizing effect on both practice and curriculum development. In other instances, the lack of comparability of certification procedures across states has had and will continue to exert an uneven and often capricious influence on both education and practice.

THE NURSE PRACTITIONER AND THE CLINICAL SPECIALIST: ROLE DIFFERENTIATION OR ROLE FUSION

To date, many university master's programs, often within the same school, produce two streams of graduates prepared to assume advanced clinical positions: nurse practitioners and clinical specialists. As described in Chapter 1, hospitals and nursing homes are increasingly less tolerant of the nuances used to differentiate these two advanced-level practitioners.

In the 1986 edition of this text, we suggested three possibilities for the future role development of the clinical specialist and the nurse practitioner in the acute and long-term care setting: continued role differentiation, role fusion, or role elimination. Given wide geographical variation in practice policies, availability of practitioners, and types of acute and long-term care institutions, it is unlikely that any one practice model will apply nationally. Nevertheless, there is now clear evidence that role fusion is the evolving model for advanced nursing practice (Elder & Bullough, 1990; Wright, 1990). Practice distinctions between clinical specialists and nurse practitioners are discussed at length in Chapter 1. These distinctions are already sufficiently blurred to suggest that remaining differences will disappear within the next decade (U.S-.D.H.H.S., 1990). This blurring of roles obviously will have a profound impact on the preparation for advanced practice.

Educational Implications of Role Overlap and Role Divergence: An Analysis

Despite the early lack of master's program consistency and the original emphasis on the CNS's indirect care role in inpatient settings and NP's direct care role in ambulatory facilities, several recent examinations of graduate program content reveal startling similarities. A survey of all graduate nursing programs (Forbes, 1990a) preparing for advanced practice roles produced data on 60 NP and 195 CNS programs, comparing them on core course content and required hours and clinical practice. In the 21 content areas examined, 15, including developmental assessment, psychosocial concepts, and community care, were similar. While both types of programs included pharmacology, primary care, physical assessment, history taking, and nutrition, the NP programs put greater emphasis on them, although the required hours of content were almost the same. These findings were even more conclusive when pediatric and gerontology CNS and NP programs were examined. With the exception of pharmacology, geriatric nurse practitioner preparation closely resembled that of gerontological nurse clinicians, and with the exception of community and primary care, PNP preparation resembled that of pediatric clinical specialists.

The major difference between the two types of programs was the clinical practice setting. In terms of practice settings for graduates, NP's were more likely to be employed in ambulatory practice and CNSs in secondary or tertiary care settings (Forbes, 1990). The survey, as reported by Forbes did not reflect on the degree of similarity in program objectives or teaching strategies, but did conclude that with respect to required knowledge and skills, there is little or no difference between nurse practitioner and clinical nurse specialist program content.

Preparation for Comprehensive Versus Circumscribed Role

Nurse practitioners are prepared as generalists to deliver comprehensive health services. While practice settings modify how individual practitioners spend their time, nurse practitioners' education teaches them to expect their greatest satisfaction in those positions that afford an opportunity to practice in a holistic manner, balancing opportunities to address both physical and emotional concerns of patients. As nurse practitioners begin to work in acute care settings, the medical and technological complexity of the setting, coupled with high physician demands for "physician assistant" activities, leave insufficient time for teaching, counseling, and guidance, activities taught in nurse practitioner programs and highly valued by most nurse practitioners. This issue is compounded because to date nurse practitioners have not been taught content to prepare them for the reality that their authority in acute care hospitals derives from their relationship with physicians. Because they receive little preparation in management, nurse practitioners are unprepared for the ambiguity of their positions within departments of nursing, adding to feelings of professional isolation.

Clinical specialists, on the other hand, are prepared as specialists to practice within a circumscribed area of practice. They expect their authority to be derived from their positions within departments of nursing. While clinical specialists report adequate time to counsel patients and staff, they experience frustration with their inability to sufficiently influence the course of the patient's recovery. Although well prepared educationally in a specialized area of practice, such as cardiovascular or respiratory nursing, they often are less well prepared in pharmacology and clinical management, content which limits their authority to directly influence patient outcomes. Moreover, recent evidence suggests that the broad range of expertise implicit in the preparation of the CNS, i.e., subroles plus expertise in a clinical specialty, may not be appropriate or possible (Arena & Paige, 1992). The rather extensive literature addressing the individual subroles supports the impression that there is no consistent expectation for performing all roles in a comprehensive manner. Research, as one example, is frequently targeted as an important area of educational preparation for CNS function, though it is not clear how CNSs are particularly well prepared with one or two courses, or how the usual expectation for doctoral preparation is compatible with this CNS expectation.

The balance between generalist versus specialist preparation for advanced nurse clinicians will be the primary educational debate of the 1990s. On the one hand, evidence suggests a need for generalist preparation. A recent study (Report to Congress, 1990) anticipates that nurses with advanced preparation should be prepared to function as case managers, primary nurses, consultants, role models, educators, and researchers. Moreover, patients with similar levels of disabilities are increasingly cared for in different practice settings; for example, patients on respirators can be cared for at home, in nursing homes, and in hospitals. The master's prepared nurse who will manage such patients must have skills which are broad, flexible, and encompass a wide base of knowledge. Almost all master's programs preparing nurse practitioners include content on theory, teaching, consultation, and leadership. The fact that nurse practitioner students do not value this content to the same degree that they value acquisition of traditional NP skills (Hupcey, 1990) has implications for curricula which seek to encourage generalist preparation.

On the other hand, several factors seem to favor an educational-specialization model. Follow-up studies of graduates of primary care programs indicate that most graduates work primarily with distinct population groups. Many graduates, in fact, have had to acquire specialized knowledge in the work setting, and would welcome additional specialization within the curriculum if it could be incorporated without sacrificing other necessary content. Moreover, while in the past students entering practitioner programs encountered almost all primary care skills for the first time, many of these skills have now been successfully incorporated into undergraduate programs, allowing time within master's programs for additional content. Finally, given the high degree of probability for future reimbursement for nursing services, attention needs to be paid to appropriate credentialing for nurse practitioners. In tertiary care settings, their ability to compete can only be assured by providing evidence of knowledge and skills in a specific practice area, which will almost assuredly require specialized knowledge.

Educational Preparation for Role Fusion

It is unlikely that ambulatory, acute, and long-term care institutions will continue to support two divergent job positions for master's-prepared nurses whose primary activities are clinical. The preceding discussion suggests areas of role satisfaction on the part of both clinical specialists and nurse practitioners. Both value direct involvement with patients. Nurse practitioners value their knowledge of clinical management and authority to take action, while clinical specialists see these as areas of deficiencies in their practice. On the other hand, clinical specialists value their specialized knowledge, the flexibility of schedule which allows time for patient and family teaching, and their strong nursing identity, deficiencies identified by nurse practitioners in their practice.

Leaving aside the obvious need to clarify terms, the most plausible resolution of this dilemma is the fusion of the two roles of nurse practitioner and clinical specialists into one new advanced nurse clinical practice role. This practitioner would have clear responsibility within the table of organization, competency in the skills of assessment and management, specialized knowledge consistent with the needs of patients in acute and long-term care settings, strong linkages with medicine, and primary responsibility and authority for a full range of patient care activities.

FUTURE CONSIDERATIONS IN THE EDUCATION OF NURSE PRACTITIONERS

Curriculum planning is a somewhat hazardous process. While there is some truth in the warnings that nursing education should be cautious in responding to the many small fluctuations of nursing practice (Gothler, 1983), there remains a need to predict trends and consider their impact on curriculum development.

Projections for the future are based on an understanding and interpretation of the present. Prior to suggesting issues for future curriculum development, it seems appropriate to summarize conclusions formulated in this chapter and in Chapter 1, which form the basis for the projections.

1. *Nurse practitioners and primary care.* The time has come to clearly differentiate between the terms *practitioner* and *primary care.* Within the health care system, primary care reflects a constellation of services and a mode of service delivery for patients needing ambulatory care services (Secretary's Committee, 1972). Within nursing, primary care denotes concepts such as comprehensive, individualized, and coordinated care which are universally consistent with the definition of nursing practice and form the basis for practice for both the beginning nurse generalist and the advanced nurse practitioner. The term *nurse practitioner* (or pos-

sibly *advanced nurse practitioner*) designates a nurse specialist prepared at the master's level who delivers direct and indirect nursing services to patients irrespective of setting. The scope of practice of these practitioners derives from a blend of knowledge and skills which originated in both primary care and clinical specialist practice.

2. *Nurse practitioners and service delivery.* The role of nurse practitioner encompasses more than solely a primary, that is, ambulatory, practice focus. While opportunities for employment of nurse practitioners in ambulatory settings can be expected to expand, the unmet health needs of adults and children with chronic health problems, the vertical integration of health care services, and financial incentives that favor cost saving, prospective and institutional reimbursement create demands for coordinated, efficient, and comprehensive provision of services in all components of the health care system. The proven ability of nurse practitioners to successfully respond to such demands in ambulatory settings favors their increasing utilization in hospitals, nursing homes, and home health care. Since most nurse practitioners have previously worked in hospitals, there is reason to believe that they will respond positively to such initiatives if issues of independence, role variability, and ability to influence patient care can be adequately addressed.

Direct reimbursement for services will increasingly be dependent on identification of qualified practitioners who have achieved certification indicating advanced preparation as nurse practitioners. The potential for reimbursement for nurse practitioner services requires mechanisms to assure competency and favors a larger influence of credentialing bodies on the development of curriculum for nurse practitioner programs.

3. *Nurse practitioners and nursing education.* The applicant pool seeking admission to nursing programs is increasingly heterogeneous, encompassing those persons who come directly to college following completion of high school and persons who choose nursing following completion of college and having had extensive life experience. Many of the more mature applicants are familiar with and seek nurse practitioner preparation. The presence of such students favors the development of curriculum models which expedite the time needed to achieve specialty, that is, nurse practitioner, status.

Indications are that the schism between nursing education and practice will continue to narrow. Unification activities serve to redefine traditional faculty and practice roles, increasingly placing responsibility for the education of nurse practitioners in the hands of faculty holding dual appointments. Moreover, such a model creates an expanded pool of mature, clinically competent, and practicing nurse-faculty available to provide supervision and leadership to newly graduated practitioners.

4. *Nurse practitioners and clinical specialists.* The infusion of nurse practitioners into acute and long-term care institutions dictates a role fusion of practitioners and clinical specialists. Over 15 years' experience with these two roles has provided direction as to the process and content for the development of one practitioner with an advanced nursing degree.

Issues for Future Curriculum Development

For the most part, existing nurse practitioner programs prepare generalists in the delivery of health care. While presentation and management of specific diseases are included within the curriculum, current nurse practitioner preparation assumes a general practitioner approach to patient problems (Diers & Molde, 1983). Although some beginning specialization of nurse practitioners has been long evident (e.g., the preparation of adult and pediatric nurse practitioners), the issue for future curriculum development is how to accommodate even further shifts in emphasis from a generalist to a more specialized preparation, given the projected emergence of new practice opportunities and the fusion and blending of the practitioner's and clinical specialist role.

Most master's programs preparing nurse practitioners have three curriculum components: content necessary for all nurses prepared at the master's level; "core" content appropriate for all nurse practitioners; and a component of content reflective of specialty preparation (i.e., pediatrics and adult). It is within these three curriculum components that changes in preparation will need to be incorporated.

Content for All Master's-Prepared Nurses

The content appropriate for all master's graduates fluctuates, depending on the philosophy, conceptual framework, and a host of other factors, such as NLN accreditation guidelines and state regulations. Suffice it to say that there are areas of knowledge needed for all master's-prepared nurses irrespective of area of concentration. For example, an understanding of statistics, research methods, and ethical issues in practice are seen as essential for all master's-prepared nurses. Also included in the overall program curriculum are opportunities for electives that provide flexibility and concern for individual learning needs.

Core Content for Nurse Practitioner Preparation

The Federal Guidelines for Preparation of Nurse Practitioners have served as the foundation for identification of core content for nurse practitioner programs (Secretary's Committee to Study Extended Roles for Nurses, 1972). Designation of core content addresses the commonality of nurse practitioners' functions irrespective of setting but excludes specific management strategies reflective of specialized areas of practice. Current trends and future needs suggest that the core content for nurse practitioner preparation falls into five general categories.

1. *The philosophy and concepts underlying nurse practitioner practice.* The historical development of the nurse practitioner role; knowledge of interdisciplinary functioning, including the roles of other health professionals; knowledge of current and pending legislation influencing nurse practitioner functioning; nurse practice acts and boundaries of practice; legal parameters and trends; and knowledge of the professional organizations and political influence which address the needs of the nurse practitioner.

2. *The nurse practitioner's role within the health care system.* Understanding the intricacies and shifting interrelationships across the health care system, and the nurse practitioner's role within such a system. Included are an appreciation of the tensions between acute and chronic care constituencies in vying for diminishing health care dollars.

3. *The scientific base for nurse practitioner functioning.* Background in biological, behavioral, and social sciences sufficient to assure an adequate basis for nurse practitioner functioning. This background incorporates both general and specific knowledge of areas such as anatomy, physiology, pathophysiology, pharmacology, nutrition, and family systems. While most nurse practitioner programs require a separate course in advanced pharmacology, some question remains as to what constitutes appropriate pharmacology content for advanced nursing practice. Rather than using what is taught in medical and dental school as the basis of comparison (Waigandt & Chang, 1989), pharmacology content should reflect the prescribing patterns of nurse practitioners. Most nurse practitioners prescribe a small number of medications (Grey & Flint, 1989), but spend a large amount of time teaching patients about drugs and drug interactions.

4. *Components of role implementation.* Sufficient content to allow the practitioner to compile a data base on individuals and family members; the process of clinical decisionmaking; and those components of role that apply across settings: health promotion and maintenance; teaching strategies for individuals and groups of patients and providers; and collaborative practice issues.

5. *Common management concerns of nurse practitioners.* Some identified management issues occur in all areas of practice and therefore lend

themselves as appropriate for core content inclusion. For example, issues such as substance use and abuse and compliance and noncompliance are generic to nurse practitioner practice, irrespective of setting.

Specialized Content for Nurse Practitioner Preparation

It is within the third component of the curriculum that the need for specialization is currently addressed. Programs preparing adult, pediatric, and geriatric nurse practitioners have developed a variety of curriculum models. In some instances, both separate didactic courses and clinical placements have been developed. More commonly, at least for the lesser-subscribed specialties such as geriatrics, specialized knowledge is imparted through clinical placement and related clinical seminars.

The issue at hand is how to teach content effectively and adequately to prepare practitioners for new areas of specialization. Specialized content refers to knowledge and skills specific to function in a distinct area of practice. It requires the ability to recognize common signs and symptoms of illness, gather additional data needed to confirm a diagnosis, and implement an appropriate plan for management. While these are characteristics of all nurse practitioner practice, the specialized content is limited and circumscribed to a bounded area of practice. Some examples of specialized nurse practitioner practice are presented in Chapters 7 and 8. The following in-depth examples further highlight the specific curricular issues involved.

1. *The emergency care nurse practitioners.* Several teaching hospitals employ nurse practitioners in the emergency room. The emergency care nurse practitioner focuses on patients who seek care in the emergency departments of tertiary care centers around the country. Many of these patients present nonacute, self-limiting problems as well as long-term chronic illness problems which happen to be in a stage of exacerbation. Emergency care clinicians have the capacity to cope effectively in diagnostics, supportive, and educational ways with such patients. In addition, they can cope with short-term critical care problems until other tertiary care resources can be summoned (Alongi, 1979; Jones, 1985; Rogers, Sweeting, & Davis, 1989).

2. *Geriatric nurse practitioners.* The changing health care system suggests that geriatric nurse practitioners (GNP) must be prepared to function in three overlapping service settings: ambulatory settings, hospitals, and nursing homes. Anecdotal reporting by currently employed GNPs indicates that the level of acuity and the deployment of technology to care for the elderly, for example, oxygen, respirators, and nutritional support, is becoming increasingly comparable across all service

sites. Expectations for discharge and/or rehabilitation and efforts to facilitate placement of patients in the least restrictive environment requires the preparation of geriatric nurse practitioners who have an appreciation for the continuum of care and are able to respond to both chronic and acute care needs (Garrard et al., 1991; Henderson, 1984).

3. *Nurse practitioners working with chronic illness.* The health problems of people with chronic illness are both similar to those of the general population and different in that they are complicated by the presence of a chronic illness. These persons are affected by acute problems superimposed on chronic ones, the increased possibility of iatrogenic complications, unexpected presentations of common complaints, often difficult social and/or economic circumstances, and a great need for coordination among many specialized providers. Nurse practitioners are already successfully employed in specialty clinics, such as those serving patients with diabetes, arthritis, and substance abuse (Lewis & Resnick, 1967; Rogers, Sweeting, & Davis, 1989; Stein, 1983; U.S. Congress Office of Technology Assessment, 1986). Such a specialty designation offers opportunities to further expand practitioner involvement into rehabilitation and acute care settings.

4. *Nurse practitioners in home care.* Home care is the fastest growing sector of the health care system. Within home care, care of children and adults with highly complex health care is increasing disproportionately. To date, reimbursement and complex physician linkages have discouraged the development of a role for nurse practitioners in home care. Recently, however, the climate of home care has changed. As a consequence of early hospital discharge, home care agencies manage large numbers of patients with complex and often unstable conditions. Fiscal responsibility imposed by managed care systems make it attractive for agencies to improve the care at home in order to avoid hospitalizations. Reductions in Medicaid funding have caused marked reductions in services offered by hospital clinics and private physicians serving the urban poor. Home care agencies have begun to employ nurse practitioners and clinical specialists, and several schools of nursing have introduced programs to prepare home care nurse practitioners (Riner, 1989).

Several issues related to specialty preparation are highlighted in the preceding examples. The first relates to the extent of the similarity and differences between new and existing content. Practitioner programs need sufficient didactic and clinical content to provide a sound basis for practice. Faculty need to decide if the knowledge base of a new specialty is sufficiently similar to existing content such that it can be adequately incorporated by arranging for specialized clinical placement alone (e.g., in an emergency room), or it is sufficiently dissimilar to warrant the development of totally new and separate didactic and clinical courses.

A second issue relates to the organization of content. As practitioners move into acute and long-term care institutions, a question arises as to how to identify the strong and most logical bonds around which to organize the curriculum.

The third issue highlighted in the above examples is the continued significance of quality clinical placements in achieving the overall objectives of nurse practitioner preparation. Precepted experiences need to be individualized and of sufficient length and intensity to allow for adequate role development. When clinical experiences are supervised by an individual or a team of clinician-faculty, students have the opportunity to work alongside exemplary role models and to share in practice responsibilities rather than entering the setting with "guest status." Clinical experiences need to be of sufficient breadth to allow hands-on experiences with a variety of problems encountered within the area of specialization. Opportunities to interact with physicians and other health professionals are essential for learning components of collaborative practice.

The fact that faculty with dual practice and teaching responsibility will have increasing responsibility for education should serve to enhance the clinical experience of students. Students will have opportunities to interact with faculty who exhibit a wide range of interests in practice, research, and teaching. Such experience will allow students to acquire an understanding of both the science and art of nursing and the incorporation of inquiry and research into practice activities.

The increasing presence of faculty-practitioners in the clinical settings, coupled with the expansion of nurse practitioner activities into home care, acute, and long-term care settings, has the potential to diminish past concerns regarding the degree of competency needed by nurse practitioner graduates. To date, most new graduates have taken first positions in ambulatory settings where they are expected to perform as advanced practitioners. Faculty, therefore, have been concerned that practitioner students function proficiently and independently. In most instances this is an unrealistic expectation for students completing a 1-year academic program. The expansion of nurse practitioner faculty practice activities opens opportunities for enhanced supervision of first-level practitioners, possibly in the model of internships or fellowships. Should such opportunities develop, they will significantly influence planning of the total nurse practitioner educational experience.

Accelerated Curriculum Models

Several strategies have been suggested earlier in this chapter that respond to the need for accelerated curriculum for second-degree students. One strategy is exemplified in existing programs preparing nurse practitioners with the master's degree as the first professional degree. A second strategy involves curriculum modifications that accelerate acquisition of the BSN degree. A third strategy is to admit applicants directly into master's programs as submatriculated students. In this instance, master's level courses substitute for equivalent course content required in the BSN program; for example, statistics, research, pharmacology, nutrition, nursing issues, conceptual systems, and electives which fulfill requirements in both bachelor's and master's programs. In such a model, students exit with a master's degree, having acquired the bachelor's degree "in passing" on the way to completion of the advanced degree. The major need now is for model development and careful evaluation of such strategies to determine their efficacy in preparing accelerated students as competent nurse practitioners.

CONCLUSION

Since nurse practitioners first successfully demonstrated their ability to deliver quality primary care to children, the concept of nurse practitioner practice has spread across the nation and across the spectrum of health care needs of the population. The quality of care delivered by nurse practitioners has received public, professional and legislative recognition.

In the 1970s, schools of nursing responded vigorously to the need for additional practitioners capable of providing primary care services by developing family, adult, and pediatric nurse practitioner programs. With many people, especially the poor and minorities, still without primary care services, the demand for nurse practitioners in primary care will continue to expand (Safriet, 1992).

The health care agenda for the 1990s, however, reflects shifting service needs. Chronic illness competes with ambulatory and episodic health problems for public attention and the shrinking health care dollar. Prospective payment and other attempts at cost containment have spurred the development of what were previously thought to be impossible linkages among disparate components of the health care system. Within academic nursing circles, there is an appreciation that the education pendulum has swung too far from our clinical practice roots, and practicing nurses are now increasingly welcomed as partners in educational endeavors. Nursing is moving rapidly to a single model for advanced practice which combines the best of nurse practitioner and clinical specialist preparation.

The urgent health care problems of the 1990s are emerging in areas of ambulatory, acute, long-term, and home health care. Now is the time for nursing education to modify and expand the preparation of nurse practitioners and clinical specialists in order to forcefully contribute to the solution of society's pressing health care concerns.

REFERENCES

Alongi, S., Geolot, D., Richter, L., Mapstone, S., Edgerton, M. T., & Edlich, R. F. (1979). Physician and patient acceptance of emergency nurse practitioners. *Journal of the American College of Emergency Physicians, 8,* 357–359.

American Nurses Association. (1988a). *The role of the clinical nurse specialist.* Washington, DC.

American Nurses Association. (1988b). *The scope of practice of the primary health care nurse practitioner.* Washington, DC.

American Nurses Association. (1988c). *Standards of practice for the primary health care nurse practitioner.* Washington, DC.

American Nurses Association. (1991). *Certification for advanced practice.* Washington, DC.

Arena, D., & Page, N. (1992). The imposter phenomenon in the clinical nurse specialist role. *Image: Journal of Nursing Scholarship, 24,* 121–125.

Arvino, A. (1989). *Nursing centers: Meeting the demand for quality health care.* (NLN Publ. 21–23(1)). New York: National League for Nursing.

Barnard, K. E. (1983). *Structure to outcome: Making it work. First Annual Symposium on Nursing Faculty Practice* (pamphlet). American Nurses Association Publication, American Academy of Nursing.

Bates, B., & Lynaugh, J. (1973). Laying the foundations for medical nurse practice. *American Journal of Nursing, 78*(8), 1375–1379.

Bates, B., & Lynaugh, J. (1975). Teaching physical assessment. *Nursing Outlook, 23,* 297–302.

Beecroft, P., & Papenhausen, J. (1989). Who is a clinical nurse specialist? *Clinical Nurse Specialist, 3,* 103–104.

Bozett, F., & Forrester, D. (1989). A proposal for a men's health nurse practitioner. *Image: Journal of Nursing Scholarship, 21,* 158–161.

Christman, L., & Grace, H. (1981). Unification, reunification: Reconciliation or collaboration. *Modes for Collaboration.* Fall Conference Proceeding, Midwest Alliance in Nursing, September 1980–1981. Unpublished.

Dellinger, C., Zentner, J. P., McDowell, P. H., & Annas, A. W. (1986). The family nurse practitioner in industry. *AAOHN Journal, 34*(7) 323–325.

Department of Health, Education and Welfare. (1980). *Longitudinal study of nurse practitioners: Phase III.* Washington, DC: US Government Printing Office.

Diamond, M. (1992) Personal communication. University of Washington, School of Nursing.

Diers, D. (1992). Nursing reclaims its role. *Nursing Outlook, 30,* 459–463.

Diers, D., & Molde, S. (1983). Nurses in primary care: The new gatekeepers? *American Journal of Nursing, 83,* 742–745.

Elder, R., & Bullough, B. (1990). Nurse practitioners and clinical nurse specialists: Are the roles merging? *Clinical Nurse Specialist, 4,* 78–84.

Fagin, C., & Goodwin, B. (1972). Baccalaureate preparation for primary care. *Nursing Outlook, 20,* 240–244.

Forbes, K., Rafson, J., Spross, J., & Kozlowski, D. (1990a). Clinical nurse specialist and nurse practitioner core curricula survey results. *Nurse Practitioner, 15,* 45–48.

Forbes, K. (1990b). Merge. *Momentum, 8,* 4–6.

Ford, L. C. (1981). Creating a center of excellence in nursing. In L. Aiken (Ed.), *Health Policy and Nursing Practice* (pp. 430–451). New York: McGraw-Hill.

Garrard, J., Kane, R., Ratner, E., & Buchanon, J. (1991). The impact of nurse practitioners on the care of nursing home residents. In P. Katz, R. Kane, & M. Mezey, (Eds.), *Advances in long-term care: Vol. 1.* New York: Springer Publishing Co.

Gothler, A. (1983). Nursing education and practice: Idealism and reality, an educator's reaction. *Journal of the New York State Nurses' Association, 14,* 40–43.

Graduate Medical Education National Advisory Committee, U.S. Department of health and Human Services. (1980). *Summary report to the secretary.* Washington, DC.

Grey, M., & Flint, S. (1989). 1988 NAPNAP membership survey: Characteristics of members' practice. *Journal of Pediatric Health Care, 3,* 336–341.

Hedrich, V. (1978). A national survey: Education for the expanded role. *Nurse Practitioner, 3,* 13.

Henderson, M. (1984). A GNP in a retirement community. *Geriatric Nursing, 5,* 2.

Herman, C., & Krall, K. (1983, July). *University sponsored home care agency as a clinical site.* Paper presented at Clinical Experience Today and Tomorrow: A Conference for Baccalaureate Nurse Educators, St. Paul, Minnesota.

Hill, B. (1989). The development of a master's degree program based on perceived future practice needs. *Journal of Nursing Education, 28,* 307–313.

Hupcey, J. (1990). The socialization process of master's-level nurse practitioner students. *Journal of Nursing Education, 29,* 196–201.

Jones, L. C. (1985). In-patient nurse practitioners. *Nurse Practitioner, 10,* 48–50.

Kane, R., Garrard, J., Skay, C., Radsswith, D., Buchanon, J. L., McDermott, S., Arnold, S., Kepferle, L. (1989). Effect of a geriatric nurse practitioner on the process and outcomes of nursing home care. *American Journal of Public Health, 79,* 1271–1277.

Kitzman, H. (1983). The clinical nurse specialist (CNS) and the nurse practitioner. In A. Hamric & S. Spross (Eds.), *The Clinical Nurse Specialist in Theory and Practice* (pp. 275–290) New York: Grune and Stratton.

Leininger, M., Little, D. E., & Carnevali, D. (1972). PRIMEX. *American Journal of Nursing, 72,* 1274–1277.

Levine, S. (1991). The development of nurse practitioners. *Nursing, 2,* 25.

Lewis, C. E., & Resnick, B. A. (1967). Nurse clinics and progressive ambulatory patient-care. *New England Journal of Medicine, 277,* 1236–1241.

Lowery, B. (1983, October). Knowledge builders: Faculty appointments. Paper presented at the Sigma Theta Tau National Convention.

Lynaugh, J., Gerrity, P., & Hagopian, G. Patterns of practice: Masters prepared nurse practitioners. *Journal of Nursing Education, 27*(7), 291–295.

MacPhail, J. (1972). *An experiment in nursing: Planning, implementing, and assessing in planned change.* Cleveland: Case Western Reserve University Press.

McGivern, D. (1974). The nurse practitioner: Preparation and practice: Baccalaureate preparation of the nurse practitioner, *Nursing Outlook, 22,* 2. 94–98.

McGivern, D., Mezey, M., & Baer, E. (1976). Teaching primary care in a baccalaureate program. *Nursing Outlook, 24,* 7, 441–445.

Mezey, M. (1992). Nursing homes: Resident's needs, nursing's response. In L. H. Aiken & C. M. Fagin (Eds.), Charting nursing's future: Agenda for the 1990s (pp. 198–215). Philadelphia: J. B. Lippincott.

Mezey, M., & Lynaugh, J. (1989). The Teacher's nursing home program: Outcome of care. *Nursing Clinics of North America.*

Mezey, M., Lynaugh, J., & Carter, M. (Eds.). (1988). Aging and academia. In *Nursing homes and nursing care: Lessons from the teaching nursing homes.* New York: Springer Publishing Co.

Mezey, M., Lynaugh, J., & Cherry, J. (1984). Teaching nursing homes: A report of joint ventures between schools of nursing and nursing homes. *Nursing Outlook, 32,* 136–140.

National League for Nursing. (1979). *Position statement on the education of nurse practitioners.* New York: National League for Nursing.

National League for Nursing. (1990). *Graduate education in Nursing: Route to opportunities in nursing.* New York: National League for Nursing.

National League for Nursing. (1991). *Nursing agenda for Health Care Reform.* New York: National League for Nursing.

Nelson-Conley, C. (1990). Role development of the clinical nurse specialist within the Indian Health Service. *Clinical Nurse Specialist, 4,* 142–146.

Nolan, J., Beaman, M., & Sullivan, J. (1988). Activities and consultation patterns of nurse practitioners with master's and certificate preparation. *Public Health Nursing, 5*(2), 91–103.

Special anniversary issue: 25 years later (1990). *Nurse Practitioner, 15,* 9–31.

Omnibus Budget Reconciliation Act. (1989). (OBRA: Public Law 101–239).

Prescott, P., & Driscoll, L. A. (1978). Nurse practitioner effectiveness: A review of physician nurse practitioner comparison studies. *Evaluation of the Health Professions, 2,* 387–418.

U. S. Department of Health and Human Services, Health Resource and Services Administration (1990, March).

Report to Congress on the Study of Need for Nurse Advanced Trained Specialties. (Department of Health and Human Services Publication No. HRS-P-OP-90-1). Washington, DC: U.S. Government Printing Office.

Rew, L. (1988). Affirm the role of clinical specialist in private practice. *Clinical Nurse Specialist, 2,* 26–30.

Riner, M. B. (1989). Expanding services: The role of the community health nurse and the advanced nurse practitioner. *Journal of Community Health Nursing, 6,* 223–230.

Robert Wood Johnson Foundation. (1980). *The primary care nurse faculty fellowship program: Final report.*

Rogers, B., Sweeting, C., & Davis, B. (1989). Employment and salary characteristics of nurse practitioners. *Nurse Practitioner, 14,* 58–66.

Rogers, M. (1975). Nursing is coming of age through the practitioner movement: Con. *American Journal of Nursing, 75,* 1844–1847.

Rosenaur, J., Stanford, D., Morgan, W., & Curtin, B. (1984). Prescribing behaviors of primary care nurse practitioners. *American Journal of Public Health, 74.*

Safriet, B. (1992). Health care dollars and regulatory sense: The role of advanced practice nursing. *Yale Journal on Regulation, 9,* 417–488.

Secretary's Committee to Study Extended Roles for Nurses. (1972). *Extending the scope of nursing practice. Nursing Outlook, 20,* 46–52.

Shortridge, L. M., & McLain, B. R. (1983). Levels of intervention for a coexistence model. *Nurse Practitioner, 8,* 74–80.

Siegel, H., & Elsberg, N. (1979). Masters preparation for joint practice. *Nursing Outlook, 27,* 57–60.

Slavinsky, A., Diers, D., & Dixon, J. (1983). College graduates: The hidden nursing population. *Nursing and Health Care, 4,* 373–377.

Smith, D. M. (1965). Education and service under one administration. *Nursing Outlook, 13,* 54–58.

Sparacino, P., & Durand, B. (1986). Specialization in advanced nursing practice. *Council of Primary Care Health Care Nurse Practitioners/Council of Clinical Nurse Specialist Newsletter, 4,* 3.

Stein, R. (1983). A home care program for children with chronic illness. *Chronic Health Care, 12,* 190–92.

Sultz, H., Henry, O. M., Bullough, B., Buck, G. M., & Kinyon, L. J. (1983a). A decade of change for nurse practitioners: Part I. *Nursing Outlook, 31,* 137–142.

Sultz, H., Henry, O. M., Bullough, B., Buck, G. M., & Kinyon, L. J. (1983b). Nurse practitioners: A decade of change: Part II. *Nursing Outlook, 31,* 216–219.

Sultz, H., Henry, O. M., Bullough, B., Buck, G. M., & Kinyon, L. J. 1983c). Nurse practitioners: A decade of change: Part III. *Nursing Outlook, 31,* 266–269.

Sultz, H., Henry, O. M., Bullough, B., Buck, G. M., & Kinyon, L. J. (1984). Nurse practitioners: A decade of change: Part IV. *Nursing Outlook, 31,* 158–163.

U. S. Congress, Office of Technology Assessment. (1986). Nurse practitioners, physician assistants, and certified nurse-midwives: A policy analysis (Health Technology Case Study 37), OTA–HCS–37, Washington, DC: US Government Printing Office.

Waigandt, A., & Chang, J. (1989). Pharmacology training in nurse practitioner programs: A comparative analysis. *Evaluation and the Health Professions, 12,* 47–60.

Williamson, J. (1983). Masters education: A need for nomenclature. *Image, 15,* 99–101.

Wright, J. (1990). Joining forces for the good of our clients. *Clinical Nurse Specialist, 4,* 76–78.

Yedidia, M. (1981). *Delivering primary health care.* Boston: Auburn House.

Yoest, M. A. (1989). The Clinical nurse specialist on the psychiatric team. *Journal of Psychosocial Nursing and Mental Health Services, 27*(3), 27–32.

Zammuto, R., Turner, E. R., Miller, S., Shannon, I., & Christian, J. (1982). Effect of clinical settings on the utilization of nurse practitioners. *Nursing Research, 28,* 98–102.

Chapter 3

RESEARCH IN SUPPORT OF NURSE PRACTITIONERS

Cynthia M. Freund

POLITICAL CONTEXT

T HE political context which influenced nurse practitioner practice in the 1980s differed considerably from that in earlier years. During the 1960s and 1970s, practitioners, researchers, and policy-makers involved in the nurse practitioner movement were excited about its potential; many saw it as a reform movement, or even a revolution. While the movement was in its formative stages, some supporters saw it as a way to enhance nurses' stature within the health care community and with patients and consumers; others saw nurse practitioners as a quick solution to the physician shortage and the lack of primary care services, particularly in rural and other underserved areas.

In the beginning, although there was wide support for nurse practitioners, there was also resistance. Thus the research of the 1960s and 1970s was motivated not only by scientific objectives, but also by the need for evidence to support the claims of the advocates of nurse practitioners, or to refute the claims of those opposed.

Early research primarily addressed nurse practitioners' impact in four areas: (1) access and availability of services; (2) consumer and employee acceptance; (3) productivity, profitability, and cost of care; and (4) quality of care (Freund, 1986). In general, this research yielded positive findings in all four areas. The majority of nurse practitioners distributed themselves in underserved areas (Sultz, Henry, & Carroll, 1977; Weston, 1980). They increased the availability of primary care services (Morris & Smith, 1977; Repicky, Mendenhall, & Neville, 1980). Patients (Alonzi, et al., 1979; Charney & Kitzman, 1973; Day, 1970; Levine, Orr, Sheatsley, Lohr, & Brodie, 1978; Lewis & Resnick, 1967; Morris & Smith, 1977; Pender & Pender, 1980; Physician Extender Work Group, 1977; Schulman & Wood, 1972; Storms & Fox, 1979; Sultz, Henry, & Carroll, 1977) and physicians (Alonzi et al., 1979; Congressional Budget office, 1979; Connelly & Connelly, 1979; Lawrence et al., 1977; Schiff, Fraser, & Walter, 1969) were satisfied with nurse practitioner care. The care provided by nurse practitioners was found to cost less than the same care provided by physicians (Freund, 1981; Record, McCally, Schweitzer, Bloomquist, & Berger, 1980; Schneider & Foley, 1977). And the quality of care provided by nurse practitioners equaled and, in some instances, exceeded that provided by physicians (Bessman, 1973; Freund, 1986; Lewis, Resnik, Schmidt, & Waxman, 1969; Merenstein & Rogers, 1974; Perrin & Goodman, 1978; Runyan, 1976; Sox, 1979; Spector, McGrath, Alpert, Cohen, & Aikens, 1975).

These conclusions could not be drawn without qualifications. Many of these studies were case examples, with small samples of nurse practitioners, physicians, and patients; random assignment, was rarely used; control over variables such as patient acuity, practice type, provider training, and experience was not exercised; and definitions and measurements varied, making cross-study comparability difficult. Nevertheless, by the end of the 1970s, many asserted that several questions about nurse practitioner practice had been answered satisfactorily. The policy initiatives of the decade had been to provide increased quality primary care services at reasonable cost; nurse practitioners had contributed to that end.

The same factors which motivated research on nurse practitioner practice in the 1970s (access, acceptance, productivity, cost, and quality) continued into the 1980s. During the 1980s, however, the conditions that had provided a fertile environment for the development of the nurse practitioner movement changed. The physician shortage of the previous decades became a physician glut: physicians who once could not be enticed to rural and underserved areas now sought them out. Community and state agencies established to help rural communities develop primary health care services had embraced nurse practitioners in the 1960s and 1970s; in the 1980s, they abandoned them in favor of physicians seeking new practice options. Further, the availability and accessibility of primary care services lost favor as a national health policy issue, in part because of the physician surplus. In the eyes of those who viewed them merely as physician substitutes, there was no further need for nurse practitioners.

Although the physician shortage was easing into a surplus, escalating health care expenditures were modifying the nation's goal of quality health care as a right for all. Quality health care at reasonable cost became the new health policy goal, and throughout the 1980s, a variety of cost containment measures were studied and implemented. Policies aimed at stimulating a market economy in the health care sector were introduced, and competition among health care providers began. Although procompetition policies were directed primarily at institutional providers, because of the increase in their number, physicians found themselves competing with each other—and with nurse practitioners. Issues of encroachment and territoriality became prominent, and the earlier emphasis on collaboration and collegiality faded.

Another noteworthy change in the sociopolitical environment during the 1980s was the growing influence of business and industry on health policy. As health care costs continued to rise, corporations—as underwriters of these costs—began to work for the development of policies to contain costs. Insurers, feeling the pressure from both business and government, instituted their own cost containment strategies.

Although a variety of cost containment strategies were introduced, those that limited access to services and the volume of services had the greatest impact on nurse practitioners. On the assumption that nurse practitioner services represented an increase in the quantity of services provided (and thus an increase in overall costs), legal barriers and restrictive reimbursement policies were established; these limited patients' access to nurse practitioners, provided a disincentive for employers of nurse practitioners and, in some instances, actually prohibited nurse practitioners from engaging in their trade. These restrictive policies designated the physician as the gatekeeper for health care services, assuming that the physician would limit the volume, and hence the costs, of the services provided (an assumption not founded, however, on fact). Thus, not only did procompetition policies put nurse practitioners in competition with physicians, but policies of cost containment put nurse practitioners at physicians' mercy.

Although many policymakers saw nurse practitioners as purely physician substitutes, the nursing profession never viewed them in that way. On the contrary, the profession took advantage of the physician shortage, the lack of access to and availability of primary care services, and the maldistribution of providers in the 1960s to introduce an innovation that not only met the pressing needs of the time, but went beyond them. Nurse practitioners could safety and effectively provide the bulk of primary care needed by most people and thus could substitute for and replace physicians; and nurse practitioners would and did practice in underserved areas. But in the profession's view, nurse practitioners would do more than that: they would change the nature of primary care services. With their focus on the traditional nursing values of health promotion and prevention, teaching and counseling, and family involvement, nurse practitioners would improve both the quality of services provided and patient outcomes. Unfortunately, policymakers did not agree.

As has been noted, research during the early period of the nurse practitioner movement addressed questions dictated by political realities and policy considerations, and as a result did not focus on the "added" advantages of nurse practitioners, that is, those aspects of the nurse practitioner's performance that go beyond traditional medical services. However, towards the end of the 1970s, research initiatives began to address more encompassing questions related to nurse practitioner practice, and this broader focus has continued.

Given the political climate of the 1980s and the restrictions on further expansion of the nurse practitioner innovation during that period, the question might be asked: what purpose have these new research initiatives served? If the time frame is limited to the 1980s, then the new initiatives appear to have advanced the nurse practitioner movement very little. However, as we move into the decade of the 1990s, there are already signs of change. For certain programs and under certain conditions, direct reimbursement is now provided to nurse practitioners for services rendered. Legal barriers to nurse practitioner practice have been tested in courts, and the courts have ruled that nurse practitioners engage in legal practice. Further, there are indications that the role of the nurse practitioner as originally conceived by the nursing profession is beginning to be understood, accepted, and endorsed by policymakers, business and community leaders, and consumers.

The research of the 1980s, like that of previous decades, provides testimony to the effectiveness of nurse practitioners. Many of the research initiatives begun earlier continued (for example, emphasis on availability, acceptance, economic impact and quality of care). A move both toward greater scientific rigor and toward broader conception of primary care and the nurse practitioner role began towards the end of the 1970s (Diers & Molde, 1979; Sullivan, Dachelet, Sultz, Henry, & Carroll, 1979; Williams, 1975); much of the research of the 1980s has been characterized by this broader focus. Recent research has also added to the already large accumulation of evidence about nurse practitioners—evidence that will be vital in deciding the policy questions of the 1990s.

Thus, even though the political climate for nurse practitioners was not overwhelmingly positive during the 1980s, the research of the period will serve the nurse practitioner movement in the years to come.

RESEARCH INITIATIVES

The purpose of this section is not to provide an exhaustive review of the literature. Several comprehensive review articles, by Edmunds (1978), Prescott and Driscoll (1979, 1980), Goodwin (1981), Abdellah (1982), Yankauer and Sullivan (1982), Shamansky (1984), Molde and Diers (1985), Crosby, Ventura, & Feldman (1987), Feldman, Ventura, & Crosby (1987), LaRochelle (1987), and Stanford (1987), provide extensive discussions of the research. Their work will not be repeated here.

The authors of report after report have concluded that nurse practitioners are successful and effective, no matter what measure is used or what question is addressed—access, availability, acceptance, satisfaction, cost, or clinical outcomes. There are studies that could be more methodologically rigorous, but more recent studies are both methodologically and conceptually sound. True, there are some reports whose findings are not favorable to nurse practitioners, but the overwhelming majority of findings support their effectiveness.

The purposes here are, first, to highlight the significant new findings from research in the 1980s which give us new knowledge about nurse practitioners, their practice, and their effectiveness; and, second, to examine these findings in the context of the policy issues of the time.

Access and Availability

Access and availability of primary care services were no longer predominant concerns in the 1980s. The physician shortage had abated, and the physician surplus that was predicted for 1990 had actually occurred early in the mid-1980s. In five years, from 1975 to 1980, the number of primary care physicians nearly doubled (Graduate Medical Education National Advisory Committee, 1978). Not only were more physicians providing primary care services, but some even went to rural underserved areas and replaced nurse practitioners (Brooks, Bernstein, DeFriese, & Graham, 1981; Brooks & Johnson, 1986). As early as 1981, it was suggested that if nurse practitioners were viewed as physician substitutes, ". . .they may serve their purpose only temporarily before their usefulness expires and before they are displaced by physicians" (Brooks, Bernstein, DeFriese, & Graham, 1981, p. 254). Thus, from the perspective of many policymakers, the basic reason for nurse practitioners—to increase access to and availability of primary care services—no longer existed.

Cost containment strategies to limit the utilization of health care services contributed to the diminished concern over access and availability in the 1980s. Controlled utilization became a policy goal, replacing access and availability. With the increase in the number of physicians, it was argued that an increase in the number of nurse practitioners would only lead to increased utilization and consequent increases in costs. Nevertheless, a study of nurse practitioner-staffed clinics across the country over a 10-year period found that when nurse practitioners were replaced by physicians or physicians were added to the staff, the clinics experienced greater patient utilization, charged more for office visits, had larger budgets, and generated more of their budgets from fees for services (Brooks & Johnson, 1986). Thus, it is doubtful whether the physician surplus which drove physicians to rural underserved areas to replace nurse practitioners actually resulted in cost savings—or even cost neutrality.

The debate in the 1980s as to whether nurse practitioners should continue to be supported also involved their distribution in rural and underserved areas. The factors that influence choice of practice location for nurse practitioners do not differ from those that influence physicians and dentists (Beck & Gernert, 1971; Bible, 1970; Cooper, Heald, Samuels, & Coleman, 1975). Nurse practitioner location in rural areas is affected by clinical training experiences in rural areas (Hafferty & Goldberg, 1986), the rural background of the nurse practitioners, and the rural background of their spouses and families (Moscovice & Nestegard, 1980). Also, salaries of nurse practitioners in rural areas are 38% lower than those of their counterparts in nonrural areas—another factor affecting practice location choice (Roos & Crooker, 1983). Nevertheless, nurse practitioners do locate in rural and inner-city areas at a higher rate than do physicians (Weiner, Steinwachs, & Williamson, 1986), even though the actual percentage in these areas is low. In one state, the number of nurse practitioners in rural areas was found to be 9.2%, compared to 7.1% of primary care physicians (Salmon & Stein, 1986).

Some policymakers expected that a still greater proportion of nurse practitioners would choose practice locations that physicians found undesirable, that is, rural and inner-city locations. Weston (1980), however, noted that the ratio of nurse practitioners to the rural population is higher in states with more liberal legal sanctions and reimbursement policies, suggesting that nurse practitioners do not avoid underserved areas; rather, they are excluded from underserved areas by legal prohibitions and restrictive reimbursement policies. Further, it is unlikely that these legal sanctions and reimbursement policies will change in order to stimulate nurse practitioner practice in underserved areas, as nurse practitioner acceptance is no longer related to access and availability, but to the increasing number of physicians competing for similar opportunities (Weiner et al., 1986).

Career Patterns

Even though access and availability were not policy concerns of the 1980s, questions about nurse practitioner distribution and career patterns remained. With increasing competition from physicians for similar opportunities, were nurse practitioners practicing in primary care settings? Were they in underserved locations? Was the scope of their practice fully realized, or was it constrained? Did master's degree and certificate degree program graduates differ? Were nurse practitioners, a predominantly female group, fully employed? Though these questions had less relevance for policy considerations in the 1980s, they continued to be relevant for the profession.

In the 1960s and early 1970s, most nurse practitioners were pediatric and family nurse practitioners. By the end of the 1980s, nurse practitioners were differentiated by a number of additional specialties—for example, adult, geriatric, occupational health, women's health, school health, and psych/mental health. They were employed in a variety of settings—rural clinics and physician offices as well as health departments, hospitals (in ambulatory care, emergency departments, and inpatient units), industry and business, schools, nursing homes, and home health agencies (Bellet & Leeper, 1982; Bennett, 1984; Brooks & Johnson, 1986; Cruikshank & Lakin, 1986; Glascock, Webster-Stratton, & McCarthy, 1985; Hayden, Davies, & Clare, 1982; Martin & Davis, 1989; Scharon & Bernacki, 1984; Sobolewski, 1981; Weston, 1980; Wilbur, Zoeller, Talashek, & Sullivan, 1990; Zimmer, Groth-Juncker, & McCusker, 1985). This differentiation and broadening of the scope of practice of nurse practitioners clearly points to the fact that the nurse practitioner role is an advanced practice role in nursing, not merely a physician substitute role.

Several investigators have surveyed graduates of nurse practitioner training programs. Others have studied nurse practitioners in a particular state or region to explore employment opportunities and career patterns (Bullough, 1984; Cruikshank & Lakin, 1986; Cruikshank, Clow, & Lakin, 1986; Hayden et al., 1982; Radosevich et al., 1990; Roos, 1979;

Sirles, Leeper, Northrup, & O'Rear, 1986). These investigators report unemployment among nurse practitioners in the range of 2% to 22%. Reasons given for unemployment are similar to those for all nurses—pregnancy, childrearing, family responsibilities, and family relocation. However, barriers to practice as a nurse practitioner are also cited as reasons for unemployment.

The most comprehensive recent survey of nurse practitioners was conducted by the American Academy of Nurse Practitioners in 1989; 12,000 nurse practitioners were sent questionnaires, and close to 59% responded (Towers, 1989a, 1989b, 1990a, 1990b). Respondents represented all nurse practitioner specialties; 47% held master's degrees, and most were in primary care practices. Of those in rural areas and small communities, 37% held a master's or higher degree. Of those in urban areas, 53% held a master's or higher degree, and close to half (45%) worked in inner city locations (Towers, 1990a).

Only 30% of the respondents had a physician on site 100% of the time, but most had access to a physician by phone; nevertheless, 70% reported asking physicians to see fewer than 20% of their patients (Towers, 1990b). A similar rate of physician consultation has been found by others (Cruikshank et al., 1986; Record, McCally, Schweitzer, Blomquist, & Berger, 1980), and these findings support the claim by Steinwachs et al. (1986) that the need for primary care physicians cited by the Graduate Medical Education National Advisory Committee was overestimated, whereas the need for nurse practitioners was underestimated.

Charges for nurse practitioner services have been reported to be considerably less than charges for comparable physician services: first visit charges ranged from 12% to 45% less than first visit charges for a physician, and regular visit charges ranged from 7% to 40% less. The variability in the nurse practitioner-physician difference in charges is a factor of the particular specialty, with the least difference noted between pediatric nurse practitioners and physicians and the greatest difference noted between psych/mental health nurse practitioners and physicians (Towers, 1989a).

The national survey of nurse practitioners found that they were managing pharmacologic therapeutics in all 50 states, across all specialties and in all locales—rural areas, small communities, and urban areas. Most used written protocols to guide their prescriptive activity, the extent of which was governed by state laws. In rural areas and small communities, 58% and 55%, respectively, of nurse practitioner respondents wrote prescriptions under their own name, whereas 43% of the urban nurse practitioner respondents did so. Fewer than 1% had been primary defendants in malpractice claims (Towers, 1989b).

Most nurse practitioners reported being responsible for taking histories, performing physical exams, ordering and evaluating lab tests, and prescribing medications—traditional medical services. All the nurse practitioners also reported nursing activities such as patient teaching, family counseling, and group education for health promotion and disease prevention.

Thus, during the 1980s, the comprehensive nature of nurse practitioner practice was becoming more apparent, and nurse practitioners were more clearly demonstrating an advanced practice nursing role. They were providing a broad range of services in underserved areas and were doing so at less cost than physicians.

Acceptance

Patient Acceptance

Studies of patient acceptance of nurse practitioners conducted in the mid-1980s confirmed the findings of previous studies: patients are accepting of and satisfied with nurse practitioner services, and their acceptance increases after they have had experiences with nurse practitioners. For example, in a study of nurse practitioners and patients in the Army health care system, Southby (1980) found that patients who had had experience with nurse practitioners were more accepting of them than were patients who had not had such experience. Furthermore, patients who had had experience with nurse practitioners had higher expectations of them than did patients with no experience.

Investigators also began to examine factors associated with this acceptance, to determine which patients were more accepting of nurse practitioners. Some investigators found that women (Smith & Shamansky, 1983) and others found that men were more accepting (Enggist & Hatcher, 1983); and still others noted no difference between men and women (Shamansky, Schilling, & Holbrook, 1985). Findings on the relationship between income level and nurse practitioner acceptance were also inconsistent (Enggist & Hatcher, 1983; Hogan & Hogan, 1982; Shamansky, Schilling, & Holbrook, 1985; Smith & Shamansky, 1983). However, findings on the relation of educational level and age to nurse practitioner acceptance were more consistent. Generally, patients with more education were more accepting of nurse practitioners (Brands, 1983; Fox & Storms, 1980; Pender & Pender, 1980; Schilling, Shamansky, & Swerz, 1985) and younger people were more likely to accept nurse practitioners than older persons (Enggist & Hatcher, 1983; Hogan & Hogan, 1982; Smith & Shamansky, 1983).

However, higher educational level, younger age, and previous knowledge of our experience with nurse practitioners are likely to be interrelated. This interrelationship was noted by Fox and Storms (1980), who found that persons age 65 and older were less likely to have heard about nurse practitioners than were younger persons. Whether or not older persons had heard of nurse practitioners, after the services provided by nurse practitioners were described, 68% said they would accept their care; however, the percentage who would accept care by nurse practitioners was significantly higher among those who had heard of nurse practitioners than among those who had not. Fox and Storms found that more younger people would accept care by nurse practitioners (76%), but more younger people had heard of nurse practitioners prior to the study. Brands (1983) noted that among older persons, those with formal education beyond high school were more accepting of nurse practitioners than those with less formal education. These findings reflect the fact that exposure to and acceptance of innovations (such as nurse practitioners) is more likely to occur among younger persons and those with higher educational levels.

Some of the studies of patient acceptance provide additional insights into why and under what conditions patients are accepting of nurse practitioners. Brands (1983), for example, who studied patient acceptance of nurse practitioners among older persons, differentiated patient acceptance between traditional, transitional (health maintenance and promotion) and nontraditional (physical assessment and management of health problems) nursing activities. Most of the older persons surveyed would accept nurse practitioners for traditional activities; three-quarters preferred nurse practitioners for transitional activities; and proportions ranging from 15% to 63% (depending on the specific activity) would accept nurse practitioners for nontraditional activities.

A study by Molde and Baker (1985) provides further evidence of the type of services patients desire from nurse practitioners. These authors studied 128 patients in a primary care center to determine whether their visit was motivated primarily by their "chief complaint" or whether they had hidden agendas. They found that 30% of the patients had hidden agendas, but did not verbalize these hidden agendas unless sanctioned to do so; the hidden agendas—often the real reason for the visit—were related to their need for nursing care. These findings suggest that patients may need the services of nurse practitioners more than the services of physicians, even if they do not recognize this. Further, if patients do recognize their need for nursing services, to seek such services outright is not sanctioned, and thus they must mask their real need, making appointments for visits under the guise of having traditional medical problems.

A series of studies of potential nurse practitioner consumers in New Haven, Connecticut, identified the characteristics of services most likely to predict intent to use nurse practitioners among consumers of all ages (Shamansky et al., 1985). Although fewer than 33% of the survey respondents had heard of nurse practitioners and fewer than 10% had had actual experience with them, 62% said they would use nurse practitioner services, while 24% were unsure and 13% would not. Prior knowledge or experience was not a significant predictor of intent to use nurse practitioner services. The strongest predictor was dissatisfaction with present care, and the most frequently expressed areas of dissatisfaction were availability and cost of care.

Holbrook and Shamansky (1985) examined the market for nurse practitioner services among women 18 to 40 years of age, a subsample of the consumers surveyed in the larger Connecticut study. Eighty percent of the women said they would use nurse practitioner services if they were covered by insurance. Shamansky and St. Germain (1987) also studied acceptance of nurse practitioners by the elderly; they found that although 73% had no prior knowledge of nurse practitioners, 51% thought there were no differences between physician and nurse practitioner services and were accepting of nurse practitioners.

These investigators also found that cost of care and health insurance coverage were significant predictors of intent to use nurse practitioner services. Prior knowledge of nurse practitioner services and perceived differences between physician and nurse practitioner care were not significant predictors. Shamansky and St. German (1987) conclude that patient acceptance and utilization of nurse practitioner services may not depend on prior knowledge or preference of provider, but on characteristics of the service which meet the particular needs of a population group, such as time spent during a visit, cost of care, convenience, and whether the services were covered by insurance.

The studies by Brands (1983), Molde & Baker (1985), and Shamansky et al. (1985) all suggest that health care consumers are discerning. They not only evaluate providers in determining their choice of services; they also evaluate the cost of the care provided, insurance coverage, accessibility and convenience of services, and inclusion of services beyond those traditionally provided. The question of patient acceptance of nurse practitioners is thus a marketing question—what kinds of services, at what cost and convenience, are the determining factors? The question involves the benefits sought by consumers and the relative advantage of nurse practitioners and the services they provide over other alternative forms of health service.

Physician Acceptance

Physicians tended to be accepting of nurse practitioners in the early 1970s when there was a shortage of physicians and they were over worked. However, towards the late 1970s, nurse practitioners began to be viewed as a threat.

As with patient acceptance, physician acceptance is thought to be related to prior experience with nurse practitioners. Several studies support this view (Pierce, Quattlebaum, & Carley, 1985; Sharpe & Banahan, 1982; Weinberger, Greene, & Mamlin, 1980). Two studies that examined the effect of working with nurse practitioners during residency training on physicians' acceptance of nurse practitioners found that house staff acceptance and expectations of these practitioners increased during the residency period; further, these physicians indicated a willingness to employ nurse practitioners (Sharpe & Banahan, 1982; Weinberger et al., 1980). However, despite these findings, there are few reports in the literature of nurse practitioner involvement in residency training programs.

It has been suggested that physician acceptance is also related to traditional hierarchical structures, particularly gender hierarchy, which limits physicians' ability to view nurse practitioners as colleagues (Campbell-Heider & Pollock, 1987); at the same time, gender bias leads physicians to see nurse practitioners as less of a threat than physician assistants (Johnson & Freeborn, 1985). Both Weinberger et al. (1980) and Sharpe and Banahan (1982) have noted that physician acceptance of nurse practitioners is influenced by the effect of nurse practitioners on physician income and by issues of licensing, legal status, and reimbursement for services. More than likely, gender is and will remain a factor in physicians' acceptance of nurse practitioners. However, during the 1980s, with the physician surplus and various efforts at cost containment, the question of physician acceptance became clouded by issues of encroachment, territoriality, and competition.

Economic Impact

By the early 1980s, there was conclusive evidence that nurse practitioners were cost effective. However, questions continued to be raised about their economic impact: Were nurse practitioners as productive as physicians? Were there true cost savings associated with nurse practitioners? Some argued, for example, that nurse practitioners were not economically viable because in many remote (and nonremote) settings, they ". . . fail to meet expenses or produce only minimal profits" (Mendenhall, Repicky, & Neville, 1980, p. 621). In this argument, however, the primary criterion used to assess economic effectiveness was income (and profit) generation; reimbursement policies were not acknowledged as a major influencing variable.

Throughout the 1980s, the question remained: what is the *potential* economic impact of nurse practitioners—for restrictive reimbursement policies prohibited coverage of many nurse practitioner services. Investigators had to conclude from the evidence available that cost savings *could* result from the use of nurse practitioners if nurse practitioner services were reimbursed by third-party payers. For example, in a study of nurse practitioners in one state with very restrictive reimbursement policies, investigators noted that in most settings, nurse practitioners could, if reimbursed, generate at least two to four times their salary and benefits; however, they could not realize this income because of restrictive reimbursement policies (Sirles et al., 1986).

Several studies conducted during the 1980s in settings not dependent on third-party reimbursement demonstrated actual cost savings associated with nurse practitioner services. Over a four-year period, Dellinger, Zentner, McDowell, & Annas (1986), for example, reported a net savings of $273,986 a year when nurse practitioners were used to provide primary care and prevention services to company employees. They also noted that dependents who had the benefit of nurse practitioner services had lower insurance claims than did other dependents. The company is now considering extending nurse practitioner services to dependents, with the prospect of further cost savings. Since in industry many companies are self-insured and, for others, insurance rates are determined by the actual claims made by employees, any program that reduces health care expenditures and insurance claims results in cost savings.

Savings similar to those reported by Dellinger et al. have also been reported by others. At Tenneco, Inc., nurse practitioners provide a comprehensive program of services to 3,622 employees. On an annual basis, their services cost $469,562, compared to $978,057 for equivalent services provided by community physicians (Scharon & Bernacki, 1984; Scharon, Tsai, & Bernacki, 1987). Caward (1981) reported a net savings of $43,452 for a company of only 165 employees. Touger and Butts (1989) showed a substantial reduction in employer health care costs with a nurse practitioner primary care clinic at the worksite—from $120 per month per employee to $87 per month per employee between 1984 and 1987. It is important to note that during this same period, on average, employer health care costs rose as much as 20% to 30%. Lawler and Bernhardt (1986) argue convincingly that the marginal benefit (extra benefit realized for each added dollar spent, taking into account marginal productivity and cost) of nurse practitioners in occupational settings is substantial.

Studies have also been conducted in other settings not dependent (or not solely dependent) on third-party reimbursement for financial viability. Yeater (1985) noted that a 1980 CHAMPUS evaluation found that reimbursed expenses to nurse practitioners were 31% less than those for physicians. Brodie, Bancroft, Rowell, & Wolf (1982) compared care provided by nurse practitioners and physicians in a military pediatric outpatient clinic and found no differences except that the mean nurse practitioner cost per visit was 38% less than the mean physician cost per visit. A study of the costs of care for services in a jail compared program costs before and after the inclusion of nurse practitioners on the staff. Volume of care doubled, while the average cost per visit was reduced one-third and various measures of quality improved (Hastings et al., 1980). And in HMOs per episode costs for pediatric patients with nurse practitioners as the initial provider were 20% less than with physicians as the initial provider; general examination costs for women ages 40 to 55 were 52% less for nurse practitioners than for physicians (Salkever, Skinner, Steinwachs, & Katz, 1982).

All of these studies demonstrate that when reimbursement from third-party payers is not an issue, the use of nurse practitioners results in cost savings, as well as other added benefits. Yet while most of the studies to date provide evidence of nurse practitioner cost-effectiveness, they are limited in one respect. Except for those conducted in industrial settings, most have measured cost-effectiveness on a per-visit, episode-of-illness or total-program basis, without considering costs incurred in other health care sectors, such as for hospitalization. In one study, however, both the costs for primary care services and the costs for hospitalization were examined for patients with congestive heart failure. The study examined costs at a Veterans Administration Center before and after the institution of a nurse practitioner clinic. Even though outpatient costs increased from $5,518 to $16,555, inpatient costs decreased from $153,450 to $22,275, resulting in a net savings of $120,138. These savings were largely attributed to a 60% reduction in the number of hospitalizations and an 85% reduction in the mean number of hospitalized days of nurse practitioner patients (Cintron, Bigas, Linares, Aranda, & Hernandez, 1983).

In the Veterans Administration study, the sample was small and patients were not randomly assigned to the nurse practitioner clinic. However, several other studies have reported similar results. In two studies of geriatric nurse practitioners in nursing homes, fewer hospital transfers from the nursing home were noted after the employment of a geriatric nurse practitioner (Garrard et al., 1990; Wieland, Rubinstein, Ouslander, & Martin, 1986). A 48% reduction in hospital transfers resulted in a reduction of 250 acute bed-days (Wieland et al., 1986). Also, in a randomized controlled trial of a home health care team using nurse practitioners, average daily costs were significantly less for patients cared for by the team with a nurse practitioner, due to the lower hospital utilization rates for these patients (Zimmer, Groth-Juncker, & Mc-

Cusker, 1985). These findings indicate that cost savings associated with nurse practitioners increase if expensive institutionalization costs are considered. The findings also suggest that more comprehensive studies of nurse practitioner cost effectiveness may show that the true cost savings may have been underestimated.

In 1980, in perhaps the most rigorous and conclusive study of nurse practitioner cost effectiveness (Record, McCally, Schweitzer, Blomquist, & Berger, 1980), the authors noted that one full-time nurse practitioner can provide the same care as a .63 full-time equivalent (FTE) physician at one-third the cost. When the training cost differential between nurse practitioners and physicians is added in, the savings are staggering.

In 1986, the U.S. Congress Office of Technology Assessment (1986) published its report on nurse practitioner and certified nurse midwife cost and quality. The policy analysis was directed by a 20-member interdisciplinary advisory committee and was based on an extensive review of the research. The report repeatedly affirmed the cost-effectiveness of nurse practitioners for society, and stressed the effects of prohibitive legal constraints and restrictive reimbursement policies in limiting the true cost savings of nurse practitioners.

Sweet (1986) and Jacox (1987) thus suggest that the challenge is to change laws and reimbursement policies. Despite enabling federal legislation for nurse practitioner reimbursement, in 1990 only 26 states had mandatory benefit laws to reimburse nurse practitioners, and even in those states, implementation of the laws was stalled and reimbursement limited (Scott & Harrison, 1990). State licensing laws meant to protect the public are actually serving to limit competition (Jacox, 1987). Licensing laws limit nurse practitioner practice by prohibiting certain activities, or by making their performance dependent on physician supervision—both of which protect the physician's monopoly and direct the reimbursement to the physician. Further, these laws result in a double charge to society, which Jacox (1987) illustrates:

> For example, an NP working in a hospital may perform an admission history and physical on a newly admitted patient who has a private attending physician. The hospital pays the nurse's salary; the attending physician "validates" the history and physical exam and collects a fee, so that consumers or payers pay twice for a single service, hence raising the total cost of care. (p. 266)

For close to 30 years, nurse practitioners have been under extensive scrutiny—to determine their cost-effectiveness, to assess the quality of care they provide, and to determine if they practice in underserved areas in greater proportions than other care providers. For these 30 years, study results have for the most part provided evidence in favor of nurse practitioners. Yet barriers continue to restrict their full contribution to the health care system in this country.

Quality of Care

The quality of care provided by nurse practitioners continued to be studied extensively during the 1980s. "From the beginning, the quality of services delivered by the new health professionals was a source of concern, receiving far more attention than the quality of services delivered by physicians had ever received" (Yankauer & Sullivan, 1982, p. 263). Many studies continued to use physician care as the standard for quality (Goldberg, Jolly, Hosek, & Chu, 1981; Hall et al., 1990; Hickman, Sox, & Sox, 1985; McDowell, Martin, Snustad, & Flynn, 1986; Palmer et al., 1985; Powers, Jalowiec, & Reichelt, 1984; Ramsay, McKenzie, & Fish, 1982; Thompson, Basden, & Howell, 1982; Watkins & Wagner, 1982). In other words, if nurse practitioner care, in terms of process or outcome or both, was equivalent to physician care, it was considered safe, competent quality care (Prescott and Driscoll [1979] provide an excellent review of earlier studies).

In the comparison studies of the 80s, subtle and important differences between nurse practitioners and physicians were noted. For example, nurse practitioners had fewer missed appointments and higher return rates for follow-up visits (Becker, Fournier, & Garner, 1982; Bibb, 1982; Fosarelli, DeAngelis, Kaszuba, & Hafferty, 1985) and they prescribed fewer medications (Rosenaur, Stanford, Morgan, & Curtin, 1984). In a study comparing physician and nurse practitioner care for hypertensive patients, nurse practitioners had more success in managing obesity: nurse practitioner patients tended to lose weight, while physician patients tended to gain weight. In addition, nurse practitioner patients had better control of their hypertension (Ramsay, McKenzie, & Fish, 1982). The investigators concluded that successful outcomes were contingent on more than technical skills.

Hall et al. (1990) asked whether some of the more favorable outcomes associated with nurse practitioners were attributable to gender, since in most studies, nurse practitioners were female and physicians were male. In a randomized controlled clinical trial of 16 ambulatory clinics, they compared the practices of female physicians and nurse practitioners. "Comparable or superior performance for nonphysicians was found for all tasks but one [cancer screening in women]" (Hall et al., 1990, p. 489).

In comparing nurse practitioners to physicians, investigators have also noted differences in caseloads between nurse practitioners and physicians (Barkauskas, Chen, Chen, & Ohlson, 1981; Chen, Barkauskas, Ohlson, Chen, & DeStefano, 1983; Diers, Hamman, & Molde, 1986; Dunn & Higgins, 1986). In some studies, caseload differences were by design, nurse practitioners were assigned "well" visits (Sackett, Spitzer, Gent, & Roberts, 1974); or, in contrast, they were assigned patients with multiple chronic conditions (Runyan, 1976). In other studies, however, more nurse practitioner patients had problems not included in the ICD-9 codes (Barkauskas et al., 1981; Diers, et al., 1986; Chen et al., 1983). Also, fewer nurse practitioner patients had private insurance, and 84% of the nurse practitioners' patients received public assistance, as compared to 62% of physicians' (Diers et al., 1986).

In some of these studies, investigators looked at differences in style or pattern of practice between physicians and nurse practitioners, rather than focusing solely on medical variables. Chen et al. (1983), for example, noted that pediatric nurse practitioners emphasized wellness more than their pediatrician counterparts. Diers et al. (1986) noted that nurse practitioners attended more to symptoms of nonpathological conditions, comfort, and comprehensiveness of care than did physicians. Campbell, Neikirk, et al. (1990) noted that nurse practitioners exhibited more concern with psychosocial issues than did physicians. However, in this study, when the type of visit (acute care, chronic care, well care and follow-up) was controlled, differences between nurse practitioners and physicians were not significant (Campbell, Mauksch, Neikirk, & Hosokawa, 1990; Campbell, Neikirk, & Hosokawa, 1990). Nonetheless, in many studies, differences have been apparent in nurse practitioner and physician style, emphasis, and pattern of practice.

Since the late 1960s, nurse practitioners have claimed that their style or pattern of practice is different from that of physicians, and that they are more than physician substitutes. Several studies have supported this view. However, results from one study suggest that this assertion requires questioning. In a study of nurse practitioner-patient interactions during well-child visits, taped interactions were analyzed. Pediatric nurse practitioners conducted comprehensive assessments and gave mothers a wealth of educational information. "However, the process of assessing and intervening was dominated by PNP questions, commands, and opinions" (Webster-Stratton, Glascock, & McCarthy, 1986, p. 249).

In a review of the Webster-Stratton et al. study, Lynn (1987) says:

> One of the early arguments for the creation of the nurse practitioner was that nurses would bring to the diagnosis and management of common

health problems a more holistic approach to the patient. A preponderance of closed questioning of patients, the lack of patient input into the "nurse-patient" interaction, the lack of description of or rationale for interventions suggested, and the nonrecognition of the patient by name or actions would seem to bring this holistic orientation into question.

Webster-Stratton et al. attribute their findings to the educational preparation of nurse practitioners, suggesting that nurse practitioners are knowledgeable about and committed to holistic care, but have less skill in the areas of counseling and teaching.

Results from many studies over the last three decades have produced evidence of the quality of care provided by nurse practitioners, particularly when physician care is used as the standard. More recent studies have begun to identify the differences in both process and outcome between nurse practitioners and physicians (Mezey & Lynaugh, 1989). In an editorial in the *American Journal of Public Health*, Sullivan (1982) noted: "Nurse practitioners continue to show an uncanny ability not only to provide primary care equivalent to that of physicians, but also to offer something special that increases adherence . . ." (p. 8) and results in fewer prescribed medications and hospital days, decreased symptoms, and improved nutritional changes. Identification of practice style differences between physicians and nurse practitioners, and examination of their effects on patient outcomes and satisfaction, are clearly research priorities for the future. As Diers et al. (1986) suggest, these are important questions, because policy decisions about substitution and reimbursement rest on the answers.

In 1979, Diers and Molde (1979) called for more conceptual and methodological rigor in nurse practitioner research, and suggested that more attention be paid to sampling, measurement of chronically ill and well populations, definition of comparison groups, and consideration of new sources of data and more relevant standards of care. Stanford (1987) and Sullivan (1982) called for studies of process related to outcome and studies of the nursing component of nurse practitioner practice. While much of the research in the 1980s was conceptually sound and addressed these methodological issues, major gaps in the literature still exist.

Crosby et al. (1987) conducted a synthesis of the literature on nurse practitioner effectiveness, and noted that studies to identify current conditions that either enhance or impede nurse practitioner practice were needed. These researchers noted that studies addressing barriers to nurse practitioner practice were reported in the early 1970s, but "a reassessment of this issue in view of the changes that have occurred would contribute to an awareness of current factors having an impact on nurse practitioners" (p. 79). As one of the expert reviewers in the study concluded, the research agenda is the policy agenda.

SUMMARY AND CONCLUSIONS

In 1986, in an examination of the factors influencing the workplace encroachment experienced by nurse practitioners, Ostwald and Abanobi (1986) wrote: "After 20 years of nurse practitioners' participation in the delivery of primary care services, the questions asked are no longer about their cost-effectiveness, the quality of services, or, for that matter, their viability" (p. 154). Researchers had made the same assertion five years earlier, many continue to make the same assertion today. The review in this chapter and the reviews by others note that there is ample evidence of the quality of services provided by nurse practitioners in all types of settings, as well as their cost effectiveness and their acceptance by consumers. However, the full potential of nurse practitioners has never been accepted, according to Yankauer and Sullivan (1982) because it is too threatening.

Despite the evidence, Ostwald and Abanobi note:

> stupendous growth in the supply of primary health care providers in the face of declining utilization raises serious questions about the professional autonomy of nurse practitioners and about practice domains between nurse practitioners and physicians. Although nurse practitioners have won social acceptance from consumers, resistance from conservative policy makers, physicians, and health-care administrators, as well as restrictive reimbursement systems, continue to pose serious barriers to optimal utilization of nurse practitioner services, favoring more costly alternatives instead. (p. 154)

Early in the history of the nurse practitioner movement, resistance was attributed to reluctance to try a new, innovative role because questions of quality, cost, and patient acceptance were unanswered. These were legitimate questions. Today, 25 years later, the questions have been answered, but the resistance continues.

That resistance has recently been described as "encroachment" or as "restraint of trade." In one state, 38% of the nurse practitioners have experienced job encroachment (Ostwald & Abanobi, 1987). Another study of nurse practitioners in emergency rooms found that 57% left for practice in other settings because of resistance to their roles by physicians and hospital administrators (Hayden, Davies, & Clore, 1982). Bullough

(1984), in an examination of major legal actions against nurse practitioners over a period of 10 years, found that of 17 major legal actions, only 2 were malpractice claims. The remainder were actions brought by medical societies and medical boards in an attempt to restrict nurse practitioner practice. Bullough concluded that most of the actions "look like harassment of nursing" (p. 441).

Kelly (1985) recommends that nurse practitioners turn to the judicial system to challenge restraints on their practice. She cites four major obstacles to the practice of nurse practitioners—or in other words restrictions that restrain their trade: (1) licensing restrictions; (2) denial or restrictions of third-party reimbursement; (3) denial of access to medical facilities; and (4) restrictions on access to physician back up services. The Sherman Act has great potential for correcting abuses in the marketplace, and antitrust actions can now be brought against licensing boards, third-party payers, health care organizations, and physicians. Success in any such antitrust action, however, is dependent on a new kind of evidence.

Evidence supporting nurse practitioner competence and safety, and the quality and cost-effectiveness of their services, will not withstand judicial scrutiny under the antitrust doctrine. In any judicial challenge, evidence must be case-specific. In addition, evidence is needed to support the demand for nurse practitioner services and limitations on consumers' free choice. In her review of restraint of trade challenges in the health care industry with relevance to nurse practitioners, Kelly (1985) describes several arguments that can be made by nurse practitioners in support of restraint of trade claims. Evidence to support such claims is being accumulated (note particularly the studies reviewed in the Patient Acceptance section), though more is needed.

In 1981, after reviewing the nurse practitioner research literature, this author concluded that much of the research from 1965 to 1980 was directed by political realities and policy imperatives. Her recommendation was that future research be directed toward methodological and conceptual issues directly related to the essence of nurse practitioner practice.

During the 1980s, a great deal of research did address the essence of this practice, focusing on both its process and its outcome. The findings confirm that nurse practitioners, in all types of settings, and with various patient populations, provide care and services that lead to positive patient outcomes; in many instances, when compared to physicians, nurse practitioner outcomes are better.

Despite the findings, more research is still needed. What nurse practitioners do that results in better patient outcomes is an important question. They do it for less cost, or at least they have the potential of providing services at less cost, which could be fulfilled if system barriers were removed so that savings could be passed on to consumers and society. Furthermore, it is unlikely there will ever be enough nurse practitioners to meet societal needs. Consequently, if what nurse practitioners do that leads to positive patient outcomes can be identified, this knowledge can be transferred to other health care providers who, along with nurse practitioners, will make up the constellation of health care professionals working to meet society's needs.

In 1991, after reviewing the literature from 1980 to 1990, it is apparent that encroachment and restraint of trade are real issues that inhibit the full use of nurse practitioners. Although the questions are slightly different from those of the late 1960s and 1970s, questions derived from political considerations are perhaps even more important today than previously. Evidence to support claims of encroachment and restraint of trade is crucial if nurse practitioners are to realize their full potential.

REFERENCES

Abdellah, F. (1982). The nurse practitioner 17 years later: Present and emerging issues. *Inquiry, 19*(2), 105–116.

Alonzi, S., Geolot, D., Richter, L., Mapstone, S., Edgerton, M. T., and Edlich, R. R. (1979) Physician and patient acceptance of emergency nurse practitioners. *Journal of the American College of Emergency Physicians, 8*, 357–359.

Barkauskas, V., Chen, S., Chen, E., & Ohlson, V. (1981). Health problems encountered by nurse-practitioners and physicians in obstetric-gynecologic ambulatory care clinics. *American Journal of Obstetrics and Gynecology, 140*(4), 393–400.

Beck, J., & Gernert, E. (1971). Attitudes and background values and predictors of urban-rural practice location. *Journal of Dental Education, 35*(9), 45–53.

Becker, D., Fournier, A., & Garner, L. (1982). A description of a means of improving ambulatory care in a large municipal hospital: A new role for nurse practitioners. *Medical Care, 20*(10), 1046–1050.

Bellet, P., & Leeper, J. (1982). Effectiveness of the pediatric nurse practitioner well-baby clinics in West Alabama. *The Alabama Journal of Medical Sciences, 19*(2), 126–128.

Bennett, M. L. (1984). The rural family nurse practitioner: The quest for role-identity. *Journal of Advanced Nursing, 9*(2), 145–155.

Bessman, A. (1974). Comparison of medical care in nurse clinician and physician clinics in medical school affiliated hospitals. *Journal of Chronic Disease, 27*, 115–125.

Bibb, B. N. (1982). Comparing nurse practitioners and physicians: A simulation study on processes of care. *Evaluation of Health Professions, 5*(1), 29–42.

Bible, B. L. (1970). Physicians' view of medical practice in nonmetropolitan communities. *Public Health Reports, 85*(1), 11–17.

Brands, R. (1983). Acceptance of nurses as primary-care providers by retired people. *Advances in Nursing Science, 5*(3), 37–49.

Brodie, B., Bancroft, B., Rowell, P., & Wolf, W. (1982). A comparison of nurse practitioner and physician costs in a military out-patient facility. *Military Medicine, 147*(12), 1051–1053.

Brooks, E. F., Bernstein, J. D., DeFriese, G. H., & Graham, R. M. (1981). New health practitioners in rural satellite health centers: The past and future. *Journal of Community Health, 6*(4), 246–256.

Brooks, E. F., & Johnson, S. L. (1986). Nurse practitioner and physician assistant satellite health centers: The pending demise of an organizational form? *Medical Care, 24*(10), 881–890.

Bullough, B. (1984). Legal restrictions as a barrier to nurse practitioner role development. *Pediatric Nursing, 10*(6), 439–442.

Bullough, B., Sultz, H., Henry, O. M., & Fiedler, R. (1984). Trends in pediatric nurse practitioner education and employment. *Pediatric Nursing, 10*(3), 193–196.

Campbell, J. D., Mauksch, H. O., Neikirk, H. J., & Hosokawa, M. C. (1990). Collaborative practice and provider styles of delivering health care. *Social Science Medicine, 30*(12), 1359–1385.

Campbell, J. D., Neikirk, H. J., & Hosokawa, M. C. (1990). Development of a psychosocial concern index from videotaped interviews of nurse practitioners and family physicians. *Journal of Family Practice, 30*(3), 321–326.

Campbell-Heider, N., & Pollock, O. (1987). Barriers to physician-nurse collegiality: An anthropological perspective. *Social Science and Medicine, 25*(5), 421–425.

Caward, J. (1981). Economics of the nurse practitioner role in an industrial setting. *Nurse Practitioner, 6*(6), 17–18.

Charney, E., & Kitzman, H. (1973). The child health nurse (pediatric nurse practitioner) in private practice: A controlled trial. *New England Journal of Medicine, 108*, 998–1003.

Chen, S. Barkauskas, V., Ohlson, V., Chen, E., & DeStefano, L. (1983). Health problems encountered by pediatric nurse practitioners and pediatricians in ambulatory care clinics. *Medical Care, 21*(2), 168–179.

Cintron, G., Bigas, C., Linares, E., Aranda, J., & Hernandez, E. (1983). Nurse practitioner role in a chronic congestive heart failure clinic: In-hospital time, costs, and patient satisfaction. *Heart and Lung, 12*(3), 237–240.

Congressional Budget Office. (1979) *Physician Extenders: Their current and future role in medical care delivery*. Washington, DC: U.S. Government Printing office.

Connelly, S. V., & Connelly, P. A. (1979). Physician's patient referrals to a nurse practitioner in a primary medical clinic. *American Journal of Public Health, 69*, 73–75.

Cooper, J., Heald, K., Samuels, M., & Coleman, S. (1975). Rural or urban: Factors influencing the location decision of primary care physicians. *Inquiry, 12*(1), 18–25.

Crosby, F., Ventura, M., & Feldman, M. J. (1987). Future research recommendations for establishing NP effectiveness. *Nurse Practitioner, 12*(1), 75–79.

Cruikshank, B. M., Clow, T. J., & Lakin, J. A. (1986). Use of physician consultation by nurse practitioners in community health and ambulatory clinic settings. *Journal of Community Health Nursing, 3*(4), 211–223.

Cruikshank, B. M., & Lakin, J. A. (1986). Professional and employment characteristics of NPs with master's and non-master's preparation. *Nurse Practitioner, 11*(11), 45–52.

Day, L., Egli, R., & Silver, H. (1970). Acceptance of pediatric nurse practitioners. *American Journal of Diseases of Children, 119*, 204–208.

Dellinger, C. J., Zentner, J. L., & Annas, W. (1984). A report on the use of a family nurse practitioner to reduce industrial health care costs. *North Carolina Medical Journal, 45*(12), 800–802.

Dellinger, C. J., Zentner, J. P., McDowell, P. H., & Annas, A. W. (1986). The family nurse practitioner in industry. *American Association of Occupational Health Nursing Journal, 34*(7), 323–325.

Diers, D., Hamman, A., & Molde, S. (1986). Complexity of ambulatory care: Nurse practitioner and physician caseloads. *Nursing Research, 35*(5), 310–314.

Diers, D., & Molde, S. (1979). Some conceptual and methodological issues in nurse practitioner research. *Research in Nursing and Health, 2*(2), 73–84.

Dunn, E. V., & Higgins, C. A. (1986). Health problems encountered by three levels of providers in a remote setting. *American Journal of Public health, 76*(2), 154–159.

Edmunds, M. W. (1978). Evaluation of nurse practitioner effectiveness: An overview of the literature. *Evaluation and the Health Profession, 1*(1), 69–82.

Enggist, R. E., & Hatcher, M. E. (1983). Factors influencing consumer receptivity to the nurse practitioner. *Journal of Medical Systems, 7*(6), 495–512.

Feldman, M., Ventura, M., & Crosby, F. (1987). Studies of nurse practitioner effectiveness. *Nursing Research, 36*(5), 303–308.

Fosarelli, P., DeAngelis, C., Kaszuba, A., & Hafferty, F. (1985). Compliance with follow-up appointments generated in a pediatric emergency room. *American Journal of Preventative Medicine, 1*(3), 23–29.

Fox, J. G., & Storms, D. (1980). New health professionals and older persons. *Journal of Community Health, 5*(4), 254–260.

Freund, C. M. (1981). *The economic impact of new health practitioner patient delegation patterns.* Unpublished doctoral dissertation, The University of Alabama at Birmingham.

Freund, C. (1986). Nurse practitioners in primary care. In M. Mezey & D. McGivern (Eds.), *Nurses, nurse practitioners: The evolution of primary care.* Boston: Little, Brown. 305–333.

Garrard, J., Kane, R. L., Radosevich, D. M., Skay, C. L., Arnold, S., Kepferle, L., McDermott, S., & Buchanan, J. L. (1990). Impact of geriatric nurse practitioners on nursing-home residents' functional status, satisfaction, and discharge outcomes. *Medical Care, 28*(3), 271–283.

Glascock, J., Webster-Stratton, C., & McCarthy, A. M. (1985). Infant and pre-school well-child care: Master's- and nonmaster's-prepared pediatric nurse practitioners. *Nursing Research, 34*(1), 39–43.

Goldberg, G., Jolly, D., Hosek, S., & Chu, D. (1981). Physician's extenders' performance in Air Force clinics. *Medical Care, 19*(9), 951–964.

Goodwin, L. (1981). The effectiveness of school nurse practitioners: A review of the literature. *The Journal of School Health, 51*(11), 623–624.

Graduate Medical Education National Advisory Committee (1978). *Supply and distribution of physicians and physician extenders* (DHEW Publication No. HRA 78–11) Washington, DC: Government Printing Office.

Hafferty, F. W., & Goldberg, H. I. (1986). Educational strategies for targeted retention of nonphysician health care providers. *Health Services Research, 21*(1), 107–125.

Hall, J. A., Palmer, R. H., Orav, E. J., Hargraves, J. L., Wright, E. A., & Louis, T. A. (1990). Performance quality, gender, and professional role: A study of physicians and nonphysicians in 16 ambulatory care practices. *Medical Care, 28*(6), 489–501.

Hastings, G., Vick, L., Lee, G., Sasmor, L., Natiello, T., & Sanders, J. (1980). Nurse practitioners in a jailhouse clinic. *Medical Care, 18*(7), 731–744.

Hayden, M. L., Davies, L., & Clore, E. (1982). Facilitators and inhibitors of the emergency nurse practitioner role. *Nursing Research, 31*(5), 294–299.

Hickman, D., Sox, H., & Sox, C. (1985). Systematic bias in recording the history in patients with chest pain. *Journal of Chronic Disease, 38*(1), 91–100.

Hogan, K., & Hogan, R. (1982). Assessment of the consumer's potential response to the nurse practitioner model. *Journal of Nursing Education, 21*(9), 4–12.

Holbrook, T., & Shamansky, S. (1985). The market for nurse practitioner services among women 18 to 40 years of age. *Health Care for Women International, 6*(5) 309–325.

Jacox, A. (1987). The OTA report: A policy analysis. *Nursing Outlook, 35*(6), 262–267.

Johnson, R., & Freeborn, D. (1986). Comparing HMO physicians' attitudes towards NPs and PAs. *Nurse Practitioner, 11*(1), 39, 43–46, 49.

Kelly, K. (1985). Nurse practitioner challenges to the orthodox structure of health care delivery: Regulation and restraints of trade. *American Journal of Law and Medicine, 11*(2), 195–225.

LaRochelle, D. (1987). Research studies on nurse practitioners in ambulatory health care: A review, 1980–1985. *Journal of Ambulatory Care Management, 10*(3), 65–75.

Lawler, T., & Bernhardt, J. (1986). Nurse practitioners and HMOs in occupational health. *AAOHN, 34*(7), 333–336.

Lawrence, R. S., DeFriese, G. H., Putnam, S. M., Pickard, C. G., Cyr, A. B., & Whiteside, S. W. (1977). Physician receptivity to nurse practitioners: A study of the correlates of the delegation of clinical responsibility. *Medical Care, 15*, 298–310.

Levine, J. I., Orr, S. T., Sheatsley, D. W., Lohr, J. A., & Brodie, B. M. (1978). The nurse practitioner: Role, physician utilization, and patient acceptance. *Nursing Research, 27,* 245–254.

Lewis, C. E., & Resnik, B. (1967). Nurse clinics and progressive ambulatory patient care. *New England Journal of Medicine, 277,* 1236–1241.

Lewis, C. E., Resnik, B., Schmidt, G., & Waxman, D. (1969). Activities, events and outcomes in ambulatory patient care. *New England Journal of Medicine, 280,* 645–649.

Lynn, M. (1987). Pediatric nurse practitioner-patient interactions: A study of the process. *Journal of Pediatric Nursing, 2*(4), 268–271.

Martin, A., & Davis, L. (1989). Mental health problems in primary care: A study of nurse practitioners practice. *Nurse Practitioner, 14*(10), 50–56.

Master, R., Feltin, M., Jainchill, J., Mark, R., Kavesh, W., Rabkin, H., Turner, B., Bachrach, S., & Lennox, S. (1980). A continuum of care for the inner city. *New England Journal of Medicine, 302*(26), 2622–2627.

McDowell, B., Martin, D., Snustad, D. & Flynn, W. (1986). Comparison of the clinical practice of a geriatric nurse practitioner and two internists. *Public Health Nursing, 3*(3), 140–146.

Mendenhall, R., Repicky, P., & Neville, R. (1980). Assessing the utilization and productivity of nurse practitioners and physician's assistants: Methodology and findings on productivity. *Medical Care, 18*(6), 609–623.

Merenstein, J. H., & Rogers, K. D. (1974). Streptococcal pharyngitis: Early treatment and management by nurse practitioners. *Journal of the American Medical Association, 227,* 1278–1282.

Mezey, M., & Lynaugh, J. (1984). The Teaching Nursing Home program: Outcomes of care. *Nursing Clinics of North America, 24*(3), 769–780.

Molde, S., & Baker, D. (1985). Explaining primary care visits. *Image, 17*(3), 72–76.

Molde, S., & Diers, D. (1985). Nurse practitioner research: Selected literature review and research agenda. *Nursing Research, 34*(6), 362–367.

Morris, S. B., & Smith, D. B. (1977). The distribution of physician extenders. *Medical Care, 15,* 1045–1057.

Moscovice, I., & Nestegard, M. (1980). The influence of values and background on the location decision of nurse practitioners. *Journal of Community Health, 5*(4), 244–253.

Ostwald, S., & Abanobi, O. (1986). Nurse practitioners in a crowded marketplace: 1965–1985. *Journal of Community Health Nursing, 3*(3), 145–156.

Ostwald, S., & Abanobi, O. (1987). Strategies used by nurse practitioners to adjust to workplace encroachment. *Pediatric Nursing, 13*(3), 189–190.

Palmer, R., Louis, T., Hsu, L–N, Peterson, H., Rothrock, J., Strain, R., Thompson, M., & Wright, E. (1985). A randomized controlled trial of quality assurance in sixteen ambulatory care practices. *Medical Care, 23*(6), 751–770.

Pender, N., & Pender, A. (1980). Illness prevention and health promotion services provided by nurse practitioners: Predicting potential consumers. *American Journal of Public Health, 70*(8), 798–803.

Perrin, E., & Goodman, H. (1978). Telephone management of acute pediatric illness. *New England Journal of Medicine, 298,* 130–135.

Physician Extender Work Group. (1977). *Report of the Physician Extender Work Group*. (No. 017–022–00555–6) Hyattsville, MD: U.S. Government Printing Office.

Pierce, M., Quattlebaum, T. G., & Corley, J. (1985). Significant attitude changes among residents associated with a pediatric nurse practitioner. *Journal of Medical Education, 60*(9), 712–718.

Powers, M., Jalowiec, A., & Reichelt, P. (1984). Nurse practitioner and physician care compared for nonurgent emergency room patients. *Nurse Practitioner, 9*(2), 39–52.

Prescott, P., & Driscoll, L. (1979). Nurse practitioner effectiveness: A review of physician-nurse comparison studies. *Evaluation and the Health Professions, 2*(4), 387–411.

Prescott, P., & Driscoll, L. (1980). Evaluating nurse practitioner performance: The nurse practitioner. *American Journal of Primary Health Care, 28*(4), 32–53.

Radosevich, D., Kane, R., Garrard, J., Skay, C., McDermott, S., Kepferle, L., Buchanan, J., & Arnold, S. (1990). Career paths of geriatric nurse practitioners employed in nursing homes. *Public Health Report, 105*(1), 65–71.

Ramsay, J., McKenzie, J., & Fish, D. (1982). Physicians and nurse practitioners: Do they provide equivalent health care? *American Journal of Public Health, 72*(1), 55–57.

Record, J., McCally, M., Schweitzer, S., Blomquist, R., & Berger, B. (1980). New health professions after a decade and a half: Delegation, productivity and costs in primary care. *Journal of Health Politics, Policy and Law, 5*(3), 470–497.

Roos, P. (1979). Nurse practitioner employment, unemployment, reemployment. *Nursing Research, 28*(6), 348–353.

Roos, P., & Crooker, M. (1983). Variables affecting nurse practitioner salaries. *Nurse Practitioner, 8*(5), 36–44.

Rosenaur, J., Stanford, S., Morgan, W., & Curtin, B. (1984). Prescribing behaviors of primary care nurse practitioners. *American Journal of Public health, 74*(1), 10–13.

Runyan, J. W., (1976). The Memphis chronic disease program: Comparisons in outcome and the nurse's extended role. *Nurse Practitioner, 1*(5), 27–30.

Sackett, D. L., Spitzer, W. O., Gent, M., & Roberts, R. S. (1974). The Burlington randomized trial of the nurse practitioner: Health outcomes of patients. *Annals of Internal Medicine, 80,* 137–142.

Salkever, D., Skinner, E., Steinwachs, D., & Katz, H. (1982). Episode-based efficiency comparisons for physicians and nurse practitioners. *Medical Care, 20*(2), 143–153.

Salmon, M. A., & Stein, J. (1986). Distribution of nurse practitioners and physician assistants: Are they meeting the need for primary care? *North Carolina Medical Journal, 47*(3), 147–148.

Scharon, G. M., & Bernacki, E. J. (1984). A corporate role for nurse practitioners. *Business and Health, 1*(9), 26–27.

Scharon, G., Tsai, S., & Bernacki, E. (1987). Nurse practitioners in an occupational setting: Utilizing patterns for the delivery of primary care. *American Association of Occupational Health Nurses Journal, 35*(6), 280–284.

Schiff, D. W., Fraser, C. H., & Walter, H. L. (1969). The pediatric nurse practitioner in the office of pediatricians in private practice. *Pediatrics, 44,* 62–68.

Schilling, L., Shamansky, S., & Swerz, M. (1985). Profiles of the consumer and nonconsumer of pediatric nurse practitioner services: New Haven, Connecticut. *Journal of Community Health Nursing, 2*(2), 79–92.

Schneider, D. P., & Foley, W. J. (1977). A systems analysis of the impact of physician extenders on medical cost and manpower requirements. *Medical Care, 15,* 277–297.

Schulman, J., & Wood, C. (1972). Experience of a nurse practitioner in a general medical clinic. *Journal of the American Medical Association, 219,* 1453–1461.

Scott, C., & Harrison, O. A. (1990). Direct reimbursement of nurse practitioners in health insurance plans of research universities. *Journal of Professional Nursing, 6*(1), 21–32.

Shamansky, S. (1984). Nurse practitioners and primary care research: Promises and pitfalls. *Annual Review of Nursing Research, 3,* 107–125.

Shamansky, S., Schilling, L., & Holbrook, T. (1985). Determining the market for nurse practitioner services: The New Haven experience. *Nursing Research, 34*(4), 242–247.

Shamansky, S., & St. Germain, L. (1987). The elderly market for nurse practitioner services. *Western Journal of Nursing Research, 9*(1), 87–106.

Sharpe, T., & Banahan, B. (1982). Evaluation of the use of rural health clinics: Attitudes and behaviors of primary care physicians in service areas of nurse practitioner clinics. *Public Health Reports, 97*(6), 566–571.

Sirles, A., Leeper, J., Northrup, R., & O'Rear, M. (1986). The education, employment situations and practice activities of nurse practitioners in Alabama. *The Alabama Journal of Medical Sciences, 23*(4), 379–384.

Smith, D., & Shamansky, S. (1983). Determining the market for family nurse practitioner services: The Seattle experience. *Nursing Research, 32*(5), 301–305.

Sobolewski, S. (1981). Cost-effective school nurse practitioner services. *The Journal of School Health, 51*(9), 585–588.

Southby, J. (1980). Primary care nurse practitioners within the Army health care system: Expectations and perceptions of the role. *Military Medicine, 145*(10), 659–665.

Sox, H. C. (1979). Quality of patient care by nurse practitioners and physician's assistants: A ten-year perspective. *Annals of Internal Medicine, 91,* 459–468.

Spector, R., McGrath, P., Alpert, J., Cohen, P., & Aikens, H. (1975). Medical care by nurses in an internal medicine clinic. *Journal of the American Medical Association, 232,* 1234–1237.

Stanford, D. (1987). Nurse Practitioner research: Issues in practice and theory. *Nurse Practitioner, 12*(1), 64–74.

Steinwachs, D., Weiner, J., Shapiro, S., Bataldon, P., Coltin, K., & Wasserman, F. (1986). A comparison of the requirements for primary care physicians in HMOs with projections made by the GMENAC. *New England Journal of Medicine, 314*(4), 217–222.

Storms, D. M., & Fox, J. G. (1979). The public's view of physicians' assistants and nurse practitioners. *Medical Care, 17*, 526–535.

Sullivan, J. A., & Dachelet, C. Z. (1979). Evaluative research and the nurse practitioner: Where we've been, where we are and what's ahead. In H. Sultz, O. M. Henry, & J. A. Sullivan (eds.), *Nurse practitioners: USA* (pp. 276–000). Lexington, MA: Lexington Books.

Sullivan, J. (1982). Research on nurse practitioners: Process behind the outcome? *American Journal of Public Health, 72*(1), 8–9.

Sultz, H., Henry, O. M., & Carroll, H. (1977). Nurse practitioners: An overview of nurses in the expanded role. In A. Bliss & E. Cohen (Eds.), *The new health professionals* (pp. 41–76). Germantown, MD: Aspen Systems.

Sweet, J. B. (1986). The cost-effectiveness of nurse practitioners. *Nurse Economics, 4*(4), 190–193.

Thompson, R., Basden, P., & Howell, L. (1982). Evaluation of initial implementation of an organized adult health program employing family nurse practitioners. *Medical Care, 20*(11), 1109–1127.

Touger, G. N., & Butts, J. K. (1989). The workplace: An innovative and cost-effective practice site. *Nurse Practitioner, 14*(1), 35–42.

Towers, J. (1989a). Part I: Report of the American Academy of Nurse Practitioners national nurse practitioner survey. *Journal of the American Academy of Nurse Practitioners, 1*(3), 91–94.

Towers, J. (1989b). Report of the national survey of the American Academy of Nurse Practitioners, part II: Pharmacologic management practices. *Journal of the American Academy of Nurse Practitioners, 1*(4), 137–142.

Towers, J. (1990a). Report of the national survey of the American Academy of Nurse Practitioners, part III: Comparison of nurse practitioner characteristics according to education. *Journal of the American Academy of Nurse Practitioners, 2*(3), 121–124.

Towers, J. (1990b). Report of the national survey of the American Academy of Nurse Practitioners, part IV: Practice characteristics and marketing activities of nurse practitioners. *Journal of American Academy of Nurse Practitioners, 2*(4), 164–167.

Office of Technology Assessment. (1986). *Nurse practitioners, physicians' assistants, and certified nurse midwives: Policy analysis.* Washington, DC: U.S. Government Printing Office.

Watkins, L., & Wagner, E. (1982). Nurse practitioner and physician adherence to standing orders criteria for consultation or referral. *American Journal of Public Health, 72*(1), 22–29.

Webster-Stratton, C., Glascock, J., & McCarthy, A. M. (1986). Nurse practitioner-patient interactional analyses during well-child visits. *Nursing Research, 35*(4), 247–249.

Weinberger, M., Greene, J., & Mamlin, J. (1980). Changing house staff attitudes toward nurse practitioners during their residency training. *American Journal of Public Health, 70*(11), 1204–1206.

Weiner, J., Steinwachs, D., & Williamson, J. (1986). Nurse practitioner and physician assistant practices in three HMOs: Implications for future U.S. health power needs. *American Journal of Public Health, 76*(5), 507–511.

Weston, J. L. (1980). Distribution of nurse practitioners and physician assistants: Implications of legal constraints and reimbursement. *Public Health Reports, 95*(3), 253–258.

Wieland, D., Rubenstein, L., Ouslander, J., & Martin, S. (1986). Organizing an academic nursing home. *Journal of American Medical Association, 255*(19), 2622–2627.

Wilbur, J., Zoeller, L., Talashek, M., & Sullivan, J. (1990). Career trends of master's prepared family nurse practitioners. *Journal of American Academy of Nurse Practitioners, 2*(2), 69–78.

Williams, C. A. (1975). Nurse practitioner research: Some neglected issues. *Nursing Outlook, 23*(3), 172–177.

Yankauer, A., & Sullivan, J. (1982). The new health professionals: Three examples. *Annual Review of Public health, 3*, 249–276.

Yeater, D. (1985). 1985 health care cost management update. *Occupational Health Nursing, 31*(12), 594–599.

Zimmer, J. G., Groth-Juncker, A., & McCusker, J. (1985). Randomized controlled study of a home health care team. *American Journal of Public Health, 75*(2), 134–141.

Chapter 4

PRIMARY CARE AS AN ACADEMIC DISCIPLINE*

Claire M. Fagin

T HE chapter "Primary Care as an Academic Discipline" was written at the invitation of the Robert Wood Johnson Foundation for presentation at their first annual symposium highlighting the work of the Nurse Faculty Fellows in Primary Care. The title was theirs; the content was mine. I doubt that I would have articulated the view of early ownership of the primary care arena by nursing had I not had the opportunity to reflect on the meaning of the term "academic discipline," offered me by the Foundation.

It was clear then, and it is even clearer now, that nurses are educated to be superb primary care practitioners; and that the skills and knowledge required to practice are imparted in most of our undergraduate programs and continued in many of our graduate programs. Research over the past two decades has proven that nurses can deliver cost-effective primary care that can substitute for physician care in many situations. Further, nurses can provide new and important services in long-term care and nursing homes (Fagin, 1990).

*"Primary Care as an Academic Discipline" slightly adapted by Claire Fagin from her chapter in *Primary Care: A Contemporary Nursing Perspective*, edited by Ingeborg Mauksch (1981). Reprinted and adapted by permission of the publisher, Grune & Stratton, Inc.

Other chapters in this book bring the numerical record about nurse practitioners up to date. This is not my aim in this Chapter. Rather, I would like to put several other issues into a contemporary perspective. First, the issue of direct reimbursement of nurse practitioners: Over the last eight years two nursing groups have been extremely successful, on a national level, in achieving direct reimbursement for their work. They are Certified Nurse Midwives (CNMs) and Certified Registered Nurse Anesthetists (CRNAs). Others have been only moderately successful, despite extensive evidence to support direct reimbursement. During the 1980s two large-scale reviews of the literature provided evidence that nurses' styles of delivering care are extremely suited to people's needs in terms of health teaching and counseling, follow-up care, use of fewer diagnostic tests, and per-episode costs (Office of Technology Assessment, 1986). Yet, in recent national deliberations, the issue of recommending reimbursement did not benefit much from this exhaustive data. Now new questions are raised as obstacles to reimbursement. They have to do with "sameness" of work and "human capital" theory. However, human capital theory as it applies to nurses seems, at this time, to be referring exclusively to opportunity costs of training. Opportunity costs are not seen as appropriate for differences in physicians' backgrounds.

It is interesting to note that studies have found that there are diminishing returns to education as it increases: the return on elementary school education is highest and the return on graduate studies (excluding professional degrees) lowest (PPRC, unpublished manuscript). The issues of sameness linked with the human capital theory have not been used in establishing relative costs for different specialties among physicians, to clinical psychologists, or to limited license practitioners.

It is hard to believe that these are the true issues which stand in the way of recommending direct reimbursement to nurse practitioners. Nurses are the only group which has produced a large volume of convincing evidence about care and outcomes of care. Yet others have achieved the goal of direct reimbursement without such evidence. Clearly, this issue, raised in the chapter that follows, is still a problem.

Over the past decade we *have* brought primary care into the mainstream of nursing education. Preparation begins at the undergraduate level, and most nurses and others accept the view that graduate education is needed to prepare the nurse practitioner for generalist and specialized roles.

A critical mass of faculty *have* been prepared for teaching primary care content. Thanks to the Robert Wood Johnson Foundation, the Kellogg Foundation, the Commonwealth Foundation, and the Joshua Macy Foundation (and others), cadres of nurses have been prepared for both practice and teaching.

While organized medicine's stance in relation to collaboration has not changed significantly, there are thousands of examples of collaborative relationships between nurses and physicians which attest to major change at the patient care level.

There are numerous clinical settings appropriate for learning, and educational resources to provide diverse knowledge and skills in teaching, administration, and research have increased exponentially.

Medical school output increased markedly and, health systems costs, as predicted, have increased dramatically. Both service based and provider based reimbursement are being examined and new payment structures (such as the Resource Based Relative Value Scale) are in place for implementation.

Much work has been done on the relative merits of community care versus institutionalization. Home care alternatives and hospice are part of many third-party reimbursement programs, and home care has been found to be cost effective as compared with hospital care. Early discharge programs for low-birth-weight infants have led to replications with other populations, and nursing has led the way in these studies.

Nurses are increasingly involved with the "power brokers" of the health care and political systems. They do sit on boards, and in various national, state, regional, and local policymaking bodies.

A new issue that emerged in the 1980s with regard to primary care and the nurse practitioner is the extent to which the international community has come to recognize nursing's importance in meeting health care needs. Work on the international scene in primary care is increasing in importance. United States nursing's maturity is permitting it to help meet needs of nurses and health care systems in other countries through collaborative efforts. The World Health Organization is cognizant of nursing's role in primary care, and has named several United States universities and programs in other countries as WHO Collaborating Centers. We can expect, therefore, the international activities of nurse practitioners, and CNMs in particular, to increase.

There is more to be done. Given the extraordinary changes that have occurred in the past decade, by the year 2000 nursing should be at the point of achievement in primary care where nurses are making the maximum contribution to our nation's health and in the international community.

I said in 1978 that primary care is the generic discipline of nursing. Nothing has happened to alter that view. What has occurred is that nursing has proven the statement, in its practice, education, and research, and no longer needs to make a claim as rhetoric that is readily seen in reality.

Primary care as an academic discipline is a vital issue for nursing and medicine to address for reasons that have to do with intellectual considerations as well as political, social, and financial factors. More striking, however, is its importance as an issue that permits the conceptualization of a distinction between the medical and nursing models. It should be said at the start that the author does not believe that primary care is a separate academic discipline within nursing nor, based on nursing's history and meaning, should it be. Primary care is an integral part of nursing in all its aspects and is the academic discipline of nursing. How the author arrived at this conclusion will be discussed by defining the term, explaining why the issue is of interest to nursing and medicine, taking a brief look at the major relevant historical events of this century, and examining nursing's past and present focus (Fagin, 1992; Fagin & Goodwin, 1972). It is the author's belief that nursing and medicine have followed, and must follow, separate routes to the goal of primary care.

DISCIPLINES, DEPARTMENTS, AND DISTINCTIONS

To begin from a common understanding of this subject, it is necessary to define what is meant by "academic discipline." There are some cases where semantics *do* make a difference, and this is one of them, since reactions to the concept of primary care as an academic discipline will be based in no small part on the terminology involved. Disciplines reflect distinctions between bodies of knowledge. The *Oxford Dictionary* (1990) defines the word *discipline* as "a branch of instruction or education; a department of learning or knowledge"; note that there are two parts for that definition.

Donaldson and Crowley state:

> Disciplines have evolved as a consequence of a distinct perspective and syntax, which determine what phenomena or abstractions are of interest, in what context such phenomena are to be viewed, what questions are to be raised, what methods of study are to be used, and what canons of evidence and proof are to be required. (p. 114)

Looking at primary care within the strict context of such a definition, as well as that part of the *Oxford Dictionary's* definition that describes "a branch of instruction or education," the idea of primary care as an academic discipline seems reasonable. While its body of knowledge has not been fully developed through theoretical exposition and research, the parameters of this area, which lend themselves to investigation and theory development, have been identified by many writers. Thus, the potential for establishing a theoretical body of knowledge that relates to primary care exists even if all of it is not available to us at the present time.

It is the second part of the definition that is a subject for debate, that is, a discipline as a "department of learning or knowledge." In centers of learning, such as universities, there appears to be a natural transition between the identification of a particular area as a discipline and the belief that this discipline should be administratively or organizationally set up as a department. It is in this area that questions must be raised as to the appropriateness of such an organizational structure for nursing. What are the factors that create, defeat, or blur the formation of a content area as an academic discipline or, in this case, as an academic department? Are these factors dominated by the intellectual force of argument that pertains to the body of knowledge of the area, or are there other considerations?

An examination of the ways in which the basic sciences are organized in medical schools may clarify the point. In examining the organization in medical education of basic science disciplines—"a branch of instruction or education"—one can note from school-to-school the blurring of discipline lines and the lack of a commonality of discipline groupings; that is, the lack of "a department of learning or knowledge." In one school, for instance, the department of anatomy was closed, and two new divisions were created in cell biology and cytology. In other schools, biochemistry may be linked with biophysics, while still other institutions maintain all of the above as separate departments (Kohler, 1982).

Why this lack of consistency? Various factors, such as competition for support, prestige, historical circumstances, perception of problems, and social interactions, contribute to this situation. So do the power of external forces, such as financial support from governmental and private agencies, that influence the growth and specific labeling of academic disciplines. Medical schools across the country have responded to these external pressures by increasing their emphasis on education for primary care. It is interesting to note that a 1977 survey by the American Association of Medical Colleges of trends in primary care education that indicated no well-defined locus for coordinating efforts for institution-wide, primary care training through specific departmental structures (Giacoloni & Hudson, 1977) still applies. While no corresponding survey for nursing has been published, the author is confident that a similar conclusion can be made.

Thus, while both medicine and nursing have shown increasing interest in the primary care area, in most cases the educational component has been discretely organized without a corresponding organization within the school's administrative structure.

HISTORICAL PERSPECTIVE

Two distinct lines of development can be identified as we examine the professional health care scene of this century: These are the public health movement and the growth of medical school—hospital establishments—each of these developments with its own priorities. By the late nineteenth century, the public health movement had achieved major success in controlling the spread of infection and in microbiology; early in the twentieth century, it began to focus on the health needs of the poor and on maternal-child health care. During this same period, there were a large number of poor-quality programs that prepared physicians. Flexner's report of 1910 had profound influence on the nature and the content of medical schools and medical education. It set the stage for the stress on research, which later became the *sine qua non* of the quality medical school. The rising professionalism of the medical group coincided with the growing power of the hospital group and the decline in power of the physicians involved in the public health movement.

In medicine, the forerunner of today's primary care practitioner was, of course, the general practitioner. Although declining somewhat in numbers in the first 30 years of the post-Flexner period, the almost total extinction of the general practitioner on the American scene occurred after World War II. At that time, a variety of developments pushed the health care system into an emphasis on, and power in, the secondary and tertiary care areas. The extraordinary research and technological process during the decade of the 1940s had stunning implications for the civilian population. There was a growing assumption that the development of technology would be tantamount to the control of illness. With the increase in technology and research, there was a subsequent need for physicians and others to become more specialized as they advanced their knowledge base. It became impossible to know all things about all medical problems.

The financing of hospital growth through the Hill-Burton Act, as well as governmental funding for medical education, grew geometrically during this period. Furthermore, the availability of governmental and private funds for research reinforced the already growing development of an academic role model for the physician-scientist. These faculty members, as the status members of the medical school group, had an enormous influence on medical students who were choosing their future paths. Although attempts were made to revise, or at least maintain, a general practice group within the American Medical Association, these attempts met with little success for reasons such as "the absence of an academic base, the undefined role of the general practitioner in relation to the specialist, and the difference in working conditions and status between the general practitioner and the specialist" (Lewy, 1977, p. 875).

In addition, the decades from the 1940s through the 1960s were dominated by the health care providers, with few consumer efforts to stop the extraordinary growth of the medical and hospital establishment. In past years, however, some countertrends had begun to develop—among them, the notion of the Great Society, with health care seen as a right rather than a privilege. The funding of health centers connected with the Office of Economic Opportunity exposed gaps in health care; in particular, the gap that we now label the "primary care needs of people."

These developments reawakened medicine's interest in general practice, and during the 1960s several study commissions set out to explore its future. One such commission indicated that the graduate education of physicians for what had now acquired the label of "family practice" required training equivalent to that of other specialties, as well as the development of a specialty board to give certifying examinations (Millis, 1966). The evolution of a new specialty, it was stated,

> requires a definition of content, the development of graduate training programs, the development of specialty departments in medical school, the establishment of standards, the development of mechanisms to insure adherence to the standards, the development of continuing education programs to insure maintenance of these standards, and the generation of research programs to further the unique body of knowledge. (Lewy, 1977, p. 875)

It was not easy to establish such programs, especially in universities, since there was no uniform process whereby the content of fields such as community medicine and behavioral science could be taught; besides, there was a severe shortage of qualified teachers in family medicine.

NURSING'S DEVELOPMENT

Nursing's role in the two lines of development in the health scene were in sharp contrast to that of medicine. Whereas medicine developed its power base in the medical school-hospital establishment, nursing became dominated by the same establishment.

Although the early hospital schools of the late nineteenth century were based on Nightingale's model and were educational apprenticeships, by the twentieth century many became what Joanne Ashley calls "successful instruments for women's oppression" (Ashley, 1977, p. 23). As early as 1915, some leaders in nursing were recommending that nursing education be placed on a professional basis within colleges and universities. Yet well into the 1930s and 1940s, hospitals simply increased the number of students in their schools to meet the demands for immediate nursing service.

There were great leaders in nursing during the first half of the century, but most of these leaders developed outside of the hospital group and were closely aligned with the public health movement, a movement that in nursing is the historical antecedent of the primary care movement. (Lillian Wald, the founder of the Henry Street Settlement and the Visiting Nurse Service, coined the terms *public health nurse* and *public health nursing*).

The first national nursing organization to have a headquarters and a paid staff was the National Organization for Public Health Nursing (NOPHN), which was established in 1912. For quite some time the public health movement in nursing continued to grow in power, to set standards for practice, and to influence education by requiring certain content, including degrees, as a condition of employment. In the 1940s, the National League of Nursing Education established its own accrediting committee, which was a very significant development in the history of nursing. It ended the proliferation of hospital schools and the student labor method of instruction. The influence of the NOPHN was very strong on the League, and many leaders in nursing education prior to 1950 came out of the public health movement.

Now, however, it is sometimes difficult to distinguish public health nurses from other university-educated nurses, since more and more nurses work outside hospital walls and nursing education increasingly focuses on a holistic view of patient, family, and community. This can be said despite the fact that nursing followed the medical path in becoming specialized from the late 1940s through the 1960s. The knowledge explosion identified areas of need, such as psychiatric nursing, and federal dollars accelerated specialization in graduate education. But as their knowledge increased, nurses frequently rejected the kind of technical tasks that the new technology created, resulting in an expressed need for different kinds of manpower; that is, technical aides who were task- and physician-oriented. One unfortunate result of this movement was the increase in fragmentation in hospital care; another was the separation of most nursing leaders from the hospital establishment. The absence of bridges from university to nursing service militated against nursing leaders having an influence on improving hospital nursing care. Fortunately, there are new moves in this direction at the present time.

By the late 1960s in fact, nursing programs had become both generalized and comprehensive, stressing public health and mental health. Had it not been for political factors and nursing's resistance to recognizing its own natural progression, nursing could have conceivably moved very rapidly to prepare for primary health care. The few imaginative nurses who carved out roles in primary care were frequently scorned by their nursing colleagues, and other groups jumped in to fill the primary care gap.

Despite this backing and filling within the profession, or perhaps because of it, pressures from governmental and other groups for a rapid method of preparing nurses to meet primary care needs resulted in the establishment of 100 or more "nurse practitioner" programs of varied duration, content, and type. In this situation, as in others before, nursing's adaptation to meet immediate needs solved some problems but created or perpetuated others. Over the past 30 years, 40,000 nurse practitioners have been prepared. Considerable funding has also gone into the preparation of other health care practitioners and into increasing the number and capability of medical schools. By now, nursing has changed its stance and sees itself as playing a major role in the delivery of primary health care.

AN ACADEMIC DISCIPLINE

We are now at a point where there is interest in primary care on the part of both medicine and nursing. But are the two fields comparable in this area? The author has tried to build a case that indicates they are not comparable, and the analysis will now be completed.

It has become increasingly apparent that for real change to occur, primary care must be seen as a respected part of the academic scene. The mass of data attesting to the influence of high-status medical faculty members on the socialization of medical students supports the importance of establishing the academic centrality of primary care. In both nursing and medical education, in other words, primary care must be part of the mainstream, with its content and faculty constituting an integral part of the academic power structure.

In medical education, however, two problems have been cited as greatly inhibiting the growth and development of comprehensive care. These are the assumptions that comprehensive care (particularly pri-

mary care) is solely a function of an attitudinal set and a kind of no-
blesse oblige that does not require specific training, and "the lack of
professionalization of the role required to provide comprehensive care
in the role of the primary physician" (Magraw, 1971, p. 475).

The Nature of Nursing

Despite the admission by medical educators of the need to educate for
primary care, the attitude in most medical centers toward this field, as
Alpert pointed out, continues to be condescending (Alpert & Charnay,
1974; Mullan, 1993). The subspecialist researchers-clinicians are the tail
that wags the dog in every academic clinical department, be it medicine,
pediatrics, or obstetrics-gynecology. A conceptual move to equalize the
status between the primary care physician and the specialist in internal
medicine or pediatrics would have been hard enough. However, since
specialists are now considered generalists in their respective fields and
the subspecialists are the predominant powers, the gap between the
subspecialist group and the primary care group is a wide one indeed. It
is therefore understandable that pressures exist resisting the establishment of primary care as an academic discipline within the medical profession. If indeed the establishment of an academic discipline, and subsequently a specific department, to coordinate and develop the primary
care component of the curriculum would help to solve some of the political and status issues faced by those devoting themselves to primary
care, then this may well be a legitimate goal—for medicine, that is.

For nursing, however—given its natural evolution from a concept of
public health and a concern for the individual, family, and community
to a concept of primary care—the situation is different, and the solution
to the problem is almost the antithesis of the medical solution. In nursing, primary care is *not* low man on the totem pole. Rather, it is increasingly recognized as the integral core of nursing rather than one of its
specialties.

The nature of nursing as described by Nightingale and others following her has been too close to the nature of primary care as described by
almost everyone else for primary care to be conceptualized as a discrete
academic discipline within nursing. Primary care is so multifaceted that
it cannot be considered the domain of any one nursing specialty group,
nor would it be possible for any one group to cover all its aspects. If we
were forced to define it as a separate entity, we would be robbing its
strength from all other groups in nursing. What is the body of knowledge for primary care, for instance, that can be differentiated from the
body of knowledge needed in nursing in general?

As the author sees it then, primary care as an academic discipline within nursing is *the* generic discipline. The care of people with actual or potential health problems and the manipulation of the environment to contribute to optimal health have long been seen as the generic base of nursing practice. Nursing is defined as including the promotion and maintenance of health, prevention of illness, care of persons during acute phases of illness, and rehabilitation or restoration of health. Are these not also the functions of primary care as described by most writers, and do they not also suggest the knowledge required? As Donaldson and Crowley (1978) stated,

> Nursing has traditionally valued humanitarian service. But in addition, the self-respect and self-determination of clients are to be preserved. The goal of nursing service is to foster self-caring behavior that leads to individual health and well-being. These values and goals, which are intrinsic to professional practice, have shaped the value orientation of the discipline. (p. 114)

Primary care has now moved into the mainstream of nursing education. The stopgap measures to prepare nurses as primary practitioners have accomplished short-term goals. There is a need to continue to incorporate teachers and leaders in educational and service programs who have a strong commitment to primary care. To do this, six ingredients must be present in the educational organization: (1) an understanding of the nature and scope of primary care nursing; (2) faculty prepared for teaching in primary care; (3) philosophical commitment to primary care as the core of nursing; (4) appropriate clinical settings with arrangements for faculty practice; (5) collaborative relationships with physicians that provide for consultation and referral; and (6) educational resources that provide diverse knowledge and skills in teaching, administration, and research. Where nursing faculty in primary care seek and do not find these ingredients, they must help to create them.

Although primary care as the appropriate focus of nursing is a comfortable concept, the issue becomes more complex, more difficult, when one considers the complementary and interdependent roles required to flesh out this concept. The question of the collaborative or collegial relationships of the two major disciplines involved in primary care—medicine and nursing—is important to study. The lack of coordinated planning in primary care has exacerbated this issue and the situation can be expected to worsen unless it is directly addressed. In the guidelines for federal support of primary care residency programs, the definition of primary care content is virtually identical to every nursing description of this area since 1968. Clearly we must come together in education and practice to utilize the best each discipline has to offer, to build on our individual strengths, and subsequently to collaborate in meeting health needs in a rational manner.

Nurses and physicians involved in primary care have not been sufficiently involved in health policy-making bodies or in health planning. Health planning is an area studied by many. However, a one-sentence summary indicates that we have neither a national health policy nor a national health plan or planning process (Falkson, 1978). Proof of this can be found in the way primary, secondary, and tertiary care have developed in the past three decades. If a collaborative and rational plan had been drawn up at the start, it is not inconceivable that a different system of health care could have been organized that would have had a major impact on the nature of primary care services as well as total-systems costs.

If the readings from the professional and public market places are correct, there are three periods of change that relate to identifying and meeting primary care needs. The first one occurred in the 1960s with the recognition of the need, and there were a variety of solutions planned and implemented. All were without any connection to one another or any consideration of their long-term effects in areas such as the nurse practitioner movement, the development of the physician's assistant, and the infusion of money into medical schools to expand enrollment with a heavy focus on preparation for primary care. The view commonly held during this period was that a nurse practitioner was to be prepared as a physician-extender, therefore, a physician substitute.

The findings from the next period of change have been very clear in indicating that the nurse practitioner in primary care can indeed fill the vast majority of needs commonly identified. Phase two is replete with studies of the effectiveness of nonphysician providers. Toward the end of this period, we begin to see data that indicate that long-term systems' costs can be affected by extended community care versus hospitalization; that is, by assisting people to remain in their own homes through supportive services. On the other hand, the question of how long-term systems' costs are affected by the relative expense of educating various practitioners has not been explored. We are now into phase three, which is the realization that physician-students already in the pipeline have caused an oversupply of specialist physicians in this country within the next few years. What effect this will have on primary care, on the development of the nursing profession, or on health system costs is unknown. Several hypotheses can be posed. One is that since physicians control the marketplace, we can expect health systems costs to increase with the abundance of physicians. Economists are examining this issue closely, and various alternatives are being posed, such as service-based (Enthoven, 1993) rather than provider-based reimbursement. Further, the extraordinary expansions of the for-profit sector with a concomitant growth in the percentage of salaried physicians may create other employment possibilities for nurse practitioners. At any rate, in phase three it would be well to examine the issues posed by the already known variables and to pressure for participation in policy development.

It is the author's belief that the expansion of the primary care effort in medicine was in error. This, incidentally, is not because of my lack of good memories about the general practitioners of the late 1930s but, rather, because the author's consumer bias is to get her money's worth for dollars spent. If indeed, at a maximum of six years, a nurse practitioner can deliver at least as good, or in some cases better, primary care than a physician—whose educational costs are much higher, length of education close to double, and income expectations correspondingly greater—then serious questions must be raised about this kind of luxurious approach (Fagin, 1993). Further, many of the reasons for medical specialization *were cogent*. The explosion of knowledge did indeed make it impossible to know all things about all medical problems. Given the nature of medical education and training, it is entirely appropriate to expect this kind of expertise from the physician. However, this kind of thinking is clearly ex post facto and will have little effect on the present situation. This is all the more reason for a clear identification of where we stand in nursing and medicine in relation to primary care and for a more open and complete discussion of these issues in interdisciplinary and consumer groups.

Conclusions

Primary care within nursing is the academic discipline of nursing. It cannot be separated from the other components of nursing into a new part but *is* the dominating force of the discipline itself. An examination of the contents and the concepts of primary care clarifies the difference between the professions of nursing and medicine in relation to primary care. Primary care is not a focus of nursing; it is nursing's major focus.

REFERENCES

Alpert, J., & Charnay, E. *The education of physicians for primary care.* Rockville, MD: U.S. Public Health Service.

Ashley, J. (1977). *Hospitals, paternalism, and the role of the nurse.* New York: Teachers College Press.

Donaldson, S. K., & Crowley, D. (1978). The discipline of nursing. *Nursing Outlook, 26,* 113–120.

Enthoven, A. C. (1993). A history and principles of managed competition. *Health Affairs, 12,* 24–48.

Fagin, C. M. (1977). Nature and scope of nursing practice in meeting primary health care needs. In *American Nurses Association (Ed.), Primary care by nursing: Sphere of responsibility and accountability* (pp. 35–51). Kansas City: American Nurses Association.

Fagin, C. M. (1990). Nursing's value proves itself. *American Journal of Nursing, 90,* 10, 17–30.

Fagin, C.M. (1992). Collaboration between nurses and physicians: No longer a choice. *Nursing and Health Care, 6,* 25–31.

Fagin, C. M., & Goodwin, B. (1972) Baccalaureate preparation for primary care. *Nursing Outlook, 20,* 240–244.

Falkson, J. L. (1978) We need a national health policy. *Journal of Health, Politics, Policy & Law, 4,* 311.

Giacoloni, J. J., & Hudson, J. I. (1977). Primary care education trends in U.S. medical schools and teaching hospitals. *Journal of Medical Education, 52,* 971–981.

Kohler, R. (1982). *From medical chemistry to biochemistry: The makings of a biomedical discipline.* Cambridge, New York: Cambridge University Press.

Lewy, R. M. (1977). The emergence of the family practitioner: An historical analysis of a new specialty. *Journal of Medical Education, 52,* 875–881.

Magraw, R. M. (1971). Implications for medical education. *American Journal of Diseases of Children, 122,* 475–486.

Millis, J. S. (1966). *The graduate education of physicians.* Report of the Citizens Commission on Graduate Medical Education. Chicago: American Association.

Mullan, F., Rivo, M.C., & Politizer, R.M. (1993). Doctors dollars and determination: making physician work-force policy. *Health Affairs, 12,* 138–151.

Office of Technology Assessment. (1986). Physicians' assistants and certified nurse-midwives: A policy analysis. Washington, DC: U.S. Government Printing Office.

Physician Payment Review Commission (PPRC). Report on non-physician practitioners. Washington, DC (unpublished).

Oxford English Dictionary. (1990). R. E. Allen (Ed.), Eighth Edition. New York: Oxford University Press.

Schweitzer, S. O., & Record, J. C. (1977). Third-party payments for new health professionals: An alternative to fractional reimbursement in outpatient care. *Public Health Report, 92,* 236–242.

Chapter 5

PHILOSOPHICAL AND HISTORICAL BASES OF PRIMARY CARE NURSING

Ellen D. Baer

SINCE the enactment of Medicare/Medicaid legislation and the growth of consumer's rights movements, the expansion of health services has placed the health care system in a bind. The supply and distribution of primary care physicians does not meet the demand for services. In addition, the services demanded are broader in scope than those contained within the domain of medicine prior to the 1960's. They now include supportive functions, such as counseling, once considered the province of multigenerational families, clergy, and the like. The nursing profession asserts that it possesses the history, organization, and educational facilities to provide knowledgeable and licensed individuals to meet the growing and broader demand for primary care. The major objection raised to the utilization of nurses in primary care roles comes from those in medicine, hospital administration, and government who believe that nurses do not have the expert knowledge, *authority* and its derivative, *autonomy*, on which primary practice rests.

Application of the principles of authority and autonomy to any human activity is problematic. In the context of the dynamic interactions of human experience, authority and autonomy fluctuate as do all processes that involve people. No one is always and absolutely autonomous, just as no one is completely devoid of autonomy. What is at issue is a continuum of authority and autonomy and the contextual boundaries of that continuum.

Nursing[1] as an occupational category is also problematic. In the generic sense, it encompasses multiple levels of philosophy, educational preparation, and practice that have developed over time as society's complexity increased. Because newer nursing educational and practice models did not totally replace earlier ones, and because nursing has resisted the mandatory university-based preparation that society recognizes as legitimating all other professions, multiple nursing levels exist. These levels, by definition and quasi-design, occupy different positions on the continuum of authority and autonomy, and their differences are not clear to the public. Organized nursing's inability to enforce stated desired educational levels for beginning or advanced nursing practice understandably raises questions about its ability to assure the practice quality of yet another kind of nurse. However, although variations in the education of nurses seeking to practice in primary care exist, by the mid 1990s almost all nurse practitioners (NPs) will be Master's-prepared, and the ANA certification examinations will require Master's preparation. Therefore, the focus of this chapter is the nurse who received initial professional preparation at the baccalaureate or higher degree level, and additional specific graduate education to be a primary care provider or to engage in independent nursing practice, which rests on the same authoritative base as does primary care, but is specified as a nursing practice.

Within the limits so described, this chapter will discuss some philosophical issues raised by nursing's assertion of its role in providing primary health care. The discussion will support appropriately prepared nurses practicing in primary care roles.

Definition of Primary Care

Drawing on Federal guidelines, primary care has been defined as including:

> either or both of two components: (a) the care the patient/client receives at the point of contact with the Health Care Delivery System, and (b) the continued care of the individual as an ambulatory patient/client. The continued care is two-dimensional: (a) the identification, management and/or referral of the health problems; and (b) the maintenance of the patient/client's health when symptomatic illness is not apparent, by means of preventive and promotive health care actions.[2]

Expanded commentary suggests that the application of the primary care role is made by the:

> generalist who is well prepared to deal with commonly occurring prob-
> lems, referring on those patients requiring the knowledge and skills of the
> specialist. . . . [the generalist] scope of practice tends to be broad since
> they serve as entry points and the locus of contact with the health care
> system [for both sexes and all ages, and] . . . includes psychosocial as well
> as physiological dimensions of care.[3]

These definitions will serve as reference points for the discussion of philosophical issues in this chapter. The definitions suggest three general, fundamental assumptions regarding the primary care role: (1) It is not specific to any one health profession; (2) it is not limited as to population served, health problems encountered, or duration of practitioner-client relationship; and (3) it requires from its practitioners independent and autonomous decision making based on professional knowledge.[4] It is this third assumption that causes the major delays and dilemmas encountered by nursing when it attempts to assume the primary health care role.

Despite some model legislation,[5] nursing has most commonly been defined legally as a dependent practice that delivers health care services under the supervision of a duly authorized physician or dentist. As the demand for primary care service expands, many institutions have inaugurated solutions in which nurses, under titles such as nurse practitioner, act in primary care roles, but operate under a system of protocols designed in advance in conjunction with physicians. Such compromises cloud the autonomy issue, because protocols are external constraints that suggest the inability of the nurse to choose correctly among "alternative possibilities of action . . . in accordance with [appropriate] inner motives and ideals."[6] Protocols merely extend the distance between the nurse in practice and the physician in supervision. They act essentially as "standing" or "PRN" orders, and implicitly reinforce the dependent model of practice for nursing.

As is prescribed by Freund in this volume (Chapter 4) there is no dispute that nurses have the requisite knowledge and training to provide quality primary care services. The central issues blocking widespread use of appropriately prepared and truly autonomous nurses to meet people's primary health care needs are political. They are hidden behind protests of whether or not nursing is a true profession, capable of safely caring for patients in an independent manner. This chapter will address both the stated and the hidden issues.

Autonomy, Authority, and Nursing Knowledge

Independent, autonomous practice rests on the assumption that the agent of such a practice has the expertise from which that agent derives the authority to act.[7] In the case of autonomous practice, this reliance on authority is essential to the protection of citizens in situations where knowledge is utilized about which the lay consumer has little understanding.

There is a substantial body of literature that discusses the notion of authority.[8] Issues of power, morality, the consent of the subject, the limits to authority, and the interactions among the concepts of authority, reason and freedom form the core of centuries of philosophical debate that cannot be addressed adequately in this chapter. The piece of the debate that seems most relevant to this chapter is that which addresses the legitimacy of authority: that is, how an individual or group justifies its claim to an authoritative position on certain bodies of knowledge, and the behaviors or actions that derive from that legitimating base. Sociologist Max Weber's conceptual base will be utilized in this chapter to clarify nursing's authority.

Weber described three basic legitimating models for the construct authority: legal, charismatic, and traditional for legal authority, "the legitimacy of the powerholder to give commands rests upon rules that are rationally established by enactment, by agreement, or by imposition."[9] For charismatic authority, the legitimacy of the powerholder rests on "an *extraordinary* quality of a person, regardless of whether this quality is actual, alleged, or presumed."[10] This personal model has been exemplified by "the prophet with the mark of grace" and has its basis in theological experience.[11] Finally, for traditional authority, the legitimacy of the powerholder rests on "the psychic attitude-set for the habitual workaday and . . . the belief in the everyday routine as an inviolable norm of conduct."[12] This basis of authority rests on the principle that certain authority has always existed, or is alleged or presumed to have always existed. The most important example of this model is patriarchy.

Medicine possesses an authority aura that encompasses all three types described, while nursing's authority base is less broad. Nursing is recognized as having legal and traditional authority to a point. It has charismatic figures such as Nightingale, Dock, Wald, and Sanger, but its overall aura is not charismatic in the same life saving, dramatic sense that characterizes the aura of medical practice.[13]

When nursing asserts its right to occupy the primary health care role which is more obviously occupied by medicine, it invites comparisons to medicine in the extent of its authority to act in that role. In that comparison, in the context of the previously described types, nursing is seen as having less authority. But that is a false issue. In comparison to medicine, every profession is seen as having less authority. The important question is: does nursing have appropriate, or sufficient, authority to act in the primary health care role? Returning to the definition, the foci of the primary care role are: (1) providing care to clients at the point of entry to the system, and/or providing continuing care to clients of all ages and both sexes; (2) delivering health maintenance and promotional services to the well; (3) managing the commonly occurring problems and referring appropriately to specialists when symptoms of illness appear; and (4) including psychosocial as well as physical care.

These health care goals have been part of modern nursing since its Nightingale origins. At the 1893 World's Fair, Nightingale's paper described "Sick nursing and health nursing . . . nursing proper is . . . to help the patient suffering from disease to live—just as health nursing is to keep or put the constitution of the healthy child or human being in such a state as to have no disease."[14] At the same meeting, Isabel Hampton (later Robb) spoke of the nurse's "three-fold interest in her work—an intellectual interest in the case, a (much higher) hearty interest in the patient, a technical (practical) interest in the patient's care and cure."[15] Nightingale's focus on environmental conditions, and their manipulation to ensure health, was responsible for her legendary work as a reformer of England's sanitation laws. Nurses were defined as the "ministers of health" who were "not only caring for the sick, but teaching the principles of cleanliness, ventilation and economy" to their patients and the families of patients.[16] The district nurse of nineteenth-century England and the visiting nurse of early twentieth-century America clearly provided primary care services to underserved populations.

The same objectives characterize certain current standards of collegiate nursing education and state Nurse Practice Acts.[17] Therefore, the stated foci of the primary care role have historical, educational, and legal bases in nursing practice, and are substantiated as within the context of nursing's legal and traditional authority. The question, then, must lie not with the existence of nursing authority, but with people's recognition of that authority.

A distinction is drawn between de facto and de jure authority: "de jure presumes a set of rules, according to which certain persons are competent (authorized) to do certain things, but not to do other things. . ." De facto, on the other hand, exists when one person *"recognizes* [sic] another as *entitled* [sic] to command him."[18]

Medicine and nursing each possess elements of both de jure and de facto authority. What matters to the practice of each is the extent to which each is accepted by the public, and the point at which the practice of each profession is seen as reaching the limits of its authority. A general practice physician is not expected to perform neurosurgery, but would be considered competent to suture a small wound. Nurses in primary care pose a similar dilemma. In the primary care role, nurses are seen as pushing the perimeter between the professions of medicine and nursing. Sociologist William Goode described this process as "encroachment," whereby "a new occupation claims the right to solve a problem which formerly was solved by another." The claim of the new group is interpreted by the old as an "accusation of incompetence, and the outraged counteraccusation is, of course, 'encroachment'."[19]

Nursing's reasons for its primary care interests should be effective in defusing the "accusative" nature of its claim to the role. Historically, nursing has essentially always occupied this role. Currently, it is identifying the role more clearly because: (1) Nurses now know better how to assert their rights and claims, and they must make overt those practices that have been covert for generations of the "doctor-nurse game"; (2) Nurses have the expertise to meet the expanding health care needs of society in the face of the declining numbers, not the incompetence, of primary care physicians; (3) Primary care practice presents nursing's qualified members with practice roles more consistent with their rigorous preparation; and (4) By providing a competitive delivery system, nurses can help contain the costs of primary care.[20]

The restrictions on nursing's de facto authority derive largely from the public's lack of knowledge about what nursing is, what nurses know, do, and are capable of doing. Nurses' expanded educational preparation, for example the requirement of a master's degree for advanced practice, their research-based knowledge, and their highly sophisticated practice roles are not generally recognized by the public, which still thinks of nurses in the bedside, maternal, handmaiden role of a much simpler era. Development of expert authority occurs interactionally between the group needing a service and the group providing that service. Medicine has been the group recognized as interacting with society's need for primary care. Nursing's role has been seen as necessary, but as secondary and dependent, not primary and independent. When educated nurses present themselves as a group prepared to fill the gap in primary health care services, cognitive dissonance may occur for those who have older views of nursing. A new group without nursing's historical image might have less difficulty occupying the role, but would lack the trust that nurses have earned from the public. The term "Nurse Practitioner" has been successful because it manages to keep the nurse-trust component, yet simultaneously presents a new image for nurses in new roles.

Accountability Operationalizes Authority

One way to demonstrate authority is through accountability.[21] One cannot, in justice, be held answerable for behaviors, actions, and events over which one has no authority or control or for which one is not responsible.[22] Therefore, nursing is documenting its perceived areas of accountability through conceptual model development, nursing diagnosis taxonomies, quality assurance programs, nursing audits, outcome criteria measurement, and legal and legislative action.

These measures demonstrate some areas for which nurses accept accountability. They do not answer other questions regarding accountability, such as to whom one is accountable. When reference groups or issues conflict, to which is one accountable under which circumstances? Must one act counter to one's own beliefs in order to be accountable to the goals of a particular group for whom one is the service provider? Nurses often find themselves in conflicts of accountability. A model has been described[23] which helps to clarify conflictive accountability, based on one's definition of health care:

1. If health care is a commodity for sale in a hospital, the patient is a customer, the physician is an outside contractor, and the nurse is a "straight" employee with responsibility only to the institution and the immediate supervisor.
2. If health care is a series of medical cases, then the physician is the scientist in charge of the project, the hospital is a laboratory, and the nurse is a subproject participant or assistant who is accountable only to the physician.
3. If health care is seen as the patient's right to relief from pain or illness, and the hospital is the locus of that relief, then the nurse is accountable to the patient.
4. If health care is defined as promoting the general well-being of persons,

[T]he patient, nurse and physician form a triad around the single enterprise of furthering that patient's well-being. The patient is the focus, but is expected to . . . aid in his own recovery; the physician is primarily a scientist, oriented towards the body's disease; and the nurse is a completely different professional, holistically oriented toward the patient's entire growth as a person. . . . In this conception, the nurse cannot be accountable for her performance as a nurse to any but her own professional standards.[24]

Professional standards begin with the personal ethical system of the nurse as an individual. These standards develop in individuals in the context of their membership in many groups within the larger society. People are socialized culturally in various ways and carry those customs with them into other parts of their lives. Most nurses are women, their gender carries cultural demands for behavior that affects later, professional behavior. Many nurses are also members of groups that have varying experiences of child rearing, socioeconomics, national origin, education, and other factors that influence nurses before they begin the professional socialization process. In addition, each nurse is a member of a social system that legally defines accepted behavior of the nurse as a citizen, resident, and nurse.

The nature of accountability, therefore, is multileveled and complex, and nursing's heterogeneity increases that complexity. The professional level on which nurses hold themselves accountable is most often the last area of accountability to develop. It may carry a weaker personal commitment when in competition with earlier developed senses of accountability; for example, women's accountability as mothers versus women's accountability as nurses. In addition, the nature of accountability changes over time in relationship to changes in the person, the society, and profession. For example, increased responsibility for patient care carries with it increased professional accountability, including increased legal accountability (see Eccord, Chapter 12). Conflicts among and between various aspects of accountability have been part of nursing since its earliest years, as this 1893 statement by Isabel Adams Hampton demonstrates:

> The superintendent of a training school is under a three-fold obligation: first to the hospital in which she works; secondly, to the patients who are entrusted to her care; and thirdly, to the women for whose education as nurses she is responsible.[25]

Though Hampton encouraged all persons connected with the hospital to "resolve that they will work harmoniously together . . . [that] justice may be done to all,"[26] the historical evidence is abundant that accountability to the hospital dominated the others. As times and gender customs have changed, nurses have become more aware of these conflicts, and more skillful in asserting their professional rights, but the conflicts still exist. A major source of such conflict is the difficulty in quantifying what nursing is and what nurses do in a system that relies heavily on quantifiable data. The essence of nursing—caring—defies measurement, and quality of life does not take precedence when survival is at stake, which is often the case of acute care settings. In primary care delivery circumstances, immediate survival threats are not as likely, which allows "care" and "quality of life" foci to take precedence.

Additionally, as the population ages, and increased numbers of people need supportive care for chronic illnesses and acquired immune deficiency syndrome (AIDS), nurses' broader range of practice is in greater demand.

Nursing as a Discipline

The major argument put forth by those who oppose independent nursing practice is that because nursing uses knowledge from the physical, behavioral, social, and biomedical sciences, it cannot be regarded as having its own unique, independent, and professional knowledge base. There is no question that nursing integrates knowledge from other disciplines. But nursing adds its own special knowledge to the gestalt, and applies it in practice in a manner uniquely its own. As a discipline, nursing's recurrent themes and concerns focus on the wholeness of people, the interaction between people and their environments, and nursing's management of people and environment to enhance comfort, quality of life, and general well being during, and beyond, illness.[27] In fact, and with irony, it must be noted that this very breadth of background is what makes nursing so clearly suited to the primary health care provider role. It is a breadth not possessed by any other health care delivery group because, though medicine also integrates knowledge from other fields, these fields are more limited to the biochemical and physical sciences. While the advances created in medicine by the merger of these sciences cannot be denied, concurrent losses of the supportive, caring functions of healing have been significant.[28] Though increased technology has also affected nursing, the supportive, caring functions of healing have continued to be central to nursing. Since doctoral preparation has become more common for nurses, and a corps of nurses have been prepared as researchers, rigorous scientific inquiry into the knowledge that validates nursing action has reduced the relevance and legitimacy of arguments raised against independent nursing practice (See Freund, Chapter 3). Such arguments must rest, then, not on concerns for science or authoritative knowledge, but on power considerations.

Power, Professionalism, and Nursing's Reluctance to Protest

A social process, professionalization, evolved at the end of the 19th century to organize knowledge growing out of the scientific and industrial revolutions. Professions developed as a means to protect uninformed citizens required to place their trust in expert authorities; they also controlled valued information and access to that information, which gave them power. Able to choose and socialize new members, the professions became regulating bodies for their practices and reference groups to which society addressed questions regarding certain areas of knowledge. New professions continue to emerge as technological advances created expert knowledge for those activities formerly conducted according to intuition or trial-and-error experience. Sociologists describe a continuum of professionalism on which occupations fall by virtue of the two primary characteristics of professions: the extent of their unique knowledge base and orientation to service.[29]

As the "new" professions emerge, the balance of power is disrupted, particularly between groups that share clients, content, and workplaces. The territorial protectiveness stimulated in the older group against the "encroachment" of the newer has already been identified. A new profession that provides a service to a client once "belonging" to another will derive income from and gain influence over that service and client. This economic and political threat is, not surprisingly, fought by the older group. The incongruity of this reaction by medicine to nursing as nurses enter primary care roles is, first, that most of what is changing is the overtness of nurses' activities, and second, that the physician practitioners being "threatened" are not those actually delivering the disputed service. Physicians are not providing primary care services in needy areas or in adequate numbers, but they do not want nurses to provide them either—probably because nursing is an independent profession, with a growing militancy in its refusal to be dominated by medicine. As a consequence, medicine created, and is supporting with its vast resources, physician-extender or assistant groups, through which it seeks to maintain control over services and clients without having to use its legitimate professional resources to do so. This creates another irony. Groups clearly labelled "assistant" are given legitimacy to act independently, and even to write orders that nurses are pressured to follow.

Such obvious maneuvering led this author toward class and gender interpretations of these power plays. The majority of medical practitioners are more affluent than their nursing counterparts, and constitute an elite, dominant group in American society. Medicine uses its greater economic and influential resources to lobby among legislators and consumers to protect its position. Because medicine is also predominantly male, while nursing is 97% female, sexism, as a societal and historical feature, contributes its piece to what is, in essence, a political struggle. Related to sexism, but derivative of a technologically worshipful society as well, are the different values attached to the two major functions of health care—care and cure. The nurturant, supportive behaviors fundamental to caring and nursing do not engage the American interest or value to the degree that the more instrumental technology of curing and medicine does. Nursing has only begun to address these concerns in the last decade. The complex social history of nursing suggests why political issues and activities have been avoided by nurses in prior eras.

Modern nursing emerged as an acceptable occupational alternative for women during the Victorian era. As single women, living away from their homes, earning salaries, and ministering to the bodily needs and functions of both sexes, usually strangers, nineteenth-century nurses were social revolutionaries who dared not breach too many more conventions for fear of losing their basic footholds. The notions of self-effacement, deference, hours of toil for small wages, and political reticence, which began as sociopolitical necessities to establish the work in one generation, became habits and customs associated with, ascribed to, and even required of nursing in subsequent generations. With the rise of science and the professionalization of knowledge at the turn of the twentieth century, certain individuals and groups of nurses became more politically aware and active. But the majority of nurses avoided issues like sexism, power, and politics.

Nursing, as a group, did not support the Nineteenth Amendment (for women's suffrage) in the early 1900s, equivocated on civil rights in the 1960s, and only belatedly and half heartedly backed the Equal Rights Amendment of the 1980s. Despite their large numbers that could have exerted noticeable pressure, nurses' reticent behavior cost them the reciprocal support of other disadvantage groups—women, African-Americans, even health care consumers—who might have added strength to nursing's political muscle. Isolated in a "Little World of our Own,"[30] and often divided amongst themselves as to the best action for nursing to take, nurses have not been effective advocates for their own positions.

Some women's groups, attempting to confront sexism in the professions, recommend increasing the number of the underrepresented sex, such as increasing the number of men in nursing and women in medicine. But that is a false solution and has not worked in nursing. It is the underlying attitude that must change, such as increasing the acceptance of assertiveness in nurses and nurturance in physicians. Otherwise, the stereotypes of relative dominance, achievement, independence, and power remain intact, and the traditionally male, white, elite choices continue to be the more desirable ones.

The negative effect of stereotype-driven choices is confounding in multiple ways. Some women who enter the more prestigious field of medicine experience conflict and disillusionment when they discover that physicians do not spend as much time with patients as they had expected. These young physicians who desire to be supportive and nurturant of their clients may be discouraged and even denigrated. Simultaneously, nursing suffers the loss to its ranks of well-qualified and highly motivated women. Similarly, men who enter the more nurturing field of nursing may experience social and economic discrimination. Society is the ultimate loser in this chain of events.

Conclusions and Suggested Actions

The question central to this chapter has been: Does nursing have the appropriate authority to act in the primary health care provider role? The evidence presented supports the conclusion that it does—within the context of specific educational preparation for specific nurses, legal sanction by legislative bodies, and public recognition by consumers of health services. Through these three mechanisms, the primary practice role for nurses will be advanced.

Organized nursing must establish specific educational programs and certification criteria on a national basis. A baccalaureate degree to enter general professional nursing practice and master's degree preparation for specialization in areas like primary care is essential. Nursing must discriminate among its own levels of preparation and practice in ways that are standard in all other disciplines.

The extension of legislative activity that would permit such practice by properly prepared nurses is necessary in all states. This may necessitate legal encounters that challenge existing restrictions, and it will require some nurses to allow other nurses to earn a different status. Having asserted that some of its members possess specific, independent expertise, nurses cannot then insist that all nurses gain the benefit of that expertise, nor can they hide behind physicians when the outcomes of their actions are challenged. In fact, if nurses seek the status of professionals, they must insist on being held accountable for the appropriateness of their actions on all levels.

Public education that alerts consumers to health issues is a well-used and demonstrably successful strategy in the United States. Similar strategies can be employed to familiarize the public with the importance of nursing in health care, and the specific nursing services available in primary care. Probably most important, nurses must demonstrate the positive health care outcomes and economic value of their practice, and then publicize those results for legislators and consumers through sophisticated use of the media.

Nurses' contributions must be acknowledged, even promoted. How many people know that Margaret Sanger was a nurse; that the current head of Planned Parenthood is a nurse (Pamela Maraldo); that the

Henry Street Settlement was started by a nurse (Lillian Wald); that the first president of the National Organization for Women was a nurse (Wilma S. Heide); that nurses run major government agencies and control 100 million dollar budgets in medical centers? We have allowed the nurse who moves out of the dependent model to cease to be identified as a nurse, thereby tacitly reinforcing the public image we now deplore.

A major concern expressed by some nurses who oppose primary care practice by nurses is fear of loss of the nursing role and identity. This is a worthy consideration. Some nurses who enter primary care practice become seduced by the power of the stethoscope to provide instant status. This misuse of the model must not be permitted. A stethoscope is only a tool, as is a pencil or a thermometer, with which competent data can be collected and the nursing process activated. The best reason for nurses to provide primary care is because they are nurses. Nursing's focus on people; its blend of medical, behavioral, and social science expertise; and its commitment to caring, teaching, counseling, and supporting patients are the characteristics of nursing that make nurses so uniquely qualified to provide primary health care services.

NOTES

1. Assumed throughout this chapter is the ANA definition of nursing as "the diagnosis and treatment of human responses to actual or potential health problems."

2. *ANA Guidelines for Short-Term Continuing Education Programs Preparing Adult and Family Nurse Practitioners* (Kansas City: American Nurses Association, 1975).

3. Linda H. Aiken, "Primary Care: The Challenge for Nursing," in Norma L. Chaska (Ed.), *The Nursing Profession: Views Through the Mist* (New York: Mc-Graw-Hill, 1978), p. 248.

4. Dagobert D. Runes, *The Dictionary of Philosophy* (New York: Philosophical Library, 1942), p. 29, defines autonomy as "freedom consisting in self-determination and independence of all external constraint."

5. New York State Education Law, Article 139—Nursing, amended Subsection 6902 in 1990 to include within the definition of nursing a subtext on nurse practitioner practice "in collaboration with a licensed physician" whereby nurse practitioners can diagnose illness and physical conditions, perform corrective and therapeutic measures, and prescribe drugs, devices and immunizing agents. However, the relationship with a physician must be written and is tightly bound. Additionally, the educational preparation of the nurse practitioner is "certificate" based rather than university mandated.

6. Runes, *op. cit.*, p. 112.

7. Stanley I. Benn, "Authority," in *The Encyclopedia of Philosophy*, Paul Edwards (Ed.), Vol. I (New York: Macmillan and the Free Press, 1967), p. 215, defines authority as meaning: "to possess expert knowledge and therefore the right to be listened to." Further, "The authority of the expert . . . involves the notion of someone qualified to speak. It presumes standards by which expertise is expressed and recognized, for example, degrees or professional reputation."

8. Ibid, pp. 215–217 briefly reports on this literature.

9. *From Max Weber: Essays in Sociology*, translated, edited, and with an introduction by H. H. Gerth and C. Wright Mills (New York: Oxford University Press, 1946, 1958), p. 294.

10. Ibid, p. 295.

11. Benn, *op. cit.*, p. 216.

12. *From Max Weber*, op. cit., p. 296.

13. Magali Sarfatti Larson, *The Rise of Professionalism: A Sociological Analysis* (Berkeley: University of California Press, 1977). On p. 31, the author asserts that occupational tasks that are more familiar in ordinary life have less magical allure, and therefore seem to require less expertise.

14. Florence Nightingale, "Sick Nursing and Health Nursing." In *Hospitals, Dispensaries and Nursing*, Papers and Discussions in the International Congress of Charities, Correction and Philanthropy, Section III, Chicago, June 12th to 17th, 1893, Under the Auspices of the World's Congress Auxiliary of the World's Columbia Exposition, John S. Billings, M.D., and Henry M. Hurd, M.D. (Eds.), (Baltimore: the Johns Hopkins Press, 1894), p. 446.

15. Isabel A. Hampton (1949), Educational Standards for nurses. In L. Petry (Ed.), *Nursing of the Sick 1893 papers and discussions from the International Congress of Charities, Correction and Philanthropy, Chicago, 1893. Published under the sponsorship of the National League of Nursing Education* (pp. 1–11). New York: McGraw-Hill.

16. Irene Sutliffe, "The History of American Training Schools." In Billings and Hurd, op. cit., p. 511.

17. For an example of educational standards, see the University of Pennsylvania School of Nursing Statement of Philosophy and Conceptual Framework: "The faculty believes that nursing is an autonomous profession whose focus is caring for persons throughout the life cycle during periods of wellness and illness" and specifies nursing actions in health maintenance, promotion, and teaching as well as therapeutic interventions. For an example of Nurse Practice Acts, see New York's Education Law, Section 6902 as amended in 1990: "The practice of the profession of nursing as a registered professional nurse is defined as diagnosing and treating human responses to actual and potential health problems through such services as case-finding, health teaching, health counseling, and provision of care supportive to or restorative of life and well-being, and executing medical regimens prescribed by a licensed physician, dentist or other licensed health care provider legally authorized under this title and in accordance with the commissioner's regulations. A nursing regimen shall be consistent with and shall not vary any existing medical regimen." Note that while

execution of the medical regimen requires medical prescription, other nursing acts do not. See footnote 5 for nurse practitioner definitions in the same act.

18. Benn, op. cit., p. 215.

19. William J. Goode, "Encroachment, Charlatanism and the Emerging Professions: Psychology, Sociology and Medicine," *American Sociological Review* 25(1960), p. 902.

20. Claire M. Fagin, "Nursing's Value Proves Itself," *The American Journal of Nursing* 90 (October 1990), pp. 17–30. See also Claire M. Fagin, "Nursing as an Alternative to High-Cost Health Care," *The American Journal of Nursing* 82 (January 1982), pp. 56–60. See also, Monica Wolcott Choi, "Nurses as Co-providers of Primary Health Care," *Nursing Outlook* 29 (September 1981), p. 521.

21. Leon M. Lessinger (1971). Accountability and Humanism in L. M. Lessinger and R. W. Tyler (Eds.), *Accountability in Education* (pp. 3–20). Worthington, OH: Charles A. Jones Publishing Co., p. 29, defined accountability as meaning: "that an agent . . . [agrees] to perform a service [and] will be held answerable for performing according to agreed-upon terms, within an established time period and with a stipulated use of resources and performance standards."

22. Richard D. Adkins, "Reponsibility and Authority Must Match in Nursing Management," *Hospitals* 53:3 (February 1, 1979), pp. 69–71.

23. Lisa H. Newton, "To Whom is the Nurse Accountable? A Philosophical Perspective," *Connecticut Medicine Supplement* 43 (October 1979), pp. 7–9. Presented with permission of the author and the journal.

24. Ibid, p. 9.

25. Isabel Adams Hampton (later Robb), *Nursing: Its Principles and Practice for Hospital and Private Use* (Philadelphia: Saunders, 1893), p. 17.

26. Ibid.

27. Sue K. Donaldson and Dorothy M. Crowley, "The Discipline of Nursing," *Nursing Outlook* 26 (February 1978), p. 113: "A discipline . . . is characterized by a unique perspective, a distinct way of viewing all phenomena, which ultimately defines the limits and nature of its inquiry."

28. Edmund D. Pellegrino, "The Sociocultural Impact of Twentieth Century Therapeutics," in *The Therapeutic Revolution: Essays in the Social History of American Medicine*, Morris J. Vogel and Charles E. Rosenberg (Eds.), (Philadelphia: University of Pennsylvania Press, 1979), p. 262, identifies the "discontent with medicine today" as related to conflict between ideals of technology and "the Aesculapian physician."

29. Everett C. Hughes, "Professions," *Daedalus* 92 (1963); William J. Goode, "Community within a Community: The Professions," *American Sociological Review* 22 (April 1957), pp. 194–200. William J. Goode, "Encroachment, Charlatanism and the Emerging Professions: Psychology, Sociology and Medicine," op. cit.

30. Nancy Tomes, "'Little World of Our Own:' The Pennsylvania Hospital Training School for Nurses, 1895–1907," *Journal of the History of Medicine and Allied Sciences* 33(1978), pp. 507–530.

PART II

THE PRACTICE ARENA

Chapter 6

CAMEOS

Joan E. Lynaugh, Barbara Medoff-Cooper,
Ann L. O'Sullivan, Henry L. Barnett,
Marianne Warguska Reilly, Elizabeth A. Kuehne,
Jo Anne Staats, Jane Kimmerer Butler, William Kavesh

INTRODUCTION—THE PRACTICE PARADIGM

Joan E. Lynaugh

"Practitioner . . . one qualified by practice . . . a person who practices a profession, art. . . ." (Webster's New World Dictionary, 1982). Not much help to be found there when trying to understand species *practitioner* of genus *nurse*, that is, nurse practitioner. Perhaps that is because a practitioner can be truly defined only by being and doing.

The "cameos" in this chapter provide explicit examples of current nursing practitioner practice. It is helpful, in reading these first-hand experiences, to examine the role of the nurse practitioner using a three-part analysis. First, and most important, is the encounter between nurse and patient. What counts in clinical nursing is what happens there. Second, using the care encounter as a framework, the relevance and com-

119

petence of nurse practitioners in primary health will be discussed. Finally, there will be a look at the nurse practitioner in his or her practice environment with its various conflicts and opportunities.

THE ENCOUNTER

Nursing cannot be practiced at a distance; access to patients and time alone with patients are both essential. Thus, the simplest and most fundamental aspect of the nurse practitioner movement of 25 years ago was the establishment of nursing control over some of the time people devote to the care of their health. Time alone with patients in an office with the door closed was a novelty to nurses in ambulatory care, even though their colleagues, community health nurses, always enjoyed the care opportunity inherent in their visits in their patients' homes. For patients visiting offices or clinics, however, nursing care was bound to remain peripheral, until the care giving system allowed ambulatory patients and their nurses planned time together. What goes on in these encounters? An ideal encounter between nurse and patient includes at least six elements:

1. The nurse discovers and addresses the need or problem that the patient hoped to solve by seeking health care.
2. The patient tells or shows the nurse what the nurse needs to know in order to understand the patient's situation.
3. The nurse tells or shows the patient what the patient needs to know in order to understand the situation as the nurse understands it.
4. A course of action is agreed upon by both parties.
5. The course of action is beneficial.
6. An effective transfer of trust and recognition occurs between both parties.

Let me illustrate with a case example. Mrs. H refers herself to see a nurse practicing in a hospital-based general care clinic. Mrs. H chose the nurse because her husband (Mr. H) was already receiving care from that particular nurse and she found the setting and practitioner familiar and relatively convenient.

Mrs. H wants a general check-up because she is feeling fatigued and because "there is a lot of heart disease in my family." She is 50 years old and feels that now is the time she should be getting some advice about her health.

The nurse practitioner and Mrs. H sit down together to review Mrs. H's current health, her past health, her family's health, her social situation, and her reasons for seeking professional care at this time. Then the nurse examines Mrs. H, following the traditional head-to-toe format of the physical examination. Next, if appropriate, Mrs. H and the nurse agree to some routine laboratory studies, such as urinalysis, blood work, or an electrocardiogram.

What is happening here is part of an implicit, occasionally explicit, negotiation between two persons; one person seeks help and the other offers it. These people are strangers to one another, yet they will try to establish a trusting relationship. As in all negotiations, each party comes to the meeting with an agenda. In a care encounter such as this, the agendas of the nurse and patient will probably be only partially revealed to each other. Of the two, perhaps the nurse's agenda is the more predictable.

Since the nurse is interested in the life processes, well being, and optimal functioning of human beings, he or she will try to compare Mrs. H's situation with some concept of health that seems clinically useful. Does Mrs. H present any overt or covert indications of dysfunction or disease? Is she in any other kind of trouble? Does she need to know something about herself or her situation that she does not know that will help her stay well or improve her health? As the nurse analyzes Mrs. H's situation, he or she will make a number of diagnoses (one could substitute the word *hypotheses*), any one of which could come not only under the rubric of nursing but also of medicine, social work, education, or theology.

Mrs. H, on the other hand, may well have a more subtle agenda. Since she sought this encounter with a health care professional, she might safely be assumed to be concerned about some aspect of her health. But whether her objectives for this encounter match those of the nurse is something they both must discover. Personal and social problems beyond the nurse's scope of practice are presented by patients. It is crucial that Mrs. H reveal her real reason for seeking care early in the encounter.

An ideal encounter demands excellent verbal and nonverbal communication, a shared goal of decisionmaking, and some degree of trust on both sides. Since the nurse is the professional in the situation, he or she has the burden of creating this ideal encounter.

From the nurse's viewpoint, the most critical first step is to find out, in detail, the story of the problem that concerns the patient. Two obstacles invariably crop up here. One is the requirement of listening and withholding judgment. The second is the problem of taking time. Listening carefully will help both participants identify the real reason which prompted the patient's visit. Problems that interest the nurse can be dealt with, of course, but unless they are urgent they should not take precedence over those that brought the patient to the nurse. Once the story is fully shared, an appropriate examination should be done. The physical examination provides useful clinical information often vital to a correct hypothesis; importantly, in the context of this discussion, the examination reduces the distance between two persons, allows the nurse to touch the patient, and validates for the patient the nurse's competency, concern, and interest.

Only when the patient's story is fully heard and the examination is finished should the nurse explain his or her findings and beliefs about the patient's problem. The discussion should include the nurse's perspective on what is and what is not occurring.

For the patient to understand the situation as the nurse understands it, the patient needs to know what significant hypotheses the nurse has rejected. It is entirely likely that the patient has already thought of the most frightening possibilities and will need clarification before proceeding to the next step.

This is the negotiation of a plan of care. The plan may be simple or complex; it may involve more data collection, treatment, referral, or education. Whatever it is, it must be consistent with the objectives of both parties in the encounter.

Numerous constraints limit achievement of the ideal nurse-patient encounter. One major limitation is the knowledge gap between the two parties. The nurse has a conceptual grasp of biophysical and psychological knowledge shared by few patients. Some patients lack the ability to absorb new information and apply it to themselves. On the other hand, the patient has social and cultural knowledge that may be entirely outside the experience of the nurse, but crucial to problem identification and the plan of care. Finally, no transfer of knowledge between two persons is absolutely complete, forcing both participants to operate on incomplete data.

There are social and attitudinal constraints as well. Some patients, frequently those of lower income, different language group, or minority status, may feel intimidated by the nurse, the care setting, or the whole situation. If patients feel powerless, it is substantially harder for them to participate effectively in any negotiation. Some patients and professionals may believe that the professional knows best what the problem is, what the patient fears, and so on. This yearning for caretaking omnipotence is likely to be ungratified. Unmet expectations will lead to unhappiness on both sides. Shared responsibility in decisionmaking requires shared power. As is evident in several of the "cameos," often the nurse must deliberately give the patient decisionmaking power to create more parity in the relationship.

Both nurse and patient must deal with uncertainty and ambiguity in most primary health care situations where clear cut, correct approaches are rare. Mutual participation in care planning is crucial to long-term success. Still, patients have a right to expect an informed and clear opinion. It is an abrogation of responsibility to abandon a patient to his or her own uninformed judgment. The nurse is required to share knowledge, to teach, to persuade, and to "help others do what they would do for themselves if they had the skill, energy, or will" (Diers, 1982, p. 12).

What is at stake in a care giving encounter is the right of the patient to his or her own personal liberty—a natural and inalienable right in Western culture. The task of the nurse practitioner is to recognize this right while at the same time fulfilling the professional obligation to do no harm.

To place this task in perspective, both in its simplicity and its complexity, it is helpful to review the two functions of what is now called *primary health care.* First the primary health caregiver is the initial contact with the health care system. Second, he or she helps patients over a continuum of care: maintenance of health, evaluation and management of common health problems, and referral to other health care professionals and agencies.

ENVIRONMENT FOR PRACTICE

Primary care nurse practitioners work in outpatient clinics, health maintenance organizations, neighborhood health clinics, long-term care facilities, occupational health, schools, homecare, private practice, and public health agencies. A common thread underlying their various practice environments is that most nurse practitioners care for patients who are complex and have a range of chronic illnesses. The first-hand experiences in the following "cameos" depict nurse practitioners working with people with AIDS, children at home with high tech needs, teenage mothers and children, and the frail elderly in nursing homes. A significant number practice in foreign countries, thereby participating in the world wide emphasis on primary health care for all people.

As is reflected in the "cameos," four major influences affect the practice environments of these practitioners: time and money; physician relationships; and recognized need for their services. With the exception of private duty, nurses in the past rarely dealt directly with any of these issues, because most were employed in relatively large bureaucratic organizations. In contrast to hospitals, the primary care practice environment is influenced by serial one-on-one relationships, direct trade of units of time for money, and broad and open-ended accountability to consumers. Now that the nurse practitioner is recognized as a significant provider of primary care, these environmental issues loom larger.

Trading time for money implies that professional time used to diagnose, advise, teach, or treat can be assigned a price. Nurses are learning that time is the unit by which they measure productivity; we are also discovering that to measure out exemplary nursing within a 20-minute visit is difficult, and sometimes impossible. The key to reducing the dilemma is to apportion realistically the number and length of visits, taking into consideration the predictable care needs of one's patient population. Similarly, a realistic price must be attached to caregiving time. It has often been said that no one makes any money doing primary care; this truism holds because primary care involves little technology and Americans have long been more willing to pay for X-rays than for advice. Nevertheless, nurses must be reimbursed adequately to maintain themselves and their share of the practice overhead, or they will not survive professionally. Any care system, as noted by Rogers (1977), must be able to reward its practitioners and attract new ones.

This simple premise underlies the current drive to obtain direct third-party insurance or insurance reimbursement for nurses providing primary care. To the extent that this goal continues to be achieved, nurses will be able to fulfill their commitment to the public.

Relationships between nurses and physicians span the century since nursing came on the American scene in the 1880s, and are characterized by a mix of interdisciplinary struggle and mutual support (Lynaugh, 1988). This ambivalence persists among nurses and physicians practicing in primary care today.

The evolution of the nurse practitioner concept in primary care was characterized by innovation and cooperation between nurses and physicians; Ford and Silver (Silver, 1968), Lewis and Resnick (1967), and Andrews and Yankauer (Yankauer & Sullivan, 1982) are examples of but a few of those pioneer teams. An interdisciplinary effort to integrate medical and nursing practice developed, inspired by a common goal of improving health care to Americans. The complementary functions of medicine and nursing were stressed in recognition of the fact that many patient needs in primary care settings fell well within the realm of nursing (Mechanic & Aiken, 1982). When personal care, counseling, support, and educative interests of nurses were meshed with the diagnostic and therapeutic interests of physicians, it became clear, not surprisingly, that the majority of patients in primary care could be fully cared for by nurses most of the time. Within a relatively short time (between 1965 and 1975) worries about the competence of nurses and patient acceptance disappeared from the literature (Prescott & Driscoll, 1978).

Other problems remain, however. There is clear competition between nurses and physicians in those instances where they cannot organize to share patients. Physicians who aspire to support themselves by seeing the 80 percent of primary care patients that could be cared for by nurses will try to prevent nurses from practicing. An equitable adjustment in reimbursement practices to give nurses access to the third-party dollar will put this competition on a fair footing. It is crucial to resolve this issue because a truly effective primary care system rests on the availability of both excellent nursing care and excellent medical care to all the people. Nurses and physicians must not neglect their social obligation to give care because of distractions stemming from territorial infighting. The blurred line between medical practice and nursing practice is always shifting—always being renegotiated. The advent of the nurse practitioner, like that of the nurse midwife and the nurse anesthetist, is a visible sign that conditions in health care are again changing.

To really understand the phenomenon that is the nurse practitioner, it may be necessary to remind ourselves that all professionals exist at the bidding of the society that supports them. Nurse practitioners exist because someone was needed to provide services to children, to the chronically ill, to the aged, and to the sick poor.

The demand for nursing services in primary care must be continually reevaluated. Currently there is a modest demand for personal health maintenance and educational services, in contrast with the incessant demand for caretakers for the chronically ill and the aged (Mezey & Lynaugh, 1991). Some nurses feel that the care of the sick in primary care is the responsibility of physicians, and that when nurses assume that care they are using a medical model. Alternatively, we know that the definition of nursing is to substitute for those things the person *cannot* do for himself or herself, which makes the primary care arena the perfect place to practice the full scope of our discipline. We must be careful not to limit our services to those things people *can* do for themselves in our effort to proclaim a unique function. Primary care nursing practice is whatever nurses and patients agree that it is; it is created during the basic encounter outlined above.

This chapter began with a definition of "practitioner" and has developed around that species of nurse. But in all likelihood, the transitional form we call nurse practitioner is just that—a transition, likely to disappear in a decade or so.

In retrospect, there was a certain inevitability in it all. Improve the education of nurses, remove other sources of general care from families (extended family, church, neighbors, family doctor), stir in a sense of affluence, add a demonstration or two of what nurses could do, and in no time we had a nurse practitioner movement. That the nurse practitioner and his or her primary care medical colleagues remained on the edge of nursing (and the edge of medicine) for a few years is evidence that, no matter how inevitable, change is resisted when it disrupts the existing order.

These days it is quite uncommon for nurse practitioners to be verbally attacked as they once were, as traitors to nursing. With acceptance has come assimilation and change. Nurse practitioners are better prepared and more clear concerning their function; the schools where nurse practitioners now teach and practice are changed by the experience. The accountable, patient-centered, clinically focused attitude of the nurse practitioner influences curriculum and faculty values. The conceptual stimulation and research opportunity afforded by full faculty status has strengthened and improved the basis for primary care nursing practice.

So why should the nurse practitioner disappear? Because the knowledge, skills, attitudes, and values of the nurse practitioner form of practice as refined in primary care will become (or are becoming) the norm for advanced nursing practice at the master's level. If nursing is primary care, as Claire Fagin announced in 1978 (Fagin, 1978), then obviously some predictable, consistent level of ability to care for patients must span graduate preparation. And, increasingly, that is just what is happening.

In many senses, though the analogy is by no means perfect, the nurse practitioner movement is like the trained nurse movement of the 1880s or the visiting nurse movement of the turn of the century. When an opportunity appears, for example, a public desire for hospital care, a social need to help the poor in their homes, or a demand for accessible health care, nurses respond. In the process, nursing and nurses are changed, and so is society. We are too close to this most recent change to see it in perspective, but the personal "voices" of practitioners in the "cameos" which follow provide a rich documentary of these responses. In all likelihood, by the year 2000 we will find the benefits outweighing the problems, and will wonder why it took so long for the practitioner to appear.

REFERENCES

Diers, D. (1982). Between science and humanity: Nursing reclaims its role. *Yale Alumnae Magazine & Journal, 65*, 8. March 82 Vol. XLV #5, p. 12.

Fagin, C. (1978). Primary care as an academic discipline. *Nursing Outlook, 26,* 750–753.

Lewis, C. E., & Resnick, B. (1967). Nurse clinics and progressive ambulatory patient care. *New England Journal of Medicine, 277,* 1236–38.

Lynaugh, J. (1988). Narrow passageways: Nurses and physicians in conflict and concert since 1875. *The physician as captain of the ship: A critical reappraisal.* Boston: D. Reidel.

Mechanic, D., & Aiken, L. (1982). A cooperative agenda for medicine and nursing. *New England Journal of Medicine, 307,* 747–780.

Mezey, M., & Lynaugh, J. (1991). Teaching nursing home program: A lesson in quality. *Geriatric Nursing, 12,* 76–77.

Prescott, P., & Driscoll, L. (1978). Issues in evaluation of nurse practitioner effectiveness: A review of physician nurse comparison studies. *Evaluating Health Professions, 2,* 387–418.

Rogers, D. (1977). The challenge of primary care. *Daedalus, 106,* 81–103.

Silver, H. K. (1968). Use of new types of allied health professionals in providing care for children. *American Journal of Diseases of Children,* 116:486.

Webster's New World Dictionary. (1982). New York: Simon and Schuster (p. 118).

Yankauer, A., & Sullivan, J. (1982). The new public health professionals: Three examples. *Annual Review of Public Health, 3,* 249–276.

PEDIATRIC GROUP PRACTICE

Barbara Medoff-Cooper

BACKGROUND

After graduating from a baccalaureate program in June of 1970, I worked on a pediatric unit for the summer. I was the first BSN graduate to work on this particular unit. All of the staff knew that I was entering a master's program in September, which increased the level of tension already felt by the staff toward someone from outside their diploma program and hospital. Most of my colleagues thought I was too concerned about the families and not about technical nursing skills. They could also not imagine why I wanted to go to graduate school.

When I completed my master's degree in nursing of children in January, 1972, the role of the clinical specialist did not seem to exist in the largest city near my home. I began calling all of the university-based hospitals with pediatric units. Finally, a nursing administrator from one of the two children's hospitals told me that a physician in the OPD was looking for nurses with at least a BSN. I was later to find out that the hospital had a Model Cities grant which included not only primary care for an indigent patient population, but also money to train 6 nurses to give primary care as pediatric nurse practitioner. Advanced nurse practice was much discussed in my master's program, but I was not sure how this concept could be integrated into the role of the practitioner. I was soon to find out that much of the role of the PNP was not very different than the work I did as a clinical specialist student in the pediatric outpatient department during my graduate student experience, except that I added more physical assessment and patient management skills to my newly acquired advanced nurse practice repertoire.

My PNP program was, of course, a certificate program, started in 1970 by a physician who had a vision that nurses could deliver care to a group of underserved patients that up to this point had never received any form of continuity in their care. The program was one year in length, and was registered with the American Academy of Pediatrics and the American Nurse's Association. This was an acceptable method of practitioner education in the early 1970s, as the two organizations set guidelines to help establish an educational program which met the approval of each group. The only other programs that were available at that time were Bunker Hill and Colorado. All participants in the class of six had at least a bachelors degree. I was the only one with a MS in pediatric nursing.

During the first six months the nurse practitioner students had classes together every morning and met two to three times a week with the medical students and residents. Classes were taught by house officers or attending physicians. The rest of the morning was spent in the outpatient department seeing patients with our preceptors, who were fellows or attendings. The assistant director of the outpatient department was responsible for our clinical learning experience. On some mornings we would make rounds on the floors to hear or see a particular medical problem presented which was related to the content we were receiving in the classroom. The afternoons were spent entirely with patients. During the last 6 months of the program. we began to build a practice and have more independence in clinical decisionmaking. We each had a caseload of 500 families, some of which we shared with a team of first-year residents. The families that were shared with the residents had a child with a chronic problem which was jointly managed by the PNP and the resident. In most situations the PNP saw the patient with the chronic illness and used the resident as a consultant for management issues. At the end of the year program we all completed an oral and written examination. We were then awarded a certificate, which allowed me to sit for the NAPNAP and ANA exam for formal certification as a PNP when these examinations became available in the mid-1970s.

PEDIATRIC NURSE PRACTITIONER

After completing the PNP program, I practiced at the same children's hospital for 2 1/2 years. Late in 1974, I left the hospital setting to join a private practice, with which I have been associated for the last 19 years, at first full-time and then after the first four years on a more limited basis.

This practice was the first practice in the state to employ a nurse practitioner, and continues to be one of the few to support the role. Prior to my joining the practice another nurse practitioner had been able to gain hospital privileges in the local community hospitals. It was virtually unheard of for a nurse to write on the physician order forms until the time that the PNP role was first accepted by the hospital medical boards. I was granted hospital rights, including visiting rights to see mothers and their infants, and to examine the infants in the newborn nursery. These privileges had come about after a long struggle, but fortunately, the conflict had been completed years before I arrived.

My practice is in a middle-class community surrounded by working-class neighborhoods, I see middle-class families and families who are college educated as well as families on medical assistance. The ages of the children range from newborns through college age students returning home. We discourage young adults from returning to our practice after graduation from college, but will see them until they find another care provider.

Every family in the practice has an option to see all of the care providers or to request to see only one individual for all well child visits. The scheduled sick visits are randomly assigned to the provider(s) not giving well child care. When I was full time, I would see most of the newly delivered mothers and their infants. It was a concerted effort on the office staff to schedule all 1 month-old infants with me for the first office visit. If a family was scheduled to see me, they would not routinely see any other provider unless I consulted with the physician for a particular concern. I was able to function fairly independently, seeing both well children as well as children with chronic illnesses.

A patient who has never seen a nurse practitioner is often confused about the role. After 19 years, I still hear the ambivalence in their voice about seeing a nurse instead of a doctor. Once a family has one appointment with me, there is seldom a time in which they will not schedule another future appointment with me. There are also mothers who feel I am appropriate to consult for certain childrearing issues, and would call me for all their health concerns. Despite their confidence in my advice, they still prefer seeing the pediatrician for the physical exam.

During the time that I was practicing full time, each day would start with hospital nursery rounds. This would give me the opportunity to do some initial anticipatory guidance for our new mothers. I would then return to the office for a phone hour, then begin seeing patients. Every Friday afternoon I would go to the local public health clinic with one of the physicians to provide primary care to children whose family could not afford private pediatric practice, but were not qualified for medical assistance.

On most days I would be scheduled for routine well visits beginning after my phone hour. Usually I was able to spend one half hour with each family, although occasionally I would see five families in two hours. Some of my responsibilities included routine primary care activities such as well baby visits, counseling adolescents about a variety of health or family issues, and even some family counseling to new mothers. Occasionally I was asked by community agencies to teach a class on some developmental issue such as newborn care, or child development during the first year of life.

In most cases, the pediatricians would refer all "difficult moms" to me. In the beginning years I saw most of the behavior and family problems, including children not doing well in school or families with some relational problem. In addition, I would do developmental screening on any child in the practice who was not reaching developmental milestones in a timely manner. In general, I saw most babies under a year of age every other visit, alternating with one of the pediatricians. There were also mothers who preferred to see me for all visits, which was perfectly acceptable.

As a primary care provider I was in contact with the larger community outside of the practice, such as school nurses and nurses in the hospital and community health settings. It is difficult at this point to remember the initial responses of these various nurses to my role. I do know that there certainly was some role confusion for them in the early years of my practice. Nurses in the hospital were not sure how to treat me. For example, after I examined a baby it was very natural for me to change the diaper, replace the shirt and rewrap the infant. The nurses were very uncomfortable with me doing these tasks. This was their task and not mine. Somehow I convinced them that I could not leave an infant undressed, and they needed to forgive me for my habits. Fortunately we were able to work out this role confusion through a lot of diplomacy. I always made an effort to include the nurses in my decisions concerning a plan for an individual infant. Slowly, they realized that I was treating them as a colleague, and trust was established.

In the community, I had contact with school nurses as well as the local Visiting Nurses Association. In many ways I believe that these nurses saw me as an advocate. This was true especially for the school nurse, who, more than any other nurse at this time, was working independently. I would often get calls from a school nurse for help with family about which she had some concerns. The community health nurses would also ask for my participation in newborn care classes, as well as a variety of other topics.

The mechanism for reimbursement has remained relatively unchanged over the years, except for the time I was a full-time employee, when I was paid a salary not unlike other primary care positions of the time. As a part time care provider, I am paid per patient, with the income generated from fee-for-service patients and by third-party reimbursements. There is a single fee for all office visits, and patients are charged this one fee irrespective of the provider. I am not paid for such services as phone consultations, or hallway discussion.

A REFLECTION OF PAST SUCCESSES AND ACCOMPLISHMENTS

As I look back on the past 20 years of practice as a primary care provider, I feel quite good about the quality of care which I have delivered to many families. In many cases I have been the first person to ask a mother how she is coping with life and motherhood. So much of my care has been concerned with mothering: mothering sick infants, premature infants with colic, infants and children with difficult temperaments, children with problems in school, and the list goes on. Almost anyone can learn to complete a physical assessment of a child or adolescent, but what makes a nurse practitioner a good care provider is what we do and ask in addition to examining bellies and ears.

When I hear a mother of a preterm infant who has been particularly difficult to parent tell me that she was sure she was doing a terrible job and my help in understanding her infant has given her great relief; or a mother of a very difficult child says that I was the first care provider to assure her that parenting a difficult child is hard work and it is okay for her to feel angry, then I feel like I have made a contribution to a family's well being.

It seems as if I have always been a practitioner. As I reflect on the last 20 years, I marvel how things in my professional practice have changed, and yet there are many components of my care that have remained constant. Despite a level of independence, I have never been immune to all of the struggles in defining the nurse practitioner role for my physician colleagues as well as the community. It has never been clear where I fit into the informal structure of the practice. It is easy to understand the hierarchy of physician, receptionist, office nurse (usually a LPN), but no one knew where I should fit. This became even more of a problem once I received my Ph.D.

The role of the nurse practitioner does have inherent frustrations as well as gratifications. Even after these many years in one practice there are times where it is clear that as a nurse I am not always considered a colleague, or that as a care provider I am less than the first choice of some parents. As I continue this ongoing effort to maintain a collegial working relationship and patient acceptance, an effort made harder by my part-time status, I have always appreciated the level of independence which allows me to deliver high quality of care to families. It is the positive rewards from meeting previous unfulfilled needs of many families which continues to override the constant struggle often inherent to advanced nurse practice.

Joint Practice and Teaching Responsibilities

I cannot envision a time when I would ever not practice as a PNP. Yet there are moments when the demands as a university faculty member, director of a master's level practitioner program, and researcher become quite overwhelming. However, not giving care has never been an option for me. I have been able to accomplish many tasks as I give care. During one semester a year I have students with me. It is during this experience that students begin to understand the role of the nurse practitioner in a setting very different from the inner-city clinics where most students practice. I also conduct funded research projects in the practice, which involves all care providers.

I like to believe that my students value my role as a practitioner who continues to give care on a regular basis. Without an ongoing practice I do not believe that I would be able to maintain my credibility with students who are, for the most part, very experienced nurses. As would be expected, my practice allows students to have first-hand knowledge about the care of high-risk infants during the first years of life, and not just in the neonatal intensive care unit.

It is an interesting interaction between the role of a faculty in a research-based institution and a nurse practitioner providing care. The role of PNP provides first-hand knowledge about the care of families, which in turn influences my teaching. On the other hand, in my role as faculty member and researcher, I have access to continuously updated knowledge and research. It is rewarding to say to a parent that, based on the literature or perhaps on my own research, I believe that a particular practice or approach should work for his/her child.

As a doctorally prepared and an experienced researcher I have assumed a unique function of mediator in the practice. Physicians in the practice ask me to provide research or conduct a Medline search on a topic which they know that I am familiar with. This literature review and subsequent discussion determines the practical approach or intervention to a particular health issue.

Throughout the years there continues to be a redefining of my role, most of which has been very rewarding, although occasionally frustrating. I cannot imagine a time when I would not have the opportunity to hold those small hands or feel those wonderful soft bellies. I will always in some way define myself professionally as a nurse practitioner as well as a researcher and educator.

ADOLESCENT FAMILY PRACTICE

Ann L. O'Sullivan

BACKGROUND

My professional career has been spent almost exclusively in positions that combine opportunities for practice and teaching in pediatric nursing. Following my diploma and baccalaureate education, I worked as a staff nurse at a large metropolitan children's hospital until completing a master's program as a pediatric clinical nurse specialist. On completion of this program, I accepted a position that combined my responsibility as a nurse clinician with that of instructor in the graduate division of a family nurse clinician program. At the same time, I continued a 4-hour per week collaborative practice with an internist in order to maintain my skills as a nurse practitioner. In 1978 I was accepted as a Robert Wood Johnson Foundation nurse faculty fellow, spending the subsequent year in the Primary Care Department at the University of Maryland.

It has been gratifying to continue to maintain clinical and faculty activities since completion of the fellowship program. My practice experiences have included those of a pediatric nurse practitioner and of director of a Teen-Tot Program, while faculty activities have centered around participation in a Primary Care-Family Nurse Clinician Program. My dissertation capitalized on my clinical interests, and consisted of case studies using qualitative methods of interviewing to describe how six adolescent mothers decided to return to school after the birth of their first infant. Each of the six families, including the adolescent mother, the baby's grandparents, friends, school nurse, counselor, and gym teacher were interviewed several times until I was able to describe how the adolescent mother made decisions regarding herself and her infant.

Adolescent mothers' behavior regarding returning to school, delaying second pregnancies, and providing appropriately timed immunizations for their infant continues after eight years to provide me with incredible challenges as teacher, clinician, researcher, and community advocate.

PRACTICE WITH ADOLESCENT FAMILIES

Characteristics and Components

The practice with which I am currently involved services the special needs of adolescent families. Located within the ambulatory clinic of a large teaching hospital, at their satellite office just five blocks from the main hospital, the practice addresses comprehensive health needs of both babies and young parents. Presently, most young mothers choose to use the hospital's adolescent clinic or local family planning clinics for their own care. Formerly funded by the Robert Wood Johnson Foundation and Mary D. Rockefeller, presently by the PEW Memorial Trust, the project consists of a randomized control study of families who attend either a special care program (the Teen Parent Program) or a routine community clinic and are followed for 18 months after the birth of their infants. Infants over 18 months from former programs are followed on a separate day at the same setting. Outcome measures assessed at the end of each study are the level of immunization and development of the infant and whether the mother has returned to school and delayed a subsequent pregnancy.

Our current caseload includes 244 mothers, 12 to 17 years of age, and their babies. The practice consists of myself, another nurse practitioner, a social worker, and a pediatrician working together in a collaborative practice arrangement.

The practice is structured so that the social worker and either the nurse practitioner or pediatrician see the adolescent family on every visit to the clinic setting. Patients see the pediatrician and a nurse practitioner on the first visit to the clinic, which takes place 2 weeks after the discharge of the baby from the hospital. This visit is scheduled in order to make an early assessment of the mother and baby and to provide an orientation to the health setting. The scope of the clinic services and the practice model are described, including an explanation of the home visit to the baby's grandmother, or the woman in the adolescent mother's life who helps her make decisions. A 45-minute time slot is customarily set aside to allow for adequate interaction and questions. This introductory visit eases the family into the system and helps to prevent abuse of the emergency room for common problems, such as low-grade fever, spitting up, and other primary care problems of the newborn period.

Whom the patient sees after that is a matter of which of us is free. The nurse aide, after weighing and measuring the infant, places the charts in a rack in the order of arrival at the clinic. Those families with problems with their medical assistance card coverage are seen by the social worker prior to the visit by a clinician. We try to arrange alternate visits, so that if I encounter the chart of a client whom I have just seen the last two or three times, I switch it to the pediatrician's door. Occasionally, if a client asks to see one or the other of us, we accommodate that request. Then we explain to them why we might not have scheduled them with me or with the pediatrician, and that if they want to participate in this program, it is to their advantage as well as ours that they see both nurse and physician providers. But there are just some days when somebody wants to see one or the other of us for some personal reason, and the practice group feels it necessary to meet that need.

The nature of the practice is such that truthfully 95 percent of the problems could be managed with the skill and knowledge of a nurse practitioner. Nevertheless, while the practice is wellness-oriented, what we are trying to accomplish with adolescent mothers is more than providing wellness care. Within this context, and given the aura that still exists around physicians, there is a real need to have a pediatrician integrally involved in the practice. In actuality, there is very little that differentiates the pediatrician's practice from my own, either in areas of management or referrals. This degree of overlap between the role of nurse practitioner and physician is not restricted to our practice, but seems to be true with pediatricians in general. Pediatricians tend to be easier to work with than other medical providers, perhaps because of the nature of the patients served and the ambulatory work environment, as well as the personal preferences of persons choosing pediatric specialization.

Consultation and Referrals Among Providers

Because of the interaction of the client with several health providers, the mechanism for introducing new management strategies and for referrals must be explicit and adhered to by all of the practice professionals.

In the practice, both the nurse and physician treat illnesses as they arise, and therefore there is no differentiation in who does the initial screening. Based on our practice model, the pediatrician and the nurse are expected, whenever possible, to deal with the problems at hand.

One level of consultation involves the confirmation of findings that must take place during the patient encounter. For example, if I think that a burn ought to be treated with antibiotics, I seek consultation with the physician at the moment. In such a situation, the burn is a medical problem beyond my skill and knowledge, and I want to make sure it is managed appropriately. Other kinds of problems for which I might seek immediate consultation include orthopedic problems of the hip or feet and suspected pneumonia in infants under three months of age. In some instances, such as dermatological manifestations, I might seek immediate consultation and confirmation from a specialist in an adjacent clinic.

A second level of consultation is that of referral to another provider during a return or subsequent visit. If a problem is not urgent and needs more than a 2-minute consultation, then the client is asked to make a return visit. This situation typically arises concerning problems of toilet training, spanking, and other disciplinary issues; the physician might schedule the next or an interim visit with the nurse practitioner. Another example of purposeful alternating visits is in determining the possibility of child abuse. In such a situation the pediatrician will finish up the visit and say something like "Now the next time I think you ought to come in and see Ann. The routine visit is scheduled for two months, but we are going to have you come back in two weeks because we have some concerns about the things we talked about today."

There are two major reasons for the way that referral patterns have evolved in the practice. In the first place, the pediatrician and I know and feel comfortable with each other and we recognize and capitalize on each other's strengths. Unfortunately, every time a team member changes, this trust, which forms the basis for collaborative practice, must be reestablished. Because of physician mobility, we have had four changes in pediatricians in as many years that I have been in the practice. Our present pediatrician is a 35-year-old male who has no children of his own and has been with us for four years. Previously two of our pediatricians were female, each staying only six months during residency, and one male, 55 years old, who had grown children of his own, and stayed for three years. Role negotiation and establishing trust, therefore, is a process that absorbs a large amount of both individual and group consultation time.

The second reason underlying our current referral pattern relates to the environment in which we practice. Specialty clinics are accessed only through the primary care referral, based on a federally funded pilot of managed care for two neighborhoods in our city. Because these specialty clinics are located at the main hospital, both the pediatrician and I refer out problems that in other settings the pediatrician might be more prone to handle on his or her own. This has helped to establish a practice model in which the practice boundaries for the pediatrician and the nurse are virtually identical. I am not seen as less of a provider than the pediatrician because of an inability to, say, ligate extra digits with a suture. We both take full advantage of the available specialty support staff.

The Teaching Program

Much of what we do in management of adolescent families includes both informal teaching, concerning such issues as feeding problems, and formal teaching sessions.

Although we have always recognized the need for a strategy for formal teaching, our initial notion as to how to present content has changed markedly since the inception of the program. Originally, we attempted to conduct a class at each clinic visit. We literally shut down the clinic and had the providers and the clients come into the teaching setting. People came at 12:30 p.m., were seen by the social worker and pediatrician, and then attended a class which lasted from 2:00 to 3:00 p.m.

Other people came at 2:00 pm and had appointments scheduled following the class. Constant disruptions further added to the chaotic atmosphere. The providers were rattled, the infants were exhausted, and the mothers were worried about keeping their appointments. No one could pay attention to what was going on, and it just did not work!

We then tried a series of eight classes. The content was primarily a mother-infant stimulation program, whereby mothers were encouraged to be the primary teachers for their newborns. This series of classes covered the growth and development phase of the infant's development, beginning when the baby is 5 weeks to 3 months of age and continuing until the child is 14 to 16 months old.

The content was based on a series of 20 classes developed by Dr. E. Badger, at the University of Cincinnati. The series has been used successfully for about 10 years in Cincinnati and has been replicated around the country. We incorporated components of those 20 classes into our series, along with additional content intended to build up the adolescent mother's self-esteem and provide additional information about contraception. The series provided for repetition of content. Infant stimulation, strategies for handling and managing a baby, and the importance of the mother as teacher were incorporated into each of the eight sessions.

Older parents "goo" and "coo," stick out their tongues, play peek-a-boo, and in general carry on a show-and-tell scene with their infants. Adolescents are too inhibited to behave this way with their newborns. It takes a lot of work to teach adolescent fathers and mothers the importance of these behaviors to their babies' development. Reinforcement of the class content, therefore, was done during each clinic visit.

Regretfully, the attendance was so poor, whether in the summer, fall, spring or winter, early or late in the afternoon, that we have now returned to our earliest model: informal teaching by the nurse in the waiting room, based on the age of the infants present, or a special discussion after a short video on such topics as safety, birth control, or sexually transmitted diseases. In addition, graduates of the research program (18 months and older) are invited to a one-hour weekly play session on the floor of the waiting room with the social worker and nurse, in order to model the appropriate play to develop fine motor and language skills for these infants and toddlers. Understanding comes in small doses, and requires ongoing attention on the part of all the practice participants.

Collaborative Practice Issues

It is the nature of practice with adolescent families that they need a sense of regularity, continuity, and similar expression of concern, irrespective of who is providing their care. These attributes, therefore, become the basis for the group practice.

One of the things that people bring up frequently about interdisciplinary provider groups is that it is difficult for the client to integrate into the group and adjust to the different approaches of group members. Our clientele could, potentially, have such a difficulty but for the fact that we as a team are particularly aware of the problems inherent in interdisciplinary practice. My practice and that of the pediatrician are similar. We ask the same questions and stress the same issues. Therefore, the client has a very similar experience on each visit, and the practitioner's approach does not overwhelm the visit. It is our experience that adolescents can get used to more than one provider, as long as the approach remains relatively constant.

The practice is therefore a concentrated effort on the part of four individual providers with special interest in adolescent families. If one of the providers is not interested in adolescents, the practice does not hold together. This becomes especially apparent when an alternate provider substitutes for one of us when we attend meetings or are on vacation.

The importance of uniformity of philosophy and the ability to come to some general consensus as to management of adolescents is especially visible during the group conferences. At the end of each clinic session, the four of us sit down and go over all of the charts of the families who have been seen that afternoon, both to identify problems that have come up since the past visit and to identify special resources that might be needed. We also meet to share information obtained by the social worker and other providers, since by sharing we are able to pull together information not necessarily available to each individual.

The decision making process in the group conference is very fluid. The primary care providers take turns presenting what they found on history and physical examination of the infant and the psychosocial information they have gotten from the mother. The social worker adds to that profile. Subsequent discussion is aimed at resolving differences in management styles. Sometimes one nurse practitioner or physician is more alarmed by a lack of weight gain or an actual loss of weight than is another provider. Sometimes I may want to bring someone back in two weeks, while the pediatrician would not bring them back for four weeks. Provider differences in dealing with clinical problems usually are resolved in some compromise agreement. Sometimes it is the nurse who is pushing toward acceptance of his or her position on an issue, and sometimes it is the pediatrician, depending on the issue.

The important determinants of the process rest on the ego strengths of the participants. Disagreement is healthy. When my decisions are questioned, it does not mean that the other person is challenging my overall ability or me as a person. Rather, the challenge is to my knowledge or skill in handling a specific incident, and if I am unable to substantiate my position, then the challenge is warranted. The same is obviously true when the nurse questions the pediatrician's actions. But you cannot challenge people, nor can you yourself be challenged, unless everyone in the situation feels competent in their practice and comfortable with themselves.

The issue of competency and comfort within true interdisciplinary practice is one that must be addressed from the provider's initial contact with the practice. Practice positions must be filled by people who hold similar practice philosophies. During the hiring process it is important to identify what the practice group should look like, including the expectations for the nurse practitioner, pediatrician, and social worker. Professional competency, personal self-confidence, trust, and communication are equally important attributes for successful interdisciplinary practice.

PERCEPTION OF PRIMARY CARE PRACTICE

Although I am enjoying pediatric practice, I do not think that you can do primary care 9 to 5, five days a week. There is a tendency to get bored with full-time practice. When you have seen 98 mothers or young kids and number 99 comes through the door on Friday afternoon at 3 o'clock, it is extremely difficult to listen attentively to the problems at hand. I do not mean to imply that primary care is less energizing for nurses than for other providers. Rather, I mean that any full-time practice can become routine or unsatisfying unless, of course, you view it as just a day's work, and do not aspire to anything more. When you do the same job day in and day out, there is a tendency to become stagnant, and your inquisitive tendencies are blunted.

If physicians are more likely than nurses to find satisfaction in full-time practice, their motivation often stems from financial incentives, incentives which are not operative for most nurses in primary care practice. Furthermore, physicians are more socialized than nurses to engage in entrepreneurial activities. They recognize that in order to develop an ongoing practice, it is necessary to establish rapport with patients. While some physicians establish rapport because they genuinely care for people, others become somewhat artificial and theatrical in their approach, feeling that this is necessary in order to keep patients.

Lacking the financial incentives, nurses need to seek other ways of making practice exciting and varied. Special projects often serve this purpose. A project, whether administrative, clinical, or teaching, such as precepting students, helps to maintain enthusiasm about practice. Similarly, it is important to develop a special clinical interest, for example, new mothers, single parents, divorced couples, or children of divorced couples. In my own situation, my interest in adolescent families enriches my practice and involves me in new areas of knowledge and with new groups of practice. As a consultant to a national study examining nursing in hospitals, I had the opportunity to speak with staff nurses throughout the country. I was impressed with the differences in the attitudes of those nurses who did only their job and those who took on additional activities, such as committee work. When you give more, you feel better.

Although stagnation and job "burnout" may occur irrespective of setting, the problem is more evident in primary care because of the character of the practice of most nurse practitioners. In contrast to hospitals, where the routine is less predictable and the patient problems more varied, nurse practitioners work primarily in ambulatory settings. In such practice settings, health providers draw strength and rewards from patients whom they come to know over time. For example, if you are a primary care provider for a patient population with chronic illness, you see people frequently and they make you feel needed. On the other hand, nurse practitioners who work primarily with well populations, for example, with well children and young adults, who have episodic and infrequent contacts with a health provider, may not feel as much satisfaction from their practice. For these reasons it is especially important for nurses in primary care to seek out alternative activities that provide a sense of reward, satisfaction, and recognition. This year, I served as a coordinator of nurse volunteers for a large immunization campaign for our city. This project included volunteers from all over the city, in medicine, public relations, media, advocacy, and community work. It was a tremendous high after we saw 6,000 children receive the immunizations they needed in just 30 days! I highly recommend even doing volunteer work in an area that complements or informs your own teaching, clinical, or research interests.

FUTURE OF PRIMARY CARE PRACTICE

The future of primary care practice for nurses is greatly dependent on the positive resolution of reimbursement issues. Without reimbursement, it will become increasingly difficult to sustain nurse practitioners in traditional ambulatory practices. There are already limited job opportunities in some states, in Health Maintenance Organizations (HMOs), clinics, and private physicians' offices. While jobs are still available in rural areas, these too will become scarcer if physicians redistribute from urban to rural settings in search of new practice opportunities.

Nevertheless, there are several trends that may increase future employment opportunities for nurse practitioners.

In the first place, the possibilities for transferring the knowledge and skill gained in primary care into settings that have not traditionally provided health care have increased over the last few years. In truth, the potential practice options are unknown for those nurses sufficiently creative to exploit corporate, industry, community, and church interest in providing health promotion, screening, and education for their constituencies.

Second, although some nurse practitioners continue to seek work as generalists, there is increasing interest in specialization within primary care. As people familiarize themselves with one area of knowledge, their interests tend to narrow. Typically, nurses have more than one practice interest during the course of their professional careers. In essence, they become specialists in several areas of practice. With each shift in emphasis, they draw on old knowledge, the increasing self-confidence that comes with experience, and the ability to engage in life long learning gained in their generalist preparation. For example, within my area of practice, I have specialized in the care of the adolescent patient. Yet, even within this focus, there is ample opportunity for further specialization, not only because of increasing physical-biological knowledge, but also because of the need to consider changes in psychological and cultural responses in managing adolescent families.

Regardless of practice setting, the notion of flexibility is crucial to nursing practice. One of the positive results of shifting interests among nurses is the recognition that you can never have—nor do you need—all of the answers. I take the position that when I am in a new practice setting, professionals and patients alike have a responsibility to help me learn those things that will help meet their needs. I have become increasingly confident in admitting the things I do not know and seeking answers from others. A spirit of trust, cooperation, and candidness between patient and provider is crucial if nurses are to maintain the level of good will that currently surrounds the delivery of primary care.

The last trend I want to discuss is the potential for introducing nurses with primary care skills into tertiary and geriatric care settings. Within institutions, nurses can work on designated units and assume the same authority and responsibility for caseloads of patients that they have had in ambulatory settings, including management of ambulation, nutrition, sleep, and bowel and bladder function—care problems of interest to and best managed by nurses. One possibility for practice in tertiary settings is for nurses with various specialty interests to join together in providing comprehensive care to patients, in a manner similar to multi-specialty physician group practices. We look to nursing to provide for the whole patient and family. On the other hand, it is unrealistic to expect each individual nurse to be uniformly competent in all areas of practice. Nurses whose skills and interest complement each other should team together. For example, a primary and tertiary care nurse might assume joint responsibility for a caseload of patients. They would make rounds together and divide the work based on their specialty interests. The tertiary care nurse would assume the major responsibility during the critical care phase of the hospitalization, while the primary care nurse would be more involved during the recovery phase. The services rendered would be documented, and billing would reflect both nurses' contributions and time expenditures.

CONCLUSION

Many practice arenas would potentially benefit from the introduction of nurses possessing primary care skills. Success in exploiting these opportunities will be dependent on the receptivity of nurses, agencies, and funding bodies.

PRACTICE IN A CHILD WELFARE AGENCY: AN INTERDISCIPLINARY VIEW

Henry L. Barnett, Marianne Warguska Reilly, and Elizabeth A. Kuehne

Health supervision of children in foster care encompasses the major principles and practices of primary care for children with special needs.

In this chapter, the provision of primary care for children in out-of-home placement by Pediatric Nurse Practitioners (PNPs) is described and assessed from the perspective of both PNPs and a Pediatrician. The Foster Care Medical Clinic (FCMC) of the Children's Aid Society (CAS), staffed primarily by PNPs, is the model presented here.

THE CHILDREN'S AID SOCIETY

CAS is a private, nonsectarian child welfare agency with a 137-year history of providing innovative social, educational, recreational, and health services for underprivileged children in New York City. The agency has a strong commitment to the provision of high-quality health care. There are approximately 30 full-time health professionals on staff. The health staff participate in most of the agency's services, which include foster care and adoption, Head Start and after-school programs, summer day camps, a sleep-away camp for disabled children, and a mobile medical/dental van. Although PNPs are involved in all of these programs, this paper will focus on the comprehensive primary health care clinic for foster children.

Foster Care Medical Clinic

A description of the development of the health services at CAS over the past 12 years reflects the profound changes that have taken place in the medical needs of children entering foster care.

Initially, physicians and nurses came to the clinic a few days a week and social service staff coordinated referrals and follow-up. In the late 1970s, a PNP was hired to provide well child care (WCC) to children placed in foster care through the Emergency Foster Boarding Home program. This program was designed to remove children quickly into a safe home situation while allegations of abuse and neglect were investigated by the Child Protective staff. The PNP soon realized that these children came into foster care having had fragmented health care or none at all prior to placement. She immediately developed a system for obtaining past medical records, updating immunizations, and making specialty referrals. When the child left the Emergency Foster Boarding Home Program, he/she was discharged with a complete health record compiled primarily by the PNP.

It soon became very clear that the medical service required restructuring, and it was decided that a comprehensive primary care service

TABLE 6.1 Health Services of The Children's Aid Society

Director of Integrated Health Services (MWR)[a]					
(PNP)					
Medical Director (HLB)[a]					
(MD)					
Director of Foster Care Health Services (EAK)[a]					
(PNP)					
Supervisor of Foster Care Medical Clinic					
(PNP)					
PNP	PNP	PNP	MD	LPN	Secretary

[a]Positions held by authors as of May 31, 1993

staffed primarily by PNPs should be established. This model of care was developed in order to meet effectively the increasingly serious and complex health care needs of foster children.

The present FCMC is a division of the Health Services at CAS (Table 6.1). This service is responsible for health supervision of 550–600 foster children throughout the time they are in care.

A 6-month prospective survey of the health status of children at the time of entry into foster care at CAS during 1988 and 1989 was made by Marianne Warguska Reilly and Elizabeth Kuehne. A high proportion of the children were Black and Hispanic. The ages ranged from newborn to 21 years; however, most were young: 22% under 6 months of age and 60% five years or less.

The most common diagnoses at time of entry are shown in Tables 6.2 and 6.3. Many of these children needed consultation with pediatric sys-

TABLE 6.2 Most Common Diagnoses of Infants Less Than 6 Months Old Entering Foster Care

Diagnoses	Percent
Positive toxicology to cocaine	62
Lack of medical history	53
Dermatologic conditions	29
URI	29
Low birthweight	24
Neurological abnormality	21
Hernia/hydrocele	21
Congenital syphilis	15
Weight less than fifth percentile for age	15
Eye condition	9

TABLE 6.3   Most Common Diagnoses Among Children of All Ages Entering
Foster Care

Diagnoses	Percent
Lack of health history	66
Lack of immunization records	60
URI/pharyngitis	35
Dermatologic conditions	24
Positive toxicology to cocaine	16
Evidence of physical/sexual abuse	11
Acute ear condition	11
Developmental/behavioral problem	11
Dental decay—obvious	11
Weight less than fifth percentile for age	10
Heart murmur	9
Asthma	7

tem specialists. Among infants less than 6 months, 47% needed an immediate specialty referral; among all children, the proportion was 63%. The referrals made most frequently were: ophthalmology, orthopedics, neurology, cardiology, and general surgery.

The Role of PNPs in the Foster Care Medical Clinic

PNPs are the primary health care providers in the FCMC. Policies and practices in the clinic are formulated by the PNPs and the full-time staff pediatrician and medical director, who also serve as general pediatric consultants. The PNPs work closely with staff members of many other services at CAS, including social workers, dentists, psychiatrists, developmental psychologists, and the educational and vocational specialists.

All children are seen on intake and discharge from foster care. Routine care is provided according to the schedule shown in Table 6.4. Appointments for episodic illnesses are scheduled as needed. Children needing urgent care during evening or weekend hours are seen in local emergency rooms in which previous arrangements have been made for CAS patients. Each E.R. visit is followed with a phone call to the foster parent to check on the child's condition. Records are obtained from the hospital, and re-visits are scheduled at the FCMC.

Care of foster children is often complicated by the fact that a child's past medical history is unknown. In addition, there are change in foster homes for individual children and although CAS caseworkers try to minimize these changes, they do occur.

TABLE 6.4 Schedule of Regular Care for Foster Children at the Foster Care
Medical Clinic of the Children's Aid Society

The Intake Visit:[a]
  - complete physical exam within 48 hours of placement
Two-Week Follow-Up:
  - Developmental assessment
  - Bloodwork (CBC, sickle-cell screen, FEP, VDRL)
  - Urinalysis
  - Tuberculin skin test
  - Vision and hearing screenings
  - Follow-up discussion with foster parent and child
Routine Care:
  - 0–6 months: once a month
  - 6–12 months: every 2 months
  - 1–3 years: every 3 months
  - 3–10 years: every 6 months
  - 10–13 years: every 6–12 months
  - 13–21 years: every 3–6 months

[a]The intake visit is a "no hurt" visit, which begins to establish a trusting relationship
with these fragile, often frightened children and their foster parents.

It is becoming increasingly difficult for all child welfare agencies to obtain acceptable consultations for foster children with pediatric system specialists. Delays in scheduling appointments, excessive waiting periods, and especially poor communication with primary care providers are encountered frequently in hospital specialty clinics accepting Medicaid reimbursement. These problems are especially troublesome for foster children and their families.

At CAS, arrangements for acceptable consultations have been made with a few such specialty clinics. However, for most consultations, CAS has developed a roster of practicing specialists who are interested in and sensitive to the special needs of foster children and their families. They also are wiling to accept fees below their usual charges. The children are seen by appointment as private patients in the specialist's office. Each child is sent with a referral letter from the PNP that outlines the problem and includes any relevant past medical history. The consultant sends a report to the PNP summarizing the findings and making recommendations. The PNP who initiated the referral is responsible for following up the recommendations and re-visits. Consultants are also available by telephone to discuss any changes in patient status or any urgent problems.

In addition to providing direct services, making referrals, and planning discharges as described, PNPs in the FCMC coordinate all health-related activities of children coming into care; they act as medical case managers, educate foster parents and social service caseworkers about health issues in special training sessions, are available for telephone consults, make home and hospital visits as needed, and appear in court for cases of abuse and neglect.

The PNPs at CAS are board certified and active in local and national professional associations. They are invited often to give lectures on the special needs of foster children and how they are met by the medical service at CAS.

A CASE STUDY OF A CHILD IN THE FCMC

The following case provides an example of the complex care a foster child may need and the effective collegial relationship between PNPs, the staff pediatrician at CAS, and staffs of related services.

J.T. was three years old when he was placed in foster care. He had been hospitalized for two years and had been diagnosed as being HIV-positive. During his first six months in the hospital, he was repeatedly in and out of the ICU. His mother, with whom he had lived, became ill during this time and eventually died of AIDS. His father, an IV drug abuser (IVDA) visited J.T. infrequently in the hospital and finally stopped visiting completely. When J.T. was ready for discharge, social services began the difficult task of trying to find a foster home for a sick HIV-positive child with asthma. After a 6-month search, the father's sister, a single 39-year-old woman without children, and also a recovered IVDA, began visiting J.T. in the hospital. She gradually became attached to J.T. and agreed to care for him as his kinship foster mother.

A caseworker in the intake unit was notified that J.T. and his aunt were assigned to CAS for supervision. The caseworker told the PNP that a home study had been completed and that J.T. would soon be discharged to live with his aunt as a newly certified foster parent. J.T. was enrolled in a special HIV program at the hospital, where he was to be seen every two weeks for IV gamma globulin treatments. In addition, his aunt understood that he would be coming to the CAS clinic for routine and episodic health care.

At the intake visit the PNP noted that J.T. was developmentally delayed and somewhat underweight, but generally in good physical condition. He was taking Theophylline, Albuterol, Bactrim, and Nystatin. The PNP spent a great deal of time with the aunt discussing HIV infection, asthma, the medications, and the clinical service.

At the routine two-week follow-up visit, the PNP did a more detailed developmental assessment, a vision and hearing screening, and an assessment of foster home adjustment. She also asked the CAS staff pediatrician to meet J.T. and his foster mother. He did a limited examination and agreed with the PNP's plan for health care. The PNP in charge of the case also discussed each visit with the medical director.

During the remaining three years of J.T.'s life, the PNP consulted often with the immunologists and Clinical Nurse Specialist at the hospital where he was being followed for the HIV infection. Major treatment issues were discussed with the CAS staff pediatrician. The PNP also met frequently with the staff psychiatrist and the caseworker, sometimes together with the foster mother. The PNP also discussed J.T.'s progress weekly with the nurse and teacher at his day care center.

Most significant was the supportive relationship that developed between the PNP and the foster mother, who needed to learn basic parenting skills, to encourage J.T. to reach his full potential, and finally to somehow let J.T. go.

Although this case was complex and very sad, all the staff involved utilized their skills most appropriately, reaping the reward of knowing they did the best possible for J.T. and his foster mother.

THE PNPs' VIEWS

At the Children's Aid Society, nurse practitioners and physicians work together in a unique way. Since the children they serve require so much more than routine medical care, these professionals are able to provide quality care in a way that affords them tremendous personal and professional satisfaction.

Since health care is not the main focus of the agency as it would be in a hospital or clinic settings, there is much less competition between the different health professionals. Instead, a kind of camaraderie exists between physicians, nurse practitioners, nurses, mental health staff, dentists, hygienists, and support staff. This setting eliminates the barriers that have affected other physician/nursing relationships, particularly those created when each person feels they are stepping on the other's toes, or crossing professional boundaries. The cases at CAS are so complex that both PNPs and the pediatrician do very naturally what they know best, and thus a collegial relationship and unified work effort is achieved. Working within a social service agency provides an environment in which PNPs and other professionals can serve needy children while enjoying a mutually satisfying working relationship.

THE PEDIATRICIAN'S VIEW

The views expressed here are drawn from the senior author (Barnett's) ten years' experience at CAS, working with both PNPs and pediatricians in the field of child welfare. They are based on his participation in the provision of primary health care to foster children, their biological and foster parents, and to homeless children and their families living in hotels. As described earlier, foster children and their families need a special type of comprehensive health care that requires skillful diagnosis and treatment, including referral for consultation for the increasing prevalence of serious and complex medical and psychosocial problems; sensitive understanding of complex adjustments to many unfavorable environmental forces; knowledge of the child welfare system, including protective services and courts; and a high capacity to work effectively and harmoniously with related disciplines, especially social services and mental health.

The high quality of the comprehensive primary care provided by PNPs in this setting has been demonstrated in many identifiable ways. PNPs are excellent clinicians, fully capable of diagnosing and treating the medical problems in ambulatory pediatric practice, and they are well informed about recent advances. They are very keenly aware of more complicated conditions that require consultation with a general pediatrician or a pediatric system specialist. They seek these consultations in a way that encourages good communication and cooperation with the consultant. Most impressive, to this pediatrician, is their extensive theoretical knowledge and practical experience in diagnosing and treating psychosocial problems, especially in the area of early childhood development. Here, too, they handle less severe problems effectively and recognize the need for consultation and cooperation with psychiatric and psychological consultants.

Many children now entering foster care present problems of so-called social pathology, such as physical and emotional abuse and neglect, including sexual abuse, substance abuse, unwanted teenage pregnancy, homicide, and suicide. The PNPs at CAS, working with social workers and relevant specialized consultants, handle these difficult problems as effectively as possible. They also have become "street smart" in coping with the complex systems of child protective agencies and the courts.

It is in these areas that the need to work effectively with social workers and related staffs in mental health and education and in administration is so essential. By virtue of the education and training of PNPs in psychosocial aspects of health care, in several areas their role overlaps that of social workers, and it might be anticipated that interdisciplinary conflicts with social workers would be increased. On the contrary, through better mutual understanding of the professional roles of each of their disciplines, PNPs and social workers at CAS have been able to mutually complement their services effectively. Although medical care has assumed a greater share of the needs of foster children in the past 10 years, it is recognized and accepted by the medical staff that primary responsibility for the overall care of foster children and their families must remain with social services. The effectiveness of the care of foster children and their families by PNPs at CAS is enhanced by locating the medical and dental clinics and the social work, mental health, and educational services in the same building. This fortunate arrangement is not only a great advantage for the clients ("one-stop-shopping"), but also facilitates contact and communication between services.

During the last 10 years, 15 PNPs and 6 pediatricians have worked in the FCMC. Generalizing from this small sample, this pediatrician boldly offers the following impressions, assumptions, and recommendations.*

The PNP/pediatrician model is more effective than other models for providing primary care for foster children. The special professional knowledge of both pediatricians and PNPs is used in the formulation of professional policies and clinical practices. PNPs provide basic comprehensive primary care independently for almost all the foster children. The pediatrician is available for general pediatric advice and consulta-

---

* Not all pediatricians would agree with some of these views. To aid the reader in assessing them, it seems desirable to describe relevant aspects of Dr Barnett's earlier professional career. Except for three years of general pediatric practice as the pediatrician at Los Alamos from 1943–1946, he was in full-time academic pediatrics until he came to CAS in 1981. He was on the faculty of Washington University School of Medicine, Cornell University Medical College, and Albert Einstein College of Medicine, where he founded and served as first Chairman of the Department of Pediatrics and later as Associate Dean for Clinical Affairs. One of his first steps in starting the Department at Albert Einstein was to establish an ambulatory comprehensive primary care clinic as a major part of the teaching and training program for medical students and pediatric residents. Experiences in this clinic, directed by Lewis M. Fraad, M.D., and in which PNPs played a major role, attracted many of the best residents into a career in pediatric primary care.

tion. In a newly designed Medical Foster Boarding Home Program at CAS, hospitalized children with more complex chronic medical problems that could be treated at home ("boarder babies") are placed in homes with specially trained foster parents. For these children, the pediatrician is the responsible primary care provider working jointly with a PNP.

In this model of care for foster children, both PNPs and pediatrician are practicing in the professional roles for which their education and training have prepared them. The PNPs are able to incorporate their basic nursing skills and insights into their practice of primary care in this setting and they feel that their professional goals are being achieved. These aspects of their work at CAS may account for the success of the agency in recruiting and retaining highly qualified PNPs in spite of the current nursing shortage.

The personal attitudes of pediatricians working in the FCMC at CAS have been more complex. They enjoy serving as general pediatric consultants to the PNPs and as primary physicians for children with chronic illnesses and serious physical problems. When they themselves are the primary care providers for foster children with less serious physical problems but with complex psychosocial disturbances, they appear in general to be less comfortable and satisfied. In contrast, as primary care providers for these children, PNPs appear to be more effective, comfortable, and interested in dealing with them. Examples of these important components of primary care are seen in their sensitive counselling of children and their families, their conscientious follow-up of patients, and their appreciation of the need to work with related disciplines such as social work, mental health, and education.

SUMMARY

This pediatrician's assessment of PNPs in a child welfare agency is that primary health care of foster children and their families is provided more effectively by PNPs working with a general pediatrician than by other models, and that providing primary health care for foster children in a child welfare agency is a professsionally rewarding and personally fulfilling career for PNPs.

CARING FOR PATIENTS WITH HIV/AIDS

Jo Anne Staats

BACKGROUND

I am an adult nurse practitioner who has cared for people with Human Immunodeficiency Virus (HIV) infection for the past five years. The first eight years of my nursing career were spent in public health nursing in New York City. Becoming a nurse practitioner seemed like a natural extension of public health nursing, and gave me the opportunity to care for patients more comprehensively. For five years after completing the nurse practitioner program, I worked in a variety of primary care settings. In January of 1987, I started in a new program, Bailey House, a supportive group residence for persons with Acquired Immunodeficiency Syndrome (AIDS).

EPIDEMIOLOGY OF HUMAN IMMUNODEFICIENCY VIRUS INFECTION

By mid–1990, there had been 250,000 reported cases of AIDS worldwide. Considering that many more cases are not reported, the actual number is estimated to be closer to 700,000. Eight to 10 million people are believed to be infected with HIV worldwide (Berger et al., 1991). As of April 1991, the United States led the world with 174,893 cases of AIDS (Centers for Disease Control, 1991).

In the United States, 59% of AIDS cases are attributed to homosexual/ bisexual transmission and 22% to intravenous drug use (Centers for Disease Control, 1991). Intravenous drug use is also the major means of transmission of HIV infection to the heterosexual and, as a consequence, to the perinatal population.

Individuals infected with HIV may confront a myriad of social problems directly and indirectly related to HIV infection. Loss of a job, and consequently any reliable income, because of HIV-related illness may result in loss of health insurance and possible loss of a home because of inability to pay the rent/mortgage. Intravenous drug users may have had multiple problems already, and HIV infection only complicates an already difficult situation. Medical care and social services may be difficult to obtain because of discrimination directed against homosexuals, IV drug users, and persons with AIDS.

New York City has the highest number of cases of AIDS and the highest seroprevalence rate of HIV infection among IV drug users of any city in the world. (Des Jarlais et al., 1989; Evans, Beauchamp, Dayton, & Thomas, 1988). The city is unable to provide both adequate medical care and social services. There are an estimated 8,000 to 10,000 homeless HIV-infected individuals. Those without a CDC-defined AIDS diagnosis can be assigned to the city shelter system for housing. Many of these individuals have multiple health problems in addition to HIV infection; Torres, Maini, and Altholtz (1990) determined that a significant number of HIV-infected residents in one shelter also had active pulmonary tuberculosis. For some, the health care provided in the shelter is their only health care.

Through the New York City Human Resources Administration's Division of AIDS Services, attempts are made to provide housing for those with AIDS. Rent will be paid for those who have lost their source of income. For others, apartments or hotel rooms may be found. Some private agencies have developed housing programs for HIV-infected people. The AIDS Resource Center (ARC) was founded in 1983 to develop housing programs and provide pastoral care for individuals with AIDS. ARC developed a supportive housing apartment program and a supportive group residence, Bailey House. Other agencies have started similar apartment programs, but the group residence has yet to be duplicated in New York City. One skilled nursing facility and one health related facility for persons with AIDS have recently opened. Other cities (e.g., Chicago, San Francisco, and Dallas) have made attempts, some very successfully, to provide housing for persons with AIDS.

MEDICAL CARE OF HIV-INFECTED INDIVIDUALS

AIDS is now only used to refer to the end stage of HIV infection. HIV infection includes the spectrum of disease from diagnosis of positivity to death. As a result of this increased need, we are seeing fewer cases of pneumocystis carrnii pneumonia (PCP) and fewer individuals succumbing to this opportunistic infection. Current studies are also exploring other drugs to be used prophylactically against other opportunistic infections. As a result, infected individuals are living longer now than was the case several years ago, and with better treatment, it is believed that their life spans will continue to increase.

As the epidemic expands, the care of HIV-infected individuals has resulted in increased costs and limited access to specialist care by physicians. Until recently specialists, primarily those in infectious disease, were responsible for the care of persons with HIV infection. As more asymptomatic HIV-infected individuals enter the health care system it is not possible for them to be cared for by specialists, nor is it necessary. HIV-infected patients, including those with AIDS, can be well cared for by primary care practitioners who have access to consultation with specialists.

Nurse practitioners can and have stepped into the role of primary health care provider for those infected with HIV. Traditionally caring for underserved populations, nurse practitioners offer holistic care to this currently underserved group. In New York City, nurse practitioners currently care for persons with HIV/AIDS in a variety of settings. Some work in a community health clinic that originally offered counseling, testing, and follow-up to individuals at risk for HIV infection. As the epidemic has progressed, they now follow their patients when they become symptomatic. Other nurse practitioners work in shelter clinics attempting to provide counseling and testing to those individuals at risk. Many work in AIDS or infectious disease clinics with their own panel of patients. Some hospitals have nurse practitioners caring for patients on dedicated AIDS units who then follow some of these patients in their own clinic upon discharge. Nurse practitioners are also increasingly more involved in the multiple research projects associated with HIV infection.

DEVELOPMENT OF THE ROLE OF HIV NURSE PRACTITIONER

I moved into the challenging world of AIDS in 1987 when I accepted the position of part-time nurse practitioner at Bailey House. Bailey House is a supportive group residence for homeless persons with AIDS that is operated by the AIDS Resource Center. It receives funding through

New York City primarily, with some other monies coming from the state and federal government. The remainder of the budget, approximately 30%, is obtained through fundraising.

The concept of Bailey House is to provide supportive housing care in a clean and safe environment to individuals with AIDS who might not do well living alone and can tolerate community living. Referrals are made through the city's Division of AIDS Services and come from all five boroughs and most of the hospitals. Requirements for admission are eligibility for supplemental security income (SSI) and Medicaid, a CDC-defined AIDS diagnosis, and to be drug and alcohol free.

There are 44 residents at Bailey House, each with his/her own room, bathroom, television, and telephone. Three meals a day, in addition to unlimited snacks, are served in the main dining room. Each floor also has a lounge with a small refrigerator and microwave oven.

The original staffing plans for Bailey House included a part-time nurse practitioner, a master's-prepared social worker, two case managers, a substance abuse counselor, a recreational therapist, a pastoral care counselor, an intake coordinator and personal care assistants, receptionists, residence managers, housekeepers, kitchen staff, office personnel, an administrator, and an assistant administrator. Until recent funding cuts occurred, it was possible to maintain this staffing pattern.

When I began at Bailey House it had been open only one month, had only seven residents, and was not fully staffed. It was my responsibility to monitor and coordinate the health care of the residents, supervise the personal care assistants, and function as a member of a multidisciplinary team. Over a period of five months the team developed a record-keeping system, developed admission criteria, determined reasons for residents to be placed on probation or discharged, and gradually filled the 44 rooms.

My initial steps were to establish liaison with the local hospitals with AIDS clinics and develop patient data forms. Through my contacts it was possible to get appointments and contact providers when residents were ill. I developed a history and physical examination form to be used when each new resident was admitted. This helped me to establish a baseline for future comparison of functioning and for the team to use in developing a plan of care for the residents. During the initial interview, the client's understanding of the disease process, medications, the need for medical care, and knowledge about safe sex and self-care were assessed and a plan for monitoring and teaching developed.

The personal care assistants (PCAs) were responsible for assisting with the activities of daily living (ADL) of those residents who might not be feeling well enough to do for themselves. In addition, they reminded residents about medications and clinic appointments, accompanied some to clinic or the emergency room, got prescriptions filled, and did shopping as needed. These responsibilities were developed as we went along and as we assessed the needs of the residents. It was also the responsibility of the PCAs to ensure that every resident was accounted for during each 24-hour period. I saw ill residents on a daily basis, and had others referred to me for evaluation by the PCAs, other staff or residents, or by the residents themselves.

Within a month after I started it became clear that my position needed to be full-time, and after 4 months funding was found to increase my hours. It was also evident that I required an assistant to track clinic appointments, arrange transportation for clinic, order supplies, and monitor PCA assignments. It was not until two years later that funding was found for that position.

The Visiting Nurse Service of New York (VNS) provided an onsite nurse at Bailey House. Some residents required intravenous infusions of ganciclovir (for cytomegalovirus retinitis) or amphotericin B (for cryptococcal meningitis), regular dressing changes, or injections, and were referred to the VNS for those services. In addition, residents who were debilitated such that they required more assistance with ADL than assistants could provide were referred to the VNS for a home attendant or home health aide. The onsite nurse was responsible for supervising those aides and monitoring the resident. The visiting nurse and I collaborated to provide coordinated care for the residents. As a result it was possible to keep many residents at Bailey House, despite repeated hospitalizations, until they died.

In 1988 Bailey House was approached by St. Vincent's Hospital and Medical Center's Community Medicine Program about the possibility of providing us with the services of one of their physicians, Dr. Ramon Torres, who was trained in the care of persons with HIV infection. Dr. Torres would consult at Bailey House two half days a week and would arrange to see residents in his clinic at St. Vincent's Hospital. Prior to Dr Torres' coming to Bailey House, I was somewhat isolated from other AIDS caregivers, and what I had learned about AIDS was by experience and reading. My knowledge of HIV infection and ability to care for persons with AIDS was greatly enhanced by working with Dr. Torres.

Residents referred to the physician had problems that did not require an emergency room visit but could not await the next clinic visit. Dr. Torres would see these residents and arrange for appropriate testing or prescriptions or contact the primary care physician. With the early intervention provided by Dr. Torres we believe it was possible to manage many medical problems in the outpatient setting before hospitalization was required (Torres and Staats, 1989).

Dr. Torres and the other HIV physicians at St. Vincent's were readily available by telephone during the times that Dr. Torres was not at Bailey House. Through my increasing knowledge of management of HIV disease and the use of protocols developed by both the Harvard Community Health Plan (1983) and the New York State Department of Health (New York Statewide Professional Standards Review Council, 1989) it became possible for me to manage many of the residents' medical problems that had previously required an emergency room visit. Not surprisingly, the more knowledgeable I became about HIV, the fewer residents I needed Dr. Torres to see during his afternoon at Bailey House. Because we were not a medical facility, I was not able to order tests and alter treatment appreciably, so I still required his assistance in this area. I was not the primary care provider of record.

Another of my responsibilities was to visit residents admitted to the hospital to assess their condition and their ability to return to Bailey House. When a resident was admitted to a hospital the city allowed Bailey House to hold that resident's room for 30 days. If the resident's hospitalization exceeded 30 days and they were medically able to return to Bailey House at the completion of their hospitalization, they would be placed first on our admission waiting list. There were few medical reasons for a resident to not be able to return to Bailey House; the main reason was inability to ambulate. In a few instances, residents who had been hospitalized became bedbound, and since Bailey House is not wheelchair-accessible we were unable to accommodate these individuals. In most instances these persons were referred by the hospital social worker to one of the few beds available in chronic care facilities.

I was also responsible for monitoring the residents during his/her course of hospitalization. Regular contact with the attending physician or resident would allow me to report back to the resident's case manager and the team at Bailey House about the resident's condition, course of treatment, and possible length of hospitalization.

Over the four years that I worked at Bailey House I also developed increasing expertise in the area of chemical dependency. Many of our residents had a history of chemical dependency, whether their risk factor was homosexual/bisexual sexual contact or intravenous drug use. As stated earlier, a prerequisite for admission to Bailey House was an ability to live drug- and alcohol-free. A potential resident's chemical dependency history was reviewed by the intake worker during the initial interview with the resident. Applicants with questionable motivation were discussed by the entire team and a decision on acceptability made by the team.

We became more adept at identifying those residents who were using drugs and/or alcohol and at offering them various options to maintain sobriety. Very few residents needed to be discharged because of an inability to stop using drugs. I also became more experienced at distinguishing those symptoms that might be AIDS-related from those that might be related to substance use.

Pain management of chemically dependent individuals is frequently an issue for health care providers. Persons with AIDS frequently experience pain and require appropriate medication. As my expertise expanded, I became more comfortable with managing the pain of those individuals with a chemical dependency history. Currently four other nurses and I are studying the response to pain in persons with AIDS whose risk factor is intravenous drug use versus homosexual/bisexual contact.

At the end of 1990 I was approached by Dr. Torres about the possibility of my doing a fellowship at St. Vincent's Hospital that would be focused on the primary care of HIV-infected substance users. The state was funding fellowships at four hospitals in New York City with the intent of increasing the number of primary care providers for IV drug using individuals infected with HIV. I felt I needed to expand my knowledge and wanted to become more involved in direct care of HIV-infected individuals, so I accepted the 15-month fellowship.

At the time I left Bailey House the facility had lost its funding for the personal care assistant and had arranged with the Visiting Nurse Service to provide services through clustering one or more residents with one home attendant. There would be a core group of home attendants providing service. The advantages of this model of care are that the home attendant services are Medicaid reimbursable, whereas the PCA services are not, and it is more cost-effective than the previous one-on-one care provided by VNS.

Because of budgetary constraints, Bailey House was unable to hire a nurse practitioner to fill my position. However, they were fortunate to hire a community health nurse with experience caring for persons with AIDS.

In my new position I am the primary care provider for patients in my clinic. When they are admitted to the hospital I follow them in conjunction with my collaborating physician. Some of my patients reside at Bailey House and are referred to me by the staff there. I also consult there one-half day a week with Dr. Torres. Other patients are referred from the inpatient unit. Most of the patients have a history of substance use. The challenge for me will be to provide primary care to HIV-infected individuals who do not choose to stop using alcohol/drugs. At Bailey House, most residents choose not to use as usage would jeopardize their continued residency at Bailey House, and therefore my experience has been only with these people. There is a dearth of primary medical care for HIV-infected individuals actively using drugs. The increasing incidence of HIV infection in New York makes it necessary to develop care models for this population.

At the conclusion of this fellowship I plan to continue to care for persons with HIV infection and would like to be involved in educating other nurse practitioners in caring for this population.

REFERENCES

Berger, J. S., Bergeron, M. G., Elgert, K. D., & Jones P. T. (1991). *AIDS 90 Summary: A Practical Synopsis of the VI International Conference*. Richmond, VA.: Philadelphia Sciences Group.

Centers for Disease Control. (1991). *HIV/AIDS Surveillance Report*, 40: RR5.

Des Jarlais, D. C., Friedman, S R., Novick, D. M., Sotheran, J. L., Thomas, P., Yancovitz, S. R., Mildvan, D., Weber, J., Kreek, M. J., Maslausky, R., Torres, R. A., Maini, S., Altholz, J., & Brickner, P. W. (1989). HIV-1 infection among intravenous drug users in Manhattan, New York City, from 1977 through 1987. *Journal of the American Medical Association, 261* (7), 1008–1012.

Evans, C. A., Beauchamp, D. E., Dayton, L., Thomas, P., & Weber, J. (1989). *Illicit drug use and HIV infection*. Washington, DC: American Public Health Association.

Harvard Community Health Plan. (1983). *Guidelines for Clinical Practices*. Boston: Harvard Community Health Plan.

New York Statewide Professional Standards Review Council. (1989). *Criteria manual for the treatment of AIDS*. Albany: New York State Department of Health.

Torres, R. A., Maini, S., & Altholz, J., (1990). Human Immunodeficiency Virus infection among homeless men in a New York City shelter. *Archives of Internal Medicine, 150,* 2030–2036.

Torres, R., & Staats, J. A. (1989). Primary care at a residence for persons with AIDS. Paper presented at the Fifth International Conference on AIDS. June, Holland.

PRACTICE IN A CONTINUING CARE RETIREMENT COMMUNITY

Jane Kummerer Butler

BACKGROUND

In 1975 I graduated from a 2-year family nurse clinician master's program. I had completed my bachelor's degree in 1969, and had been working for 4 years in staff development at a large urban teaching center. Several factors served to whet my interest in furthering my education in nursing. Through my contacts in staff development, I had learned about a nurse practitioner program at Chapel Hill, North Carolina. The role fascinated me, but there were no local programs, and I felt unable to relocate. Another factor was the obvious move by nurses in the region to gain higher degrees.

In 1969, the hospital where I worked had only one or two nurses who had master's degrees—I was one of two who had a bachelor's degree! By 1973 all the new nurses in advanced positions similar to mine had or were working towards graduate degrees. I therefore made application to a local university, spending a year to make up the necessary prerequisites in preparation for enrolling in a program in medical-surgical nursing. While I was taking courses to fulfill the requirements for graduate study, a program in primary care was established. I changed my major and became one of the seven students in the first graduating class of family nurse practitioners.

The 2 years spent studying to be a nurse practitioner were not easy for me. All seven students were quite competitive and concerned about their performance as "pioneers." There were no stipends, and we were spending large sums on tuition while at the same time we were questioning where in Philadelphia, with its conservative medical community, we would find jobs on graduation.

Our preceptors were primarily physicians. For example, I learned to listen to hearts from a renowned cardiologist, and became quite proficient at identifying heart murmurs, although this has not been terribly useful in long-term care! We had experiences in obstetric and pediatric clinics. The only geriatrics in my graduate program was a course in gerontology, which was given by the department of Community Health at the School of Medicine. The course was filled with depressing statistics which made me feel depressed, and I distinctly remember sitting in class thinking I could never take care of old people again! Now, here I am practicing solely with the elderly. I question the psychology that says you are in control of your life. For me, it has been that "Life is what happens to you while you are making other plans"—William Gaddis.

I felt really special after I graduated as a nurse practitioner. As a hospital nurse for 10 years after diploma school, I was often frustrated by the technology and how it interfered with the provision of quality care. It seemed that I was never in charge—it was always someone else, usually the doctor, dictating how and on what I should spend my time, and many times doing so in conflict with my own values. Being a nurse practitioner made me feel more responsible for my actions and the health care I provided. In the words of one of my colleagues, my new role "empowered me to act." I had a good sense of what changes needed to be made in order to provide better nursing care. There were some gaps in the program. For example, we had no course in pharmacology (heaven forbid that nurses should ever be able to prescribe medicines!). Nevertheless, we had learned how to obtain information and had developed an attitude of life long learning.

In 1975, the year I graduated, there was no national or state process for certification of nurse practitioners. The Primary Care Council of the American Nurses Association (ANA) was formed that year, and our class went as a group to a 2-day workshop in New York City to participate in discussions that led to the development of an ANA program for certification of primary care nurse practitioners. I was in the first group of nurses that took and passed this exam. I since have become certified as a Geriatric Nurse Practitioner by exam.

On graduation we developed a Nurse Practitioner Special Interest Group in our area, the third such group within the state nurses' association. One priority issue was the goal to obtain state level certification. At the time there was little support for these activities from either collegiate schools of nursing or the state nurses' association. Nevertheless, the nurse practitioner interest groups actively participated in meetings with the State Boards of Nursing and Medical Examiners, and were successful in passing rules and regulations for state certification of nurse practitioners. The state chose to certify programs rather than individual applicants, and students graduating from a state-certified program were titled as CRNPs (Certified Registered Nurse Practitioners).

We felt that although the nurse practitioner role fell within the framework of all nursing practice, there was a need for legal sanction of our practice, especially in those instances where there was question as to whether certain components of practice, for example, diagnosis and treatment, are explicitly or implicitly allowed within the state practice act. State certification assured that we were functioning within the rules and regulations of the state, legitimizing our practice as nurse practitioners for patients and employers.

THE CONTINUING CARE COMMUNITY

The life care concept is unique in long-term care (Somers and Spears, 1992). The community consists of a continuum of care, ranging from independent living to skilled care. People enter the community healthy. The prepayment component, inherent in life care, assures complete health care for the remainder of the person's life. It is somewhat analogous to an insurance policy. If the resident remains healthy, the money is never used on his or her behalf. If, on the other hand, the person becomes sick soon after entering the community and requires long-term personal or skilled care, he or she may receive benefits far exceeding the initial life-care fee. The payment structure therefore provides security of access to a full range of services, regardless of the resident's state of health.

The life care community in which I work is comprised of approximately 350 people over 65 years of age, 250 of whom live independent lives in garden-type apartments spread out over 83 acres. The average age of the independent resident is 83 1/2 years. These residents may utilize the services of the community nurse practitioners or physicians, or may seek medical care from outside providers (at their own expense.)

Thirty-two residents, with an average age of 87 years, live in the personal care facility. Residents move to personal care when they are unable to remain safely alone in their apartments, or when they have insufficient energy or mobility to get to or from the dining room. Cart service is available for residents whose ambulation is limited, but whose functional abilities otherwise allow for independent living. Failing vision and memory loss are also often responsible for a move to personal care. Supportive nursing care is available in the personal care facility 24 hours a day. The nursing goal for these 32 residents is to promote optimum levels of self-care as long as possible.

The community also has a skilled nursing facility (SNF) of 65 beds staffed with approximately 70 full- and part-time RNs, LPNs and NAs, 2 nurse practitioners, 2 physicians, a social worker, a physical therapist, and an activities staff of 3. In addition, podiatry and dental services are provided onsite, and occupational and speech therapy is available on consultation. The physical environment in the "health center" is designed to be noninstitutional, using wallpaper, soft colored drapes, and rugs. Permanent residents may use their own furniture in their rooms.

A life care community is one of those rare instances where administrative, consumer, and professional goals coincide. There is dual motivation to emphasize health, not only to provide exemplary care, but also to promote the financial well being of the community. Our philosophy is to keep everyone as healthy as possible. Services need to be provided in the most efficient and inexpensive manner, and the least expensive means is to have a healthy community whose residents care for themselves. This becomes especially important in the present economic climate of cost containment and Medicare cutbacks. For example, of our SNF beds, only four or five at a time are reimbursed by Medicare. The major source of SNF reimbursements comes from the community itself.

Therefore, there is a real incentive to provide good health care. Self-care is promoted whenever appropriate, from the very active residents committee activities, to teeth-brushing in the health center.

DIRECTOR OF NURSING/NURSE PRACTITIONER ROLE

To say the nurse practitioner was introduced to this life care community through the back door in putting it mildly. The new medical director tried to create a position for me because he felt the practice was too large for one provider. We had worked together at a comprehensive health care clinic—he was my first employer after graduation—and he felt that we could share the practice. The administrator, on the other hand, was not familiar with the nurse practitioner role (very few people were!) and was not interested in hiring me. Then the Director of Nursing position became available and the physician suggested that I apply. The idea was rather unappealing. I had chosen to pursue practitioner education to get away from administration, and had turned down other supervisory positions because of the lack of patient contact. A position as Director of Nursing in a nursing home was not the ideal job I had envisioned after completing my master's degree. Furthermore, the administrator was intent on hiring a person familiar and experienced with the rules and regulations of long-term care in an effort to preclude federal and state problems over licensure. I started as an employee of the medical director. The administrator had one day's notice of this arrangement and hastily bestowed on me the title of Acting Director of Nursing. After 2 weeks on the job, the administrator urged me to accept the dual position of Nurse Practitioner and Director of Nursing, and we had a wonderful working relationship from then on.

In retrospect, assuming the dual titles of Director of Nursing and Nurse Practitioner worked out extremely well. I was able to facilitate change and maximize my nurse practitioner functions. I was responsible for the preparation and administration of the health care budget—which allowed more control of programs. My two positions intermeshed. Because I had an Assistant Director of Nursing, which was negotiated when I accepted the DON position, initially I spent one-third of my time in purely administrative functions and two-thirds in a clinical role. Later on, unfortunately, the balance shifted to the DON role. When I was taking care of patients in the skilled care facility, I was still very much the Director of Nursing. Many management responsibilities

individual modify his behavior, while the physician is more willing to develop a prescriptive plan of care.

PHILOSOPHY OF PRIMARY CARE IN THE NURSING HOME

Primary care is the predominant practice in a nursing home. It is comprised of chronic care and acute care and includes all the common health care problems. Although all the residents are old and many are frail, the majority of the health care problems encountered can be managed at the primary care level.

My philosophy of primary care developed as I studied for my master's degree. It became apparent very early in the program that an important part of our practice was to recognize and plan for the holistic needs of our clients. It also was clear that I would not be able to provide for all their health needs, but that I was responsible to see that my clients had access to the care that was required. In this respect, my assessment skills are vital. I need to know when to treat and when to refer to another health provider. I need to be cognizant of the costs of referrals and take responsibility for minimizing the high costs of health care. Studies conducted at the Robert Wood Johnson Teaching Nursing Home and Mountain projects show consistently that nurse practitioners in nursing homes improve the quality of care with no added cost (Garrard, Kane, Rutner, & Buchanon, 1990).

In my practice, I incorporate my nursing philosophy of self care, adapted from Dorothy Orem's model (1985), into my concept of primary care. I believe that I am here to help the elderly to care for themselves. The more independent the resident is, the more powerful he will feel. It is important that the residents feel as good about themselves as they can, despite the disabilities or infirmities age or disease imparts. The concept of patients taking care of themselves was one of the biggest changes in my philosophy as a result of my graduate program. I was trained in a hospital setting where your role was to take care of and do everything for the patient, and which in turn made me feel like a "good nurse." Now, I feel that my importance lies in recognizing the patients' strengths, and in facilitating those strengths through education and support, although at the same time remaining sensitive to their sometimes overwhelming disabilities and infirmities.

It is this philosophy of self-care which makes the job in the long-term setting challenging. It is a challenge to help people maintain or resume

continence or self-feeding and offer simple but attainable goals. I believe in the power of positive thinking. People must feel that they are in
control, both of their health and, to some degree, of their disease. I very
much believe that health care should be participative and that decisions
about health should be joint client-provider decisions. This is an area
around which the physicians and I probably have the most dialogue.
Sometimes the medical treatment plan conflicts with the quality of life
plan. I feel that if patients disagree with health care suggestions, the
necessary education and knowledge should be provided to help them
make their own decisions. It may be better in the long run, because
people are then acting from a position of strength, rather than
weakness.

Another major area for philosophical decisions in a long-term facility
concerns the dying patient. The average age in our facility is 85, which
clearly means the residents are at the end of their lives. Maggie Kuhn,
founder of the Grey Panthers, stated in a recent address that the closure
of life should be a rewarding experience (Kuhn, 1991). How do we, as
advocates of the elderly, help to insure that "rewarding experience?"
Does this mean maintaining life at any expense? Once again, the philosophy of participative health care becomes very important. Since the advent of living wills, and, more recently, the even more explicit Advance
Medical Directives, it has become easier for the care providers to follow
the wishes of their patients. At Foulkeways, a community-wide program
introduced the advance medical directives, including educational seminars and personal counseling and assistance in the completion and no-
tarization of the form. The importance of this issue to the elderly is obvious: of this community of 250 independent residents, approximately
220 completed an advance medical directive.

Nurses who have worked in an acute care hospital sometimes have
trouble adjusting to the idea that "dying in our health center" is acceptable and, most times, desirable. Residents in the community have made
it clear that they want to die when it is time. Many are tired and ready.
They want to die without tubes, and with minimal hassle. We most often hear "Just let me go as peacefully as possible." If death is inevitable,
our goal is not to prolong life artificially. When dying residents are sent
to the hospital, control is lost because the hospital operates under different constraints, legally and administratively. If capable, the resident
is involved in the decision whether to hospitalize or not. If the resident
is not able to communicate, the family is consulted. Usually, if we feel
the residents are not going to improve, the decision is not to hospitalize
but to keep them "at home" where we are in control of their care. When
you have known people for a long time and know their wishes, you feel
that you are betraying them when you send them off to a hospital

where the environment is unfamiliar and impersonal. The accusation of "playing God" often surrounds these moral and ethical decisions, but are we playing God more by trying to prevent an inevitable death, or by allowing people to die at home?

When a resident dies of a heart attack, the reaction is "Oh, I hope I go like that." Residents tell me that if they tell their family they are ready to die, the reaction often is "Oh Mother, do not say that" and so they often do not talk about death with their loved ones. A good, nonthreatening way to open this type of dialogue is to encourage the resident to discuss their Advance Medical Directive with their children.

When residents tell me they are ready to die, it is a comforting thing for me to hear. I feel this is the way the end of life should be. It is very helpful to me to listen to the elderly who, without being depressed, eloquently discuss their view of death.

ACADEMIC LIAISONS

Over the years the nature of the facility, coupled with the nurse practitioner/physician model of care delivered, has resulted in linkages between the community and neighboring universities. We have students who come for both short- and long-term educational experiences in many fields of gerontology. I precept students from a master's level geriatric nurse practitioner program. For many years a group of undergraduate students received their first nursing experience in our skilled nursing facility. We provided them with an initial positive experience in caring for the elderly.

I have been precepting graduate nurse practitioner students since my own graduation. Having this responsibility is very rewarding since it provides a continuous link with the university, challenging me to continue to learn and be the best practitioner I can. The student hopefully benefits by my tutelage and I in turn have access to *her* knowledge and insights (so far all my students have been "hers"!). Also, having nursing students has allowed us to initiate some projects of longstanding interest but for which we have not had the necessary personnel, skills, or resources. Graduate nurse students have helped initiate residents' groups, taught both informally at the bedside and formally in inservice programs and resident seminars. One student undertook a resocialization project with residents living in the personal care area. We had become increasingly concerned that these residents were more isolated than others in the community. The student was able to increase interaction among these residents by rearranging the environment and establishing group activities. Students are treated with care and affection, since we feel that a good student experience helps mold a professional committed to the special problems of aging and willing to consider the field of gerontology.

Another link with academia is through research. Residents have participated in significant research projects conducted by the Center for Aging of the University of Pennsylvania; several spent the night at the university as part of a sleep project. Many are participating in a ten-year prospective urinary tract infection study. As a result of our research interest, one resident established a university fund in his wife's name to provide seed money for nursing research in geriatrics. This, in turn, led to the appointment of a professor in the school of nursing to the governing board of our facility and to an official partnership between the school and our community.

Every aspect of the student and research relationship results in an increased awareness and pride in the care our facility provides to its residents. Residents and staff alike feel as if they are contributing to importance. Research for the future must concern the health care, quality of life, and appropriate treatment for the very old.

REFLECTIONS

Practicing as a nurse practitioner in a life care community has been by far the most rewarding time in my nursing career. Initially, when I was one of the few master's prepared nurses in geriatrics, my friends and colleagues wondered at my satisfaction. They did not understand the challenge quality care for the elderly provided and the joy which meeting the challenge brought. It is very rewarding to see the growth of geriatric nurse practitioners and geriatric medicine in long-term care.

Nurse practitioners are successful in long-term care settings because they possess a combination of nursing skills and "a hernia into medicine" (B. Bates, personal communication; 1990). The focus of long-term care is concerned not only with the medical diagnosis, but with changes in lifestyle and quality of life. Who can do that better than nurses? While the whole health care system would benefit from a similar perspective, my clientele remains this one community. I feel like the old family doctor who, rather than moving away from town to find a more lucrative or challenging practice stayed your doctor until he died. At the same time, I frequently feel challenged by the possibilities outside this one community.

The success of the nurse practitioner is also tempered by administrative support and by state and federal regulations. From the beginning I have had the support of the administration and board. At one board meeting the president asked for my "wish list;" I didn't have one! The administrator had given me freedom to design programs as needed; apparently, the board gave him a similar degree of flexibility.

It has been interesting and rewarding to see how nurse practitioner issues at the state and federal level have slowly but persistently evolved. I feel the question of what the nurse practitioner is and what can he or she do is pretty much resolved in most states. This has been largely accomplished by placing the education of NPs in graduate programs and by studies which have demonstrated the quality and consumer acceptance of NPs. Medication prescriptive privileges of NPs are increasingly recognized under various practice models. The biggest issue still to be resolved is reimbursement under Medicare. It is unacceptable to reimburse physicians for services provided by NPs. Medicare payment to long-term care facilities for NP services and direct payment to NPs in designated rural areas are, however, encouraging. The future of the geriatric nurse practitioner has no place to go but up!

REFERENCES

Garrard, J., Kane, R., Rutner, F., & Buchanon, J. (1990). The impact of nurse practitioners on the care of nursing home residents. In R. Katz, R. L. Kane, and M. Mezey (Eds.), *Advances in long term care, Vol. 1* (pp. 169–187). New York: Springer Publishing Company.

Kuhn, M. "Psychosocial Needs of the Older Adult in America." Paper presented at Gerontological Update '91/Psychiatric Nursing Update '91 Philadelphia: Medical College of Pennsylvania Continuing Nursing Education 1991.

Orem, D. (1985). Nursing: Concepts of practice (3rd ed.). New York: McGraw-Hill.

Somers, A., & Spears, N. (1992). *The continuing care retirement community*. New York: Springer Publishing Company.

PHYSICIAN AND NURSE PRACTITIONER RELATIONSHIPS

William Kavesh

I first began working with nurse practitioners almost twenty years ago at a neighborhood health center in South Boston. This was my first job after completing a medical residency and the nurse practitioner, who had been a nurse at the health center, needed a preceptor to work with her through the final portion of her training. We were both fairly new practitioners, and I had no preconceptions about what her role should be. The patients welcomed her back, and many of them comfortably accepted her new role. She was more familiar to them than I was, and spent more time with them as well. But, gradually, they also came to accept me.

We evolved a fairly standard approach to seeing patients. I saw all new patients and then referred to her the ones who had fairly stable medical problems, such as hypertension and diabetes, that were amenable to management by a set of guidelines which her teachers had written. Our sessions ran at the same time, and I always had an open door policy: if she had any questions, I would stop what I was doing as soon as I could and come in to check things out. It soon became apparent that the guidelines, or any set of guidelines for that matter, could not begin to describe all the nuances of patient care which she encountered. Instead, we dealt with situations as they arose. She became more skilled at sorting out complex problems, and we both became more comfortable with the range of her skills. But I still reviewed most of the things which she did.

It was a fairly auspicious beginning to my experience with nurse practitioners. We both stayed at the health center about three years. Soon after that, I moved on to the Urban Medical Group, a nonprofit group practice specializing in long-term care and geriatrics. The Urban Medical Group operated an innovative nursing home care program which at that time was serving over 400 residents of about a dozen Boston area nursing homes. In addition, we provided medical services to several coordinated home care programs, which cared for 500 frail elders in their own homes. All these programs employed nurse practitioners.

Though nursing home and home care differ in a number of ways, the basic rationale for using nurse practitioners was similar. Physicians found the time constraints of a typical practice inimical to the responsiveness necessary to attend to acute problems in nursing homes and at home. A physician with an office full of patients would find it virtually impossible to drop everything and run to a nursing home or make a home visit. Reimbursement was woefully inadequate for the time involved. Finally, negative attitudes toward aging and nursing home care in particular discouraged physicians from caring for nursing home residents (American College of Physicians, 1980; National Foundation for Long-Term Care, 1981).

HOME CARE

Though, as we have seen, the rationale for the use of nurse practitioners is similar in home and institutional settings, the organizational regulatory, and reimbursement environments differ from home care to nursing home. Home care programs are organized primarily to deliver direct nursing services or services requiring nursing supervision, such as those delivered by home health aides (Kavesh, 1986). Despite significant growth in the proprietary sector in the 1980s, programs under the auspices of Visiting Nurse Associations, hospitals, or other nonprofit organizations still deliver the largest portion of home care services. One of the big problems these programs encounter is getting physician participation. While the physician writes the orders authorizing services and ostensibly has responsibility for everything that happens, in reality, the previously mentioned factors discourage most physicians from making home visits. When home care dealt with fairly limited and straightforward problems, such as postoperative care of a wound, this was not necessarily a problem. But as federal efforts to restrict the growth of nursing home care have expanded, home care programs have taken on the care of elderly patients with multiple complex medical problems and frequent changes in medications. As a result, the typical VNA nurse spends hours on the phone updating different physicians and getting new orders.

In a coordinated home care program, care is delivered by a team consisting of a nurse practitioner, a social worker, a physician, and other staff as appropriate. In the programs where Urban Medical Group physicians worked, the patients usually had no private physician, or the physician realized that s/he was unable to make regular and emergency home visits to deal with the complex medical problems these patients had. Therefore, the patient was often turned over to the team.

The key member of the team in these programs was the nurse practitioner. Because her full-time job was providing home care, she was available during the day for regular visits or emergencies. Our physicians were available by beeper for backup consultation and would make home visits when necessary. If hospital admission was necessary, the physician would admit the patient as his/her private patient. If a social worker or other provider was required, the nurse practitioner would make a request, and the physician would authorize the visit at a weekly team meeting.

As a physician, I came to rely increasingly on the diagnostic skills of the nurse practitioner to detect subtle changes in the physical status of the patients and to make changes in the therapeutic regimen according to the guidelines which we used. Often, a report at the weekly meeting would consist of the following: "Mrs. Levine called on Monday saying that her legs were more swollen and that she was wheezing at night. I went out to the house and she had rales half way up both lungs. So I gave her an extra 40 mg of lasix, got her to stop using the cans of salty soup I found in the kitchen, and now she's fine." Not only had the nurse practitioner treated the problem appropriately, but she had found the source of the problem, the salty soup, and fixed it. A visit to the doctor's office might have resulted in the same treatment, but the problem would have recurred every time the patient ate the soup—or worse, her medication would have been permanently increased, leaving her at risk for dehydration if she went without the soup for several days.

From time to time, the nurse practitioner would page me to tell me that a patient had deteriorated and probably would need admission to the hospital. Occasionally, I would make a home visit to confirm the severity of the problem, but, after a while, it became apparent that she was invariably correct when she thought the patient needed hospitalization, so we simply arranged for an emergency room visit where I would also see the patient and do an evaluation for the inevitable admission.

Once a week, the team got together for a 2-hour meeting. The caseload in all four of the programs where we provided physician services was about 100–140 patients. We reviewed most of the active cases on a regular basis, and spent more time on those that were unstable. The social worker or physical therapist would add additional information as necessary. Periodic physician home visits would be scheduled at the meetings as well.

The nurse practitioner's role in the coordinated home care program would seem to meet many needs of the aging U.S. society. Studies show repeatedly that older, disabled Americans prefer their homes to nursing homes (Kavesh, 1986). Since physicians find it difficult to make home visits, the use of the nurse practitioner seems ideal. Unfortunately, in home care settings, Medicare does not recognize nurse practitioners. If a home care program wants to hire a nurse practitioner, her visits must be billed as nursing visits, an anachronism left over from a time when home care was a short-term post-hospital phenomenon for surgical problems or brief rehabilitation. Further, the visit frequencies must conform to cumbersome rules under which reimbursement will not be made if the patient is either too stable or too sick. Reimbursement for the physician backup is woefully inadequate, reflecting Medicare rules put into effect to respond to abuses in the 1970s, when some home care programs paid physicians primarily to drum up business (General Accounting Office, 1979). Finally, state laws vary considerably in authorizing prescribing privileges for nurse practitioners. Though Massachusetts permits nurse practitioners to prescribe in home care settings (see below), many other states do not, inhibiting the spread of coordinated home care programs.

NURSING HOME CARE

In 1971, a Boston City Hospital physician, who was later to become one of the founders of the Urban Medical Group, noticed that nursing home residents always seemed to be coming and going from the emergency room and primary care clinics. They did not seem especially sick and most returned to the nursing home that day. This mechanism for providing nursing home care seemed both costly and burdensome for the residents. It was clearly the outgrowth of a system of Medicare oversight, ostensibly set up in response to physician abuses, which restricted physician reimbursement to one visit per month. It was possible on occasion to get paid for additional emergency visits, but the effort involved was so cumbersome and the review mechanism so capricious that most physicians visited residents once a month and sent them to the hospital for anything else they needed.

In an effort to break this cycle of inappropriate transfers, a program was developed to utilize nurse practitioners and physician assistants teamed with a physician to provide onsite primary care to nursing home residents. The advantage of the program to the nursing home residents and families was the opportunity to have a practitioner physically at the nursing home at least twice a week, evaluating problems and meeting with families and staff. If an emergency arose at one facility, the practitioner would be able to make a special visit within a short time by simply rearranging routine visits at another home. The advantage to nursing home staff was the presence of a primary care provider who was attentive to emergency problems, provided informal education and training, and permitted staff to feel comfortable caring for sicker patients at the home because reliable backup was available.

The program began in 1972 as a demonstration project with waivers granted by the Massachusetts Department of Public Health that permitted practitioners to perform initial and followup examinations and write orders under the supervision of a physician. After three years, a controlled study of almost 500 residents enrolled in the program showed a pattern of results which have been replicated in a number of studies since then: an increase in visits to the residents of the nursing home coupled with a marked reduction in the use of hospital-based emergency room, clinic, and inpatient services (Mark, Willemain, Malcolm, Master, & Clarkson, 1976). The pattern of visits at the nursing home also changed, with a significant increase in visits required by patient need. A 1982 study of the program showed that almost half the visits were episodic, whereas the physicians in the control group invariably visited only once a month, the minimum interval for which Medicare provides reimbursement for a routine visit (Kavesh, Mark, & Kearney, 1984). The study also showed improvement in the quality of care. Nursing home administrators and nurses were very pleased with the program because they finally had someone to give them the timely medical backup that physicians alone had not been providing. Finally, and most important to later efforts to expand such models, the program proved to be cost neutral.

The success of Urban Medical Group's nursing home care program provided the impetus for the next stages in the maturation of the nurse practitioner role in Massachusetts nursing homes: legalization of the right for practitioners to write prescription in long-term care settings, and statewide expansion of the demonstration program.

By the early 1980s, a number of studies besides those of the Urban Medical Group had documented that the quality of care provided by nurse practitioners working with physicians was equivalent to that provided by physicians alone. Increasingly, efforts were being successfully undertaken in a number of states to obtain prescription writing privileges for practitioners. Urban Medical Group activists saw that waivers for prescription writing would not persist indefinitely. Therefore, with the assistance of an activist lawyer and a coalition of nursing home industry supporters, physician assistants, nurse practitioners, community advocates, and Urban Medical physicians, a campaign was undertaken to get a prescription writing law passed. It took three years to succeed, partly due to the opposition of the Massachusetts Medical Society, which felt that only doctors should be able to write prescriptions, and the Massachusetts Pharmaceutical Association, which worried about increasing liability for pharmacists and argued that if anybody other than doctors should be allowed to prescribe, it should be pharmacists. The bill allowed nurse practitioners and physician assistants to prescribe in home care settings and long-term care settings as long as a supervising physician was identified on the prescription and the physician reviewed the prescription within a certain period of time (one or two weeks, depending on the situation) (Kavesh & Bachrach, 1990).

The other step taken in response to the success of the nursing home care program was an application to the Health Care Financing Administration for a statewide expansion of the program. This demonstration, which ran through most of the 1980s, promoted the expansion of nurse practitioner (and physician assistant) activities to over 100 nursing homes throughout the state of Massachusetts. An evaluation of this program, conducted by researchers from the RAND Corporation, the University of Minnesota School of Public Health, and the Boston University School of Public Health showed that physician/practitioner teams improved the quality of care at costs that were equivalent to or, for some subgroups, less than the costs of care provided by physicians practicing in the traditional manner. The other key findings of the study were in the area of nursing home staff and administrator satisfaction. The vast majority of nursing directors and administrators who were surveyed felt that the practitioner had a faster response time than a physician, had a positive impact on nursing home staff morale, and gave residents more attention than those cared for by a physician alone (Buchanan et al., 1989a).

A PHYSICIAN PERSPECTIVE ON THE ROLE OF THE NURSE PRACTITIONER IN THE HOME CARE SETTING

Though there may be certain similarities in the roles of the nurse practitioner in home care and in the nursing home, it is useful to look first at these categories separately. From the perspective of the physician, the distribution of roles in home care includes the following features:

1. Home care is a nursing program. It is usually run by nurses, and nursing is a key component of home care in the eyes of regulators and third-party payors. Despite the physician's role mandated by regulators, the nurse practitioner operates in a nursing setting. She is involved in supervising other staff, such as home health aides, and delegating responsibilities to other professionals, such as therapists.

2. For the patient and family, the nurse practitioner becomes the primary provider and contact. She makes most of the home visits, is the first call in emergencies, and serves as the focal point for the activities of the team.

3. The physician continues to play an important role at various stages of the home care experience. If the physician has been the primary provider prior to the onset of home care. s/he plays a key role in legitimizing the role of the nurse practitioner. The tendency of the patient and family will be to call the physician first for problems. If the nurse practitioner is going to feel invested in the patient's care, the physician must

resist the urge to deal with little problems, and pass them off to the nurse practitioner. If the physician has not been the primary provider, it may be easier to get the patient and family to view the nurse practitioner as the first call.

4. Once the relationship with the patient and family is established, the physician still has overall responsibility but needs to permit the nurse practitioner to have sufficient independence in making decisions so that she remains satisfied with her role. No matter what a set of guidelines may say, personality and experience play a big role here. Some physicians are comfortable delegating a great deal of responsibility, especially as it becomes clear that the nurse practitioner can deal with problems independently, but has the self-awareness to know when she is running up against her limits. Other physicians worry more about being sued if a problem arises, and therefore want to be much more involved in details.

5. In any case, the physician must back up the nurse practitioner, both in being available by beeper for problems and in being supportive if families try to undermine the nurse practitioner's role by calling on the physician to second-guess what the nurse practitioner has done. There is nothing more destructive of the nurse practitioner's self-confidence than a physician who countermands an order when it really is a judgment call as to what the preferred option might be.

6. The physician must be available to take over the care of the patient if hospitalization is necessary. The physician should certainly stay in touch with the team to get their input concerning difficult decisions regarding limitations of care or possible institutionalization rather than a return home. But regular progress reports at the team meeting are also valuable, so that everyone can keep up with what is going on in the hospital.

7. The nurse practitioner must be aware of her key role as the hub of the care wheel and the need to keep everyone else informed as to any changes in the patient's condition. The physician's comfort level with the nurse practitioner will be directly related to the degree to which she keeps him/her informed as to potential problem situations—especially at the end of the day, when overnight coverage will usually be provided by the physician.

8. The nurse practitioner must be sensitive to the limitations of her knowledge and skills. This is not a problem unique to nurse practitioners. Physicians also need to know when to call a subspecialist in for a consultation. But, since the collaborating physician will be held accountable for any problems that occur with a patient jointly cared for with a nurse practitioner, the nurse practitioner needs to be mindful of the need to consult frequently for problems that approach her limits.

A PHYSICIAN PERSPECTIVE ON THE ROLE OF THE NURSE PRACTITIONER IN THE NURSING HOME SETTING

Nursing homes differ in significant ways from home care settings. The nursing home is a complex organization run by an administrator who usually has a business background. The nursing staff are accountable to the administrator via the director of nurses. Both the nurse practitioner and physician are outsiders. (The option for Medicaid reimbursement for the nurse practitioner to be hired by the nursing home appears to have been foreclosed by a provision of the Omnibus Budget Reconciliation Act of 1990, which precludes Medicare payment for nurse practitioners hired by the nursing home. The home could choose to hire the nurse practitioner as part of the regular complement of nurses, but there would be no option for Medicare reimbursement for visits delegated by a physician.) The physician is traditionally viewed as the lead person in providing medical care to nursing home residents. These differences in setting inevitably affect the role of the nurse practitioner.

The role of the nurse practitioner in the Massachusetts nursing home care program model is outlined in Table 6-5. In the nursing home, as opposed to home care, the nurse practitioner is an unfamiliar entity. Therefore the key requirement is for the physician to establish for the administrator, nurses, patient, and family that the nurse practitioner is the person who takes first call for all problems within regular working hours. The staff also need to know that the physician is readily available to the nurse practitioner. The success of the Urban Medical Group model in attracting and holding good practitioners hinged upon the willingness of the physicians to provide that level of support.

The nurse practitioner establishes her credibility in the nursing home by making regular visits to the facility once or twice a week and by making emergency visits at the request of the nursing staff. In the Urban Medical Group model, a nurse practitioner could have a caseload of up to 150 nursing home residents scattered in two to three facilities. The physician would visit once a week in facilities with a large caseload (over 30–40), and as infrequently as every two weeks where the case load was smaller. During the physician visits, patients are seen who require a physician examination by regulation, as well as patients whose cases the nurse practitioner wants to review because of the complexity or persistence of a problem.

The nurse practitioner strengthens her relationships to the nurses in the nursing home by her responsiveness to acute problems and her informal teaching of staff. Since, for the reasons mentioned earlier, nurses

TABLE 6.5   Role of the Nurse Practitioner in the Nursing Home

1. Primary Onsite Provider
   - Takes first call from nursing home
   - Visits to patient
     a) Initial within regulatory time limit
     b) Regular periodic
     c) Episodic/emergency at request of staff
2. Relationship to Physician
   - Works in collaboration with physician
   - Practices within scope of written guidelines
   - Telephone backup by physician
   - Regularly scheduled rounds
   - Regularly scheduled patient examinations
   - Feedback between physician and nurse practitioner
3. Relationship To Nursing Home Staff
   - Responds to requests of staff
   - Coordinate management of emergencies and critically ill patients
   - Case conferencing
   - Training sessions
4. Relationship To Patient's Family
   - Establish communication with family
   - Interval contacts

often have difficulty getting the same level of responsiveness from physicians, the role of the nurse practitioner is enhanced by her availability. Because of her frequent presence onsite and the difference in hierarchical relationships compared to the role of the physician in relation to staff nurses, the nurse practitioner is often able to establish a trusting and close relationship with nursing staff. In addition, the nursing staff becomes used to the reliability of the nurse practitioner; they often are comfortable caring for sicker patients at the nursing home because they know backup is available.

Relating to patients' families is a bit trickier. They often expect the physician to play a larger role. At the most critical moments, when hospitalization may be necessary, the physician does assume the leading role in making arrangements and providing direct primary care to the patient. Thus, the physician moves from a position of some distance from the day-to-day care of the nursing home setting to the intense involvement of the hospital setting. The family may become used to this level of physician involvement and expect it when the patient returns to the nursing home. Physician support of the nurse practitioner's renewed role becomes important at this point.

The physician's role in the nursing home is outlined in Table 6-6. The

TABLE 6.6 Role of the Physician in the Nursing Home

1. Back-up and Call Accessibility
   - To the NP
   - To the nursing home
   - To the family
2. Collaborative Relationship with NP
   - Reinforce role of NP
   - Initial examination of patient
   - Convey involvement with patient
   - Onsite visits—regularly scheduled, usually weekly
   - Consultation to NP
3. Relationship to Administration of the Nursing Home
   - Responsible for patient
   - Compliance with state and federal regulations
   - Medical Director, committee
4. Connection to the Hospital/Consultants

key features are prompt availability, regular visits, and consistent support of the nurse practitioner. The physician plays an important role in liaison to the nursing home administrator. The physician may sit on nursing home committees or be the medical director of the home and therefore have a regular relationship to the administrator. Even if this is not the case, the administrator will often turn to the physician to solve problems with families. The degree to which the physician maintains a good relationship with the administrator may affect the way in which the nurse practitioner can function within the nursing home.

REGULATORY AND REIMBURSEMENT ISSUES IN NURSING HOMES

The regulatory environment for nurse practitioners in long-term care is steadily improving. The role of the nurse practitioner is currently recognized in every state. At present, 35 states permit nurse practitioners some degree of prescriptive authority (Pearson, 1991).

At the federal level, a provision of the Omnibus Budget Reconciliation Act of 1990 permits physicians to delegate to a nurse practitioner all visits to nursing home residents required by law. The law also includes a requirement that the nurse practitioner can not be hired by the nursing home. I find this law to be a mixed blessing. In many rural states, especially those in the West, nursing homes have had trouble finding nurse practitioners and doctors. Under the auspices of the Mountain States Health Corporation, many of these nursing homes sent nurses for training as nurse practitioners, after which they could return to the home (Buchanan et al., 1989b). Acting, no doubt, to protect the consumer's interest in having the nurse practitioner free from the coercion of the ownership, the law now outlaws such arrangements. At the same time, it authorizes a minimal relationship between the nurse practitioner and the physician—at least if the state in which they practice will permit it My own view is that the patient benefits from the active involvement of both the nurse practitioner and the physician. It is hard to imagine a physician being able to provide optimal hospital care to a nursing home resident whom s/he barely knows. Nonetheless, the new law, and its accompanying regulations (Federal Register, 1991) do add a degree of flexibility that responsible physicians and nurse practitioners may find workable.

In the area of reimbursement, the Omnibus Reconciliation Act of 1989 included a provision authorizing Medicare reimbursement of nurse practitioners in nursing homes. Reimbursement is set at a rate of 85% of the rate for the least specialized physician in the area. Unfortunately, this could mean rates of $20 or lower in certain areas, which does not encourage nurse practitioners to go into long term care. The new physician fee schedule, based upon a resource based scale of relative values, could raise the base physician rate to the point where it might be financially viable for nurse practitioners to practice in long-term care settings, especially if the rate accepted for physician visits reflects the actual value of resources expended in a nursing home visit as suggested by the American Medical Directors Association (AMDA, 1991).

COMMONALITIES OF THE PHYSICIAN NURSE PRACTITIONER RELATIONSHIP ACROSS PRACTICE SETTINGS

In my experience as a physician the best aspect of working with a nurse practitioner is being freed from the need to respond to a myriad of problems, which the nurse practitioner is well equipped to handle and which would otherwise wreak havoc with my schedule. Most of the acute situations in long-term care involve infectious diseases, cardiorespiratory problems, or psychosocial crises. These are usually well suited to the development of guidelines. I have had the good fortune to work with nurse practitioners who have been astute and compassionate clinicians. They have made it possible for me to care for many more older patients than I could have done alone. Most important, they have made it possible for me to provide these patients with a higher quality of care than I could have provided alone.

If there is a down side, it is the feeling of distance that I sometimes have in caring for someone whose primary relationship is really with the nurse practitioner. Once the patient has been in the hospital, that gap is usually bridged from that point on, but, until then, I am very much aware that there is something special about the primary relationship with the patient and family that results from being the person who receives the first call. Would I give up working with nurse practitioners to get that extra measure of satisfaction? Not at all.

REFERENCES

American College of Physicians. (1980). Proceedings of a conference on the changing needs of nursing home care. Washington, DC: American College of Physicians.

American Medical Directors Association. (1991, March 6). Letter to Health Care Financing Administration, Columbia, MD: American Medical Directors Association.

Buchanan, J. L., Arnold, S. B., Bell, R. M., Witsberger, C., Kane, R. L., & Garrard, J. (1989a). *The financial impact of nursing home based geriatric nurse practitioners: An evaluation of the Mountain States Health Corporation GNP Project.* Santa Monica, CA: The RAND Corp. #R–3694–HCFA/RWJ.

Buchanan, J. L., Kane, R. L., Garrard, J., Bell, R. M., Witsberger, C., Rosenfeld, A., Skay, C., & Gifford, D. (1989b). *Results from the evaluation of the Massachusetts Nursing Home Connection Program.* Santa Monica, CA: The RAND Corporation, #JR–01.

Federal Register. (1991, September 26). *56,* 48875. General Accounting Office. (1979). Home health care services—Tighter Fiscal Controls Needed. (HRD 79–17). Washington, DC: General Accounting Office.

Kavesh, W. N. (1986). Home care: Process, outcome, cost. *Annual Review of Gerontology and Geriatrics, 6,* 135–195.

Kavesh, W., & Bachrach, S. (1990). Nursing home innovation in the public arena. *Journal of Aging & Social Policy, 2,* 87–106.

Kavesh, W., Mark, R., & Kearney, G. (1984, November). Medical care teams improve nursing home care and reduce costs. Paper presented at the 37th Annual Scientific Meeting of the Gerontological Society of America, San Antonio.

Mark, R. G., Willemain, T. R., Malcolm, T., Master, R. J., & Clarkson, T. (1976). Nursing home telemedicine project: Final Report. Vol 1. (NSF/RA 76–0282). Washington, DC: National Science Foundation.

National Foundation for Long-Term Care. (1981). Proceedings of a conference on physician involvement in nursing homes. Washington, DC: National Foundation for Long-Term Care.

Pearson, L. J. (1991). 1990–91 Update: How each state stands on legislative issues affecting advanced nursing practice. *Nurse Practitioner, 16*, 11–18.

Chapter 7

NURSE-MIDWIFERY AND PRIMARY HEALTH CARE FOR WOMEN

Joyce E. Thompson

P RIMARY care nursing for women in an outpatient setting focuses on the promotion of health and the practice of healthy behaviors by women during their years of potential reproductive activity. The health care activities of nurses include health education and self-care instructions, health screening, and health supervision relative to women of childbearing age. The principal foci for primary care are contraception, childbearing care, gynecological screening, and sexual counseling. The principal health care provider referred to in this chapter is the certified nurse-midwife.

WOMEN AND HEALTH CARE

We live in a time when individuals are more actively seeking to control their own destinies. Feelings of independence, self-control, and self-determination abound as individuals cooperate in their health care and assume self-care activities. These feelings are of special interest to women whose place in society (and in health or illness care) until recently has accorded them few opportunities for self-determination and control of their own destinies (Scully, 1980; Thompson & Thompson, 1980). Modern contraceptive means, although of some risk to the users, have given millions of women a choice in childbearing instead of almost certain motherhood. There are still some people (mostly men) who think this choice is wrong (Thompson & Thompson, 1981). But for the majority of women, freedom to choose whether and when to bear children has opened up opportunities for greater control over their lives, including wider options in career choice, improved health with the spacing of children, and improved education without interruption for childbearing.

Self-care is a process of education and action in which an individual learns to provide effectively for his or her own health care needs. It may include some screening activities, such as taking a Pap smear, and treatment of certain conditions, such as vaginitis, with natural remedies. Self-care skills are learned, and this learning can be self-initiated, group-taught, or learned through an organized educational program in a health care facility with the professionals acting as consultants. Today the types of self-care activities increasing in importance involve nutrition, exercise, self-medication, and stress management. All of these and other self-care activities important to healthy women serve as a model for primary health care. The practice of primary health care by nurses is based on a cooperative, educative, and supportive relationship with women clients.

If one accepts the premise that women need health care services during their reproductive years in order to maintain or improve their health status, it would seem to follow that provision of such services should be a national health priority, supported by lawmakers as well as by the people for whom the services are intended—women. Unfortunately, this is not the case. The question of why a mandate for health care for all women of childbearing age has not occurred is one focus of this chapter.

PROVIDERS OF PRIMARY HEALTH CARE FOR WOMEN

The Nurse-Midwife

For purposes of this chapter, the primary care nurse working most closely with healthy women of childbearing age is the certified nurse-midwife. The nurse-midwife is an individual educated in the two disciplines of nursing and midwifery; a certified nurse-midwife (CNM) is one who has been certified by examination for entry into practice according to the requirements of the American College of Nurse-Midwives (ACNM) (ACNM, 1978; DeClerq, 1992). In 1992, there were 4,100 nurse midwifes practicing in the United States, of whom 3,300 were members of the American College of Nurse-Midwives. Approximately 300 new midwives are certified annually.

Nurse-midwifery practice as defined by the ACNM (1987a) includes the independent management of the care of healthy newborns and women throughout the childbearing cycle and the care of women seeking contraceptive and/or gynecological care. Nurse-midwifery practice occurs within a health care system that provides for medical consultation, collaborative management or referral, as needed, and is in accord with the *Standards for the Practice of Nurse-Midwifery* as defined by the ACNM (ACNM, 1987b).

The CNM utilizes written policies and procedures (protocols) that have been jointly agreed upon with the collaborating physician(s). These protocols form the general guidelines for nurse-midwifery practice in a given setting. The protocols speak to areas of care (antepartum, intrapartum, family planning-gynecology), specific procedures (e.g., laboratory tests, pudendal blocks, normal delivery, intrauterine device [IUD] insertions, newborn physical examinations), medications that may be used in the treatment of specific conditions (e.g., anemia, vaginitis, analgesia for labor), and the indications for referral to a physician (e.g., placenta previa, preeclampsia, breech delivery, recurrent pelvic inflammatory disease [PID]) (American College of Obstetrics and Gynecology, 1982). This autonomy in decisionmaking is enhanced by the use of practice protocols, since the nurse-midwife must rely on clinical skills and judgment to know what to do at any given time and when to call the physician for consultation or collaboration (ACNM, 1985; ACNM, 1986; ACNM, 1991b; DeClerq, 1992).

The above definition of nurse-midwifery practice also clearly states that the CNM provides care for essentially normal newborns and women throughout the childbearing cycle, which practice is clearly the epitome of health care to this professional. Thus, the CNM is a *nurse* who provides *health* care to women seeking *primary care* services. In addition, nurse midwives practice according to a philosophy whose central theme is family-centered care, supporting the woman's right to self-determination in her health care, and in which the nurse's support of client and family as "captains" of the health care team is implicit! (ACNM, 1989). Self-determination in health care requires informed consent and responsibility for one's actions (Thompson, 1980; Thompson et al., 1989), which in turn require education and interest in self-care activities. Thus the nurse-midwife is an excellent example of a nurse who provides primary health care for women.

Education of Nurse-Midwives

The education of nurse-midwives as providers of primary health care services was begun in the United States in 1932 at the Maternity Center Association in New York City. Since that time standardization of curriculum has evolved along with a formal accreditation process administered by the ACNM. There are currently two routes to basic preparation as a nurse midwife: the 9- to 12-month certificate, and the 16- to 20-month master's degree programs (ACNM, 1991a). Four- to six-month refresher (precertification) programs exist for foreign prepared nurse midwives or those who wish to upgrade their knowledge and skills for current practice. In 1992 there were 37 programs preparing nurse midwives: 24 master's programs; 10 certificate programs; and 3 precertification programs.

The core competencies required in all nurse midwifery programs include theory and clinical practice in the care of essentially healthy women and newborns throughout the childbearing cycle and health care for women of childbearing age who are not pregnant (ACNM, 1985). In addition, knowledge of common pathological conditions of pregnancy is required, although clinical practice with high-risk clients is not. Emphasis throughout the educational program is placed on health-promotion activities, family-centered care, and development of the client's ability to screen for potential complications so they can be prevented or treated early.

The nurse-midwifery curriculum in many educational programs is based on the health model of care because nurse-midwives believe in the natural physiological state of pregnancy, and direct their care efforts toward the attainment and maintenance of optimal health for mother and fetus. Perhaps nowhere else in the health care system is the truism of personal responsibility for health more obvious than during a normal pregnancy. As long as all is going well, only the pregnant woman can maintain that optimal health state through proper nutrition, exercise, sleep, and management of life stresses. The role of the nurse-midwife is one of watchful screening, teaching, support, and supervision (Thompson et al., 1989).

Health education comprises approximately 90% of the clinical activities of nurse midwives, including the teaching of self-care skills, preparation of childbearing and childrearing, and knowledge of the anatomy and physiology of women. These educational activities also provide women with knowledge of their bodies, contraception, pregnancy, and general health care needs so that informed decisionmaking about health actions is promoted. The theoretical framework of health education builds on the woman's perception of her state of health, her view of herself as a person and as a woman, and her particular stage of growth and development (Bermosk & Porter, 1979; Rubin, 1979).

A concrete example of the nurse-midwives' belief in and promotion of self-determination for women clients is their willingness to offer care options to childbearing families. Women were encouraged to make informed decisions about the frequency of prenatal visits long before the NIH/HHS Expert Panel on the Content of Prenatal Care suggested fewer visits for healthy women (1989). Women are also asked who their support people will be during childbearing and during antepartum visits, what type of delivery they want, where that delivery will take place, and what specific procedures will be allowed on indication (e.g., episiotomy, analgesia, IV, prep, or enema). Concurrent with the nurse-midwife's encouragement of women to take an active role in decisions about their health care is the education of women for the responsibilities inherent in self-determination. For example, if a woman plans a home delivery, she must also be willing to maintain her body in optimum condition for labor, prepare herself and her family for the labor, delivery, and needs of a postpartum mother and newborn, and consent to prenatal supervision so that the candidacy for home birth can be assessed at frequent intervals.

One example of education for primary health care practice by nurse-midwives is the private nurse-midwifery practice at Pennsylvania Hospital established in 1985. It was founded on the belief in the client's right to self-determination and active participation in care decisions, and to serve as a practice base for the education of nurse-midwives. The concomitant responsibilities of both client and nurse-midwife are spelled out in the consent-for-care form, with the understanding that if either party to this contract can not or does not meet its responsibilities, then the contract is broken. This contract is possible because all the clients are healthy and not dependent on an organized health care system to keep them well.

The practice was established principally to provide an experience base for students in the master's program in nurse-midwifery, in which students can actually put into practice what they are taught in the educational program. This educational program also provides clinical experience in a variety of public and private nurse midwifery practices and in home birth and birth center settings as well. Thus, the educational and practice philosophy of nurse-midwifery as *health* care is reinforced by the curriculum following a health model, and students increase their knowledge and skills in health-promoting activities.

Other Nurse Providers of Womens' Health Care

Other primary care nurses who provide health care to women are family planning nurse practitioners (now expanded to include ob/gyn and family planning practice), usually prepared in certificate-level postnursing programs, and health care of women specialists and the family nurse clinicians, usually prepared at the master's degree level in nursing programs. All of these nurses with advanced practice provide care for women at all points in the life cycle, with varying degrees of emphasis on health care for women of childbearing age. Family planning was the original focus of many of these expanded roles, beginning in the late 1960s and early 70s. Expansion to well-woman gynecological services was a natural extension in the late 1970s. Historically, since the early twentieth century, public health nurses have provided prenatal care services; other nurses learned these same skills in advanced nursing programs in the 1970s. Use of practice protocols, common among family planning and ob/gyn nurse practitioners, are limited among the newer health care of women specialists and family nurse clinicians. The roles of family nurse clinicians within the health care delivery system are still developing and, therefore, patterns of practice, vary a great deal (American Nurses Association [ANA]), 1976; Edmundson, Jennings, & Kowalski, 1980; Gluck, 1980; Martin, 1978; Pickard, Noble, & Defiese, 1976; Rooks, 1989; Bell & Mills, 1989).

In summary, several types of nurses currently provide primary health services for women in this country. The nurse-midwife, with origins in practice extending back to Biblical times and in this country to the mid-1920s, has the benefit of being an established and legally recognized health care provider within our national health care system, who clearly represents the professional autonomy and scope of practice activities needed to provide primary health care services to women of reproductive age. This, however, by no means implies that the midwife is free of limitations or constraints on practice, or even that she or he automatically succeeds in establishing a role as a primary health care nurse. Many critical issues are raised by the concept of primary health care and by the provision of needed health care services in this country, especially when those services are provided by nurses.

MODEL OF PRIMARY HEALTH CARE FOR WOMEN

Any model of primary health care must be based on knowledge of what determines health, what activities promote health, which type of health care provider can best support or carry out these health-promoting activities, and how that health care provider should be educated for such a crucial role in our national health care system. Each individual has a responsibility for adopting health behaviors and giving up careless, self-destructive habits. Blum (1974) believes that medical care and the provision of health services are relatively minor inputs into one's state of health. He places greatest emphasis for the state of one's health on the environment (fetal and physical), and sociocultural, educational, and employment factors. The next greatest impact is from one's personal behavior, followed by health services, and then hereditary factors. McKeown (1978) de Tornyay (1978) and *Healthy People 2000* (1991) state that the main determinant of health is the way of life an individual chooses to follow.

If one's lifestyle is the principal determinant of one's state of health, what could be a more cost-effective health program than one that promotes self-care and a healthy lifestyle? A model for primary health care for women should be based on a holistic health concept fostering maintenance and/or adoption of health behaviors and habits by the woman and her significant others.

Health, in my opinion, is a continuum from most to least healthy, with the majority of us falling along the "healthy," end and without major illness or disease. Health is a separate condition from disease, but health and illness are not necessarily opposites of one another, as clearly explained by Gardner and Fiske (1981).

If health is principally determined by one's lifestyle and environment, it may be concluded that any cost-effective model of primary health care must focus on education: teaching individuals to know what constitutes health for them, how it may be achieved or maintained through alterations in their lifestyles, if necessary, and preparing each individual to assume the responsibility for self-care. Education for self-care and assuming responsibility for one's own health are key components of the proposed primary health care model, and they are the most difficult components of the model to teach and learn (de Tornyay, 1978; Millis, 1977), primarily because most of us, whether consumer or provider, tend to have some destructive habits. Perhaps we have all fallen into that mistaken notion often promoted by the medical world that disease can be treated and health regained no matter what we do to ourselves (McKeown, 1978).

A second important component of a primary health care model is a personalized, caring concern exhibited at all times by health care providers for the whole person and for that person's significant others. This *caring* concern is *not*, however, equated with a *controlling* concern by the professional (Gardner & Fiske, 1981; Garrett & Garrett, 1982; Thompson, Oakley, Burke, Jay, & Winklin, 1989). All people need exposure to health care providers who are concerned enough to allow them information and the space to make informed decisions about their health and its supervision, besides encouraging healthy people to assume health-promoting behaviors, thus maintaining control over their own bodies and lives. We health professionals are beginning to see the illogical nature of our demands that clients be "good" submissive patients and yet also become responsible adults in control of their health. Such schizophrenic demands of adults often leave them with little choice but to distrust the system and go it alone, if at all. The health care professional must also be aware of and understand the client's need for and use of natural remedies and therapies, such as herbs, acupuncture, meditation, biofeedback, and faith healing (Bermosk & Porter, 1979). It may be difficult for professional health care workers to provide all of these modalities, but it is important to know about them.

Part of this caring concern is knowing when to use a directive approach to health care, when to be supportive, and when mutual participation is indicated. During my own research (Thompson, 1980) on the process of care used by nurse-midwives to supervise the health status of primigravid women, I concluded that even though some women responded very well to learning about pregnancy and taking an active role in decisions about their care, other women seemed more responsive to being taken care of by the nurse-midwife. It seems impractical to expect all women or all people to want to and to be able to participate fully in working toward mutually agreed upon health goals, although this type of interaction is an important goal to strive toward.

The other two necessary components of any model for primary health care are the activities of health screening and health supervision. The health screening component for women includes such things as routine cancer smear, breast examination, tests for venereal disease and vaginitis, and general physical fitness exams relative to nutrition, exercise, sleep, and activity patterns. The health supervision component for women includes pregnancy and contraceptive care and well woman gynecological care for women who are neither pregnant nor practicing contraception. An integral part of health supervision is the integration of counseling activities, consultation and/or referral to other sources of care (e.g., the dentist), and ongoing health education activities.

There have been several models of primary health care proposed in the literature and used in practice these past few years (ANA, 1976; Bermosk & Porter, 1979; Choi, 1981; Fagin, 1992; Nursing's Agenda, 1991). They range from minor modifications of the medical model that include health screening activities, to global ideas of holistic health care in which the provider needs expertise in both scientific and natural remedies. The shortage of health care of the type described in this chapter led me to develop my own model.

My schematic representation of a woman's primary health care model is illustrated in Figure 7.1. Most health care activities are the responsibility of the individual woman. Supervision and screening activities of the health care provider come after the woman makes her initial contact with the nurse and seeks out these activities. Health education is the foundation of all activities carried out by the nurse care provider. The overlap of health activities between woman client and care provider is illustrated by the appearance of certain actions-needs above and below the level of interaction with the nurse, that is, the individual's point of entry into the health care system. Since there is little or no apparent need for the well woman to be taken care of by others, the health care provider (nurse) enters into the individual's mind-body-spirit system rather than providing an outside system that the woman must enter. This type of health care is represented by mutual-participation interaction providing an open system at the point of interaction with the nurse should consultation or referral to a disease-illness system become necessary.

This model of health care also clearly indicates that it is the woman who is in control of her health and that the responsibility or decision to seek out a professional health worker is also hers. The model also attempts to portray the mind-body-spirit wholeness of the woman influenced by who she is, what she believes in and values, where she lives, and who her family, friends, and community are. All of these factors are brought to bear on an individual woman's definition of her health care needs and her motivation to take health actions. The general health needs of most women of childbearing age center around nutrition, contraception, pregnancy, care of the reproductive organs, sexuality, and job-related conditions. Educational and counseling programs center on anxiety and stress management, sexual assault, abuse, or harassment, parenting skills, role identity, accident prevention, drug abuse, and self-care skills. Specific or individualized health care needs will be determined by the woman in interaction with her health care provider (Thompson, 1990).

PRACTICE OF PRIMARY HEALTH CARE NURSING FOR WOMEN

The majority of certified nurse-midwives are assisting childbirth in hospital settings (ACNM, 1991b). In 1992, 90% of nurse-midwives were sal-

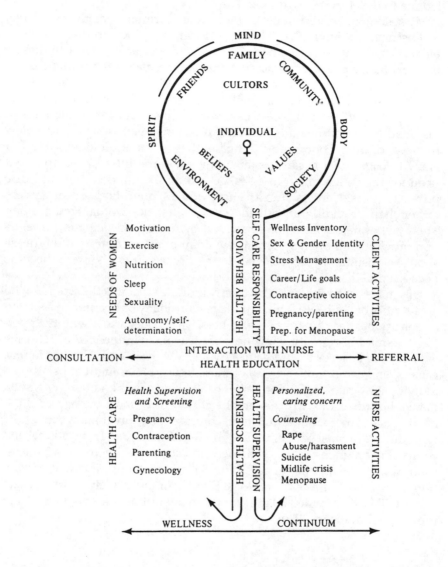

FIGURE 7.1 Women's Primary Health Care Model (reproductive age group).

aried employees of physicians, hospitals, and HMOs. Nevertheless, there has gradually been a resurgence of interest in midwifery practice in the home, as well as in other out-of-hospital settings, such as free-standing birth centers. In addition, pregnancy supervision and contraceptive and gynecological care provided by nurse midwives takes place in a variety of settings, including hospital outpatient facilities, health maintenance organizations, private offices, community centers, and self-help collectives.

The success of nurses as providers of primary health care services for women can be illustrated by the expansion of job opportunities for nurse-midwives, nurse practitioners, and nurse clinicians. Although direct reimbursement of health care services given by nurses remains a major obstacle to expansion of some services, nurse-midwives have been able to win, with difficulty, such recognition within some federal agencies and several states (Hackley, 1981; Office of Technology Assessment, 1986; Sparer, 1979). Details of the reimbursement issue will follow. The increased consumer demand for a change in our present health-illness care systems has brought renewed interest in nursing and nurses as providers of care as well as the request for nonhospital, nonillness-related health services.

EXAMPLES OF WOMEN'S PRIMARY HEALTH CARE

Childbearing Care: The Childbearing Center

A prime example of the success of health-oriented services demanded by consumers and provided by nurses is the Childbearing Center designed by the Maternity Center Association (MCA) in New York City (Lubic & Ernst, 1978; MCA, 1979). The Maternity Center Association has a long and illustrious history of meeting the needs of childbearing families since 1918 (Laird, 1955). As we have already noted, it cosponsored the first school in the United States for the education of nurse-midwives in 1932, and has continued to provide guidance and leadership in nurse-midwifery education and practice. The opening of the Childbearing Center at East 92nd Street in New York City in 1975 was another step forward in MCA's leadership in the provision of health-oriented services for childbearing families. The impetus for development of this out-of-hospital birthing unit came principally from two sources. The principal source of stimulus was from women and families who

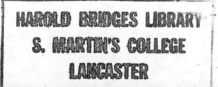

opted out of the disease-oriented hospital systems, but then had little choice left but "do-it-yourself" home deliveries. I suggest that this opting out, although certainly not risk-free, was partially the result of the refusal of health care workers to allow women to actively learn about and participate in decisions about their pregnancy care, that is, to be seen as colleagues or partners in their care. As a consequence, health care providers may have actually forced women to choose no prenatal or childbearing supervision—the antithesis of the role and function of health care—rather than submit their bodies to the control of others.

The second impetus for the development of the Childbearing Center was MCA's ongoing attempts to meet the total needs of families in a rapidly changing social scene. It became evident that the medical-hospital care system, set up to meet the needs of childbearing families, was failing in the area of personalized health-oriented services. The Childbearing Center was designed as a demonstration project to explore whether out-of-hospital childbearing care was safe, satisfying, and economical in meeting the needs of families who opted out of the hospital system. All of these measures have demonstrated success, and MCA once again has set an example for others to follow in providing safe, satisfying, and economical health care services for the nation's families, utilizing the CNM as the primary care provider teamed with public health nurses and health-oriented obstetricians (physicians) for other vital services.

The Childbearing Center, located in a converted townhouse in upper Manhattan, offers comprehensive health supervision in a homelike environment for healthy families anticipating a normal birth experience. All aspects of the primary health care model described earlier that relate to childbearing are put into practice at the Childbearing Center. The family seeking childbearing supervision requests the services of the Childbearing Center. A contract for health education and supervision is entered into with the CNM as the primary health care provider. Support of client self-determination is offered through education for self-care and informed decision making. Family members learn how to perform prenatal screening tasks, such as taking the blood pressure, assessing fetal growth and heart rate, checking urine for glucose and protein, and weighing under the watchful, supportive guidance of a CNM. Charting is done by the client or a family member and verified by the nurse-midwife, and group and individual teaching includes the psychosocial needs of pregnant families as well as preparation for childbearing and childrearing.

One of the most exciting components of this primary health care practice from its inception is the requirement that families learn parenting skills prior to "on-the-job training." Parents delivering at the Childbearing Center are eligible for discharge within 12 hours following birth, and consequently need to know how to provide at home for the needs of the mother and infant. Self-instructional modules or traditional group classes are the methods of learning available to the families, and public health nurses visit the home within 24 hours of birth to continue the health supervision component of care.

The record of safety for families choosing the Childbearing Center is superb, and this record is maintained principally by the careful initial evaluation and periodic screening of the health status of the pregnant woman, the responsible health-maintenance activities of the pregnant family, and the cooperative efforts of health care providers and clients. Satisfaction with care is evident in the growing number of clients served and in the personal testimony of families.

Perhaps one of the most significant results of the Childbearing Center, beside the quality of care and client satisfaction, has been the cost effectiveness achieved. A fiscal audit reported as early as 1979, by Blue Cross/Blue Shield of Greater New York (BCBSGNY) noted that charges for complete care of uncomplicated pregnancies at the Childbearing Center were 37.6% of the cost of in-hospital care, and the actual cost (total) to BCBSGNY families cared for at the Center were 66.1% of the cost to the plan had the same family gone to a hospital setting for their normal pregnancy. Likewise, Medicaid reimbursement costs for the Childbearing Center care were $400 to $900 less than hospital care for normal maternity experience with a 3-day hospital stay.

Another important aspect of the economy of the Childbearing Center is its success in coordinating primary health care services for women and families in a safe environment that is appropriate, accessible, available, and affordable. The comprehensive fee includes all prenatal supervision and education, individualized and continuous support and care during labor and delivery, home visits during the postpartum period by public health nurses, obstetric and pediatric physician availability, and unlimited telephone consultation. In most other settings, especially hospitals and private obstetrical practice, each of these services would be charged for separately and most likely provided by a great variety of persons.

Perhaps one of the best indicators of the success and quality of care provided at the Childbearing Center is the following excerpt from a woman who delivered her second child at the Center.

This time, I made it through labor without any chemical crutches (indeed, without uttering a single, self-pitying or angry word). . . . I feel that having faced my labor with dignity is a fact that will bolster my image of myself for the rest of my life. It was a gift not only to me, but to all those close to me. It's made me a stronger, more confident person. (MCA, 1979)

There is no better way to illustrate the effects of implementation of a primary health care model for women than this poignant response of a woman who has grown into full personhood!

Care for Prostitutes

Another brief example of the implementation of primary health care services for women is the opening of the first clinic for "professional" women in New York City, in which this author was involved. The Center for Reproductive and Sexual Health (CRASH), on Manhattan's upper east side, in collaboration with the senior minister and administrator of Judson Memorial Church in Greenwich Village, outlined a plan for providing needed health services for the women who worked in massage parlors or walked the streets. These were often the forgotten, abused, and misused women of our society, and their needs for health care and supervision had received inadequate attention. If health screening was sought, physicians who were willing to attend these women charged exorbitant fees, and then often did little more than draw weekly blood samples for syphilis testing. If screening for gonorrhea was done at all, women reported only vaginal smears being done despite the majority of sexual acts being fellatio.

With much careful planning, CRASH prepared to offer health services for the prostitutes of New York City. It was decided that the care provider should be a woman, and that the nurse-midwife would be the most appropriate care provider and the one most acceptable to the women of the street. As a member of the planning group, I agreed to be the first care provider for the Center, and we were ready for business. It took several weeks for the women to trust the Center enough to come for care, especially since we were charging a mere $20 for a complete physical examination, screening for venereal disease, contraception, and counseling (in contrast to the $50 to $100 charged elsewhere merely for a blood test.)

An average visit lasted 50 to 60 minutes, and I learned as much from the clients as they learned from me. Once again, the rewards for efforts in the provision of primary health care services included the excitement these women demonstrated when they learned about their bodies; how to check out a client for venereal disease and then protect herself; how to choose a method of contraception suitable to herself and her work schedule; and the tears exhibited because someone really cared about them and was willing to listen to their problems and lifestyle without judgment or disgust.

The services for this special group of women are still offered by nurse-midwives, with referral to staff gynecologists or staff counselors as the need arises. The model of care followed is the one outlined in this chapter. It focuses on education, mutual participation interaction, self help measures, and health screening and supervision.

BARRIERS TO PRIMARY HEALTH CARE NURSING FOR WOMEN

In spite of the positive examples cited of primary health care services given by nurse midwives, there remain many barriers to the provision of such services on a nationwide scale. These barriers take many forms, the prohibition of the practice of nurses in primary health care to a lack of support for any health care services. Let us examine some of these barriers in more detail.

One of the major reasons for the relatively low level of health in this country is that our society as a whole places limited value on health care services and prevention of disease, as opposed to illness care. Our schools for educating physicians and nurses have traditionally followed a medical or disease-oriented model of care, our hospitals have expanded beyond limits to care for the sick and dying, and most of the money spent for health and illness care goes for illness care.

Even if we developed a national program of health education and services, would people use it? The answer depends in part on the availability, accessibility, acceptability, and affordability of the education and service program; in other words, on its effectiveness. A brief review of research related to use and nonuse of prenatal care services will give one greater understanding of these three interrelated concepts.

A classic study of the effective use of nurse-midwives as health care providers was done in Madera County, California, from 1960 to 1963 (Montgomery, 1969). This 3-year demonstration project made available health care services that were accessible and acceptable to pregnant women. Significant increases in use of the services, as well as improvements in maternal and neonatal health, were seen. This successful program was not allowed to continue, however, The California Medical Association refused until ten years later to support a permanent change in the state law allowing nurse midwives to practice. In a retrospective study performed in 1968, Levy, Wilkinson, & Marine (1971) found that the level of maternal and neonatal health and utilization of traditional medical services after the nurse midwives left was worse than before the project started in 1960. In addition to a change in the principal health care provider, from nurse-midwife to resident obstetrician, a change in eligibility criteria for medical assistance was instituted, so that some women could no longer afford prenatal care even if they sought it.

Poor utilization of existing health services, especially during pregnancy, is usually a result of health care provider inadequacies (poor interpersonal skills, unfeeling or incompetent care, and a lack of confidence and continuity in the care giver) leading to client dissatisfaction; setting variables, including long waiting times, inconvenient hours, impersonal treatment, and lack of privacy; and the many motivational factors described earlier. Other factors involved in the nonuse of available prenatal care services have to do with babysitting problems, lack of transportation, financial limitations, and fears (Brown, 1988; National Institutes of Health/Health and Human Services, 1989; Perry, Youngs, & King, 1976; Poland, 1976; Slatin, 1971).

A barrier to the use of health care services during pregnancy is the public's view that health care providers pursue an illness approach to maternity care. Physicians who took over the practice of midwifery in the early part of this century applied a pathology orientation and tried to turn pregnancy into a disease condition. Many women were unwitting accomplices in this view of pregnancy and the trend toward hospital-oriented care with promises of relief from the pain and suffering associated with labor. In recent years, however, educated women and families are once again insisting on control of their childbearing experiences. They look for professionals who view pregnancy as a healthy state and who are willing to enter a cooperative partnership with them while providing health supervision.

Nurse-midwives have been in demand since the early 1970s, principally because of their focus on health activities and their support of pregnancy as a normal physiological state and life cycle event (ACNM, 1991a; Anderson, 1977; Burnett, 1972; Dillon et al., 1978; Ernst, 1979; Record & Cohen, 1972). de Tornyay (1978) noted that it is difficult for medical health care professionals to turn over responsibility for care to their clients because then they lose the monetary and psychological rewards of being the great "health gurus." Nurse-midwives and others, however, recognize different rewards in teaching others to care for themselves. They experience the excitement of others' learning to take increased control over their lives.

If one listens closely, the message coming from some sectors of our population, most notably the self-help collectives and do-it-yourself home birth families, is that traditional medical care is inappropriate and insensitive to the needs of healthy people. Several authors (American Academy of Nursing, 1977; Thompson & Thompson, 1980; OTA, 1986) have noted that consumers are increasing their demands for personalized, individualized, accessible, and affordable health care. They want a provider whom they can trust and who is willing to work with them to meet their health goals. Consumer demands created and supported the Childbearing Center described earlier, and consumer demand has increased the numbers of nurses providing primary health care services, including nurse-midwives. Nurses have developed a viable role in primary health care, and they must work in alliance with consumers to overcome current barriers to practice and to maintain the viability of their health-oriented services.

Another aspect of the unacceptability of health care practice has been the lack of coordination of services, which by law joins physician and nurse in a "forced" team approach to care. One of the most difficult experiences for me as a clinician has been the struggle to be accepted by the physician community as a person and as a nurse midwife. In an effort during the 1980s to establish a private nurse midwifery practice in a university setting, I once again experienced the difficulty of acceptance. I quickly became accepted as an expert clinician and was treated "like one of the boys." When I protested that I did ont particularly like the way physicians treated one another and wished to be treated as a human being, there was little understanding of my request. Must nurses resort to acting like physicians to be accepted as legitimate care providers? I certainly hope not, for we have so much more to offer our clients as nurses—as the professionals we were prepared to be.

Maldistribution of Services and Personnel

Despite their ability to deliver primary care services to women, which is at least equal to that of physicians, and often with greater satisfaction expressed by the clients (acceptability), the availability of nurses in primary health care will continue to be limited if they remain legally and otherwise bound by physician supervision or restrictive reimbursement. Laws governing the practice of nurses in expanded roles clearly require some degree of control of nurse practice by physicians. This is not hard to understand, since most state laws that recognize primary care practice by nurses were written and supported by physicians.

Modern nurse-midwifery did not develop in this way, although physician supervision is often still required by state law. Nurse-midwives would prefer to and do function within the concept of a consultative team relationship, but the laws are slow to reflect this mature professional collaboration. Courts often still hold physicians legally liable for all acts of care given by nurse-midwives, thus implying that the practice of nurse-midwives must be attached to that of a physician. But what about those areas of the country where physicians refuse to practice? Is there always an obvious or designated physician responsible? Can the CNM ever practice alone? The struggle for individual accountability in practice has, in fact, been won by many nurse midwives. Most midwives carry their own malpractice insurance, reflecting their willingness to be held legally as well professionally responsible for their health care activities.

One example of the negative results of mandatory physician supervision of nurse-midwifery practice comes from the 1981 congressional hearings on restraint of trade issues in Tennessee. Two nurse-midwives lost their means of practice when their consulting physician was forced to leave town. Without physician availability, their hospital privileges were withdrawn. The nurse-midwives could no longer practice in that area and were forced to seek employment elsewhere (Sparer, 1979). Ten years later this court case is completed with interim decision in favor of the CNMs. This case illustrates not only the legal issue of restraint of trade, but also the political consequences to nurse midwives who invade the private practice arena of the physicians. Bates (1975) and others have noted that where "turf" is occupied by paying patients, physicians often put up a most vigorous fight against primary care by nurses. Even when clinic (public) patients are involved, there may be costly battles over "territory." As noted earlier in the discussion of the Madera County study, physicians refused to legalize the practice of nurse-midwifery even when faced with overwhelming evidence of the quality and effectiveness of care these nurses provided. As a consequence, a very high price was paid in maternal and neonatal mortality for what appeared to be professional jealousy.

Recommendations for the Future

More than a decade has passed since Gardner and Fiske (1981) suggested that competition is needed in the health care arena to improve the quality, and, presumably, the availability and acceptability of services. Competition between nurse and physician providers of primary health care services is currently a myth, however, since the physician has all the power to determine where and whether nurses will practice. Thus, the continued existence of nurses as providers of primary care services is dependent on permission of the very group who are/or will be most affected—the physicians themselves (Choi, 1981).

The notion of competition in the health services arena has another mythical component, in that without direct reimbursement for services, nurses remain tied to and thus unable to compete with physicians. While the government has been slow to respond to payment for health-oriented services in general, reimbursement for pregnancy care has been the exception. Very possibly because of the nation's focus on health during pregnancy, nurse-midwives have achieved more success in being reimbursed for their services than have other nurses, although this has not come about easily (Ernst, 1979; Hackley, 1981; Sparer, 1979).

Obviously, new plans for financing health-oriented services are needed for full implementation and expansion of the Women's Primary Health Care Model, or any other health model for that matter. Nurse midwives have benefited from years of government support of training programs for nurses in expanded roles (Bates, 1975). Now it is time for government to support full reimbursement for the quality services provided by all advance practice nurses working to improve health care to women.

The issue of nonavailability of health-oriented services is intimately related to the ineffective use and distribution of health care providers (Levy, Wilkinson, & Marine, 1971; Montgomery, 1969; National Center for Health Services Research, 1977; OTA, 1986; Safriet, 1992). Few physicians until recent times were interested in providing primary health care to women in inner cities and rural areas, and yet physicians have also been unwilling to grant nurses legal sanction to fill this gap without their continuing presence. Financial reimbursement for such health services has also lagged in this country, so there has been minimal incentive for either physicians or nurses to provide health services. Nor has the public been willing to pay out-of-pocket for ambulatory care, such as home deliveries, when their insurance plans cover similar care when delivered in the hospital.

Nurses providing primary health care services to women are placed in an even greater financial predicament, since few states allow direct reimbursement for such services. Reimbursement mechanisms instead provide money to the physician who employs the nurse who actually provides the services. Is it any wonder we have lagged in our provision of health care services? The physician who could get paid does not want to do it, the nurses who want to provide the services cannot be reimbursed, and the people who need the services have to pay out-of-pocket unless they belong to a clinic or a managed care system such as a health maintenance organization (HMO).

The controversy surrounding the proper utilization of the nurse-midwife is illustrative of our national problems in manpower utilization (DeClerq, 1992; NCHSR, 1977). In 1971 the American College of Obstetrics and Gynecology, Nurses Association of the American College of Obstetrics and Gynecologists, and ACNM issued a joint statement on maternity care in the United States (the statement was updated in 1992). This statement was the first official recognition of the nurse-midwife as a competent provider of primary care for pregnant women, even though we have had nurses practicing midwifery in the United States since the 1920s! As late as 1976 there was still some doubt as to the role the nurse-midwife could play in the delivery of maternity care services, despite repeated demonstrations of the efficacy and quality of care given by the nurse-midwife in a variety of settings (Thompson, 1986; Thompson, 1990). The blue ribbon committee sponsored by the March of Dimes issued a report in 1976 that stated: "All deliveries should be attended by a physician or, where necessary and where acceptable, by a certified nurse-midwife under the supervision of a physician" (Meglen, 1976, p. 7). This qualified use of the nurse-midwife did little to recognize the valuable roles she or he plays in the provision of quality health care for pregnant families.

Fortunately, acceptance of the nurse midwife as a provider of quality health services in obstetrics has become increasingly recognized by physicians, consumers, and policy makers (Brown, 1988; Dillon et al., 1978; IOM, 1985; OTA, 1986). Indeed, the nurse-midwife, as one of the class of nurse practitioners providing primary care services, is now seen as one of the solutions to our health crisis both in meeting unmet health or medical care needs and in controlling or reducing health care costs (Brown, 1988; OTA, 1986). Several authors (Choi, 1981; Fagin, 1992; OTA, 1986; Pickard, 1974; Safriet, 1992) support my position that there are large numbers of individuals seeking health (and medical) care whose concerns and care needs do not require the skills of the physician. In fact, many people could receive better care from specially trained nurses whose major concern and expertise is for education, health promotion activities, and psychosocial support of clients and families and who are also proficient in clinical judgment, certain medical care skills, and the management of care.

If we are to develop primary health care services for women that are accessible, acceptable, and affordable, we must understand the barriers to the use of such services and overcome as many of them as possible. Given current constraints in expenditures for health care, the country must carefully choose the most cost efficient care providers and process of caregiving.

REFERENCES

American College of Nurse-Midwives, American College of Obstetrics and Gynecology. (1982). *Joint statement of practice relationships between obstetrician/gynecologists and Certified Nurse-Midwives*.

American College of Nurse-Midwives. (1978). *Definition of a Certified Nurse-Midwife*. Washington, DC: Author.

American College of Nurse-Midwives. (1985). *Core competencies in nurse-midwifery*. Washington, DC: Author.

American College of Nurse-Midwives. (1986). *Statement on nurse-midwifery education*. Washington, DC: Author.

American College of Nurse-Midwives. (1987a). *Nurse-midwifery practice*. Washington, DC: Author.

American College of Nurse-Midwives. (1987b). *Standards for the practice of nurse-midwifery*. Washington, DC: Author.

American College of Nurse-Midwives. (1989). *Philosophy of the American College of Nurse-Midwives*. Washington, DC: Author.

American College of Nurse-Midwives. (1991a). *Educational programs accredited by the ACNM Division of Accreditation as of 3/91*. Washington, DC: Author.

American College of Nurse-Midwives. (1991b). *Fact sheet 91–4/17*. Washington, DC: Author.

American College of Nurse-Midwives. (1991c). *Today's Certified Nurse-Midwife*. Washington, DC: Author.

American Nurses Association. (1976). *Scope of primary nursing practice for adults and families*. Kansas City: American Nurses Association.

American Academy of Nursing. (1977). *Primary care by nurses: Sphere of responsibility and accountability*. Kansas City: American Nurses Association.

Anderson, S. F. (1977). Childbirth as a pathological process: An American perspective. *American Journal of Maternal Child Nursing, 2*(4), 240–244.

Bates, B. (1975). Physician and nurse practitioner: Conflict and reward. *Annals of Internal Medicine, 82*, 702–706.

Bell, K.E., & Mills, J.J. (1989). Certified nurse-midwife effectiveness in the health maintenance organization's obstetrics team. *Obstetrics & Gynecology, 112*, 21–29.

Bermosky, L., & Porter, S. (1979). *Women's health and human wholeness*. New York: Appleton-Century-Crofts.

Blum, H. (1974). *Planning for change: Development and application of social change theory*. New York: Human Sciences Press.

Brown, S. (Ed.). (1988). *Prenatal care: Reaching mothers, reaching infants*. Washington, DC: National Academy Press.

Burnett, J. (1972). A physician sponsored communi nurse-midwife program. *Obstetrics and Gynecology, 40*, 719.

Choi, M. W. (1981). Nurses as co-providers of primary health care. *Nursing Outlook, 29*, 519–521.

DeClerq, E. (1992). The transformation of American midwifery: 1975–1988. *American Journal of Public Health, 82*, 680–684.

de Tornyay, R. (1978). Primary care in a pluralistic society: Impediments to health care delivery. *American Nurses Association Publication*. (G-133) 1–22.

Dillon, T., Brennan, B. A., Dwyer, J. F., Risk, A., Sear, A., Dawson, L., & Wick, P. L. (1978). Midwifery 1977. *American Journal of Obstetrics and Gynecology, 130*(8), 917.

Edmundson, M. A., Jennings, B. J., & Kowalski, K. A. (1980). A nurse practitioner program for women's health care. *American Journal of Nursing, 80*, 1784–1785.

Ernst, E. (1979). The evolving practice of midwifery. *Health Law Project Library Bulletin*, 4:289–294.

Fagin, C. (1992). Collaboration between nurses and physicians: No longer a choice. *Nursing & Health Care, 13*, 354–363.

Gardner, H., & Fiske, M. (1981). Pluralism and competition: A possibility for primary care. *American Journal of Nursing, 81*, 2152–2157.

Garrett, S. S., & Garrett, B. (1982). Humaneness and health. *Topics in Clinical Nursing, 3*, 7–12.

Gluck, J. (1980). Primary care: The extension of primary nursing. In K. Zander (Ed.), *Primary Nursing* (pp. 281–293). Germantown, MD: Aspen Publications.

Hackley, B. K. (1981). Independent reimbursement from third-party payers to nurse-midwives. *Journal of Nurse Midwifery, 26*, 15–23.

Healthy people 2000: A report on health promotion of disease prevention. (1991). Washington, DC: United States Department of Health, Education and Welfare Pub. No. 91-55071.

Institute of Medicine. (1985). *Preventing low birthweight: Summary*. Washington, DC: National Academy Press.

Laird, M. D. (1955). Report of maternity center association clinic, N.Y. 1931–1951. *American Journal of Obstetrics and Gynecology, 69*, 178–181.

Levy, B. S., Wilkinson, F. S., & Marine, W. M. (1971). Reducing neonatal mortality rate with nurse-midwives. *American Journal of Obstetrics and Gynecology, 109*, 50–58.

Lubic, R., & Ernst, E. (1978). The childbearing center: An alternative to conventional care. *Nursing Outlook, 26*, 754–760.

Martin, L. L. (1978). *Health care of women*. Philadelphia: Lippincott.

Maternity Center Association. (1979). *Economic aspects of the childbearing center*. New York: Maternity Center Association.

McKeown, T. (1978). Determinants of health. *Human Nature, 4*, 170–172.

Meglen, M. (1976). Final Report of the *Cost-effective potential of new maternal and infant care health team*. Jackson: University of Mississippi.

Millis, J. S. (1977). Primary care: Definition of, and access to . . . *Nursing Outlook, 25*, 443–445.

Montgomery, T. A. (1969). A case for nurse-midwives. *American Journal of Obstetrics and Gynecology, 105*, 309.

National Institutes of Health/Departments of Health and Human Services Expert Panel on Content of Prenatal Care. (1989). *Caring for our future: The content of prenatal care*. Washington, DC: United States Public Health Services.

National Center for Health Services Research. (1977). *Nurse Practitioner and Physician Assistant training and deployment*. Pub. No. 77-3173. Washington, DC: U.S. Government Printing Office.

Nursing's agenda for health care reform. (1991). Washington, D.C: American Nurses Association.

Office of Technology Assessment. (1986). *Nurse Practitioners, Physician's Assistants, and Certified Nurse-Midwives: A policy analysis.* Washington, DC: U.S. Government Printing Office.

Perry, H., Youngs, D., & King, T. (1976). Patient acceptance of a nurse-midwifery in a private group practice. *Journal of Reproductive Medicine, 16*, 21–25.

Pickard, F. D., Noble, J., & Defiese, G. (1976). Concepts of health and illness. In J. Noble (Ed.), *Primary care and the practice of medicine* (pp. 74–86). Boston: Little, Brown.

Poland, M. L. (1976). The effect of continuity of care on the missed appointment rate in a prenatal clinic. *Journal of Obstetrics and Gynecologic and Neonatal Nursing,* 45–47.

Record, J., & Cohen, H. (1972). The introduction of midwifery in a prepaid group practice. *American Journal of Public Health, 62,* 354–360.

Rooks, J.P. (1989). The national birth center study: outcomes of care in birth centers. *New England Journal of Medicine, 321,* 1802–1806.

Rubin, L. B. (1979). *Women of a certain age: The midlife search for self.* New York: Harper Colophon.

Safriet, B. (1992). Health care dollars and regulatory sense: The role of advanced practice nursing. *Yale Journal on Regulation, 9,* 417–488.

Scully, D. (1980). *Men who control women's health: The miseducation of obstetrician gynecologists.* Boston: Houghton Mifflin.

Slatin, M. (1971). Why mothers bypass prenatal care. *American Journal of Nursing, 71,* 1388–1389.

Sparer, E. (1979). Blue Shield and the nurse-midwives. *Health Law Project Library Bulletin, 4,* 281–288.

Thompson, J. B. (1980). *Nurse-Midwives and health promotion during pregnancy.* Unpublished doctoral dissertation, Columbia University.

Thompson, J. B., & Thompson, H. O. (1981). *Ethics in nursing.* New York: Macmillan.

Thompson, J. E., & Thompson, H. O. (1980). The ethics of being a female patient and a female care provider in a male-dominated health-illness system. *Issues in Health Care of Women, 2,* 25–54.

Thompson, J. E. (1986). Nurse-midwifery research: 1925–1984. In J. Fitzpatrick & R. L. Taunton (Eds.), *Annual Review of Nursing Research: Vol. 4* (pp. 153–173). New York: Springer Publishing Co.

Thompson, J. E. (1990). Health education during pregnancy. In I. R. Merkatz & J. E. Thompson, (Eds.), *New perspectives on prenatal care* (pp. 220–263). New York: Elsevier.

Thompson, J. E., Oakley, D., Burke, M., Jay, S,. & Conklin, M. (1989). Theory building in nurse-midwifery: The care process. *Journal of Nurse-Midwifery, 34,* 3, 120.

Thompson, J. E., & Thompson, H. O. (1990). *Professional ethics in nursing.* Melbourne, FL: Kreiger.

Chapter 8

MEETING THE HEALTH CARE NEEDS OF OLDER ADULTS

Neville E. Strumpf and Geraldine Paier

Compassion, patience, a sense of proportion, humor, and adequate awareness of the dynamics of human behavior are a circle of safety in which to gather strength; the elderly person needs a health care worker who is an advocate and a friend.

—*Doris Schwartz (1981, p. 104)*

A s is perhaps more painfully evident today than at any other time in our history, professionals and consumers alike live with the frustrations of a system of health services that do not meet, in any comprehensive way, the needs for primary care. This is apparent for every age group, in all parts of the United States, and in most settings, whether institution or community.

For the oldest members of American society, these failures are underscored by an unprecedented burgeoning of the elderly population. The demographic features are well known to gerontologists and providers of care, but bear repetition as we examine the impact older individuals will have on national needs for primary care now and in the future. In 1900, persons over the age of 65 comprised roughly 4% of the population. Today, that proportion if 12.4% (30 million people); by 2000 it will grow to

13% (35 million) and by 2030 to 22% (66 million) (Omenn, 1990). The majority of older people live in urban areas, one in four in housing where at least half of the residents are over 60, in what is called a naturally occurring retirement community (Lewin, 1991). Megaretirement communities such as Sun City, Arizona, and Century Village, Florida, are home to another 1 million Americans (Carlton, 1991).

Greater life expectancies mean that 13 million people will be over the age of 85 in 2040 (Gillick, 1989) and 1 million of these are projected to be 100 years and older (Schneider & Guralnik, 1990). Such staggering numbers apply worldwide as well, with an estimated 1.1 billion persons 60 and over by 2025 (Alderman & Cruise, 1989).

It is thus not surprising that the number of disabled and chronically ill are also increasing, as is the volume and complexity of their service needs. Older Americans use health care services extensively, accounting for 33% of all expenditures (American Medical Association, 1990). Rates of hospitalization and lengths of stay are greater for the elderly when compared to younger persons. Average annual Medicare costs per person rise substantially with age, from $2017 for individuals aged 65 to 74 years to $3215 for those aged 85 years and above (Waldo, Sonnefeld, McKusick, & Arnett, 1989).

Care in nursing homes cost 48 billion dollars a year in 1989, an increase of 140% during the 1980s (Nursing homes cost, 1991). This represents at least $30,000 annually for each of more than 1.6 million residents. About half of this is paid by Medicaid, and the rest by patients or their families. The risk of needing some nursing home care over a lifetime may be as great as 43% for those 65 and over (Kemper & Murtaugh, 1991), a figure some call conservative (R. L. Kane & R. A. Kane, 1991a). No accurate data on the total costs of home care or community-based ancillary services exists, but it appears in excess of 5 billion dollars per year (General Accounting Office, 1986). By 2050, the costs of long-term care could reach 150 billion dollars (Senate Special Committee on Aging, 1986; Wilensky, 1987).

These figures leave no one doubting the significant challenges which face us as we enter the 21st century. At a minimum, we will need models shaped by a philosophy of primary health care, ones where health promotion and disease prevention strategies are thoroughly understood and integrated, principles of interdisciplinary comprehensive geriatric assessment incorporated, and quality of life emphasized. This will require achievement of the essential components and ideals of long-term care—comprehensiveness, continuity, and accessibility. Although the full realization of primary health care will mean a revamping of our current, piecemeal method of delivering services, this chapter describes an existing foundation of knowledge in assessment, health promotion and disease prevention, models of care, and use of nurse specialists that could create a better future for older adults.

DEVELOPMENT OF SPECIALIZED PRACTICE IN GERONTOLOGICAL NURSING

A 1925 editorial in the *American Journal of Nursing* alerted nurses to a growing need for care of the elderly (Care of the aged, 1925), but the first text in geriatric nursing was not published until 1950. It described in detail the care of older persons, including constructive health practice and prevention of disease (Newton, 1950). Geriatric Practice was established as one of five divisions of the American Nurses Association (ANA) in 1966. The first Standards for Geriatric Nursing Practice were published in 1970; the latest evolution of these initial guidelines appeared in 1987 as *Standards and Scope of Gerontological Nursing Practice* (ANA, 1987). The current standards are congruent with the basic tenets of primary health care, with particular emphasis on data collection, planning and continuity of care, and interdisciplinary collaboration (Walker & Knapp, 1990).

Paralleling similar developments in advanced practice in the United States, gerontological clinical specialists and nurse practitioners emerged in the late 1960s. The present number of those with master's preparation in gerontology and skill in primary care, however, remains a fraction of the actual need. Recent documentation of the impact of gerontologic nurse practitioners on outcomes and costs of care (Buchanan et al., 1990; Kane et al., 1991; Kane et al., 1989; Kane et al., 1988; Mezey & Lynaugh, 1989) has intensified demand, and will, one hopes, enhance recruitment efforts and influence existing structures for reimbursement.

In an examination of roles for the gerontological nurse specialist in hospitals, home care, and nursing homes, Heine (1988) identified seventeen behaviors, including in-depth assessment, identification of problems posing a high risk for morbidity and mortality, development and implementation of a timely and appropriate discharge, support, and consultation of family members and other staff, and interdisciplinary collaboration to ensure quality of care. Among the positive outcomes resulting from such activities are timely discharge, prevention of readmission, and increased comfort and physical condition, especially with impaired mobility, depression, and altered mental status, nutritional deficits, bowel and bladder problems, pressure sores, potential for infection, and pain (Beyerman, 1989).

FROM PRIMARY CARE TO CASE MANAGEMENT

As described in greater detail elsewhere in this text, primary care can apply to practice in any setting where a mechanism exists to handle first contact into the system and to provide a continuum of care, evaluation and management of symptoms, maintenance of health, and appropriate referrals (Commission, 1972). In many ways primary care exemplifies a nursing model where measurement of success is determined by attainment by the patient of the highest level of physical, mental, and social function; the focus is on holistic approaches; and participatory roles are accorded to patients and families (ANA, 1982). Acceptance of these ideas by the wider medical community is increasingly apparent in discussions of care and case management.

Without question, a major study by the Institute of Medicine, *Improving the Quality of Care in Nursing Homes*, drew attention to gaps in care for the elderly, including problems with decision making, accountability, and quality of life (Lohr & Donaldson, 1990). More recently, the American Medical Association issued a "White Paper" summarizing the poor management of frail elderly: inappropriate institutionalization, incomplete medical diagnosis, lack of coordination with community support services, overprescription of medicines, and underutilization of rehabilitation (American Medical Association, 1990). A strong case for, and de facto an endorsement of, comprehensive geriatric assessment was made to remedy the situation. If actually carried out, this *could* represent a major shift from the traditional medical model.

In what is beginning to look like recognition and momentum concerning the primary health needs of older adults, the American Geriatrics Society (AGS) adopted, in 1991, a position statement on "care management as an important component of an effective and comprehensive geriatric service system" (Fanale, Kennan, Hepburn, & Von Sternberg, 1991, p. 431). Care planning is at the heart of the document. Rather than "case management" or "service coordination," "care management is meant to establish a certain kind of interface between individuals and the complex and often confusing array of services set up to serve them." Its primary goal is "to coordinate and integrate services and provide bridges between and among the discrete systems of acute, institutional, and home-based care" within the constraints of reimbursement and affordability. Provision of flexible service packages will be overseen by care managers (nurses and social workers) whose core activities include intake/screening, assessment, care planning, service arrangements, monitoring and evaluation. Care management embodies values such as "maintenance of individuals at optimal levels of safe functioning in the least restrictive environments" and "client-centered care." (p. 432).

Possible models for delivering care management include brokerage (assessment, planning, and packaging of available community resources); waiver programs enabling the purchase of needed services, possibly coupled with some direct care by the managers; and established organizations prospectively paid to care for a large pool of clients (Fanale, 1991). Who the care managers will be remains an open question; physicians, in the American Geriatric Society (AGS) Position Statement (1989), are suggested as the medical consultants to a care management team.

In contrast to care management, but certainly related to it, case management is an "administrative service that directs client movement through a series of planned involvements with long-term care systems" (Capitman, Mac Adam, & Abrahams, 1991, p. 124). With new incentives for controlling costs, case management programs have proliferated. Capitman et al. note that several states are allocating funds to statewide systems for community-based home care programs having case management as a central feature.

In a White Paper on Case Management prepared by the Government Affairs Committee and approved by the Board of the National Association for Home Care, nursing is seen as central to the coordination of various resources to meet client needs (Government Affairs Committee, 1991). Two very different and conflicting types of case management are described: that performed by providers as an essential part of caregiving and that used as a mechanism for controlling costs. Clinician management and fiscal management may be contradictory terms, and the Committee recommended a framework of case management incorporating client eligibility based on functional impairment, with authorization to spend up to a specific dollar amount depending on the degree of impairment.

The call for comprehensive systems serving all levels of care is not new, and discussions of care and case management now underway are but an extension of an earlier dialogue on primary care. It is a hopeful sign, however, that some version of care or case management appears to be emerging as the single most important technique for providing primary care for the frail elderly.

COMPREHENSIVE GERIATRIC ASSESSMENT

Crucial to the provision of primary care for older adults is comprehensive geriatric assessment (CGS), which has as its most basic purpose

> to serve the patient and the patient's family: through identifying the difficulties and quantifying the impact on the patient; through attention to any treatable or remediable condition; through identifying long-term care services needed and helping to arrange for them; and through reinforcing the adaptive and support mechanisms that are already in place. (Bentley, Williams, & Williams, 1982, p. 71)

Obviously a thorough history and physical are important if subtle or atypical changes, so characteristic of the older person, are to be detected (Mezey, Rauckhorst, & Stokes, 1993). An initial appraisal should be offered to all older people in any setting, with follow-up once a year or every two years, depending on the existence of problems needing intervention or referral and the age and history of the patient. Use of the problem-oriented record is an excellent way to determine status as well as to monitor progress with a form of systematic record keeping. The format provides for the collection of subjective (profile, nutritional history, family history, history of the present problem, past history, and review of systems) and objective (physical examination, laboratory and diagnostic procedures) data. Having obtained the database, a list of actual, potential, person-oriented, and health promotion/health maintenance problems can be compiled for use by all who work with the patient. As problems are dealt with, the necessary subjective and objective data are recorded, an assessment is made, and diagnostic, therapeutic, teaching, and referral plans are developed.

Certain modifications in the collection of a history, performance of physical examination, and development of an assessment and plan are necessary when working with older adults. These people have a unique and often lengthy history, and it requires time and patience to collect it. Assessment must be based on the knowledge that health is relative to the ability to function despite the presence of disease. The practitioner needs to evaluate thoroughly any personal biases or perceptions about older people; otherwise, findings of frailty, confusion, weakness, or other dysfunctions may be regarded as expected behavior, rather than as evidence of illness, worsening of underlying disease, or mismanagement of the therapeutic regime. Practitioners need to guard against preconceived expectations if complete assessments are to be done, especially when residents enter nursing homes (Lavizzo-Mourey, Mezey, & Taylor, 1991). What is normal for the patient or resident needs to be established, keeping in mind that response to illness may be muted altogether, or exacerbated by such external stimuli as altered mental status, drug prescriptions, and drug-taking behaviors. Determination of the precise nature of underlying disease may not be as significant as evaluating the functional impairment and human discomfort of chronic illness. As Williams and Hadler (1983) argue so well, maintaining a "purely disease-specific focus" interferes with thinking about strategies that best serve the individual.

The "biomedicalization of aging," with its focus on the diseases of aging and emphasis on clinical phenomena leading to a specific diagnosis, has considerably hindered the management of many problems common to older adults (Estes & Binney, 1989). In their excellent discussion of illness presentation in the elderly, Fried, Storer, King, & Lodder (1991) demonstrate persuasively the weakness of the standard medical model of diagnosis in the face of comorbidity, atypical symptomatology, compromised functioning, major psychosocial life stresses, and the physiologic changes associated with aging. Using both retrospective chart review ($n = 86$) and a prospective validation in a second sample ($n = 56$), these clinicians found that the medical model of illness led to a correct diagnosis in less than half of the patients.

The need for alternative approaches to diagnosis highlighted by the above study, and well-known to most practitioners working with older adults, strengthens the necessity for evaluation and treatment based on comprehensive geriatric assessment. Although the significance of functional assessment in health and illness has been apparent for more than 100 years, we have come far since the earliest indices of basic and instrumental activities of daily living developed in the 1960s and 1970s (Katz & Stroud, 1989). these early quantifications of function have been greatly enlarged in the last 20 years, leading to a "new technology of geriatrics" (Epstein et al., 1987, p. 299); comprehensive geriatric assessment.

Comprehensive geriatric assessment (CGA) was defined by the National Institutes of Health Consensus Development Panel (1987) as a

> multidisciplinary evaluation in which the multiple problems of older persons are uncovered, described, and explained, if possible, and in which the resources and strengths of the person are catalogued, need for services assessed, and a coordinated care plan developed to focus interventions on the person's problems. (p. 342)

Basic elements include physical and mental health, social and economic status, environmental characteristics, and functional status. The principles of comprehensive assessment and functionally oriented care were first applied as part of the National Health Service in the United Kingdom forty years ago (Barker, 1987). In the United States, comprehensive geriatric assessment is found mainly in academic centers and Veterans Administration hospitals.

Reuben and Solomon (1989) make the important point that, for optimal effectiveness, CGA must be inextricably linked to ongoing care, with objective assurance that a plan is implemented and modified as events may dictate. This means taking CGA beyond diagnostic purposes to identification of a sequence of needs and implementation on an appropriate plan of care (Bentley et al., 1982).

CGS is not to be confused with functional status assessment, which is a measure of the ability to complete basic, intermediate (instrumental), and advanced activities of daily living (Reuben & Solomon, 1989). Rather, CGA represents a compilation of many types of assessment, determined by a variety of instruments measuring physical and cognitive function, emotional status, social activities and support, adequacy of the environment, and quality of life (Applegate, Blass, & Williams, 1990; Johnson & Mezey, 1989; LeKan-Rutledge, 1988). Assessment instruments should be used with an understanding of their role in establishing baseline data, screening for risk factors or undetected problems, assisting in diagnosis, setting rehabilitation or therapeutic goals, and monitoring the clinical course. To date, CGA's greatest success has occurred with targeted groups in specialized settings with interdisciplinary expertise in aging. With a growing body of literature documenting the success of CGA, the American Geriatrics Society is calling for initiation of Medicare reimbursement for these services (Rubenstein et al., 1991).

GERIATRIC CONSULTATION TEAMS

Through the use of consultation teams consisting, at a minimum, of physician, nurse, and social worker in geriatric evaluation and management (GEM) units, targeted assessment and therapy for selected older patients is provided. In a review of inpatient geriatric consultation, Winograd and Stearns (1990) describe three ways in which the consultations are typically generated: (1) by instituting a hospital wide policy to evaluate all patients over the age of 75; (2) by responding to consultation requests only when asked; and (3) by following routinely all patients cared for by other geriatric services, e.g., home care or a geriatric clinic. Requests, most commonly, are for general medical or nursing care, discharge planning, evaluation and management of dementia or other mental status problems, "failure to thrive," and potential for rehabilitation. New diagnoses are frequently uncovered, especially those related to sensory impairment, depression, delirium, adverse drug reactions, malnutrition, and anemia. Improved outcomes for hospitalized patients receiving CGA are increasingly reported (Rubenstein et al., 1984), including better utilization of resources (Barker et al., 1985); reduced medications; improved physical and mental status (McVey, Becker, Saltz, Feussner, & Cohen, 1989; Sullivan, Wanich, & Kurlowitz, 1991), and greater survival rates (Applegate et al., 1990; Hogan & Fox, 1990).

Studies of geriatric evaluation and management in ambulatory settings have achieved similar outcomes, with a major goal to keep older persons in the community as long as possible (Williams & Williams, 1986). Selection of patients appears to be a crucial factor in achieving success with consultative interdisciplinary team care (Fretwell et al., 1990). Epstein and colleagues (1990) also caution that consultative geriatric assessment with limited follow-up may not benefit most older ambulatory patients in a health maintenance organization.

Geriatric consultation is clearly consistent with the aims of primary care, but "has yet to demonstrate its graceful utility" (Campion, 1987). As evaluation and management units multiply, several issues need to be addressed: a critical definition of desirable and realistic outcomes (Saltz et al., 1988), precision concerning interventions, identification of target groups most likely to benefit, cost-effectiveness, and resources necessary to implement decisions, including sufficient numbers of trained personnel. The best results have occurred in combined geriatric assessment and rehabilitation settings, or inpatient units, focused on individuals with potentially reversible disabilities. The entire subject of geriatric evaluation and management (GEM) is reviewed in a special supplement of the *Journal of the American Geriatric Society*, September 1991. (Rubinstein et al., 1991).

Successful outcomes resulting from comprehensive assessment through geriatric consultation suggest that the health status of frail, older persons can be improved (AGS Public Policy Committee, 1989). Looking more broadly at the health of all older people, however, means practice that emphasizes healthier life-styles and environmental improvements (Fries, 1990). This will require greater commitment to health promotion and disease prevention than presently exists.

HEALTH PROMOTION AND DISEASE PREVENTION

Broadly defined, health promotion is "any combination of health education and related organizational, political and economic interventions designed to facilitate behavioral and environmental changes conducive to health" (Green, 1980, p. 7). At a systems level, it may involve increasing problem-solving capacity of older persons or the community they live in, providing a comprehensive continuum of community and social services conducive to health and self-reliance, and helping older persons gain access to knowledge, skills, and other resources needed to meet personal health objectives (Minkler & Pasick, 1986). Health promotion, a cornerstone of primary care and the first phase of primary prevention (Lauzon, 1977), encompasses those activities contributing to general wellbeing, personal fulfillment, and self-actualization (Pender, 1982). Activities are aimed at persons without evidence of overt disease; emphasis is on facilitation or reinforcement of healthful living. In assessing the needs for health promotion, the focus should be, first, determination of practices that have enabled the person to reach a particular age and, second, discovery of those practices that might make a significant difference if incorporated or improved.

Promoting the health of older people can best be accomplished when normal age changes are differentiated from disease processes; this provides the professional with an index of wellness. It often requires sophisticated professional intervention, especially since most people, young or old, are reluctant to change their behavior, even with exposure to good health teaching. Work with persons having no discernible chief complaint remains an uncomfortable role for many in the health professions who themselves need to be educated in the skills required to promote health.

Such concepts as "successful" or "productive" aging, "preventive gerontology," and "compression of morbidity," with their connotations of enhanced social function, improved physical and mental expectations, prolonged independent living, and greater autonomy, assume strategies that promote health. Yet health promotion for older people has been largely ignored by practitioners, educators, and researchers. The policy document *Healthy People: The Surgeon General's Report on Health Promotion and Disease Prevention* (U.S. Department of Health, Education, and Welfare, 1979) thus represented a landmark with its goal to improve the quality of life and functional independence for older adults. Recommended were the following eight actions: (1) maintain an active work and social life; (2) engage in regular physical activity; (3) maintain a nutritious, well-balanced diet; (4) undergo periodic health check-ups; (5) review and minimize medications; (6) obtain consultation regarding immunization against pneumococcal pneumonia and influenza; (7) improve home safety; and (8) have access to needed community services.

Minkler and Pasick (1986) identify alterable health-related problems associated with aging and amenable to health promotion as nutrition, smoking, stress control, misuse of alcohol and drugs, accident prevention, and exercise and fitness. The authors are careful to point out, however, the sociostructural factors that heavily influence individual health practices and subsequently, the ability to comply with a health promotion plan—poverty, racism, sexism, ageism, occupational hazards, and environmental pollutants. As illustration of this reality, Minkler & Pasick give the excellent examples of being told the importance of walking, but not how to walk safely in a high crime neighborhood, or of receiving instruction about nutritious food, but not how to afford them or even how to get to a store to buy them.

Prevailing notions that health promotion isn't "worth it" for older people (the matter of cessation of smoking being a case in point) are gradually disappearing (Omenn, 1990). Recent research has demonstrated that exercise and nutrition may be critical health promotion activities associated with function (Duffy & MacDonald, 1990), and recommendations have been made by the Surgeon General's Workshop on Health Promotion and Aging (Centers for Disease Control, 1989) encouraging health care providers to develop and use physical activity assessment, prescription, and follow-up protocols for fitness and exercise. These developments draw further attention not only to the efficacy of health promotion, but to the need to support it in policy decisions, allocation of resources, continued research, and education of providers and the public. Success will depend greatly on the ability to entice those most needing to participate: older individuals who smoke, are sedentary, isolated, multiply medicated and depressed, have low income, and suffer from sensory impairment (Omenn, 1990).

Beyond basic efforts directed toward health promotion is the sizable and complex challenge of disease prevention, aimed at early detection when presymptomatic illness is likely because of factors such as genetic history, age, weight, certain health habits, or environmental exposure. Surveillance for the onset of acute illness or the worsening of chronic disease involves the identification of these risk factors. According to Breslow (1978), risk factors for disease consist of (1) personal habits, such as smoking or consumption of alcohol, and (2) actual body changes or body characteristics that can be considered precursors to disease. The latter might include a physiological change, such as elevated blood pressure, a biochemical alteration, such as increased cholesterol, or an anatomical or genetic characteristic. Breslow goes on to describe the two elements of risk factor intervention as (1) identifying and quantifying the relationship of certain personal characteristics and dealing with them to avoid disease altogether, and (2) identifying a disease process in its early stages and taking the steps necessary to avoid progression of the disease.

Half the older population reports at least one chronic illness, although 80% of those 65 and older consider themselves to be in "good" health, living full and active lives (American Medical Association, 1990). The ten most common chronic conditions include arthritis, hypertension, hearing and visual impairment, heart disease, skeletal problems or deformities, chronic sinusitis, diabetes, varicosities, and abdominal hernia (National Center for Health Statistics, 1985). Many syndromes are also frequently seen in the elderly: falls, functional impairment, incontinence, constipation, dehydration, nutritional deprivation, and sleep disorders (American Medical Association, 1990). Problems frequently overlooked by health and social services include depression, inadequate foot care, inappropriate use of drugs, loneliness, prolonged bereavement, and the effects of poor housing and limited finances; many older people receive wholly inadequate mental health care (Persky, Taylor, & Simson, 1989).

Three major sources of recommendations concerning prevention with older adults have been put forward: the Lifetime Health-Monitoring Program (Breslow & Somers, 1977), the Canadian Task Force on the Periodic Health Examination (Canadian Task Force, 1979, 1984, 1986, 1988), and the Guide to Clinical Preventive Services from the U.S. Preventive Services Task Force (Woolf, Kamerow, Lawrence, Medalie, & Estes, 1990a, 1990b).

Breslow and Somers introduced packages of selected preventive services for various age groups. For older adults, the goals are to prolong optimal physical, mental, and social activity; minimize disability, discomfort, and inactivity from chronic conditions; prepare in advance for retirement; and receive support during terminal illness. Also recommended are professional counseling about changing lifestyles, testing for specified chronic conditions every 2 years between 60 and 74 and annually thereafter, flu vaccination, and dental and podiatric care.

The U.S. Preventive Services Task Force, using categories similar to the Canadian Task Force, came up with specific recommendations about screening for 42 clinical conditions, counseling for eight health-related behaviors, and five forms of immunization or chemoprophylaxis. The U.S. Task Force differentiates primary and secondary prevention in its guidelines (Woolf et al., 1990a, 1990b).

Primary prevention refers to interventions in asymptomatic persons who lack clinical evidence of the targeted conditions, and includes counseling about behavioral risk factors, immunizations, and chemoprophylaxis. Specifically dealt with are tobacco use, physical activity, nutrition, unintentional injuries and dental health, activities similar to those associated with health promotion.

Secondary prevention, drawing on the earlier work of Breslow (1978), includes screening tests for the early detection and treatment of modifiable risk factors or preclinical disease in asymptomatic persons. Included in the discussion on secondary prevention are coronary artery, cerebrovascular, and peripheral arterial diseases; breast, colorectal, cervical, prostate, lung, skin, oral, ovarian, and pancreatic cancers; obesity, diabetes, thyroid disease, tuberculosis, urine abnormalities, anemia, visual acuity and glaucoma, hearing impairment, osteoporosis, dementia, depression and suicide, bereavement, and violent injuries.

The U.S. Task Force recommendations do little to clarify precisely which screening examinations are worthwhile and on whom they should be done (Wolf-Klein, 1989). There is no direct evidence, for example, that a nationwide cholesterol screening and treatment program for older adults would reduce overall morbidity or would justify a cost of $1.6 to $16.8 billion (Garber, Littenberg, Sox, Wagner, & Gluck, 1991). Screening is a very complex issue when considering the care of residents in nursing homes who may benefit selectively from judicious use of annual laboratory tests (Levinstein, Ouslander, Rubenstein, & Forsythe, 1987). Improvement in nursing home care rests not only on better screening, health maintenance, and preventive practices, but also on better documentation and attention to mental health issues and overuse of antipsychotic drugs (Ouslander, 1989). The positive role of rehabilitation in the promotion and maintenance of health has been vastly overlooked (Becker & Kaufman, 1988).

An editorial in a British journal makes the point that "screening," the search for asymptomatic disease, is not "case finding," which is the search for unreported problems (Denham, 1990). The writer further notes that:

> This view of screening in the United Kingdom contrasts with that of the USA where there continues to be more enthusiasm for periodic examination of patients. . . . The elderly in general welcome case finding, consider it improves their quality of life and encourages a more positive attitude towards health. (p. 181)

The need to promote and maintain health for as long as possible will intensify with the ever-increasing numbers of elderly. A disease-specific approach to geriatric preventive health care will not suffice; measures to enhance or maintain physical, mental, and social function will also need emphasis (Stults, 1984). Moreover, adequate investigation to determine efficacy of and appropriate target populations for preventive measures is urgent. Although it is unrealistic to expect health promotion and disease prevention to accomplish grand-scale cost containment, well-selected initiatives can bring improvements in health status, maintenance of functional independence, and moderation of increases in health care use and spending (Omenn, 1990).

DELIVERING OF HEALTH SERVICES TO OLDER ADULTS

Models of primary health care meeting the requirements of older people are far from fully developed. It is rare to find comprehensive services containing what Brody (1974) identified as the five essential ingredients: personal care, supportive medical services, personal maintenance, counseling, and linkages. Increasingly called for by many professional organizations, policy makers, and consumer groups is a reformed health care system providing universal access, equitable treatment for those in need, and efficient, cost-effective services (Moon, 1989). A large population of older adults will intensify demands for a long continuum of care, with the home at one end and institutional support at the other (Gillick, 1989). The present system, or more accurately the nonsystem, satisfies no one.

Despite our frustrations and dissatisfactions, we live with the existing health system, one dedicated to acute care in the hospital, and offering a fragmented array of other services through home care and community based agencies, rehabilitation, and long-stay institutions. Even with the limitations imposed by cost containment and bureaucratically maddening structures for reimbursement, primary care is somehow delivered in numerous settings, often with special funding. These exemplars represent what might be a new future in long-term care. Many of these models in the hospital, community, and nursing home depend heavily on nurse practitioners or clinical specialists and are described in some detail elsewhere (Mezey, 1991; Strumpf & Stevenson, 1991).

Notable among developments in acute care have been the geriatric evaluation and management units consultation teams already described. A consultative role for the gerontological nurse specialist in hospitals is increasingly perceived as valuable, given the complications and acuity of elderly patients (Reilly, 1989). Other types of inpatient services include hospital-based skilled care (Knapp, 1986) and comprehensive discharge planning (Naylor, 1990). Given that prospective payment has increased the likelihood of discharge to the home in an unstable condition (Rogers et al., 1990), the necessity of assessment, teaching, and planning by a competent team is crucial. Early discharge has placed unique pressures on home care agencies and nursing homes.

The most significant of the managed, community-based long-term care systems have been the multiple state National Long-Term Care Demonstration (Channeling), On Lok Senior Health Services Community Organization for Older Adults in San Francisco, Access in New York, South Carolina Long-Term Demonstration, and a national demonstration sponsored by the Health Care Financing Administration, the Social/Health Maintenance Organization (SHMO) (Fanale et al., 1991). These projects, in general, have shown that care management may improve clients' independence and reduce social isolation, may enhance quality of life, and may reduce nursing home utilization and retard entry. On a more modest scale, nurse-managed clinics have demonstrated patient satisfaction and improved health status (Pulliam, 1991). Unless services are carefully targeted, however, overall costs appear to increase.

Because of the introduction of Medicare's prospective payment system, persons served by home care programs are likely to be frail, over the age of 75, and have multiple diagnoses. In the Beth Israel Hospital Home Care Program in Boston, geriatric nurse practitioners provide "medical" aspects of care and serve as case managers, providing linkages to the health care system, assurance of adequate follow-up, and delivery of necessary services (Burns-Tisdale & Goff, 1989). The nurse practitioner's ability to provide comprehensive physical examinations and make assessments allows quick identification of changes affecting treatment plans or requiring emergency care. Collaboration with the physician enables prompt resolution of potentially critical declines in the patient's condition. LaVizzo-Mourey (1989) puts forward the idea of a traveling team approach in home health agencies, with goals of accurate and complete diagnosis, assessment and enhancement of function, reduction in nursing home placement, decreased use of medications, and improvements in cognition. Other community-based options are the Block Nurse Program, with its use of public health nurses in a neighborhood-based system of service delivery (Jamieson, Campbell, & Clarke, 1989), and day programs providing either health care and physical rehabilitation or social interaction and activities, depending on individual need (Butrin, 1985; Kaenen, 1980; Schwartz, 1979).

Provision of adequate health care for older people must be considered from the standpoint of a continuum of services, ranging across settings from home to hospital to long-stay institution. However, nursing homes dominate and symbolize the problems and dilemmas of long-term care. Criticized as being neither a real home nor providing good nursing care (Kane & Kane, 1991b), they are considered decidedly second-class and undesirable places by consumers and providers alike. The role of nursing homes, too, is uncertain: Are they to house and support frail older people with nowhere else to go, provide sophisticated rehabilitation services after hospitalization, protect the cognitively and functionally impaired, or simply offer a place to die? Earlier hospital discharge to long-term care settings has substantially increased the needs and acuity of residents in nursing homes (Kanda & Mezey, 1991; Shaughnessy & Kramer, 1990). A persistent lack of funds has affected quality of care and the ability to attract and pay professional staff. The average 100-bed nursing home has only one registered nurse and one and a half licensed practical nurses per shift, and the registered nurse delivers to each resident less than 12 minutes of care per day (Mezey & Fulmer, 1991). Here lies the greatest challenge of all: getting primary care services to these elders in greatest need.

Perhaps the most significant experiment toward improving nursing home care was the Robert Wood Johnson Foundation Teaching Nursing Home Program (Mezey & Lynaugh, 1989). This experiment in social change was conceived as a model for restructuring and enhancing clinical care. Its purposes were to upgrade care of residents using a cadre of nurse specialists; to create an environment supportive of education, and to promote research. The 5-year national demonstration project involved 11 schools of nursing and 12 nursing homes with established joint appointments. Two other demonstrations, the Kellogg Foundation's project with the Mountain States Health Corporation and the Nursing Home Connection, also used nurse practitioners and clinical specialists to deliver care to nursing home residents (Mezey, 1990). Findings from all three projects consistently supported the effectiveness of these nurses as providers of care: these nurses responded to changes in resident status, conducted assessments, monitored medication, provided direct care or supervision for the more complex patient problems, and counseled patients and families.

There is substantial evidence that geriatric nurse practitioners in all three demonstration projects significantly lowered hospitalization rates of nursing home patients (Shaughnessy & Kramer, 1989). In addition, residents had better functional outcomes, fewer urinary catheters, less incontinence, fewer nosocomial infections, and more appropriate use of medications. Reductions in psychotropic medications and use of physical restraints also occurred, along with better management of wandering and disruptive behavior. Presence of a geriatric nurse practitioner assured the transmittal of timely and accurate information to physicians and reduction in unnecessary trips to the hospital emergency room. Evaluation to date supports a significant role for geriatric nurse practitioners in nursing homes (Kane et al., 1988; Kane et al., 1989; Kane et al., 1991). Furthermore, employment of nurse practitioners does not adversely affect nursing home costs of or significantly affect profits (Buchanan et al., 1990). The effectiveness of the model is a given; it remains now to find mechanisms making possible its wide establishment in long-term care.

This brief description of health service delivery, and evolving models of primary care, demonstrates the interdependent nature of the system's constituent parts. Policies focused on one element inevitably reverberate elsewhere, adding to the urgency and desirability of an integrated system of health care that is truly responsive and accessible to the elderly (Densen, 1991).

CONCLUSIONS

Renewed interest in primary care during the 1960s was a significant development. Nursing educators quickly recognized the need for advanced practitioners skilled in data collection, health assessment, planning, teaching, counseling, and referral. These events, coupled with a rising number of older people, brought to awareness the inadequacies in the existing system of health care for the elderly. Today, neither the acute care offered by the hospital nor the long-term care provided in many nursing homes meets the health needs of the majority of older adults who, despite chronic disease or other limitations, remain in the community for as long as possible.

In 1991, both the American Medical Association and the American Nurses Association declared their support for health care reform. The American Nurses Association called for a shift from illness and cure to wellness and care, including many components consistent with primary health and better provisions for long-term care (ANA, 1991). In what promises to be a turbulent decade of revised expectations and fiscal austerity, nursing must remain steadfast in its commitment to primary care and not relinquish its important place within it. Primary care by its very nature is interdisciplinary, but that does not mean the role of nursing need be subsumed within a still firmly entrenched biomedical agenda. Nurses are an alternative to high cost care (Fagin, 1982), nurse practitioners are cost-effective (McGrath, 1990), and nurses should not be excluded from reimbursement (Harrington & Culbertson, 1990).

This chapter differs markedly from its predecessor in the prior edition. The theoretical and clinical basis of comprehensive geriatric assessment is more fully developed; models consistent with primary care have been implemented in selected hospitals, nursing homes, and community agencies; beneficial outcomes of health promotion and disease pretion are better known; and the significant contributions of nurse practitioners and clinical specialists working with the elderly are increasingly documented. Still necessary, however, is funding of a national research agenda in aging aimed at reducing disability and dependence in old age, and decreasing the burdens on a health care system strained to its limits (Institute of Medicine, 1991); reimbursement allowing for essential health and social services by the appropriate provider; and, in the absence of national health care, more sites providing primary care. Until the delivery of health services is entirely reconstructed in the United States, primary care for older adults remains an oxymoron. We must be politically committed to change if the components of care articulated in this chapter are to be practiced by all providers and offered with satisfaction and confidence to every older American.

REFERENCES

American Geriatric Society Public Policy Committee. (1988). Comprehensive geriatric assessment. *Journal of the American Geriatrics Society, 37*(5), 473–474.

Alderman, M., & Cruise, M. J. (1989). The coming of age in nursing care of the elderly. *International Nursing Review, 36*(2), 47–49, 60.

American Medical Association. (1990). White paper on elderly health. *Archives of Internal Medicine, 150*(12), 2459–2472.

American Nurses Association [ANA]. (1982). *A challenge for change: The role of gerontological nursing.* Kansas City, MO: American Nurses Association.

American Nurses Association [ANA]. (1987). *Standards and scope of gerontological nursing practice.* Kansas City, MO: American Nurses Association.

American Nurses Association [ANA]. (1991). *Nursing's agenda for health care reform.* Kansas City, MO: American Nurses Association.

Applegate, W. B., Blass, J. P., & Williams, T. F. (1990). Instruments for the functional assessment of older patients. *New England Journal of Medicine, 322*(17), 1207–1214.

Applegate, W. B., Miller, S. T., Graney, M. J., Elam, J. T., Burns, R., & Akins, D. E. (1990). A randomized controlled trial of a geriatric assessment unit in a community rehabilitation hospital. *New England Journal of Medicine, 322*(22), 1572–1578.

Barker, W. H. (1987). *Adding life to years: Organized geriatrics services in Great Britain and implications for the United States.* Baltimore: Johns Hopkins University Press.

Barker, W. H., Williams, T. F., Zimmer, J. G., Van Buren, C., Vincent, S. J., & Pickrel, S. G. (1985). Geriatric consultation teams in acute hospitals: Impact on back-up of elderly patients. *Journal of the American Geriatrics Society, 33*(6), 422–428.

Becker, G., & Kaufman, S. (1988). Old age, rehabilitation, and research: A review of the issues. *The Gerontologist, 28*(4), 459–468.

Bentley, D. W., Williams, M. E., & Williams, T. F. (1982). Assessment of the elderly for long-term care. *Journal of the American Geriatrics Society, 30*(1), 71–75.

Beyerman, K. (1989). Making a difference: The gerontological CNS. *Journal of Gerontological Nursing, 15*(5), 36–41.

Breslow, L. (1978). Risk factor intervention for health maintenance. *Science, 200*(26), 908–912.

Breslow, L., & Somers, A. R. (1977). The lifetime health-monitoring program. *New England Journal of Medicine, 296*(11), 601–608.

Brody, S. J. (1974). Evolving health delivery systems and older people. *American Journal of Public Health, 64*(3), 245–248.

Buchanan, J. L., Bell, R. M., Arnold, S. B., Witsberger, C., Kane, R. L., & Garrard, J. (1990). Assessing cost effects of nursing-home based geriatric nurse practitioners. *Health Care Financing Review, 11*(3), 67–78.

Burns-Tisdale, S., & Goff, W. F. (1989). The geriatric nurse practitioner in home care. *Nursing Clinics of North of America, 24*(3), 809–817.

Butrin, J. (1985). Day care: A new idea? Not really. *Journal of Gerontological Nursing, 11*(4), 19–22.

Campion, E. W. (1987). The merits of geriatric consultation. *Journal of the American Medical Association, 257*(17), 2336–2337.

Canadian Task Force on the Periodic Health Examination. (1979). The periodic health examination. *Canadian Medical Association Journal, 121,* 1193–1254.

Canadian Task Force on the Periodic Health Examination. (1984). The periodic health examination: 2 1984 update. *Canadian Medical Association Journal, 130,* 1278–1285.

Canadian Task Force on the Periodic Health Examination. (1986). The periodic health examination: 2. 1985 update. *Canadian Medical Association Journal, 134,* 724–729.

Canadian Task Force on the Periodic Health Examination. (1985). The periodic health examination: 2. 1987 update. *Canadian Medical Association Journal, 138,* 618–626.

Capitman, J. A., Mac Adam, M. A., & Abrahams, R. (1991). Case management in emergency approaches to long-term care. In P. Katz, R. Kane & M. Mezey (Eds.), *Advances in Long Term Care*: Vol. 1 (pp. 124–146). New York: Springer Publishing Co.

Carlton, J. (1991, August 12). Retirement villages, of all places, become hotbeds of dissent. *Wall Street Journal,* pp. 1, 8.

Center for Disease Control. (1989). Surgeon general's workshop on health promotion and aging: Summary recommendations of physical fitness and exercise working group. *Journal of the American Medical Association, 262*(18), 2507, 2510.

Commission to Study Extended Roles for Nurses. (1972). Extending the scope of nursing practice. *Nursing Outlook, 20*(1), 46–52.

Denham, M. J. (1990). Screening the elderly. *Care of the Elderly, 2*(5), 181.

Department of Health, Education, and Welfare. (1979). *Healthy people*. (DHEW (PHS) Publication No. 79–55071). Washington, DC: U.S. Government Printing Office.

Densen, P. M. (1991). *Tracing the elderly through the health care systems: An update*. (AHCPR Monograph, Report No. AHCPR 91-11) U.S. Department of Health and Human Services. Washington, DC: USDHHS.

Duffy, M. E., & MacDonald, E. (1990). Determinants of functional health of older persons. *The Gerontologist, 30*(4), 503–509.

Editorial. (1925). Care of the aged. *American Journal of Nursing, 25*(5), 394.

Epstein, A. M., Hall, J. A., Besdine, R., Cumella, E., Feldstein, M., McNeil, B., & Rowe, J. W. (1987). The emergence of geriatric assessment units: The "new technology of geriatrics." *Annals of Internal Medicine, 106*(2), 299–303.

Epstein, A. M., Hall, J. A., Fretwell, M., Feldstein, M., De Ciantis, M. L., Tognetti, J., Cutler, C., Constantine, M., Besdine, R., Rowe, J., & McNeil, B. J. (1990). Consultative geriatric assessment for ambulatory patients. *Journal of the American Medical Association, 263*(4), 538–544.

Estes, C. L., & Binney, E. A. (1989). The biomedicalization of aging: Dangers and dilemmas. *The Gerontologist, 29*(5), 587–596.

Fagin, C. M. (1982). Nursing as an alternative to high-cost care. *American Journal of Nursing, 82*(1), 56–60.

Fanales, J. E., Kennan, J. M., Hepburn, K. W., & Von Sternberg, T. (1991). Care management. *Journal of the American Geriatrics Society, 39*(4), 431–437.

Fretwell, M. D., Raymond, P. M., McGarvey, S. T., Owens, N., Traines, M., Silliman, R. A., & Mor, V. (1990). The senior care study: A controlled trial of a consultative/unit-based geriatric assessment program in acute care. *Journal of the Geriatric Society, 38*(10), 1073–1081.

Fried, L. P., Storer, D. J., King, D. E., & Lodder, F. (1991). Diagnosis of illness presentation in the elderly. *Journal of the American Geriatrics Society, 39*(2), 117–123.

Fries, J. F. (1990). The sunny side of aging. *Journal of the American Medical Association, 263*(17), 2354–2355.

Garber, A. M., Littenberg, B., Sox, H. C., Wagner, J. L., & Gluck, M. (1991). Costs and health consequences of cholesterol screening for asymptomatic older Americans. *Archives of Internal Medicine, 151*(6), 1089–1095.

General Accounting Office. (1986). Report to the Chairman, Subcommittee on Intergovernmental Relations and Human Resources, Committee on Government Operations, House of Representatives: An aging society meeting the needs of the elderly while responding to rising federal costs (GAO/HRD-86-135). Washington, DC: U.S. General Accounting Office.

Gillick, M. R. (1989). Long-term care options for the frail elderly. *Journal of the American Geriatrics Society, 37*(12), 1198–1203.

Government Affairs Committee. National Association for Home Care. (1991). *Case management*. Washington, DC: Author.

Green, L. W. (1980). *Health education planning: A diagnostic approach*. Palo Alto, CA: Mayfield.

Harrington, C., & Culbertson, R. A. (1990). Nurses left out of health care reimbursement reform. *Nursing Outlook, 38*(4), 156–158.

Heine, C. A. (1988). The gerontological nurse specialist: Examination of the role. *Clinical Nurse Specialist, 2*(1), 6–11.

Hogan, D. B., & Fox, R. A. (1990). A prospective controlled trial of a geriatric consultation team in an acute-care hospital. *Age and Ageing, 19*(2), 107–113.

Institute of Medicine. (1991). *Extending life, enhancing life.* Washington, DC: National Academy Press.

Jamieson, M., Campbell, J., & Clarke, S. (1989). The block nurse program. *The Gerontologist, 29*(1), 124–127.

Johnson, J. C., & Mezey, M. D. (1989). Functional status assessment: An approach to tertiary prevention. In R. Lavizzo-Mourey, S. C. Day, D. Diserens, & J. A. Grisso (Eds.), *Practicing prevention for the elderly* (pp. 141–152). Philadelphia: Hanley & Belfus.

Kaenen, R. E. (1980). Adult day care: A Northwest perspective. *Journal of Gerontological Nursing, 6*(4), 218–221.

Kanda, K., & Mezey, M. (1991). Registered nurse staffing in Pennsylvania nursing homes: Comparison before and after implementation of Medicare's prospective payment system. *The Gerontologist, 31*(3), 318–324.

Kane, R. A., & Kane, R. L. (1991, August 18). Time to rethink the nursing home. *New York Times*, p. 15.

Kane, R. A., Kane, R. L., Arnold, S., Garrard, J., McDermott, S., & Kepferle, L. (1988). Geriatric nurse practitioners as nursing home employees: Implementing the role. *The Gerontologist, 28*(4), 469–477.

Kane, R. L., Garrard, J., Buchanan, J. L., Rosenfeld, A., Skay, C., & McDermott, S. (1991). Improving primary care in nursing homes. *Journal of the American Geriatrics Society, 39*(4), 359–367.

Kane, R. L., Garrard, J., Skay, C., Radosevich, D. M., Buchanan, J. L., McDermott, S. M., Arnold, S. B., & Kepferle, L. (1989). Effects of a geriatric nurse practitioner on process and outcome of nursing home care. *American Journal of Public Health, 79*(9), 1271–1277.

Kane, R. L., & Kane, R. A. (1991a). A nursing home in your future? *New England Journal of Medicine, 324*(9), 627–629.

Katz, S., & Stroud, M. W. (1989). Functional assessment in geriatrics: A review of progress and directions. *Journal of the American Geriatrics Society, 37*(3), 267–271.

Kemper, P., & Murtaugh, C. M. (1991). Lifetime use of nursing home care. *New England Journal of Medicine, 324*(9), 595–600.

Knapp, M. T. (1986). Filling the gaps in health care: A hospital-based skilled nursing facility. *Nursing Management, 17*(9), 19–21.

Lauzon, R. J. (1977). An epidemiological approach to health promotion. *Canadian Journal of Public Health, 68*(4), 311–317.

Lavizzo-Mourey, R. (1989). The home team. In R. Lavizzo-Mourey, S. C. Day, D. Diserens, & J. A. Grisso (Eds.), *Practicing prevention for the elderly* (pp. 209–214). Philadelphia: Hanley & Belfus.

Lavizzo-Mourey, R., Mezey, M., & Taylor, L. (1991). Completeness of admission of resident assessments in teaching nursing homes. *Journal of the American Geriatrics Society, 39*(7), 676-682.

Lekan-Rutledge, D. (1988). Functional assessment. In M. A. Matteson & E. S. McConnell (Eds.), *Gerontological nursing* (pp. 57-91). Philadelphia: W. B. Saunders.

Levinstein, M. R., Ouslander, J. G., Rubenstein, L. Z., & Forsythe, S. B. (1987). Yield of routine annual laboratory tests in a skilled nursing home population. *Journal of the American Medical Association, 258*(14), 1909-1915.

Lewin, T. (1991, July 21). Communities and their residents age gracefully. *New York Times*, pp. 1, 16.

Lohr, K. N., & Donaldson, M. S. (1990). Assuring quality of care for the elderly. *Law, Medicine & Health Care, 18*(3), 244-253.

McGrath, S. The cost-effectiveness of nurse practitioners. *Nurse Practitioner*, 1990, *15*(7), 40-42.

McVey, L. J., Becker, P. M., Saltz, C. C., Feussner, J. R., & Cohen, H. J. (1989). Effect of a geriatric consultation team on functional status of elderly hospitalized patients. *Annals of Internal Medicine, 110*(1), 79-84.

Mezey, M. (1991). Nursing homes: Residents' needs; nursing's response. In L. H. Aiken & C. M. Fagin (Eds.), *Nursing and health policy: Issues in the 1990s* (pp. 198-215). Philadelphia: Lippincott.

Mezey, M. (1990). GNPs on staff. *Geriatric Nursing, 11*(3), 145-147.

Mezey, M., & Fulmer, T. (1991). The future of nursing home care. *New England Journal of Medicine, 325*(5), 360.

Mezey, M. D., & Lynaugh, J. E. (1989). The teaching nursing home program: Outcomes of care. *Nursing Clinics of North America, 24*(3), 769-780.

Mezey, M., Rauckhorst, L., & Stokes, S. (1993). *Health assessment of the older individual*. New York: Springer Publishing Co.

Minkler, M., & Pasick, R. J. (1986). Health promotion and the elderly: A critical perspective on the past and future. In K. Dychtwald (Ed.), *Wellness and health promotion for the elderly* (pp. 173-186). Rockville, MD: Aspen.

Moon, M. (1989). Taking the plunge: The arguments for a comprehensive long-term care system. *Journal of the American Geriatrics Society, 37*(27), 1165-1170.

National Institutes of Health Consensus Department Panel. (1988). National Institutes of Health Consensus Development Conference statement: Geriatric assessment methods for clinical decision-making. *Journal of the American Geriatrics Society, 36*(4), 342-347.

National Center for Health Statistics. (1985). Vital and health statistics: Current estimates from the National Health Interview Survey: United States, 1982 (U.S. Department of Health and Human Services publication (PHS) 85-1578). Washington, DC: National Center for Health Statistics.

Naylor, M. D. (1990). Comprehensive discharge planning for hospitalized elderly: A pilot study. *Nursing Research, 39*(3), 156-161.

Newton, K. (1950). *Geriatric nursing*, St. Louis: Mosby.

Nursing homes cost $48 billion in 1989. (1991). *Quality Care Advocate, 6*(2, 3), 11.

Omenn, G. S. (1990). Prevention and the elderly: Appropriate policies. *Health Affairs, 9*(2), 80–93.

Ouslander, J. G. (1989). Medical care in the nursing home. *Journal of the American Medical Association, 262*(18), 2582–2590.

Pender, N. J. (1982). *Health promotion in nursing practice.* Norwalk, CT: Appleton-Century-Crofts.

Persky, T., Taylor, A., & Simson, S. (1989). The network trilogy project: Linking aging, mental health and health agencies. *Gerontology & Geriatrics Education, 9*(3), 79–88.

Pulliam, L. (1991). Client satisfaction with a nurse-managed clinic. *Journal of Community Health Nursing, 8*(2), 97–112.

Reilly, C. H. (1989). The consultative role of the gerontological nurse specialist in hospitals. *Nursing Clinics of North America, 24*(3), 733–740.

Reuben, D. B., & Solomon, D. H. (1989). Assessment in geriatrics: Of caveats and names. *Journal of the American Geriatrics Society, 37*(6), 570–572.

Rogers, W. H., Draper, D., Kahn, K. L., Keeler, E. B., Rubenstein, L. V., Kosecoff, J., & Brook, R. H. (1990). Quality of care before and after implementation of the DRG-based prospective payment system. *Journal of the American Medical Association, 264*(15), 1989–1994.

Rubenstein, L. Z., Applegate, W. B., Burton, J. R., Hyer, K., Pawlson, L. G., & Winograd, C. H. (1991). Medicare reimbursement for geriatric assessment: Report of the American Geriatrics Society Ad Hoc Committee on Geriatrics Assessment. *Journal of the American Geriatrics Society, 39*(9), 926–931.

Rubenstein, L. Z., Josephson, K. R., Wieland, G. D., English, P. A., Sayre, J. A., & Kane, R. L. (1984). Effectiveness of a geriatric evaluation unit: A randomized clinical trial. *New England Journal of Medicine, 311*(26), 1664–1670.

Saltz, C. C., McVey, L. J., Becker, P. M., Feussner, J. R., & Cohen, H. J. (1988). Impact of a geriatric consultation team on discharge placement and repeat hospitalization. *The Gerontologist, 28*(3), 344–350.

Schneider, E. L., & Guralnik, J. M. (1990). The aging of America: Impact of health care costs. *Journal of the American Medical Association, 263*(17), 2335–2340.

Schwartz, D. (1981). Meeting human needs of elderly patients. *Family and Community Health, 13*(1), 101–104.

Schwartz, R. M. (1979). Multipurpose day centers: A needed alternative. *Journal of Gerontological Nursing, 5*(1), 48–52.

Senate Special Committee on Aging. (1986). Developments in aging. Washington, DC: U.S. Government Printing Office.

Shaughnessy, P., & Kramer, A. (1989). Trade-offs in evaluating the effectiveness of nursing home care. In M. Mezey, J. Lynaugh, & M. Cartier (Eds.), *Nursing homes and nursing care: Lessons from the teaching nursing homes* (pp. 127–144). New York: Springer Publishing Co.

Shaughnessy, P. W., & Kramer, A. M. (1990). The increased needs of patients in nursing homes and patients receiving home health care. *New England Journal of Medicine, 322*(1), 21–27.

Strumpf, N. E., & Stevenson, C. M. (1991). Breaking new ground in elder care: Practice, research and education. In L. H. Aiken & C. M. Fagin (Eds.), *Nursing and health policy: Issues of the 1990s* (pp. 419–432). Philadelphia: Lippincott.

Stults, B. M. (1984). Preventive health care for the elderly. *The Western Journal of Medicine, 141*(6), 832–845.

Sullivan, E. M., Wanich, C. K., & Kurlowitz, L. H. (1991). Nursing assessment: Management of delirium in the elderly. *American Operating Room Nurses Journal, 53*(3), 820–828.

Waldo, D. R., Sonnefeld, S. T., McKusick, D. R., & Arnett, R. H. (1989). Health expenditures by age group: 1977 and 1987. *Health Care Financing Review, 10*(1), 111–120.

Walker, S. N., & Knapp, M. T. (1990). Development and use of the ANA standards of gerontological nursing practice. *Journal of Nursing Quality Assurance, 4*(3), 1–14.

Wilensky, G. R. (1987, February 24). Statement before the U.S. Senate Finance Committee, Subcommittee on Health.

Williams, M., & Hadler, N. (1983). The illness as the focus of geriatric medicine. *New England Journal of Medicine, 308*(22), 1357–1359.

Williams, M. E., & Williams, T. F. (1986). Evaluation of older persons in the ambulatory setting. *Journal of the American Geriatrics Society, 34*(1), 37–43.

Winograd, C. H., & Stearns, C. (1990). Inpatient geriatric consultation: Challenges and benefits. *Journal of the American Geriatrics Society, 38*(8), 926–932.

Wolf-Klein, G. (1989). Screening examinations in the elderly: Which are worthwhile? *Geriatrics, 44*(12), 36–47.

Woolf, S. H., Kamerow, D. B., Lawrence, R. S., Medalie, J. H., & Estes, E. H. (1990a). The periodic health examination of older adults: The recommendations of the U.S. preventive service task force: Part I: Counseling, immunizations, and chemoprophylaxis. *Journal of the American Geriatrics Society, 38*(7), 817–823.

Woolf, S. H., Kamerow, D. B., Lawrence, R. S., Medalie, J. H., & Estes, E. H. (1990b). The periodic health examination of older adults: The recommendations of the U.S. preventive services task force: Part II: Screening tests. *Journal of the American Geriatrics Society, 38*(8), 933–942.

Chapter 9

INCORPORATING PRIMARY CARE CONCEPTS INTO PSYCHIATRIC NURSING ROLES

Madeline A. Naegle

PRIMARY CARE AND PSYCHIATRIC NURSING

THE model of psychiatric nursing which must closely approximated, and predated, the primary care role emerged in the 1970s in the community mental health center. Mandated to provide basic services to people with a wide scope of mental health needs, these centers provided inpatient and outpatient care, day care, 24-hour crisis intervention, and consultation and education to people living in the community. Nurses who implemented new roles in these centers (1) worked primarily in ambulatory care; (2) were highly autonomous; (3) delivered treatment modalities traditionally reserved for psychiatrists, social workers, and others; and (4) provided mental health teaching, education, and consultation to schools, social agencies, and service centers. The nurse was often the first contact with the health care delivery system for the client and assumed responsibility for continuing care. This care necessarily included identification, management, and referral of health problems coexisting with acute or chronic mental illness, and required the utilization of knowledge germane to both the generalist and specialist preparation of the nurse. The contemporary characteristics of psychiatric nurses continues to include (1) autonomous function, (2) client advocacy, (3)

232

accountability, and (4) collaborative activities with nurses and members of other disciplines.

Although primary care continues to be viewed as the realm of the generalist, there is considerable discussion of primary care activities by mental health specialists. Leininger (1973), for example, saw lowering the rate of new incidence of mental disorders as a primary care activity. The psychiatric nurse does this by identifying and caring for high-risk populations and developing preventive strategies. Teaching about stress and mental health risks would constitute a central activity of psychiatric nursing (Jennings, 1977). Mitsunaga (1982) and Martin (1984) also advocate that primary care, holistic approaches be incorporated into the education of psychiatric mental health nurses. Their suggestion coincides with an increasing emphasis on biophysiologic research and understanding of mental illness. Cadoret and King (1974) compared the functions associated with primary care to first contact interventions traditionally utilized in psychiatry (Bellak, 1976). They advocated broadening assessment to include a comprehensive medical history on first contact, and a multidisciplinary approach to assessment and diagnosis. Furthermore, they emphasized the need to coordinate referrals, the usual consequences of psychiatric evaluation in a comprehensive care setting.

More recently, McEnany (1991) urged psychiatric nurses to strengthen the specialty by expanding the biological bases for practice beyond the narrowly defined parameters which continue to govern practice. He notes that psychiatric nurses need to use new scientific knowledge to update and broaden their knowledge base and to understand human behavior from a richer perspective. Such an approach emphasizes the importance of generalist skills and the health concepts basic to primary care (Murphy & Hoeffer, 1987).

Thus, psychiatric nursing integrates a wide variety of approaches, including primary care approaches, into care delivery. The degree to which this integration occurs is determined by the health needs of the client and the functional autonomy of the nurse.

GENERALIST NURSING PERSPECTIVES INTEGRATED INTO SPECIALIST ROLE FUNCTIONS

The value of a model that combines generalist skills, including primary care, with specialist training in psychiatric nursing is that it enables the nurse to deliver broad-based care while maintaining a relationship that addresses a client's psychotherapeutic needs. The appropriateness of such a model is most clearly demonstrated in the nursing management of certain illness. Illnesses which involve complex psychophysiologic relationships are manifested in both dysfunctional behavior and physiologic changes. Sensory deprivation dysfunction and alcoholism are in this category (Ruffin, 1975). Others have suggested the integration of primary care concepts into specialty services for drug abuse (Klerman, 1980), gerontological nursing (see Strumpf, Chapter 8) geriatric psychiatry (Ebersole, 1989). The traditional psychotherapeutic relationship is enhanced when nursing goals incorporate elements of primary care. The scope of the relationship extends to include family and "community" as recipients of care as well as collaborators in care provision. Opportunities increase, as well, for the involvement of other health and social service workers, and consultants, to the client's benefit. Lazarus (1988) notes the importance of the therapist (specialist) assuming an active role with client and family. The role changes at different stages of therapy, and must be flexible enough to include primary care delivery, coordination of care providers, and advocacy behaviors for the client within a variety of community and health care delivery systems.

The use of primary care activities by the specialist can be explored through brief reviews of the care of the depressed elderly client and the alcoholic client. Both depression and alcoholism are multidimensional disorders and highly prevalent in our society. Depression, in varying degrees, occurs in as much as 20% of the elder population and is frequently identified in populations seeking care in primary care facilities (Ells, 1991). Alcoholism occurs in as many as 18 million individuals, most of whom are untreated because the disease goes unrecognized by care providers and denied by the client. Eating disorders and narcotic dependence are equally suited to nursing care delivered in this model.

Perspectives fundamental to nursing provide a framework within which psychiatric nurses assess, treat, and evaluate client outcomes. Three of these perspectives of relevance to geriatric and alcoholic clients are (1) a health orientation; (2) relevance of psychosocial and environmental factors; and (3) a focus on family relationships and interrelationships among family members' health needs. These three perspectives and their incorporation into psychiatric nurse practice are specifically applied in the following examples.

SPECIFIC APPLICATION: THE DEPRESSED ELDERLY CLIENT

Health Orientation

Most older persons consider themselves in good mental and physical health and are reluctant to acknowledge or admit to psychological difficulty (Reiff, 1980). They are hesitant to talk about feelings of depression, apathy, or discouragement, and tend not to seek psychological interventions even when feeling sad and/or dejected (Blumenthal, 1980). The nursing orientation toward health promotes the formulation of goals which reflect the client's overall concerns rather than singling out separate symptoms. Clients' concerns about activities of daily living and social isolation are good examples. These clients tend to place greater emphasis on meeting basic survival needs than on their mental and physical health needs. The nurse works to develop an overall plan which encompasses all concerns, but acknowledges the client's priorities (Pfeiffer, 1976; Ebersole, 1989). For example, teaching about the importance of easily prepared, well balanced, and diverse meals shared with others introduces a means of both decreasing boredom and promoting good nutrition.

Psychosocial and Environmental Factors

Primary care activities and efforts to prevent depression in the elderly take into consideration the elder individual's mood changes secondary to alteration in cerebral function and the depletion of physical coping energies (Ebersole, 1989). Irrespective of age, illness, when it occurs, always has some depressive components. In addition, elderly clients' preoccupation with economic security, social relationships, and social conditions are indicators that they might benefit from greater involvement with the community.

For older people, decreasing social and physical mobility, awareness of increasing dependence, and a limited capacity to manipulate the environment create feelings of being trapped and a sense of helplessness to change environmental circumstances. The nurse's efforts to increase community involvement can often prevent a client from feeling increasingly isolated and/or confined. When the nurse is at ease and familiar with obtaining information about the community for the client, greater activity is promoted. Outreach efforts, essential to delivering primary care, are evident in a readiness to visit the client at home and/or assess factors such as safety and stability of the home environment and the community.

Focus on the Family System

The elder's family system is often diminished in size and spirit by death and other types of loss and separation. Protective, supportive relationships are few in number, and their positive effects of maintaining self-esteem by reflected appraisal may be limited. "Family" may consist of friendships or relationships with neighbors or former business associates because the client is estranged from, or without, kin. Knowledge of families, the dynamics of family relationships, and the interrelationships of family members' health care needs undergird planning and intervention. Individuals who provide emotional and practical resources for the client are included in health teaching. Family counseling in which the psychotherapist intervenes to facilitate problem solving and decisionmaking is recommended for the depressed elderly client (Bellak, 1976). Family support groups provide arenas in which to work out feelings about the many care-related issues faced by family members (Ebersole, 1989). By including family members in the initial assessment, the nurse acknowledges the importance of the family structure and its members as sources of support for the client, as well as sources of data for the development of a care plan.

Psychiatric Nursing Care of the Elderly Depressed Client

First Contact with the Health Care System

First contact for depressed elderly clients is often a general medical clinic, home care setting, or social service agency, since this population is less likely to seek assistance for psychological difficulty. Rather, the client seeks treatment for physical complaints such as fatigue, headache, and insomnia, while experiencing concurrent symptoms of dysphoric affect, and feelings of helplessness, hopelessness, and worthlessness. Memory impairment is common, and it is important to differentiate depressive symptomatology from organic changes. A broad-based assessment helps to identify possible physical illnesses contributing to depression, and to rule out secondary effects of infection, cerebral trauma, malnutrition, misuse of prescribed drugs, and alcohol intoxication, all of which can produce acute brain syndrome (Blumenthal, 1980; Naegle, 1983; Ebersole, 1989).

Evaluation of physical health is a first priority and can be conducted by the psychiatric specialist utilizing generalist skills. If the nurse does not wish to perform the screening history and physical, referral to a physician or nurse colleague is appropriate, as is accessing information about recent evaluations from a private provider or clinic where the client has been seen.

A mental status assessment is then conducted, with special attention to age-specific themes often associated with depression. These include multiple complaints and demands, hypochondriasis, and anxiety. Related occurrences include multiple losses, disappointment with one's life, a sense of futility, and anticipation of one's own demise (Beyer, 1981). Such themes should be evaluated for their links to depressive symptoms. Suicidal ideation and self-destructive thoughts are exacerbated by poor health and limited, unsatisfactory support systems. In interpreting the mental status examination, consideration is given to the effects of aging, chronic medical conditions, and social conditions as culturally derived perspectives (Lazarus, 1988). The material is then incorporated into the database.

Continuity of Care

Continuity of care is a key primary care component and one of particular importance to the elderly client. Feeling devalued, angry, and lonely, the elderly depressed individual withdraws even further from investing in relationships. The care provider must engage in outreach and invest time and patience in building a trust relationship. Cognitive changes, diminished sensory and learning capacities, and social losses make these individuals especially vulnerable to the confusion caused by fragmentation in the health care delivery system and brief, superficial contacts with a wide variety and number of health care personnel (Bellak, 1976). When the single health care professional who is both therapist and primary care provider assumes multiple role functions, the client's security is enhanced.

By assuming a central coordinating role, communication, interpretation of the plan for care, and emotional and psychological support are provided by one familiar and trusted care provider. Maintaining a primary relationship and consolidating the emotional investment in one caregiver provides further security that counteracts ongoing fears of desertion, loss, and fear of death experienced by the elderly (Levin, 1967; Lazarus, 1988).

Management of Symptoms

Psychotherapeutic interactions with the elderly can be subsumed under three goals: amelioration of symptoms, restoration of functioning, and enhancement of the perceived quality of life (Lazarus, 1988). Amelioration of symptoms requires an evaluation of the symptom itself and the capacity of the care provider to address it. For the nurse who is prov iding both primary care and the therapeutic relationship, questions may arise regarding the management of related medical illness as well as the prescription of medication. A well-established network of other care providers is, then, most beneficial in its potential as a resource for referral and collaborative care. If the nurse is not licensed to prescribe medication, the utilization of referral networks and assumed responsibility for monitoring medication responses becomes the mode of operation. Overall, the management of symptoms and restoration of functioning is best handled within the context of the nursing relationship, providing that the role functions include both primary care activities and specialist related functions, such as psychotherapy.

Restoration of functioning evolves from the success of nurse/client interaction and relates to the implementation of the nursing care plan. Psychotherapeutic interactions are crucial here and encompass the goals which support positive quality of life changes. Nursing interventions are established and derived on the basis of individual needs.

Health Maintenance

For the elderly depressed client, health maintenance activities that can be implemented by the psychotherapist include (1) establishing networks supportive to the provision of primary care, including health education and health screening; (2) psychotherapeutic work to identify and manage feelings of depression; and (3) planning and coordination of multidisciplinary services essential to the client's support in daily functioning. Because the elderly client needs multiple services, often from private and public agencies, collaborative and coordinating functions by the therapist may become primary, at times. Information sharing and interpretation of client needs, collaboration with social workers, clergy, public health nurses, and/or agency volunteers are necessary to restore and maintain whatever functional level is possible for the client (Mezey, Stokes, & Rauckhorst, 1993). Since the client is often overwhelmed by the activities necessary to meet practical needs, the therapist can work to effect change on several levels through information sharing and the interpretation of services and necessary activities. Such coordination of service connotes a broad understanding of the relationship between comprehensive care and psychotherapeutic goals. In the ongoing relationship, the therapist offers opportunities for the client to have increasing participation in health maintenance activities. Simultaneously, client and therapist can evaluate the effectiveness of implemented plans and modify care plans as treatment progresses. Interested other individuals, including family and other care providers, may be included in this process as necessary. Such an approach extends the therapeutic activity beyond the one-to-one relationship.

Referral

Depression in the elderly client is a complex phenomenon. Depending on the age of the client, extenuating medical problems, and the availability of support services, care provision is time-intensive. Components of the database may, necessarily, be obtained by specialty consultation with a variety of care providers, such as neuropsychologists, psychiatrists, physical therapists, social workers, and others. The primary care provider must be skilled in identifying the need for and making the appropriate referrals to other providers. Examples of frequently needed services include short-term hospitalization, psychopharmacologic evaluation, and diagnostic testing. At times such treatment may be subsumed within the goals of the therapeutic relationship, with greater goal-directed activity being initiated at a later date. Continuity of contact with client and family during these times is essential to offset fears of abandonment and loss in the life of the elderly client.

SPECIFIC APPLICATION: THE CLIENT WITH ALCOHOL PROBLEMS

A Health Orientation

Alcohol-related problems can be described on a continuum from early problem drinking to alcoholism. Nursing interventions along the continuum take into consideration the beginning level of severity, intermediary stages, and progressive changes toward an entrenched pattern of alcoholism during which the client experiences varying degrees of health and illness. The nurse who understands patterns of illnesses in acute and chronic stages is able to assist the client during phases of sobriety as well as preliminary stages of recovery and periods of relapse. Primary prevention and basic health care inhere in a drug-free life style, and health education is utilized to promote physical and mental well being. The emphasis on health is particularly helpful for the individual whose physical signs will lessen as recovery proceeds, and for the chronically ill individual for whom hope is an essential cornerstone of continuing struggles to achieve sobriety and recovery.

Psychosocial and Environmental Factors

The disease of alcoholism results from multiple interrelated factors and affects many aspects of the client's life and the lives of those with whom he/she lives, works, and interacts. Occupational, legal, and social spheres are arenas within which the disease and its associated behaviors are played out, and its ramifications take on a variety of meanings. Nurses, by virtue of their basic education, are sensitive to the psychological impacts of socially stigmatic attitudes about individuals with drinking problems, know the long-term effects of heavy alcohol consumption, and are aware of the legal difficulties frequently encountered through driving while intoxicated (DWI) and threats to professional licensure and/or employment. Because nurses understand both the implications for the community and community patterns and resources, they are able to identify support systems as well as lifestyle factors and community patterns that support drug-using behaviors. This knowledge facilitates the development of an invaluable network of community agencies and care providers, which, with guidance and information, the recovering alcoholic can access and utilize.

Focus on the Family System

Heavy drinking and alcohol dependence in one or more members of a family has the effect of distorting emotional relationships and ultimately disrupting relationships within the family system and the community. The alcoholic member may manifest problems at work and is often involved in legal infractions and problems related to compliance with taxes and other indebtedness, as well as engaging in behaviors which result in alienation of the family from the community.

Dysfunctional relationships within the family have implications for day-to-day living as well as for the future of the family and its members. These implications include familial predispositions to alcohol and other drug dependence which may be genetic and/or environmental, as well as learned patterns of relationships which are dysfunctional and compromise the family members' abilities for successful interpersonal interactions (Ells 1991). Although supporting research data is limited, adult children of alcoholics report many life problems, and a significant number of them develop dependencies on alcohol and other drugs. The generalist nurse is well educated in assessing family systems and equipped to develop strategies for health education, support, and counseling needs of the family with an alcoholic member.

Psychiatric Nursing Care of the Alcoholic Client

First Contact

The majority of clients with alcohol problems do not seek treatment in specialty care settings. They are inclined to enter the health care delivery system through the emergency room, general medical clinics, and occupational health settings. Alcoholism afflicts approximately 20% of male and 6% of female individuals in the general population (Colligan, Davis, Morse, & Offord, 1988). These persons will seek care in general settings, and are encountered by the generalist practitioner most frequently.

The management of the alcoholic's encounter with the health care delivery system is crucial. It is precisely because of the client's defensiveness and denial about excessive drinking that the contact with health care professionals must be positive. Generally, because of negative attitudes on the parts of health care personnel, drug and alcohol dependent clients receive inadequate assessments. This is partly due to the limited knowledge on the parts of health care providers about the signs and symptoms which indicate the presence of disease. These are (1) physiological and clinical signs, and (2) behavioral, attitudinal, and psychological characteristics associated with stages of alcoholism (National Council on Alcoholism Criteria Committee, 1972; Estes & Heinemann, 1986)

Irrespective as to whether the psychiatric nurse acts as consultant or as primary care provider, a comprehensive history and physical examination includes a drinking/drug history. The basic drug/drinking history consists of:

1. Alcoholic beverages and types of drugs consumed.
2. Frequency and amount of alcohol/drugs consumed daily, weekly, and monthly.
3. The function that the drug/alcohol use serves for the client.
4. Description of a typical drinking/drug-using day.
5. Client's perceptions/concerns about drinking/drug use.
6. Changes/disturbances in social, legal, and occupational spheres linked to drinking/drug-using behaviors.

The care provider should be particularly alert to signs observed in the physical examination of the alcoholic. These include:

1. Palmar erythema
2. Spider angioma

3. Numerous burns, lacerations, petechiae, ecchymoses
4. Acne rosacea
5. Dental caries; gum disease
6. Cheilitis
7. Rhinophyma
8. Muscular atrophy
9. Vein scarring and circulatory disturbance
10. Abnormalities of uric acid, free fatty acids, and macrocytosis (Schuckit, 1989, p. 60)

Findings suggestive of alcoholism should be discussed with the client, and be presented as part of the overall health assessment. The need for intervention, whether through modification of drinking habits or hospitalization for intensive treatment, must be acknowledged in a caring, nonpunitive manner, and options available to the client clearly spelled out.

Continuity of Care

Social stigma, frequent interpersonal and economic losses, and the continuing and generally unsuccessful struggle to control drinking result in diminished self-regard and feelings of hopelessness for the alcoholic. Given the frequency with which other drugs are combined with alcohol, legal problems, and job performance problems may further reinforce feelings of low self-esteem. The constancy of one primary care-nurse therapist facilitates the development of a trusting relationship characterized by accessibility and commitment. Since "slips" or relapses occur in all phases of recovery, the therapist must carefully establish a contract with the client about the commitment to abstinence from alcohol and other drugs, and the consequences of relapse. An open agreement will support honest reporting and diminish expectations about punishment or rejection if relapse should occur. Long-term working relationships increase opportunities to achieve personal growth as well as in sobriety.

The therapeutic nursing relationship with the alcoholic and drug abuser develops around three central concerns:

1. Breaking the addictive cycle.
2. Treating immediate medical and social problems.
3. Treating core problems of psychological dependence (Blumenthal, 1980, p. 34; Schuckit, 1989).

Each concern requires that the interrelated psychophysiologic experiences be addressed. Interrupting the addictive cycle, when the client is both psychologically and physiologically dependent, may result in effects of alcohol withdrawal and disturbing and compelling physical cravings for the drug. The nurse must be alert to signs of withdrawal and provide or coordinate appropriate treatment as well as interpret elements of the disease process to the client. The long-term effects of alcohol abuse, such as anemia, gastritis, fatty liver disease, or cirrhosis, pose serious medical problems, and the client must be treated comprehensively. The client may require inpatient hospitalization or medical supervision for outpatient detoxification. The nurse assumes responsibility for identifying the client problem, recommending treatment, and establishing the channels through which the client and/or family can obtain specific services. Preeminent needs for medical care will interrupt the nurse-client relationship to some degree, but continuity is provided through the nurse's involvement in coordination and the integration of new information into the data base that remains the context of the primary care relationship.

Health Maintenance

Although alcoholism is a chronic disease, the client, through abstinence, can achieve a significant level of health. Sobriety is most effectively attained through the use of self-help groups as an adjunct to treatment, Alcoholics Anonymous and other programs developed according to this twelve-step model provide structure, support, social aspects of a fellowship, and a program for establishing a drugfree life style. Referring the client to twelve-step programs and supporting or even requiring their attendance enhances treatment and provides a means of around-the-clock access to an understanding person when drug cravings and other use-related behaviors emerge. Education about the disease of addiction makes up a major component of prevention and ongoing health maintenance. In addition, a comprehensive self-care plan should be developed with the client. Since alcohol and other drug use has persisted for long periods, clients have often neglected self-care, such as exercise regimens, dental hygiene, and nutrition. The nurse not only imparts important information about these areas, but interprets their importance in the context of positive self-regard and support for sobriety.

Health maintenance includes new learning in the psychotherapeutic relationship. The prominence of alcohol or some other drug in the life of the individual results in distorted and neglected relationships with co-workers, family, and friends. Relearning interpersonal patterns requires that the trusting nurse-client relationship include an examination of en trenched dysfunctional patterns of lifestyle and relationships. These dysfunctional patterns will soon be evident to the nurse, not only as they are manifested in the psychotherapeutic relationship, but in the manner that the client utilizes guidance and referrals as he/she accesses other services. When friends and family members have enabled the client's illness to progress by participating in drug use and/or supplying the drug in an effort to abort negative behavior by the client, these individuals profit from learning the errors of their ways. Al-Anon provides a group setting in which to understand how efforts to "keep the peace" or "save the client" also serve to support the client's continued drug use and lead to poor mental health for everyone.

Similarly, modifying one's own behaviors, such as not expressing or meeting one's own emotional needs, results in behavioral distortions known as "codependence." Many patterns of interaction, inappropriate problem solving approaches and social attitudes develop as a function of a family or group member's use of drugs. Approaches useful with non-traditional or traditional "family systems," such as family therapy, are strategies for creating behavioral change. Nurse-therapists may be equipped to practice these approaches, but more likely will refer the family to appropriate agencies and care providers. Nurses who function as the primary caretaker must be skilled at assessing individual and family system with health problems, understanding the interface of patterns which support the continuation of health problems, and envisioning the most effective strategies to resolve old and dysfunctional behaviors on the parts of clients and family members. If change to a drug-free life style is to persist for the addicted individual, efforts must be made to modify old patterns of relating to family, social, and occupational systems.

Coordination and Collaboration

Optimally, nurses who assume the role of primary care/psychotherapy provider give direct care to clients. Involvement with the family is relevant, but the primary care providers' role, more often, is that of coordinator of services, collaborator with family and several care providers, and advocate for client and family. For the recovering person, coordination is particularly important. While twelve-step groups complement the therapeutic work of client and nurse, families and others significant to the patient easily become involved in complicated systems within the community. It is important that nurses interpret the availability and appropriate use of resources to clients and families.

Referral

Because alcoholism and other drug dependencies have wide ramifications for the client's life, it is important to utilize many resources in planning and implementing change. The focus of the psychotherapeutic work is to address the client's drug use and central psychological problems, as well as changing the self-concept. Supports and learning opportunities which move the individual toward a new view of self are particularly important. As primary therapists and providers of primary as well as specialty care, nurses facilitate appropriate opportunities for change at various stages of recovery. Vocational counseling, and/or subsequent job training or education, legal counsel, sheltered workshops, and halfway houses are examples of resources that the client needs assistance in utilizing. In addition to identifying resources, it is important for nurses to follow up and note outcomes related to involvement in various agencies, with other care providers and with self-help groups. The capacity for independent choice by the client must be supported; at the same time, the therapist is knowledgeable in a variety of ways about resources and professional roles, and this knowledge should be used to the advantage of the client and his/her family.

FUTURE PSYCHIATRIC NURSING ROLES

Community health-oriented nursing roles, including community mental health, have moved psychiatric nursing away from institution-based interventions, with a focus on pathology, to a view of the nursing role as it relates to mental health along a continuum. Psychiatric nursing liaison and consultation, and now the possibility of combining primary and specialty modes of care, provide new opportunities to demonstrate nursing's contributions to improving mental health services. Earlier in nursing's history, autonomy in practice and collaborative modes of working were viewed as more readily achievable in psychiatric nursing. These role characteristics, along with prescriptive privileges, client advocacy, and accountability are now fully integrated into advanced practice nursing in most specialties. Parallel changes are also occurring in psychiatric nursing (Naegle, 1983; McEnany, 1991).

The need for an expanded role for psychiatric nursing was described as early as 1976 by the American Nurses Association. (American Nurses Association [ANA], 1976). The American Nurses Association noted that trends toward shorter hospitalization, deinstitutionalization of psychiatric patients, and an increased emphasis on prevention, as well as professional trends emphasizing quality care, consumer advocacy, and accountability, all supported greater independence of practice and role changes toward more comprehensive care delivery.

Current changes in psychiatric nursing are timely when one considers that: (1) psychiatric nurses now have greater educational preparation, including broader knowledge of generalist and practitioner skills as the foundation for their practice; (2) complex health care needs of populations require practitioners with diverse skills who are comfortable practicing in a wide variety of settings; and (3) communication and psychotherapeutic skills are of increasing importance to effective delivery of care.

The need for major change in the way in which health care is delivered in this country is now widely acknowledged. Large numbers of individuals fall victim to acute and long-term problems, including HIV infection, substance abuse, and age-associated illnesses, such as Alzheimer's Disease. There is a greater recognition of the importance of psychosocial needs manifested by clients seeking care in general medical clinics (Martin, 1984), and the prevalence of emotional disturbance and mental illness in clients seeking care in primary care clinics and emergency rooms. In addition, a growing number of individuals with chronic mental illness, alcoholism, and other substance abuse disorders are seeking care in settings such as nursing homes and home care agencies, which are ill equipped to meet their needs.

Psychiatric nurses capable of blending both primary care and psychosocial skills offer unique talents in meeting these consumer health care needs. Implementing such a role is an unprecedented opportunity for nurses to garner public support for their practice (Mechanic, 1982).

Originally, as psychiatric nurses moved toward greater specialization, their generalist skills were underutilized. Now, however, psychiatric nurses are particularly well suited to implement an expanded role. Their traditional grounding in a biologic axis of patient and family oriented care links them with a holistic approach to care delivery. Advanced education in crisis intervention equips them to confront client responses to stressful life situations; skills in assessment and management of illness further broadens this base.

This combined generalist-specialist preparation, with its capability for complex decisionmaking, offers a potential for cost-effective health care delivery (Murphy & Hoeffer, 1987). When nurses function as primary therapists, more psychosocial issues are addressed, supporting the value of psychotherapy in reducing hospital stays and maximizing patient responses to treatment. Such an approach emphasizes the interface between generalist and specialist approaches to care. The acknowledgement of psychiatric nursing's contribution has been further reinforced by greater accessibility to third-party reimbursement and more open attitudes of younger nursing graduates, willing to implement their generalist nursing skills in psychiatric care settings.

An ongoing reality of care is that the setting for practice continues to exert a strong influence on the freedom with which nurses implement their role. The philosophical tenets of primary care—a health orientation and commitment to total care in a continuing relationship—lend themselves most readily to independent practice. However, because independent practice is not readily accessible, the freedom of nurses to practice autonomously must be negotiated on an ongoing basis within institutions and with other members of the health care team. Within the confines of these practice boundaries, the ability to function as a colleague is essential. Rodgers' (1981) observations suggest directions for growth that are necessary milestones if nurses are to function as colleagues.

The concept of collegiality can be viewed as having three dimensions: interpersonal relations, professionalism, and decisionmaking. A professional identity is a prerequisite if nurses are to participate as colleagues with other professionals. Within psychiatric nursing, nurses must be ready to articulate their role in relation to that of other mental health professionals. Issues of territoriality restrict the potential for professionals to function together. Established roles, if rigidly defined, may artificially divide tasks when what is needed are flexible boundaries in order to meet client needs.

Recruitment to the specialty of psychiatric nursing would be enhanced by the sanction and support of the specialty within primary health care settings. With an increasing emphasis on quality care and cost savings, the role of psychiatric nurses can assume an importance not previously acknowledged. More careful attention to articulating the links between the goals of prevention, primary care, and treatment is the key to opening doors for psychiatric nurse specialists.

CONCLUSIONS

Primary care as a health care delivery model presents challenging opportunities to specialists in psychiatric nursing. The broad-based, client-focused nature of primary care suggests a more holistic approach to planning and delivery of care. A focus on collaboration, coordination, and direct care delivery suggests a central role for psychiatric nurses.

Their skills lie in addressing client/family problems, organizing environmental patterns to support treatment approaches, and facilitating circumstances to influence the client's ability to attain optimum wellness.

Contemporary factors, including greater awareness of the psychological aspects of illness and changing health care needs in large segments of the populations, support the potential for expanded psychiatric nursing practice. Efforts to achieve third-party reimbursement, and increasing evidence of accountability and autonomy, further underscore the vision and resolve of psychiatric nurses to create a more flexible and responsive health care system.

REFERENCES

Aiken, L. (1978). Primary care: The challenge for nursing. In N. Chaska (Ed.), *The nursing profession: Views through the mist* (pp. 242–255). New York: McGraw-Hill.

American Nurses Association [ANA]. (1976). Statement on Psychiatric Mental Health Nursing Practice. Kansas City, MO: Author.

Bellak, L. (1976). Geriatric psychiatry as comprehensive health care. In L. Bellak & T. B. Karasu (Eds.), *Geriatric psychiatry: A handbook for psychiatrists and primary care physicians* (pp. 3–12). New York: Grune and Stratton.

Beyer, J. E., & Marshall, J. (1981). The interpersonal dimension of collegiality. *Nursing Outlook, 29,* 662–665.

Blane, H. T. (1978). Psychotherapeutic approach. In B. Kissin & H. Begleiter (Eds.), *Treatment and rehabilitation of the chronic alcoholic* (pp. 105–160). New York: Plenum Press.

Blumenthal, M. D. (1980). Depressive illness in old age: Getting behind the mask. *Geriatrics, 35,* 34–43.

Cadoret, R., & King, L. (1974). *Psychiatry in primary care.* St. Louis: C. V. Mosby.

Chychula, N. M. (1984). Screening for substance abuse in a primary care setting. *Nurse Practitioner, 9*(7), 15–24.

Colligan, R. C., Davis, L. J., Morse, R. M., & Offord, K. P. (1988). Screening medical patients for alcoholism with the MMPI: A comparison of seven scales. *Journal of Clinical Psychology, 44,* 582–592.

Ebersole, P. (1989). *Caring for the psychogeriatric client.* New York: Springer Publishing Co.

Eisenman, E. (1976). Primary care in a mental health facility. *Nursing Outlook, 24,* 640–645.

Ells, M. A. W. (1991). Family therapy. In G. E. Bennett & D. Woolf (Eds.), *Substance abuse* (pp. 267–279). Albany: Delmare.

Estes, N. J., & Heinemann, M. E. (1986). *Alcoholism: Development, consequences, and interventions* (3rd ed.). St. Louis, C. V. Mosby.

Fagin, C. M. (1983). Concepts for the future: competition and substitution. *Journal of Psychosocial Nursing and Mental Health Services, 21*, 36–40.

Glover, B. A. (1967). A psychiatrist calls for a new nurse therapist. *American Journal of Nursing, 67*, 1003–1005.

Jennings, C. (1977). Primary care and the question of obsolescence. *Journal of Psychiatric Nursing and Mental Health Services, 15*, 9–17.

Keller, N. (1978). The whys and whats of private practice. In N. Chaska (Ed.), *The nursing profession: Views through the mist* (pp. 279–286). New York: Mc-Graw-Hill.

Klerman, G. (1980). Klerman outlines goals of ADAMHA programs. *Psychiatric News, 40*, 279–286.

LaGodna, G. (1981). In A. Burgess (Ed.), *Psychiatric nursing in the hospital and community* (pp. 629–636). Englewood Cliffs, NJ: Prentice-Hall.

Lazarus, L. W. (Ed.) (1988). *Essentials of geriatric psychiatry.* New York: Springer Publishing Co.

Leininger, M. (1973). *Contemporary issues in mental health nursing.* Boston: Little, Brown.

Levin, S. (1967). Depression in the aged. In M. Berezin & H. Cath (Eds.), *Geriatric psychiatry: Grief, loss and emotional disorders in the aging process* (pp. 203–229). New York: International University Press.

Martin, E. J. (1984). A specialty in decline? Psychiatric nursing: Past, present, and future. *Journal of Professional Nursing, 1*, 48–53.

McEnany, G. W. (1991). Psychobiology and psychiatric nursing: A philosophical matrix. *Archives of Psychiatric Nursing, 5*, 255–261.

Mechanic, D. (1982). Nursing and mental health care: Expanding future possibilities for nursing services. In L. Aiken & D. Mechanic (Eds.), *Nursing in the 1980s: Crises, opportunities and challenges* (pp. 343–358). Philadelphia: Lippincott.

Mezey, M., Stokes, S., & Rauckhorst, L. (1993) Community and home assessment. In *Health assessment for the older individual* (2d. ed.). New York: Springer Publishing Co.

Mitsunaga, B. K. (1982). Designing psychiatric-mental health nursing for the future: Problems and prospects. *Journal of Psychosocial Nursing and Mental Health Services, 20*, 12, 15–21.

Murphy, S., & Hoeffer, B. (1987). The evolution of subspecialty in psychiatric and mental health nursing. *Archives of Psychiatric Nursing, 1*(3), 145–154.

Naegle, M. (1983). The role of Psychotherapist within the primary health care model. In L. Breslau & M. Haug (Eds.), *Depression and aging* (p. 86). New York: Springer Publishing Co.

National Council on Alcoholism, Criteria Committee, 1972.

Nightingale, F. (1859). *Notes on nursing: What it is and what it is not.* London: Harrison and Sons.

Pfeiffer, E. (1976). Psychotherapy with elderly patients. In L. Bellak & T. B. Karasu (Eds.), *Geriatric psychiatry: A handbook for psychiatry and primary care physicians* (pp. 191–206). New York: Grune and Stratton.

Raskin, A. (1979). Signs and symptoms of psychopathology in the elderly. In A.

Raskin & L. Jarvik (Eds.), *Psychiatric symptoms and cognitive loss in the elderly* (p. 21). Washington, DC: Hemisphere.

Reiff, T. R. (1980). The essentials of geriatric evaluation. *Geriatrics, 35,* 59–68.

Rodgers, J. (1981). Toward professional adulthood. *Nursing Outlook, 29,* 478–481.

Salzman, C., & Shader, R. (1979). Clinical evaluation of depression in the elderly. In A. Raskin & L. Jarvik (Eds.), *Psychiatric symptoms and cognitive loss in the elderly* (pp. 39–72). Washington, DC: Hemisphere.

Schmidt, C. W. (1974). Psychiatric problems of the aged. *Journal of the American Geriatric Society, 22,* 355–359.

Schuckit, M. A. (1989). *Drug and alcohol abuse: A clinical guide to diagnosis and treatment.* New York: Plenum Medical Book Company.

Sulsky, S., Jacques, P., Otradovec, C., Hartz, S., & Russell, R. (1990). Descriptors of alcohol consumption among noninstitutionalized elderly patients. *Journal of the American Geriatrics Society, 9*(4), 326–331.

Chapter 10

NURSING CENTERS: THE NEW ARENA FOR ADVANCED NURSING PRACTICE

Eileen Sullivan, Bonnie Fields, Joseph Kelly, and
Ellen-Marie Whelan

A LTHOUGH nurse practitioners and educators of nurse practitioners
have been relatively successful in controlling the scope of practice,
opportunities to control the practice environment have been more elu-
sive. To be sure, a growing number of nurse practitioners and nurse-
midwives have established private practices, but the majority of nurse
practitioners and mid-wives, even today, are not self employed.

Nursing centers provide one opportunity to control both the scope of
practice and the practice environment. Nursing centers (or nurse managed centers) are today's model for autonomous nursing practice. Congruent with *Nursing's Agenda for Health Care Reform* (National League for
Nursing [NLN]/MET Study, 1991), there is limited but compelling evidence that nursing centers provide quality, accessible, and affordable
ambulatory services. This chapter reviews the history of nursing centers, describes their characteristics, and discusses fiscal issues critical to
their survival.

EVOLUTION OF NURSING CENTERS

Numerous definitions of nursing centers are reported in the literature (Fehring, Riesch & Schulte, 1986; Fields, Kelly, Sullivan, & Whelan, 1991; *Legislative Network for Nurses*, 1992). All definitions have in common the following elements: (1) care is client/patient focused with direct access to professional nurses; (2) practice is controlled by and preferably managed by nurses; (3) services are reimbursed directly, or from third-party payers; (4) a referral network is established; and (5) practice is evaluated.

The concept of a nurse managed center continues a tradition of health care settings in which nurses have both clinical and fiscal responsibility for care (Henry, 1978). Hospice care and childbirth centers are just two examples of such care. In contrast with these specialized services, reports of centers providing more general health care services began to appear in the literature in the late 1960s (Riesch, 1986; Riesch, 1992a, 1992b). Early reports described nurse-managed care in hospital clinics (Lewis & Resnick, 1962), and programs providing care to diverse populations in the community centers (Delaware Nursing Center, 1983, personal communication; Lundeen, 1986). Often using nurse practitioners and primarily serving underserved populations, centers from their inception emphasized health promotion and wellness, identification of health/illness needs, management of health care problems, and referral.

In the 1970s, nursing faculty within universities began to establish nurse-managed centers to encourage faculty practice and to provide controlled clinical sites for nurse practitioner students (Culang, Josephson, Marcus, & Vezina, 1980; Mezey & Chiamulera, 1980; Ossler, Goodwin, Mariani, & Gilliss, 1982; Riesch, Felder, & Stauder, 1980; Vezina, 1986). In these academic nursing centers, faculty could demonstrate primary nursing care which was autonomous and client-focused. In a position paper at the American Public Health Association convention, Henry (1978) emphasized that academic nursing centers provided a model for linkage of practice and education and promotion of research leading to the advancement of knowledge in nursing practice.

In 1981, 63 schools of nursing indicated that they were affiliated with or sponsored a nurse-managed center. In 1982, the National League for Nursing (NLN) Council for Nursing Centers was established, and the first national conference on nursing centers was held in Milwaukee, Wisconsin (Riesch, 1983). While useful for sharing information, these and subsequent meetings underscored the infancy of the movement, the small number of clients served, and the precariousness of funding. Nevertheless, spurred by growing interest in nursing centers within academic settings, in 1981 the Division of Nursing of the United States Public Health Service (USPHS) funded the establishment of the first federally supported university based nursing center at the University of Connecticut.

Optimism about nurse-managed centers peaked in 1983 when Senator Inouye introduced a bill to provide coverage for community nursing center services under Medicare and Medicaid (S410, 98th Congress, 1983; Lang, 1983). This bill failed to gain legislative support through two sessions of Congress. Subsequent to this effort, a few centers were successful in gaining foundation support (Delaware Nursing Center, 1983).

Currently, the renewed interest in nursing centers is evident in legislation passed in Section 4079 of the Omnibus Budget Reconciliation Act of 1987 (OBRA–87), which directs the Health Care Financing Administration (HCFA) to *test* prepaid, capitated payments to Community Nursing Organizations (CNOs) under the Medicare program (Community Nursing Organization, 1991). Through this funding, contracts were awarded to four CNO demonstration sites to provide community nursing and ambulatory care services to Medicare beneficiaries. The current call for proposals by HCFA was an opportunity for both academic and entrepreneurial nursing centers to demonstrate the quality and cost advantages of independent primary nursing care.

Most centers, however, continue to operate by pulling together packages of support from diverse funding streams. Many centers, in conjunction with schools of nursing, seek sites for creative, independent faculty practice and research, student education, and a desire to deliver care in the community (Boettcher, 1991; Henry, 1978; Lang, 1983; Lundeen, 1986; Mezey, 1983; Riesch, 1986). More recently, health care agencies such as community health clinics, service agencies, and hospitals have developed nursing centers to address unmet health care needs in their communities. Some individual nurses have also started centers as private, entrepreneurial businesses (Dickerson & Nash, 1985; Ethridge, 1991; Parker & Secord, 1988).

The NLN Council for Nurse Managed Centers has continued as a national forum for the identification, categorization, and dissemination of information about nursing centers. Its publication, *Connections*, is mailed to over 200 sites and individuals associated with nursing centers.

DIVERSE CHARACTERISTICS OF NURSING CENTERS

Two recent studies provide data concerning the varied characteristics of nursing centers currently in operation.

A study funded by the Metropolitan Life Foundation reports that, in 1990, more than 118,000 Americans received care in an estimated 250 community nursing centers (NLN/MET Study). The average budget per center is estimated to be about $750,000. Forty-three percent of the centers served the general population, while other centers served specific groups such as the elderly, women, and children, and clients with need for mental health services. At least 45% of center clients were minorities. Most clients were uninsured and 13% were covered under Medicaid. Fifty-two percent of the nursing centers studied were affiliated with a second community facility such as a home health agency, retirement community, or public health department.

Close to 45% of the centers provided primary care. Other services included assessment and screening (19%); education (14%); counseling (7%); and home health care (3%). Approximately 3% of the centers primarily served clients with psychological and mental health needs. The average number of clients served by a center annually was 1,900, each client being seen for an average of five visits. Centers served clients of all income groups, ages, and racial/ethnic backgrounds. The fact that half the centers were founded within the past five years and that half the clients are middle-class suggest that community nursing centers appeal to a wide range of consumers and are competitive with other available health care services.

A second study (Fields et al., 1991) consisted of in-depth telephone interviews with 20 operating centers representing 25% of all centers listed in the NLN's Council on Nurse Managed Centers (NLN/MET Study, 1991). Fourteen centers were recruited from those participating in the first National Conference on Nursing Centers conducted by the Council for Nurse Managed Centers. One hundred and ten people attended the conference representing 30 centers. Participants completed a pilot survey to elicit information about the type of center, description of services, client volume, employees, and revenue sources. In-depth telephone interviews were requested with centers meeting the following criteria: (1) actively operating; (2) providing patients direct access to professional nurses; and (3) practice controlled by nurses. Six centers were in the development phase or indicated no interest in follow-up interviews. In order to comprise a total sample of 20 centers, 6 centers were selected for interviews from those listed on the NLN mailing list of nurse-managed centers.

Thirty percent of centers in the total sample of 20 were in the Midwest, 25% in the Mid-Atlantic region, 20% in the Southeast, 15% in the Southwest, and 5% in both the Northwest and the Northeast. Sixteen (80%) were academic centers and 4 (20%) were freestanding, that is, not directly related to any other institution. Although most centers received in-kind support from hospitals or agencies, none were primarily hospital or agency sponsored. Eighteen (90%) were designated as not-for-profit centers. Eleven (55%) identified grants and/or foundations as their primary revenue source. The university was the primary revenue source for 6 (30%) of the centers, whereas managed care contracts and fee for service were the primary revenue source for two (10%) of the centers. One center (5%) received a significant portion of its funding from a contractual arrangement with a community health center. Contributing to the centers' revenue sources were Medicaid (6 centers), Medicare (1 center), and commercial insurance (1 center).

Existing centers received an abundance of in-kind support. Housing authorities, city and county health departments, and churches frequently donated, renovated, and furnished space and provided utilities. Some community agencies also gave monetary donations to the centers. In addition to direct support, academic centers received university support for space, secretarial support, furniture, printing services, and purchase discounts.

The type of services provided, number of clients seen, client/provider ratios, and staff support varied widely among these centers. Types of services provided can be grouped in the following categories:

1. *Health screening/promotion/education* were the primary services. provided by nine (45%) of centers surveyed. Health screening (blood pressure, cholesterol, glucose, and hemoglobin) frequently resulted in referrals to a primary provider and/or social service agency. Some centers conducted community needs assessments as part of their health screening services in order to demonstrate community health needs for local government and policy agencies. Others offered specific nursing services, such as foot care. The focus in other centers was on employee groups and injury prevention. Mobile health services were provided by two centers serving rural populations.

2. *Primary and/or basic family care* were the basic service offered by six (30%) of the centers. Primary care included multiple services such as screening and immunizations for adults and children. One center providing primary care was established as the college student health service.

3. *Family planning and prenatal care* were the focus of two (10%) of the centers surveyed. These centers indicated that they hoped to expand to provide well and sick baby care.

4. *School nurse services* were the focus of one center. Services included Early and Periodic Screening, Diagnosis, and Treatment (EPSDT) and lead screening. Anticipatory guidance for children and parents was a key component of services provided.

5. *Direct nursing care in home, hospital or private offices* was the central focus of one center. In this center, nurses provided in-home assessment and care to patients with high-risk pregnancies, either through contracts with private physicians and hospitals, or direct payment from clients who might otherwise have been hospitalized. Early postpartum discharge from the hospital was another fee-for-service provided by this center through contracts with hospitals or clients. This center also offered consultation and continuing education to agencies in the area of maternal health care. Models for creative and cost-effective high quality care were emphasized in these consultations.

6. *Education programming for professionals and assistance with nursing research* was the prime focus of one academic center. However, affiliations with schools of nursing as clinical sites for students were a component of all centers surveyed.

The primary service, number of first-time and repeat visits, type and number of providers, and number of staff for each center are shown in Table 10-1. The range of first-time and repeat visits, type and number of providers, and number of staff based on a center's primary service category are shown in Table 10-2.

COMMON CHARACTERISTICS OF NURSING CENTERS

There is now sufficient data with which to formulate some general characteristics regarding nursing centers. Typically, centers serve the medically underserved and the poor or near-poor. The clients served are predominantly women of childbearing age or the elderly. There is, however, wide variation as to the clients served. The NLN survey (NLN/ MET Study, 1992) found the centers serve a substantial number of middle-class clients. The convenience sample survey conducted by Fields et al. (1991) identified a small number of centers serving specific population groups such as university students and employee groups.

Word-of-mouth is the most common source of referral for most nurs-

TABLE 10.1 Nurse-Managed Centers: Summary Findings

Center	Primary service	No. of first visits/month	Repeat visits/month	Type/No. of providers (FTEs)
1	Screening/ Promotion/ Education	*	*	Faculty/0.5
2	Screening/ Promotion/ Education	*	* (190 live in housing unit served)	NP/1
3	Screening/ Education	50	*	NP/2
4	Screening/ Promotion/ Education	30	*	NP/0.4
5	Primary Care	Not collected	Not collected	NP/3
6	Nursing Care	Contract Basis	Contract Basis	RN/10.0
7	Screening/ Promotion/ Education	Screenings = 718 Other = *	* (529 family records)	Faculty/ student teams/2.6 Interdisciplinary
8	Screening/ Promotion/ Education	* (in planning stages)	*	*
9	Educational Programs/ Research/ Practice	*	*	Faculty/2.2
10	Family Planning/ Prenatal C.	*	*	Faculty/ student teams/3.0
11	Primary Care	86	265	NP/1.0 MD/1.0 PT MDs
12	School Nurse Programs	*	* (target 180–190 families)	NP/0.6 Faculty/ PT
13	Screening/ Promotion/ Education	*	*	RN/1.6
14	Primary Care	300–450	150–300	NP/4.0 PT MD/1.0 RN/1.0

(continued)

TABLE 10.1 (*continued*)

Center	Primary service	No. of first visits/month	Repeat visits/month	Type/No. of providers (FTEs)
15	Primary Care	150	300	NP/1.5
16	Screening/ Promotion/ Education	*	* (follow 300 fam.)	NP + Team
17	Primary Care	50	160	NP/4.0
18	Screening/ Promotion/ Education	40	20 (130 families followed)	Faculty
19 *	Family planning/ Prenatal C.	* (in planning stage)	*	*
20	Primary Care	250	250	NP/2 MD/1

*Data not available. **PT = Part Time.

ing centers. Nevertheless, centers receive referrals from physicians, county health departments and clinics, social service agencies, and churches. In the NLN survey, close to a third of referrals were from physicians, nurses and other health professionals (NLN/MET Study, 1992). Some centers advertise through newspapers or fliers.

Most centers have close relationships with other agencies within their communities which provide either direct or in-kind support. Even academic centers, which are largely supported by their respective universities, receive additional support from local housing authorities, city and county governments, and agencies serving the elderly.

While early centers emphasized health promotion and screening, current centers use nurses with advanced practice skills to provide diversified, primary care services to a variety of clientele (Igou, Hawkins, Johnson, & Utley, 1989; Lang, 1983; Pulliam, 1991; Riesch, 1986). Some centers are able to offer a range of health care services including podiatry, dental care, and counseling. By expanding the types and scope of services, centers can secure additional revenues from local and state funding agencies, charitable organizations and, albeit with difficulty, third-party payers (Ethridge, 1991; Igou, Hawkins, Johnson, & Utley, 1989; Lundeen, 1986).

Although there is a clearly recognized need, the majority of centers

TABLE 10.2 Nurse-Managed Centers: Summary Findings by Primary Service Category

Type of Service	No. of first-time visits	No. of repeat visits	Type/no. of providers (FTEs)
Health Screening/ Promotion/ Education	40–50 on average, up to 718 screenings	Data not available—follow 130–600 families	NP 0.4–2 nurse 0.4–3 faculty/ students
Primary care	50–450	150–300	NP 1.5–4 nurse 0–1 MD 0–1
Family planning/ prenatal care	*	*	Faculty/ students
School nurse programs	*	* (follow 180–190 families)	NP 0.6 faculty/ students
Direct nursing care	Contract basis *	Contract basis Faculty	RN 10.0
Educational programming/ nursing research*			

*Data not available.

do not appear to have formal quality assurance programs. Centers providing primary care employ physicians on a part-time basis to complete mandated chart reviews. When required to conduct quality assurance, for example, in response to grant funding, most centers rely on a county coalition or state health agency to perform these activities. Most centers occasionally conduct patient satisfaction surveys.

Personal risk is often reduced for the managers of many centers because of their university affiliation. The three centers not associated with a university in the study by Fields et al. (1991) assumed considerable risk. For instance, the provider at one entrepreneurial center depended on family support for nearly four years before showing a profit sufficient for her to draw a salary. Another operated for six years before the business grew sufficiently to allow hiring additional help. A third center is currently at risk of closing because the provider is unable to secure HMO contracts in an area where most clients now participate in a managed care plan.

Financing Nursing Centers

The need to broaden both goals and sources of income has been an ongoing concern of nursing centers (Mezey, 1983; NLN, 1991). While many have done so, other efforts have been thwarted by shortages of nursing faculty, cutbacks in educational resources, and decreased government funding of demonstration projects. As a case in point, the Nurse Education Link to Wellness Center, a nursing center at the University of Delaware, closed its doors in September of 1991 when the Division of Nursing, USPHS, failed to renew its funding (Harriman, 1991).

To date, most centers, particularly academic centers, have successfully competed for grant funding and have been willing to operate on "soft" monies (Fields et al., 1991). More recently, as costs of services have escalated and grant funding diminished, these centers have sought to increase that portion of their revenues which comes from fee-for-service third-party reimbursement. Lack of reimbursement by traditional third-party payers, such as Blue Shield and Medicare, is seen as a major obstacle to the financial stability of nursing centers. Yet there is some fallacy to this analysis. While it is true that nurse practitioners are eligible for private insurer reimbursement in slightly more than half of the states (Pearson, 1991), Medicare, Medicaid, and most third-party insurers do not reimburse for many of the core health promotion and education services provided by nurses. Medically defined evaluations and management, which are reimbursed, are only a small portion of the services provided at nursing centers.

Although headway has recently been made for nurse practitioners and clinicians to obtain limited payment from Medicaid and Medicare, accessing reimbursement has proven to be time-consuming and difficult. Medicare reimbursement is available only to nurse-midwives, anesthetists, and practitioners in nursing homes and rural health settings. Medicaid reimburses very little, even for traditional medical management. Thus, while additional third-party reimbursement for some services provided by nurse practitioners in nursing centers would be useful, it will supply only a small percentage of needed revenues.

Capitation has the potential to place nursing centers on a surer financial footing than fee-for-service practice. In the Community Nursing Organizations (CNO) demonstration project, for example, reimbursement is capitated. The level of capitation and who should assume risk are to be established as part of the demonstration. If such centers demonstrate quality and cost-effective care, nursing centers could benefit from this funding well into the 21st century.

Rather than rely totally on government or university funding, nursing centers would benefit by applying standard business practices. Like all business ventures, nursing centers are at risk. Thus, careful and creative business planning is an absolute necessity for survival. To date, such planning has been absent in most nursing centers.

Business planning is essential, creative, and analytical (Johnson, Sparks, & Humphreys, 1988; Manion, 1990; Vestal, 1988). Key components of a business plan include (1) a situational diagnosis of the strengths, weaknesses, opportunities, and threats (SWOT analysis) to the organization; (2) short- and long-term goals; (3) operating plans; and (4) a financial plan. In a thorough business plan, all potential funding sources for start-up and continuation of the project are identified. A business plan which includes a clear purpose and succinct goals is more readily received by investors. This strategy is helpful in keeping control of the business in the hands of the developers rather than the funding source. Moreover, utilization of business plans would assist nursing centers in maintaining their autonomy and control over the scope of practice.

When Fields et al. (1991) examined the success of centers completing their survey, a common theme was the ability of these centers to successfully use consultants, define a market, and to develop a strategic plan. These and other factors are summarized in Table 3. Successful centers, as defined by years of operation and/or client volume, used consultants in the start-up phase for clinical, accounting, and legal advice. In several instances, consultants also conducted a preliminary needs assessment of the potential market area of the center.

The majority of centers developed unique community relationships and found various revenue sources specific to their location and situation. In many cases, a university affiliation shielded the center from financial liability and the discipline of the market. Three centers responding to the survey had a high potential for closing because they lacked a solid revenue base and had no strategic plan for fiscal viability. On the other hand, those centers that recognized the need for and followed through with a business and financial plan were more apt to be successful.

Finally, a dedicated staff, giving hours over and above their salaries to meet the health care needs of the underserved, coupled with a strong rapport built between the center staff and the community, was key to some centers' success. The community provides referrals and offers a wide range of in-kind support. In the survey conducted by Fields et al. (1991), one center was identified as at risk for closing because its goals were not consistent with the needs of the community. For some centers, a strong focus on public relations helped keep them visible and in the public's mind.

TABLE 10.3 Key Success Factors

1. Use consultants during planning/start-up phase; at a minimum, seek accounting and legal advice.
2. Complete a market analysis (or at minimum a needs assessment, and look at your competition).
3. Complete a strategic plan related to long-term fiscal viability. Determine revenue sources and means of reimbursement.
4. Seek a committed core staff.
5. Develop and maintain a strong community relationship.
6. Keep center visible.
7. Be cost competitive.

Additional Success Factors Noted by Interviewees

1. Define your product/service clearly. Identify what nursing has to offer that is unique and worth purchasing.
2. Determine hours of operation based on clients' needs.
3. Determine client satisfaction on an ongoing basis.
4. Nurture relationship with referral sources.

In conclusion, both academic and freestanding nurse-managed centers are widely varied organizations designed to meet the needs of the communities they serve. In some communities, such centers are firmly established and offer a quality, cost-effective alternative to existing health care resources for both underserved and more affluent patients. The success of nursing centers is contingent on their ability to gain a solid revenue source and strong community support. Careful strategic planning can be an important mechanism for assuring the future success of nursing centers.

REFERENCES

Boettcher, J. (1991). Nurse practice centers in academe. *Nursing Management, 22,* 65.

Community Nursing Organization Demonstration Site Development. (1991, August 9). SOL HCFA–92–007/CLK POC. *Commerce Business Daily.*

Culang, T. G., Josephson, S. L., Marcus, M. T., & Vezina, M. (1980). Implementation of a campus nursing and health information center in the baccalaureate curriculum. *Journal of Nursing Education, 19,* 11–14.

Dickerson, P. S., & Nash, B. A. (1985). The business of nursing: Development of a private practice. *Nursing and Health Care, 6,* 327–329.

Ethridge, P. (1991). A nursing HMO: Carondelet St. Mary's experience. *Nursing Management, 22,* 22–27.

Fehring, R., Riesch, S., & Schulte, J. (1986). Toward a definition of nurse managed centers. *Journal of Community Health Nursing, 3*(2), 59–67.

Fields, B., Kelly, J. H., Sullivan, E. M., & Whelan, E. M. (1991). Nursing centers: Strategies for viability. Unpublished.

Harriman, J. (1991, September 26). Patients mourn as nursing program succumbs. *The News Journal* (Wilmington, DE), p. 1.

Henry, O. M. (1978, October 15). Demonstration centers for nursing practice, education, and research. Paper presented at the Annual Meeting of the American Public Health Association, Los Angeles, CA.

Igou, J. F., Hawkins, J. W., Johnson, E. E., & Utley, Q. E. (1989). Nurse-managed approach to care. *Geriatric Nursing, 10*, 32–34.

Johnson, J. J., Sparks, D. G., & Humphreys, C. (1988). Writing a winning business plan. *Journal of Nursing Administration, 18*, 15–19.

Lang, N. M. (1983). Nurse managed centers: Will they survive? *American Journal of Nursing, 83*, 1290–1291.

Legislative Network for Nurses. (1992, May 20). Community nursing centers praised as best kept health reform secret. *Legislative Network for Nurses, 9*(10 73.

Lewis, C. E., & Resnick, B. A. (1962). Nurse clinics and progressive ambulatory patient care. *New England Journal of Medicine, 277*, 1236–1241.

Lundeen, S. (1986). In Nursing Center with M. Mezey & D.O.M. McGivern (Eds.), *Nurses, nurse practitioners: The evolution of primary care.* Boston: Little, Brown.

Manion, J. (1990). *Change from within: Nurse entrepreneurs as health care innovators.* Washington, DC: American Nurses Association.

Mezey, M. (1983). Securing a financial base. *American Journal of Nursing, 83*, 1297–1298.

Mezey, M., & Chiamulera, D. (1980). Implementation of a campus nursing and health information center in a baccalaureate curriculum: Part I: Overview of the center. *Journal of Nursing Education, 19*, 7.

NLN/MET Life Study shows middle-class clients at nursing centers. (1992). *Nursing & Health Care, 13*, 318–319.

National League for Nursing. (1991). *Nursing's agenda for health care reform.* NY: National League for Nursing.

Ossler, C. C., Goodwin, M. E., Mariani, M., & Gilliss, C. I. (1982). Establishment of a nursing clinic for faculty and student clinical practice. *Nursing Outlook, 30*, 402–405.

Parker, M., & Secord, L. J. (1988). Private geriatric case management: Providers, services and fees. *Nursing Economics, 6*, 165–172.

Pearson, L. (1991). 1990–91 Update: How each state stands on legislative issues affecting advanced nursing practice. *Nurse Practitioner, 16*(1), 11–17.

Pulliam, L. (1991). Client satisfaction with a nurse-managed clinic. *Journal of Community Nursing, 8*, 97–112.

Riesch, S. K. (1983, November 9). Exercise of self-care agency: The childbearing family. Paper presented at University of Wisconsin-Milwaukee School of Nursing's 6th Annual Research Day.

Riesch, S. K. (1986). A primary care initiative: Nurse-managed centers. In M. Mezey & D. O. McGivern, (Eds.), *Nurses, nurse practitioners: The evolution of primary care* (pp. 242–248). Boston: Little, Brown.

Riesch, S. K. (1992). Nursing centers: An analysis of the anecdotal literature. *Journal of Professional Nursing, 8*(1), 16–25.

Riesch, S. K. (1992). Nursing centers: An analysis of the empirical literature. In A. Jacox, J. Fitzpatrick, & R. L. Taunton (Eds.), *Annual Review of Nursing Research*. New York: Springer Publishing Co.

Riesch, S. K., Felder, E., & Stauder, C. (1980). Nursing centers can promote health for individuals, families, and communities. *Nursing Administration Quarterly, 4,* 1–8.

Vestal, K. W. (1988). Writing a business plan. *Nursing Economics, 6,* 121–124.

Vezina, M. L. (1986). A college nursing center: Implementation to action. In M. D. Mezey and D. O. McGivern (Eds.), *Nurses, nurse practitioners: The evolution of primary care* (pp. 263–277). Boston: Little, Brown.

PART **III**

LEGISLATION, LAW, REMBURSEMENT, AND POLICY

Chapter 11

STATE NURSE PRACTICE ACTS

Bonnie Bullough

I N the United States, occupational licensure is a responsibility of the states rather than the federal government. This can result in wide variations in the scope of practice of a given occupation from one state to another. Not surprisingly, however, since a statute that seems workable in one state is often copied in other states, there is great similarity among state statutes and regulations. Communications between the state licensing bodies is facilitated by organizations such as the National Council of State Boards of Nursing. In addition, occupations communicate with each other and advise the state governments as to the kind of licensure and regulations to be used to regulate practice.

The legal precedent for occupational licensure was first established by physicians. Lobbying for legislation started in 1847 with the organization of the American Medical Association (AMA). The objectives of the AMA were to raise the level of competence of physicians and to lessen competition from other healers. In 1873 the AMA succeeded in getting a licensure act through the Texas State Legislature (Derbyshire, 1969). In 1881 a similar statue was passed in West Virginia, but was challenged by the courts. The case reached the U.S. Supreme Court in 1888, and the Court ruled that occupational licensure was a valid exercise of the political powers of the states (United States Reports, 1880). As a consequence of this decision, by the end of the nineteenth century, all states had passed medical licensure laws. That medical licensure came first has had important implications for all other health care occupational statutes, in that state acts regulating other professions in effect became amendments to the original medical practice acts (Roemer, 1973; Shryock, 1967).

THE HISTORY OF THE STATE NURSE PRACTICE ACTS

The history of the state nurse practice acts falls into three distinct phases:

1. Passage of the early nurse registration acts: 1903–1939.
2. Definition of the scope of nursing practice: 1938–1971.
3. Development of advanced nursing specialties: 1971–present. (Bullough, 1967, 1980, 1984)

Using the model established by medicine, nurses sought to use state licensure to raise standards, eliminate competition from untrained nurses, and increase the power and prestige of the profession. The desirability of achieving licensure was a catalyst for nurses to organize. The organization which became the National League for Nursing (NLN) was established in 1894; the organization which later was named the American Nurses Association (ANA) was founded in 1896. In turn, both of these nursing organizations were instrumental in lobbying the state legislatures for registration, although, because of its larger membership, most of the day-to-day work was done by the ANA. The task was difficult because women did not yet have the vote, but the membership was persistent. In 1903 North Carolina became the first state to pass a registration act, followed in the same year by New York, New Jersey, and Virginia. One by one other states followed, until by 1923 all of the states then in the union had a nurse registration act (Lesnik & Anderson, 1947). These early laws are properly called registration acts, instead of nurse practice acts, because they did not define a scope of practice. Rather, the term *registered nurse* referred to a person of good character who had completed an acceptable nursing program and passed a state board examination. In some states the individual had additional attributes, such as good health; but none of the statutes spelled out the functions of a registered nurse.

The second phase in the development of nursing licensure started in 1938, when New York State enacted the first mandatory practice act.

The law established two levels of nurses, registered professional and practical, and defined each level. Nursing functions were restricted to members of these two groups (All those who nurse, 1939; Hicks, 1938).

Although mandatory licensure had long been a goal for nursing, New York's mandatory practice act was the vehicle which made it possible to restrict the title "nurse." Key to achieving mandatory licensure was the development of licensed practical nurses. Hospital employers had argued that all nursing functions did not require three years of training. Mandatory licensure of two levels of nursing (with one year and three years of training) seemed a reasonable response to the hospitals' felt need. The New York statute served as a model which was widely copied (Jacobsen, 1940; Lesnik & Anderson, 1947).

Besides being linked with the stratification of nursing, mandatory licensure was important because it established two distinct nursing roles. Older laws had merely made it illegal for an unauthorized person to use the title *registered nurse*. Mandatory practice acts, on the other hand, made it illegal for an unauthorized person to practice nursing. Eventually a scope of function statement came to be thought of as a goal in and of itself (Lesnik and Anderson, 1947).

In order to assist state nursing organizations to establish mandatory practice acts, the ANA adopted a model definition of nursing in 1955. Professional practice was defined as

> the performance, for compensation, of any act in the observation, care and counsel of the ill, injured or infirm, or in the maintenance of health or prevention of illness in others, or in the supervision and teaching of other personnel, or the administration of medications and treatments prescribed by a licensed physician or dentist, requiring substantial specialized judgment and skill and based on knowledge and application of the principles of biological, physical and social science. The foregoing shall not be deemed to include acts of diagnosis or prescription of therapeutic or corrective measures. (ANA Board, 1955, p. 1474)

By 1967, fifteen states had incorporated this model language into their state laws, and another six states had used the model with only slight modification (Fogotson, Roemer, Newman, & Cook, 1967). A regrettable feature of the model act, as well as other similar definitions of nursing practice, was a disclaimer which clearly indicated that nursing did not include any acts of diagnosis, treatment, or prescription of therapeutic measures. At the time the model act was issued by the ANA, nurses were in fact making diagnostic decisions and acting on them in a variety of settings. If the disclaimer was included to make the model practice act more palatable to medicine, there is no historical evidence that this was necessary. Rather, it appears to have been a foolish feminine withdrawal before any challenge was made. A decade later, this disclaimer rendered all of the advanced specialty nursing roles illegal (Bullough, 1980).

THE DEVELOPMENT OF ADVANCED NURSING SPECIALTIES

Postgraduate specialty courses for nurses were popular as early as the first part of the twentieth century. An apprenticeship approach was used by hospitals for these offerings, which usually ran about 8 to 16 weeks (Bullough, 1990). Intensive upgrading of the nursing specialties started in about 1965. Basic nursing education had by that time improved to the point where about 14% of new nurse graduates completed baccalaureate programs (ANA, 1967). These graduates, along with a smaller group who earned baccalaureate degrees after their diploma training, constituted the pool of applicants available for graduate study. Realizing the importance of nursing as a national resource, the federal government in 1965 began to offer financial support for graduate nursing education, and universities responded by expanding or initiating graduate programs for nurses (Kalisch & Kalisch, 1982). Preparation for the major nursing specialties now takes place totally within university settings, where programs are offered at the master's degree level or in short-term certificate programs.

When first initiated, the primary goal of graduate programs was to prepare clinical specialists who could improve the quality of nursing care (Johnson, Wilcox, & Moidel, 1967). Most content focused on social psychological support rather than on treatment, so that the new clinical specialists could supplement the work of, rather than compete with, physicians. The only possible competition to medicine was from the psychiatric clinical specialists, because psychological support was regarded as therapy in psychiatry (Glover, 1967; Rohde, 1968). As a result, clinical specialists other than psychiatric nurses fared poorly in the clinical job market. Their avoidance of physician territory left hospital and clinical employers puzzled as to their functions, and most turned to teaching or administration (Elder & Bullough, 1990).

The first nurse practitioner program, established in 1965 at the University of Colorado, was a short-term certificate rather than a degree program. This program provided an intensive educational experience rather than an apprenticeship, yet it was outside the mainstream of nursing education because of the hostility of traditional nurse educators to nursing roles which overlapped with medicine. Federal funding through the Division of Nursing, however, helped nurse practitioner programs gain a foothold in universities. By 1980 the majority of the nurse practitioner programs were university-sponsored and awarded master's degrees (Sultz et al., 1983).

Nurse practitioners developed primarily in response to a shortage of primary care physicians, a shortage caused by a planned underproduction of physicians during the first part of the twentieth century and an unplanned reallocation of physicians away from general practice and into specialty roles (Fein, 1967). In 1971, physician specialists outnumbered general practitioners three to one (National Center for Health Statistics, 1972–73). In the past five years, although the overall physician shortage has abated, a shortage of primary care providers persists; medical specialists now outnumber generalists five to one.

Improvements in health care technology provided a further impetus for the development of specialties in nursing. Most notable were the specialized coronary and other intensive care units in hospitals (Dracup & Marsden, 1990). The early clinical specialists who staffed these units were prepared in short-term certificate programs supplemented by on-the-job training. Presently, critical care nurses are the largest group of specialty nurses (Hartshorn, 1988; Rehm, 1987). The membership of the American Association of Critical Care Nurses is more than 57,000, with 25,000 being certified as Critical Care Registered Nurses (CCRN). Only a minority of the group is as yet master's prepared, but several graduate programs focusing on critical care have recently opened, so their number is expected to grow.

Midwifery is a time-honored profession. In Europe, when trained nursing developed, most countries established a level of practitioner who was called a nurse-midwife. In the United States, physician competition delayed this process for at least a half century. When the first nurse-midwifery training program was started in 1932, in connection with the Maternity Center in New York City, the scope of this practice was limited, and confined to poor neighborhoods (Litoff, 1978; Tom, 1982). As late as 1965 nurse-midwives were licensed only in New Mexico, the eastern counties of Kentucky, and New York City (Fogotson et al., 1967).

The expansions of nurse-midwifery was greatly enhanced by many of the same factors which facilitated development of nurse practitioners: federal funding and changes in the nurse practice acts. The women's movement was also instrumental in reviving midwifery in that clients demanded the personal care long associated with midwife deliveries. By 1990, more than 3,000 practicing nurse-midwives, prepared both in certificate and increasingly in master's programs, were certified by the American College of Nurse Midwives.

Lastly, nurse anesthetists have emerged as a master's level specialty practice. Nurses started administering anesthesia as early as 1889, particularly in Catholic hospitals (Clapesattle, 1943). Using an apprenticeship format, the first formal course in nurse anesthesia was offered in Portland, Oregon, in 1909. At that time, physician anesthesiologists had no formal training; interns or colleagues were often pressed into service, and nurses were welcomed as assistants (Thatcher, 1953). As the specialty of medical anesthesiology developed, the climate changed, and two landmark law cases were brought by medical societies against nurse anesthetists. In 1917, a Kentucky judge rules in favor of a physician employer of a nurse anesthetist. The ruling indicated that licensure laws are written to benefit people rather than professions, and that people should not be deprived of the services of nurse anesthetists (*Frank v. South*, 1917). In 1937, a California nurse anesthetist was sued by the medical society, which argued she was practicing medicine. The nurse won her case with a ruling that she was not practicing medicine because she was supervised by the operating surgeon (Thatcher, 1953).

The American Association of Nurse Anesthetists established a certification program in 1945 and an accreditation program in 1952. A baccalaureate degree was mandated for certification in 1987; a master's degree will be required in 1998 (Gunn, 1984). Today there are 22,000 Certified Registered Nurse Anesthetists (CRNAs) in the United States. Approximately half of the anesthesia in the United States is administered by CRNAs working with anesthesiologists; CRNAs working alone administer 20%, and the other 30% of anesthesia is administered by physician anesthesiologists (American Association of Nurse Anesthetists, 1990).

EXPANDING STATE LAWS TO COVER NURSE PRACTITIONERS

Although professional certification is well established, more recently a movement has developed to obtain a separate level of licensure for nurse specialties. This movement developed out of a need to accommodate nurse practitioners, who were clearly diagnosing and treating patients in violation of disclaimers written into most nurse practice acts after 1955. The first nurse practitioner legislation was passed in 1971 in Idaho, instructing boards of medicine and nursing to draw up rules that would allow nurse practitioner practice. The joint boards ruled that nurse practitioner practice should be regulated by policies and procedures (protocols) written at the local level (Idaho, 1971). The board rules did not, however, give separate licensure to nurse practitioners. This precedent-setting approach was widely copied by other states.

A second approach to accommodate nurse practitioner practice was to expand a state's basic definition of all registered professional nurse practice. This is accomplished by either omitting or limiting the disclaimer in state practice acts against diagnosis and treatment by registered nurses, or by rewriting the definition of registered nursing using broader language. New York was the first state to use this approach, in 1972. Amendment of a state practice act constitutes an important legislative step, because it removes unnecessary barriers to the full use of registered nurses. Whether or not a nurse actually functions as a nurse practitioner under these amended statutes, even with the use of a protocol, depends on other state statutes and regulations.

There has been at least one favorable court ruling in relationship to amended state practice acts. A 1975 Missouri revision of the Nurse Practice Act removed the blanket prohibition to diagnosis and treatment by nurses but made no mention of nurse practitioners or other advanced specialists (Missouri, 1975). In spite of this, some nurse practitioners in the state used written protocols to guide their practice. Physicians working with nurse practitioners in a rural family planning clinic were charged by the Board of Medicine with aiding and abetting the illegal practice of medicine. The Medical Board won its case at the local level, but the State Supreme Court overturned the ruling (Greenlaw, 1984; Wolff, 1984). With impetus from the Missouri decision, a broad definition of nursing practice plus the use of protocols has been adopted by other states as the mechanism for legal coverage of advanced nursing practice.

In a third approach to facilitating nursing practitioner practice, some states have opted to give physicians more delegative powers. Even before the current phase in nursing licensure, some state medical practice acts, including those of Arizona, Colorado, Florida, Kansas, and Oklahoma, gave physicians broad power to delegate medical acts to other workers. South Dakota (1972), North Carolina (1973), and Maine (1974) added delegatory language to their practice acts to facilitate nurse practitioner practice. The Maine act permits professional nurses with additional educational preparation to diagnose, prescribe, and treat when these responsibilities are delegated to them by physicians (Maine, 1974). More recently, states have afforded physicians broader power to delegate their responsibilities to other workers in order to facilitate the work of physicians' assistants.

LICENSURE FOR THE ADVANCED NURSING SPECIALTIES

A fourth approach to accommodate advanced nursing functions is to use the statutory or regulatory power of the state to separately certify or license independent nurse specialists. Called a state certificate, this approach is actually a separate level of licensure for advanced practitioners. It provides the advanced practitioners with a separate title, a defined scope of function, and responsibility for their own actions. Since 1973, nurse practitioners in Washington, Oregon, Arizona, and Nevada have functioned under their own licenses (Washington, 1973; Oregon, 1973; Arizona, 1973; Nevada, 1973). The current pattern of certification for nurse specialties in each state is shown in Table 11-1.

Individual certification of nurse specialists is the best approach to legal coverage because it makes practitioners accountable for their own practice. Passage of laws to permit individual certification is, however, difficult to achieve, especially in the face of a physician surplus. New York State nurse practitioners struggled for eight years before they succeeded in passing such a law, in 1988. Passage of this law was impeded both by physicians and by the New York State Nurses Association. The state association lobbied against passage in support of the position of the American Nurses Association enunciated in the publication *Nursing: A Social Policy Statement* (1980) and in the 1981 model practice act (ANA, 1981). The ANA does not object to nurses with advanced preparation having an expanded scope of function which differs from that of the basic registered nurse; it simply argues that professional associations, rather than the state, should grant authorization for advanced scope of function.

The ANA model is similar to that used by medicine. State practice acts have traditionally afforded medicine very expansive practice privileges. Physician licensing is all-encompassing; controls on scope of function come from certifying boards and the fear of malpractice litigation. Consumers would probably not support such an approach if medical practice acts were being written now.

While the emergence of nurse practitioners was the impetus for nurse practice act revisions, state boards and state legislatures quickly realized that amendments should cover all advanced nursing specialties together, instead of dealing with each separately. Consequently, many states legislated umbrella advanced specialty acts, while others amended nurse practitioner statutes to include nurse-midwives, nurse anesthetists, and in some cases, clinical nurse specialists. Nurse practitioners, nurse midwives, and nurse anesthetists came under the spe-

TABLE 11.1 Authorization of Advanced Practice in the Practice Acts

States	Certification				Comments
	NP	NM	NA	CNS	
Alabama	x	x	x		
Alaska	x	x	x		
Arizona	x	x	x		
Arkansas	x	x	x		
California	x	x	x		
Colorado*		x			Broad RN definition
Connecticut	x		x	x	
Delaware	x	x	x	x	
Florida	x	x	x	x	
Georgia	x	x	x		
Hawaii					
Idaho	x	x	x		
Illinois					
Indiana					
Iowa	x	x	x		
Kansas	x	x	x		
Kentucky	x	x	x		
Louisiana	x	x	x	x	
Maine	x	x	x		
Maryland	x	x	x		
Massachusetts	x	x	x	x	
Michigan	x	x	x		
Minnesota		x	x		
Mississippi	x	x	x		
Missouri					Court decision
Montana	x	x	x		
Nebraska	x	x	x		
Nevada	x	x	x	x	
New Hampshire	x	x	x		
New Jersey			x		Board guidelines
New Mexico	x	x	x		
New York	x				
No. Carolina	x	x			Med. Practice Act
No. Dakota	x			x	
Ohio		x			
Oklahoma	x	x	x		
Oregon	x	x			
Penn	x	x	x		
Rhode Is.		x			
So. Carolina	x	x	x		

(continued)

TABLE 11.1 (*continued*)

States	Certification				Comments
	NP	NM	NA	CNS	
So. Dakota	x	x	x		
Tennessee	x	x			
Texas	x	x	x	x	
Utah	ʌ	ʌ	x	x	
Vermont	x	x	x	x	
Virginia	x	x	x		
Washington	x	x	x	x	
West Virginia		x	x		
Wisconsin		x			
Wyoming	x	x	x		
Washington, D.C.	x	x	x		Hospital licensing act

*Colorado's 1980 statute certifying NPs was repealed in 1985.

cialty umbrella of state practice acts first because their certifying bodies were outside of the American Nurses Association and supported state licensure as a way to legitimate specialist practice and protect consumers from untrained practitioners. Certification of specialties certified and represented by the ANA, including some nurse practitioners and clinical specialists, has proven more difficult because of the ideological stance of the ANA. Not only has the ANA opposed advanced licensure for nurse specialists, it has also opposed nurses' treating patients and prescribing drugs. The dominant belief system within the ANA is that the ideal role of the nurse is to "care for" rather than cure patients (Stevenson & Tripp-Reimer, 1990). Motivated by competition from already licensed specialists, such as social workers and clinical psychologists, some ANA-certified clinical specialists, especially psychiatric or mental health nurses, have sought to be included in a state's advanced practice legislation. As shown in Table 11-1, 11 states now certify clinical specialists.

The American Association of Critical Care Nurses (AACCN), with its huge work force of Certified Critical Care Registered Nurses, has behaved like a sleeping giant in relation to state certification and licensure. The AACCN has taken no ideological stance either for or against licensure and has not sought coverage for its members under advanced practice statutes. Rather, the AACCN has relied on the use of protocols and standing orders. When their practice extends beyond such safeguards, which is not rare, critical care nurses assume that physicians will "cover" for them. There is evidence that physicians in fact are willing to back up (and take credit for) nurses' actions which save patients' lives. It is unclear whether physicians are similarly inclined to cover nurses' actions which result in negative outcomes. As more master's level recruits enter the field, critical care nurses as a group in all likelihood will become more politically active and vocal regarding licensure.

SUMMARY AND CONCLUSIONS

Recent activities in the development of nursing licensure has been characterized by efforts to legitimate specialty nursing practice. In some states the existing registered nurse statutes have been stretched to cover the advanced specialists by allowing or mandating protocols or by augmenting physicians' rights to delegate their responsibilities. In other states, nurse specialists carry their own license; their titles are protected, and they are responsible for their own actions.

State statutes ordinarily recognize the certification of "specialist" granted by the national certifying organizations. All specialists are registered nurses with additional education. While the amount of additional education varies from short certificate courses to master's preparation, the trend is in the latter direction. Only women's health care nurse practitioners and certified critical care nurses are still prepared primarily in certificate programs. As educational requirements become longer, more intensive, and more expensive, these specialists will increasingly fall within the collegiate system.

The development of educational programs and state licensure of advanced specialty nursing practice has substantively changed the stratification pattern of nursing. The law now recognizes three levels of nursing:

1. Licensed Practical Nursing
2. Registered Nursing
3. Advanced Registered Nursing Practice: nurse practitioners, nurse-midwives, nurse anesthetists, and clinical nurse specialists.

Although the titles for advanced practitioners vary from state to state, the three-level pattern becomes more clearly defined each year. The efforts begun five years ago to change credentialing for baccalaureate nursing have resulted in some changes. Within the next two years, two states, Maine and North Dakota, will accept only baccalaureate prepared practitioners as Registered Nurses. Perhaps surprisingly, the nursing credential which has changed most rapidly is master's degree preparation and legal recognition of advanced specialty practice.

REFERENCES

All Those Who Nurse for Hire! (1939). *American Journal of Nursing, 39,* 275–277.

ANA Board Approves A Definition of Nursing Practice. (1955). *American Journal of Nursing, 55,* 1474.

American Association of Nurse Anesthetists. (1990). *The report of the National Commission on Nurse Anesthesia Education.* Park Ridge, IL: American Association of Nurse Anesthetists.

American Nurses Association. (1967). *Facts about nursing: A statistical summary.* New York: American Nurses Association.

American Nurses Association. (1980). *Nursing: A social policy statement.* Kansas City, MO: American Nurses Association.

American Nurses Association. (1981). *The Nursing Practice Act: Suggested state legislation.* Kansas City, MO. American Nurses Association.

Arizona Revised Statutes. (1973). Section 32-1601.

Bullough, B. (1967). Alienation in the ghetto. *American Journal of Sociology, 72*(5), 469–478.

Bullough, B. (1980). *The law and the expanding nursing role* (2d Ed.). New York: Appleton-Century-Crofts.

Bullough, B. (1984). The current phase in the development of nurse practice acts. *The St. Louis University Law Journal, 28,* 365–395.

Bullough, B. (1990). Advanced specialty practice: Its development and legal authorization. *The nursing profession: Turning points* (pp. 375–386). St. Louis: C. V. Mosby.

Clapesattle, H. (1941). *The Doctors Mayo.* Minneapolis: University of Minnesota Press.

Derbyshire, R. C. (1969). *Medical licensure and discipline in the United States.* Baltimore: Johns Hopkins Press.

Dracup, K., & Marsden, C. (1990). Critical care nursing: Perspectives and challenges. In N. Chaska (Ed.), *The nursing profession: Turning points* (pp. 304–311). St. Louis, MO: C. V. Mosby.

Elder, R. G., & Bullough, B. (1990). Nurse practitioners and clinical specialists: Are the roles merging? *Clinical Nurse Specialist, 4,* 78–84.

Fein, R. (1967). *The doctor shortage: An economic analysis.* Washington, DC: The Brookings Institution.

Fogotson, E. H., Roemer, R., Newman, R. W., & Cook, J. L. (1967). Licensure of other medical personnel. *Report of the National Advisory Commission on Health Manpower, Vol. 2* (pp. 407–492). Washington, DC: U.S. Government Printing Office.

Frank v. South. (1917), Kentucky Rep. 175:416–428.

Glover, B. H. (1967). A new nurse therapist. *The American Journal of Nursing, 67*, 1003–1005.

Greenlaw, J. (1984). Commentary: Sermchief v. Gonzales and the debate over advanced nursing practice legislation. *Law, Medicine, and Health Care, 12*, 930–931.

Gunn, I. (1984). Professional territoriality and the anesthesia experience. In B. Bullough, V. Bullough, & M. C. Soucup (Eds.), *Nursing issues and nursing strategies for the eighties* (pp. 155–168). New York: Springer Publishing Co.

Hartshorn, J. (1988). The President's message: It's up to you. *Focus on Critical Care, 15*, 67–69.

Hicks, A. (1938). Crusade for safer nursing: How New York's new nurse practice law was won. *American Journal of Nursing, 38*, 563–566.

Idaho Code. (1971). Section 54–1413.

Jacobsen, M. (1940). Nursing laws and what every nurse should know about them. *American Journal of Nursing, 40*, 1221–1226.

Johnson, D. E., Wilcox, J. A,. & Moidel, H. A. (1967). The clinical specialist as a practitioner. *American Journal of Nursing, 67*, 2298–2303.

Kalisch, B. J., & Kalisch, P. A. (1982). *Politics of Nursing*. Philadelphia: Lippincott.

Lesnik, M. J., & Anderson, B. E. (1947). *Legal aspects of nursing*. Philadelphia: Lippincott.

Litoff, B.(1978). *American Midwives: 1860 to the present*. Westport, CT: Greenwood Press.

Maine Revised Statutes. (1974). Section 31–2102.

Missouri Statutes. (1975). Section 335–016.

National Center for Health Statistics. (1972–1973). *Health Resources Statistics: Health Manpower and Health Statistics*, U.S. Public Health Services Publication, No. 1509.

Nevada Revised Statutes. (1973). Section 632–020.

Oregon Revised Statutes. (1973). Section 678–410.

Rehm, A. A., (1987). Personal letter to Y. Scherer.

Roemer, R. (1973). Legal systems regulation health personnel: A comparative analysis. *Milbank Memorial Fund Quarterly, 46* (1968). Reprinted in *Politics and law in health care policy*, J. McKinley (Ed.).

Rohde, I. M. (1968). The nurse as a family therapist. *The American Journal of Nursing, 67*, 1003–1005.

Shryock, R. H. (1967). *Medical licensing in America, 1650–1965*. Baltimore: Johns Hopkins University Press.

Stevenson, J. S., & Tripp-Reimer, T. (Eds.). (1990). *Knowledge about care and caring: State of the art and future developments*. Kansas City, MO: American Academy of Nursing.

Sultz, H. A., Henry, O. M., Kinyon, J., Buck, G. M., & Bullough, B. (1983). Nurse practitioners—A decade of change, program highlights, I. *Nursing Outlook, 31*, 138–141.

Thatcher, V. S. (1953). *A history of anesthesia: With emphasis on the nurse specialist*. Philadelphia: J. B. Lippincott.

Tom, S. (1982). Nurse midwifery: A developing profession. *Law, Medicine and Health Care, 10,* 262–266.

United States Reports. (1888). *Cases adjudged in the Supreme courts.* 129 Dent v. West Virginia. *United States Reports,* 114–128.

Chapter 12

LEGAL RAMIFICATIONS FOR EXPANDED PRACTICE*

Walter T. Eccard and Edward E. Gainor

NURSES AS PROFESSIONALS

P HYSICIANS, consumers, and attorneys have become increasingly aware of the use of malpractice claims as a mechanism for regulating the quality of health care.[1] Concurrently, the escalating costs of providing medical care, the maldistribution of primary care physicians, and the growing consumer demand for affordable, quality care have brought pressure on the health care system to find and provide low-cost alternatives for the delivery of health care services. These two trends are related and have led to increased use of nonphysician providers of health care and to new statutory recognition of these health care providers. Indeed, in the past decade, two states, California and Utah,[2] adopted, for a short period, trial programs using nurses as primary health care providers in areas of physician shortage. In the face of these and future changes, courts will be required to consider the appropriate standard of

---

*"A Revolution in White: New Approaches in Treating Nurses as Professionals" by Walter Eccard from *Vanderbilt Law Review*, Vol. 30, 1977. Reprinted and adapted by permission of *Vanderbilt Law Review*.

care that nonphysicians must meet. For a surprisingly long period of time, the legal literature was almost devoid of any consideration of the nonphysician health care provider.[3] Legal commentators have now begun to fill this knowledge void.[4] As discussed in this chapter, however, many courts and most lawyers do not understand either the current state of nursing practice or its legal implications. As a result of the historical failure of the legal profession to study nonphysician health care providers, courts, not surprisingly, have adopted a variety of contradictory and often confusing approaches to questions involving the adequacy of care provided by these persons. This chapter deals with nurses and does not consider such health care providers as physician's assistants. This focus is proper and analytically sound. Nurses are health care professionals in their own right. They are separately licensed and have a professional orientation independent of medicine that is based on nursing's status as a profession. Indeed, a decision of the Washington Supreme Court is based on this distinction.[5] To lump all nonphysician health care providers together is fundamentally flawed and dilutes the status of nursing as a profession.

This chapter will review the development of nursing as a profession, discuss trends in nursing, review the current case law in light of these developments, and, finally, propose alternative approaches to the questions relating to nursing malpractice. Specifically, this chapter will examine the questions of the appropriate statute of limitations for nursing malpractice cases, the need for nurses as expert witnesses in malpractice actions, and the proper standard of care for a registered nurse. These questions will be considered in the context of the various state licensure laws, nurse certification programs, and the formal education training of nurses.

EARLY HISTORY OF NURSING

An awareness of the origin and development of nursing in this country aids in understanding why courts have failed to treat nursing as a profession. Tentative steps toward the recognition of nursing as a separate discipline were taken in the first half of the nineteenth century. In 1809, Elizabeth Seton founded the Sisters of Charity to give medical care to the poor, and in 1839, Dr. Joseph Warrington founded the first sectarian group to care for the ill.[6] He also instituted a short course to train future nurses in maternity care.[7] During the Civil War Dorothea Dix supervised a corps of army nurses.[8] Her statement of the qualifications necessary to become an army nurse indicates that nursing was still in its formative stages. To qualify as an army nurse, applicants had "to be 30 to 50 years of age; they [applicants] had to have good health and endurance; they had to have a matronly demeanor and good character; and they had to be plainly dressed."[9]

In the quarter century after the Civil War, nursing training became more formalized. This era was characterized by the development of schools of nursing and the initial effort to organize nurses in common organizations. In 1872 the Women's Hospital of Philadelphia became the first endowed school of nursing in the United States.[10] The first nursing textbook was published in 1879, and by 1885 nursing textbooks were beginning to recognize that nursing care included more than simple obedience to a physician's orders.[11] Hospitals were the major training ground for nurses, making standardization of nursing care difficult to achieve. Nurses tended to identify with the institution that trained them, rather than with the concept of belonging to an organized profession. Steps to remedy this lack of professional identification began in 1893, with the first national meeting of nurses,[12] and the formation, in 1896, of the first national organization of nurses.[13]

THE LICENSURE MOVEMENT

Nursing, along with other groups aspiring to professional status at the end of the nineteenth century, viewed licensure as a means of acquiring control over membership in the emerging profession.[14] This history and current status of nursing licensure has been thoroughly presented by Bullough (Chap. 11). Suffice it to say that almost all states now recognize by statute that the profession of nursing requires "substantial nursing skills, knowledge and training," and the application of "nursing principles based on biological, physical and social sciences."[15] In addition, many states go further and by statute recognize and authorize "diagnosis" by nurses.[16] This right to diagnose is often put in the context of nursing diagnosis and, in many instances, statutes traditionally continue to provide that nurses are not to act as doctors.[17] These revisions to the definition of the practice of nursing take various forms, and minor changes in working from one state statute to another can alter significantly a nurse's scope of permissible action. Nonetheless, these statutes have several important similarities. First, they all recognize that to be licensed as a nurse means that a person has obtained a minimum level of competence in a profession requiring specialized knowledge. Second, they recognize that this specialized knowledge is based on academic disciplines. Third, to varying extents, they recognize that nurses act, at least at times, independently.[18] Finally, and most critically, they recognize that nursing is a profession separate from medicine. While the two professions obviously overlap in many ways, they also are separate. The distinction between medical and nursing diagnosis, for instance, only makes sense if there is first a recognition that nursing is a profession separate from medicine. Also, as noted below, a majority of jurisdictions now provide formal recognition for nurses with advanced training.

Much remains to be accomplished, however. Three states[19] still have physicians serving on their boards of nursing. Such outdated relics of a time long past[20] cannot be justified and perhaps can only be explained by reference to the power of the state medical profession. Further changes should be expected.

THE DEVELOPMENT OF NURSING STANDARDS OF PRACTICE

The relationship of the various nursing organizations to each other and to nursing generally has had an important effect on the movements to define standards of practice and to develop a certification program.[21] There are two major national nursing organizations. The American Nurses Association (ANA), the professional organization of registered nurses, sets standards for nursing education and practice and represents nurses on legislative matters concerning health, education, and general welfare. The National League for Nurses (NLN), on the other hand, stresses improvement of nursing services and educational programs through accreditation, consultation, testing, research, and publication.[22] Besides these two major groups, there are a number of specialty organizations for individuals with special interest in a particular area of practice.[23] Although the ANA is the only national organization with the capability to institute and develop programs that are applicable to nurses generally, other organizations facilitate acceptance of these programs by all nurses.

The development of standards has been directed at setting minimum levels of acceptable performance and has attempted to provide the consumer[24] with a means of measuring the quality of nursing care they receive.[25] The certification movement, on the other hand, has had as its goal the recognition of excellence of performance.[26]

Turning first to the movement for the development and implementation of standards, the ANA defines a standard as an "authoritative statement by which the quality of practice, service, or education can be judged."[27] The ANA made rapid progress in implementing its standards following an organizational revision of the ANA in 1966 that created five divisions of practice that corresponded to distinct specialty areas.[28] Each new ANA division was charged with the development of standards in its own specialty area, following a general format developed by the joint effort of the chairpersons of each division. The development of standards came to a halt in 1970 due to the ANA's financial problems and disagreement as to the form the standards should take.[29] Once the temporary financial problems were resolved, however, work began anew on the standards. Generic standards applicable to all nurses in all areas of practice were completed by the end of 1971, and by the end of 1975 standards in the various specialty areas also had been published.[30]

At the same time that the ANA was developing standards, various specialty groups outside ANA also were involved in the process of standard making. This involvement took two basic forms. While some specialty groups worked with the ANA in the joint formulation of standards,[31] other groups developed and published their own standards.[32] These separate standards can, however, be viewed as complementary to the parallel ANA standards.[33]

The ANA standards include general standards and assessment factors that can be used to determine whether the standard has been met.[34] For instance, one standard for medical-surgical nursing is:

> The collection of data about the health status of the patient is systematic and continuous. These data are communicated to appropriate persons, recorded and stored in a retrievable and accessible system.[35]

The assessment factors used in measuring compliance with this standard include the evaluation of fluid and electrolyte balance, metabolic regulation, cardiovascular and respiratory output, and the complete collection of relevant data.[36] The standards for each specialty group developed by the ANA follow the same pattern. While the standards are similar to the one described above, and are thus general, when combined with the assessment factors that follow each standard they provide a useful framework for analyzing whether the nursing action in question complied with what the profession believes to be the appropriate standard of care.[37]

The most complete standards developed by an organization outside the ANA are those published by the Nurses Association of the American College of Obstetricians and Gynecologists (NAACOG).[38] These standards detail nursing functions during labor and delivery, and after childbirth. In addition, they specify behaviors inappropriate for nurses. For instance, standards adopted in 1974 allowed a nurse, during post-partum, to administer oral, intramuscular, or intravenous medication and to initiate blood transfusion and intravenous solutions that have been ordered by the physician. In addition, the specially trained nurse could remove sutures and remove vaginal packing. According to these standards it was inappropriate, however, for any nurse to remove uter-ine packing and suprapubic catheters.[39] Revised standards adopted in 1986 include a much longer list of more than two dozen specific func-tions that a qualified nurse may perform during postpartum.[40] The same framework is followed in describing nursing functions in antepartum, labor and delivery, and neonatal care. Standards that are this specific make it relatively easy to determine if the nurse acted within the scope of permissible activity.

ADVANCED CERTIFICATION PROGRAMS

Coinciding with the development of standards to measure nursing care, a program to define, establish, and implement a program of certification for nurses also developed. Certification recognizes the attainment of specialized knowledge and skills beyond those required for safe prac-tice. The ANA has designed its certification program to recognize excel-lence in each area of the clinical practice of nursing.[41] To qualify for certi-fication, an applicant may be a graduate from any basic nursing program,[42] must practice for a set period of time in the clinical area in which certification is sought, and must demonstrate excellence of knowledge and performance through written examinations and written documentation of nursing practice.[43] The first certification examinations were held in 1975, and by the end of that year 304 nurses had been awarded certification.[44] Controversy has surrounded the certification program. Although some specialty groups outside the ANA have worked with and assisted in the initiation of the certification program,[45] others, including the American Academy of Pediatrics,[46] have not.[47]

But while medical and nursing professionals have been unable to de-velop a uniform program of nationwide certification, the concept of sep-arate certification for nurses with advanced training has rapidly taken hold on the state level. In 1981, at least seven states, California,[48] Flor-ida,[49] New Hampshire,[50] Michigan,[51] New Mexico,[52] Oklahoma,[53] and Utah[54] provided for certification or official statutory recognition of ad-vanced practice beyond basic licenses. Since 1981, at least 19 additional states and the District of Columbia have adopted statutes that recognize the advance practice of nursing.[55] As will be discussed below, this official recognition by a majority of jurisdictions of advanced levels of competence and scope of practice is analogous to specialization in medicine, and persons obtaining this advanced level of certification should and will be held to standards of care above those of nurses who have not attained this advanced level of skill.

DIFFERENTIATION OF NURSES BY BASIC ACADEMIC PROGRAM

Without presenting an in-depth discussion of educational preparation of nurses in general, within the context of this chapter it is important to note that while traditionally hospital diploma programs have been the major source of new nurses, associate-degree and baccalaureate programs have supplanted the hospital diploma programs as the primary means of entry into the profession. Although this trend is not without controversy, there is support for the differentiation of education and levels of practice.

The ANA's Standards for Nursing Education support the dichotomy in expected levels of performance, stating that baccalaureate programs are designed to prepare nurses who can use the scientific method and apply it to nursing care problems and who can collaborate with other health care professionals.[56] ANA standards state that associate degree programs, on the other hand, are designed to train nurses to enter practice in positions focusing on direct patient care—nurses who know the limits of their knowledge base and know when to seek assistance.[57]

In summary, the different ways to becoming a nurse do not produce, and are not intended to produce, nurses with identical skills. All nurses have a basic level of proficiency to perform certain required nursing treatments, but nurses with baccalaureate and higher degrees[58] have the added ability to function at an independent level that includes selecting appropriate nursing actions based on analysis of relevant data on the patient. Perhaps of greater practical significance is the fact that, as discussed below, states have provided official recognition for nurses with advanced training. While the authors believe it is appropriate to differentiate between nurses on the basis of the nature of their initial training, the more significant differentiation has occurred with respect to certification at levels above the entry level.

Professional Discipline and Continuing Education

One measure of the professionalization of an occupation is the extent to which the occupational group enforces expected norms of behavior. In the area of professional discipline, to enforce standards, and in the area of continuing education, to maintain and increase competence, nursing is reflecting a growing sense of professionalism.

Scott v. State ex rel. Board of Nursing[59] reflects that in recent years the nursing profession, through its state boards of nursing, has begun to examine the conduct of its members and to measure the conduct against certain norms. In *Scott* a nurse was licensed in another state and applied for licensure in Nebraska. The applicant met the objective statutory standards for licensure.[60] The state board of nursing, nevertheless, refused to grant the license because it found that the applicant was guilty of unprofessional conduct.[61] In reaching this conclusion the board received evidence that the nurse-applicant had provided inadequate care to a patient,[62] had left her patients unattended, did not follow procedures for admitting patients, and failed to cooperate with patients or fellow nurses. The board also heard testimony from several nurses that this kind of behavior constituted unprofessional conduct. The board refused to issue the license[63] and the disappointed applicant sought judicial redress. The Supreme Court of Nebraska, rejecting the contention that the board's finding was subject to de novo review by the courts, affirmed the board's decision. The court noted that the board of nursing was composed of professional nurses and concluded that the legislature, in granting licensure authority to the board of nursing, intended the board to use this expertise in making licensure decisions.

Scott is significant for two reasons. First it demonstrates that state boards of nursing, through their licensure power, have the authority to enforce professional norms.[64] While it is impossible to generalize on the basis of one case, *Scott* at least reflects the kinds of behavior that can be examined in determining whether an individual is guilty of unprofessional conduct. In this case the behavior questioned involved patient care and thus was an evaluation of the nurse's professional behavior. Although *Scott* was set in the context of an application for licensure by a nurse licensed in another state, most boards have been given authority not only to deny such license requests but also revoke or suspend currently issued licenses.[65] The second significant aspect of *Scott* is the response of the court. By refusing to allow de novo review by the trial court, the Nebraska Supreme Court has granted a great deal of power to the state board of nursing. This deferral by the courts is appropriate, especially when state boards of nursing are composed of nurses who bring their own expertise to bear in determining questions of professional performance.

In the last several years, continuing education has become an important force in the practice of nursing. At the present time continuing education in nursing exists as a voluntary program in the majority of states.[66] Continuing education is, however, increasingly being used as a mandatory requirement for relicensure, with fifteen states already adopting the mandatory system.[67] Continuing education for nursing is viewed as a means of ensuring that all nurses are exposed to new developments in the field. In addition, the technological nature of health care and the critical importance of understanding new discoveries in providing safe and effective health care argue in favor of a continuing education program.[68]

THE COURTS AND THE NURSE

The Appropriate Statute of Limitations

In determining the appropriate statute of limitations in claims against nurses, courts necessarily must confront the question of whether nurses should be treated as professionals. If nurses are professionals, actions against them should be based on malpractice theory, rather than on usual negligence standards. The standards to be used, in turn, will affect the selection of an appropriate statute of limitations; the need for, and quality of, expert testimony required to establish culpability; and the selection of a proper standard of care.

The continuing spate of malpractice litigation has led to statutory change in many states to provide greater protection against malpractice claims. Many states, in adopting these changes, have established a much broader definition of potential defendants protected by the malpractice statute.[69] Other states specifically have limited their statutes to professional groups that do not include nurses.[70] A third category of states does not define the group of individuals subject to the malpractice statutes.[71] Many of these statutes have been challenged and some have not withstood constitutional scrutiny.[72] Thus, in those states whose new malpractice statutes have been rejected by the courts and in those states that have not defined the group subject to the malpractice statute, the courts will have to determine whether nurses are subject to the malpractice statute of limitations,[73] which is shorter than the negligence statute of limitations. Further, the discussion below indicates that those state legislatures that have failed to make their malpractice statutes applicable to nurses should reconsider that exclusion.

In *Richardson v. Doe*,[74] the leading Ohio case dealing with statutes of limitation,[75] the court determined that a nurse was not subject to the shorter malpractice statute of limitations. The decision rested on two lines of analysis. The court based the first line of analysis on its view of nursing practice and its second on two earlier New York cases. Neither line of analysis supports the conclusion reached by the *Richardson* court, and the result is clearly wrong and should not be followed today.

The court first determined that nurses did not need the protection of the malpractice statute of limitations because a nurse:

> is to observe and record the symptoms and reactions of patients. A nurse is not permitted to exercise judgment in diagnosing or treating any symptoms which the patient develops. . . . A nurse by the very nature of her occupation is prohibited from exercising an independent judgment in these areas.[76]

These conclusions, although based on a limited and incorrect view of nursing practice, were perhaps understandable in 1965. The nursing profession itself, in its first definition of nursing practice, claimed that nurses did not perform acts of diagnosis.[77] While that definition was, in the view of current commentators, unnecessarily restrictive and inaccurate,[78] it does give historical basis for the Ohio court's conclusions. Whatever historical validity the decision might have had, however, has been eroded by the licensure and certification movements, which specifically recognize that nurses function independently and indeed perform acts of diagnosis.[79] Thus conclusions based on historical ideas of nursing practice should be modified to reflect current reality.

The second basis of the *Richardson* decision, New York precedent, is also suspect. In *Isenstein v. Malcomson*[80] the court refused to apply the malpractice statute of limitations to a nurse who left a hot water bottle on the exposed flesh of an unconscious patient. The *Isenstein* court implied that malpractice actions were limited to physicians and attorneys. Although the rationale of the court in *Isenstein* also is understandable and the result appears correct based on the facts of the case, the case was decided prior to the second phase of nursing licensure laws[81] at a time when many nurses did not have even a high school education.[82] Again, results that are correct in a given historical period should be studied in context before being applied to a different context. The second New York opinion, *Wolff v. Jamaica Hospital*,[83] is not helpful. It is a one-page opinion that concludes, without analysis, that malpractice actions are limited to physicians and surgeons.

The *Richardson* court failed to mention *Davis v. Eubanks*,[84] a decision four years earlier by a lower level Ohio court that concluded that nurses were subject to the malpractice statute of limitations. In *Davis* the court found that since the legislature defined nurses as professionals, the courts should accept this legislative determination.[85] This approach, focusing on the current level of nursing practice and the legislative recognition of that practice, appears sound. Once it is recognized that nursing is founded on an independent, specialized core of knowledge and theory and that nurses use this body of knowledge to prescribe and to diagnose, it is only logical to treat them as professionals and apply a malpractice statute of limitations to nurses.

Unfortunately, *Richardson* remains good law in Ohio. In 1982, a majority of the Ohio Supreme Court in *Lombard v. Good Samaritan Med Center*[86] retained the restrictive reach of Ohio's malpractice statute of limitations. However, the rationale supporting the position of the Ohio courts has been undercut, not only by the evolution of the nursing profession, but also by a New York Court of Appeals decision overruling the cases on which *Richardson* depended for support.

In *Bleiler v. Bodnar*,[87] New York's highest court was called upon to consider the scope of a recently enacted state statute establishing a two-and-a-half year statute of limitations for medical malpractice actions. The statute did not define "medical malpractice," and did not specify to what groups of medical professionals the statute applied. Plaintiff in *Bleiler* alleged negligence on the part of a hospital, a physician, and an emergency room nurse; the court held that all three defendants were protected by the medical malpractice statute of limitations.

The court said the role of the nurse has changed since *Isenstein* and other cases, which held that a nurse may be liable for negligence, but not for malpractice. A registered nurse is no longer merely a "passive, servile employee," said the *Bleiler* court, but has become "an assertive, decisive health care provider."[88] The court said:

> Today, the professional nurse monitors complex physiological data, operates sophisticated lifesaving equipment, and coordinates the delivery of a myriad of patient services. As a result, the reasonably prudent nurse no longer waits for and blindly follows physicians' orders.[89]

Still, not every negligent act committed by a nurse in the care of a patient should constitute medical malpractice. The court established this test: "[A] negligent act or omission by a nurse that constitutes medical treatment or bears a substantial relationship to the rendition of medical treatment by a licensed physician constitutes medical malpractice."[90] The defendant nurse in *Bleiler* had allegedly failed to take a proper medical history—a failure that would "unquestionably" constitute medical malpractice by a physician, said the court, and so should be classified in the same manner when the alleged offender was an emergency room nurse, "functioning in that role as an integral part of the process of rendering medical treatment to a patient."[91]

Bleiler is indicative of modern courts' approach to nursing. The *Bleiler* court appropriately recognized the changes that have taken place in nursing in reaching its determination that nurses are medical professionals. Nevertheless, it is unfortunate that the test adopted by the court, in relying on an analogy to acts of physicians, fails to explicitly recognize the independent nature of nursing practice.

Another state whose medical malpractice statute is vague regarding what professional groups are protected is Nebraska. The Nebraska statutes set a 2-year statute of limitations for malpractice actions, but do not specify which groups are subject to the statute.[92] In determining whether nurses should be subject to this statute, one must turn to the section defining nursing practice. That section states:

> The practice of nursing shall mean the performance for compensation or gratuitously of any act expressing judgment or skill based upon a systemized body of nursing knowledge. Such acts shall include the identification of and intervention in actual or potential health problems of individuals or groups. These acts are directed toward maintaining health status, preventing illness, injury, or infirmity, improving health status, providing care supportive to or restorative of life and well-being through nursing assessment and through the execution of diagnostic or therapeutic regimens. . . .[93]

It can therefore be argued that by defining nursing in the above described terms, the legislature intended to treat nurses as professionals, and that demonstrable legislative intent to treat nurses as professionals should be followed by applying the shorter malpractice statute of limitations to nurses.

The best solution to this question is for states explicitly to include nurses in the group of professionals covered by a state's malpractice statute. Such an approach removes all doubts as to whether the legislature intended to include nurses in the class of protected professionals. Furthermore, since most states recently have modernized their definition of nursing to recognize its increasingly complex and independent nature, explicit statutory recognition of nurses as within the protected class of professionals is a proper corollary to that modernizing change.

Hawaii and Utah are examples of states that have attempted this direct approach.[94]

The Need for Expert Witnesses in Nursing Malpractice Actions

The traditional rule in malpractice actions requires expert testimony to support a finding of negligence.[95] Although a variety of rationales has been offered to support this requirement,[96] the most convincing rationale is the respect and deference that the courts have for the learning of another profession.[97] One commentator, in expanding on the justification for this rationale in the medical malpractice area, has suggested that since a large measure of judgment enters into the practice of medicine, this judgment should be free to operate in the best interests of the patient.[98] He contends that if every judgment made by the physician were subject to second guessing on the part of laypersons, the physician would be reluctant to exercise that degree of independent judgment necessary to benefit the patient.

Any discussion of the need for expert testimony in a malpractice action presents the question whether a profession should be allowed to set its own standard of care.[99] As noted by Prosser,[100] this is a unique concession to professional groups. Keeping in mind that the major reason for requiring expert testimony and for allowing a profession to set its own standards is to encourage the exercise of independent professional judgment, the majority of courts have extended this privilege to the medical profession. Since nursing has published its own standards of practice, which can serve as the basis for evaluating nursing actions, the privilege of a profession to set its own standards should be extended to the nursing profession as well.

In considering malpractice actions, two major questions must be confronted. The first is whether the rationale described above applies to nurses. The second question is, assuming the first question is answered in the affirmative, who is qualified to serve as an expert witness? The correct solution to both inquiries depends, in large part, on the determination of whether nursing is a profession.

The nature of traditional nursing practice has caused a fair amount of confusion as to whether expert witnesses are necessary in nursing malpractice actions. This confusion results from the realization that traditionally nurses have performed both routine, nontechnical tasks and specialized nursing tasks. If, in considering the case law in this area, the dispute is analyzed in terms of what action by the nurse is being complained about, it is possible to make some sense out of the relevant decisions. Indeed, as discussed above, just such an analytical approach was adopted by the New York Court of Appeals in *Bleiler*. In addition, it is possible to use these precedents accurately in view of the current changes taking place in nursing.[101]

Jones v. Hawkes Hospital[102] is one of the classic cases dealing with the issue of expert witnesses in nursing malpractice litigation. In *Jones* the plaintiff was in the hospital's labor room prior to the birth of her first child. She was sedated and had made previous attempts to climb out of bed. After the plaintiff's contractions ended, the nurse primarily responsible for her care temporarily left the room in order to check information concerning the plaintiff and to respond to a request for assistance from a physician. During the nurse's five-minute absence, plaintiff fell out of bed and was injured.[103] The defendant hospital appealed the trial court's finding of liability, claiming that the plaintiff needed to produce expert testimony to show that the nurse, the hospital's employee, failed to meet the applicable professional standard of conduct. The majority of the Ohio Supreme Court rejected this contention.[104] In justifying this result the court noted that six members of the jury in the instant case were women and took judicial notice of the fact that most women jurors were mothers or grandmothers and that "they know probably as much if not more about childbirth than many witnesses who might be put on the witness stand."[105] Thus, under the majority approach it was unnecessary to resort to expert testimony to determine that the nurse in question was negligent. This argument, as the dissent correctly noted, missed the point.[106] In view of the paramount justification for demanding expert witnesses in malpractice actions—encouraging the exercise of independent judgment[107]—the dissent's approach is sound. In this case the nurse's decision to leave the room in order to perform other nursing tasks and to assist in the care of others might have been erroneous. If so, that judgment should have been evaluated by fellow nurses instead of by a jury of laypeople. This malpractice approach will benefit the health care consumer because care will be administered according to these principles.

Cases subsequent to *Jones* that have attempted to focus on the nature of the nursing action have not required expert testimony when the court concludes that the action at issue is within the ordinary and common knowledge of lay jurors. In *Hundemer v. Sisters of Charity*[108] the court considered a claim that resulted from the infiltration of the drug Levophed (norepinephrine bitartrate) into the tissues surrounding the plaintiff's veins. The court in *Hundemer* distinguished *Jones* and concluded that expert testimony was necessary to determine if the drug had been administered correctly. The court's unstated distinction seems to center on the conclusion that although unattended falls may be within the scope of an ordinary juror's knowledge, administration of drugs is not.

A more difficult case is *Johnson v. Grant Hospital*.[109] In *Johnson* a nurse allegedly did not lock a mentally ill patient's room, and the patient left the room and jumped from the hospital roof, committing suicide. The attending physician had left orders that the patient's room was to be locked at night. The court concluded that expert testimony existed in the record, and that a directed verdict for the defendant was inappropriate, since a genuine issue of fact existed. In reaching these conclusions the court constructed a two-tier approach to determine whether expert witnesses are needed in nursing malpractice actions. In so doing, the court recognized that this requirement varies depending on the nursing act at issue. The court noted:

> Even though specially trained, a nurse must also exercise the standard of care of an ordinary prudent person. Where the issue is one of an exercise of judgment or skill requiring the specialized training of a nurse, opinion would be required.[110]

Acceptance of this rule, however, does not resolve all controversy. For example, in *Johnson*, the majority appeared willing to conclude that expert testimony was not necessary in evaluation of the question whether the patient had received adequate attention, yet the dissent concluded that expert testimony was necessary.[111]

In *Cramer v. Theda Clark Memorial Hospital*[112] the Wisconsin Supreme Court also distinguished between acts requiring expert testimony and those acts that did not require expert testimony. In *Cramer* a postoperative patient broke his hip after a nurse had lowered the bed restraints in order to allow the patient to feed himself. The court cited *Jones* with approval and concluded that it was unnecessary to have expert testimony on the need to have the patient restrained.

Several more recent court decisions reflect a growing recognition on the part of the courts and attorneys that expert testimony is necessary to establish that a nurse is liable in a malpractice action. This growing recognition is tied to an increased awareness of the fact that there is a technical, independent component of nursing practice. For instance, in *Vassey v. Bursch*,[113] a North Carolina appellate court upheld a trial court that granted summary judgment in favor of nurses in a malpractice action. In *Vassey* a patient came to a hospital emergency room complaining of vomiting and severe abdominal pain. The nurse consulted the patient's physician by telephone and, upon the physician's orders, administered medication and sent the person home. The next day this person was readmitted to the hospital suffering from a ruptured appendix and severe peritonitis. In the resulting lawsuit the patient alleged that the nurse should have recognized that he was suffering from appendicitis. The court noted, however, that the patient had not introduced expert testimony to establish that such a failure on the part of the nurse constitutes a failure to act at the level of minimum professional competence of a nurse. In the future it is unlikely that attorneys will fail to introduce such evidence, or that courts will refuse to impose liability for the delivery of nursing care that falls below established levels of minimum pro fessional competence.

A second case underscoring the increasing use of expert witnesses to establish whether a nurse is liable for malpractice is *Maslonka v. Hermann*.[114] In *Maslonka*, a woman died several hours after giving birth. The resulting lawsuit named various doctors and nurses as defendants. In reviewing the evidence offered at the trial level, the court noted that the plaintiff had introduced as an expert witness a nurse who testified that the woman had received inadequate nursing care. Specifically, the nurse expert witness found that: (1) the nursing notes were poorly kept; (2) the nursing notes may have been made after the patient's death; (3) the nursing notes showed poor communication among the nursing staff about the patient's condition; (4) the vital signs were poorly monitored; and (5) a proper nursing diagnosis could have led the nurse to conclude that the fatal hemorrhage was possible. The nurses in question ultimately escaped liability because the appeals court concluded, in a split decision, that the plaintiff's expert witness did not establish that there was a causal link between the failure of the nurses to act in conformity with nursing standards and the patient's death. Based on the repc ted facts, this conclusion appears suspect, and another court could well impose liability on the nurses. What is significant about this case, however, is that the plaintiff used a nurse expert witness to establish that the nurses had not acted in conformity with minimum acceptable nursing standards. Also of significance is that the effect of nursing actions on individual patients is coming under increased review. It should be expected that this form of judicial review of nursing practice will continue and increase.

Once it is determined that an expert witness is required, the next question is who should qualify as an expert. The Kansas case of *Hiatt v. Groce*[115] is a vehicle for considering this question. In *Hiatt* the court considered whether a nurse attending a woman during childbirth was negligent in failing to notify the attending physician of the impending delivery of plaintiff's baby. At the trial the court found for the plaintiff, in spite of expert testimony of a nurse and physician that, on the basis of hospital records, the nurse's action comported with sound nursing care. The Kansas Supreme Court upheld this judgment on the basis of the underlying facts of the case.[116] The trial court issued the following instructions to the jury on the question of the appropriate standard of care required of a nurse:

> In determining whether a registered nurse used the learning, skill and conduct required of her, you are not permitted to arbitrarily set a standard of your own or determine this question from your personal knowledge. On questions of nursing expertise concerning the standard of care of a nurse, only those qualified as experts are permitted to testify. The standard of care is established by members of the same profession in the same or similar communities under like circumstances.[117]

In spite of this instruction, particularly its requirement of experts from the same profession as the defendant, the trial court allowed a physician to testify as an expert witness on the adequacy of nursing care provided the plaintiff. In addition, one professor of maternity nursing also testified concerning the quality of nursing care.[118]

Despite the court's failure to adhere to its own standard, its instruction is a sound statement of what the law should be. The use of physician testimony is, however, common practice. In *Mellies v. National Heritage, Inc.* an appellate court applied *Hiatt* in a reasonable manner.[119] In *Mellies* a patient sued a nursing home for pain associated with decubitus ulcers allegedly caused by inadequate care at the nursing home. These sores required approximately 40 days of hospitalization to cure. At the trial the patient attempted to have a registered nurse and instructor of nursing at Wichita State University qualified as an expert as to the cause, prevention, and treatment of decubitus ulcers. The trial court allowed this person to testify as to the standard of care for nursing practice in treating ulcers, but refused to let the nurse testify as to their cause or cure. The trial judge concluded that only a doctor could qualify as an expert on the cause or cure of decubitus ulcers. The appeals court reversed the trial court and concluded that a nurse who has had wide experience with bedsores is in fact an expert as to decubitus ulcers, since their "prevention, treatment and cure are largely nursing duties."[120] Thus, the Court in *Mellies* focused on the nature of the disease or injury in order to determine if nurses can qualify as expert witnesses. Until courts become more aware of what different levels of nurses can do, confusion and contradictory rulings at malpractice trials are likely to result. While the decision in *Mellies* is consistent with the following analysis, it does not address the problem of how to treat nurses and physicians in areas of shared expertise.

The confusion results from the fact that nursing and medicine have an overlapping knowledge base because both nurses and physicians study disease and the treatment of disease. Thus, both a coronary care specialist and a physician understand and can interpret various heart arrhythmias. This knowledge base, however, is overlapping, not coextensive. In the above example, the physician and specialist nurse would know when and how to defibrillate a patient. The physician, in addition, could determine when surgery is necessary and could select the appropriate course of medical treatment (e.g., drug selection). The nurse, on the other hand, would be able to select the appropriate intervention that would meet the patient's psychological needs, select and administer drugs according to established protocols in an emergency, plan for the patient's rehabilitation, and teach the patient self care.[121]

One nursing commentator has suggested that in areas of shared expertise, nurses could testify as expert witnesses in evaluation of a physician's action.[122] Allowing a physician to testify in nursing malpractice actions simply because they share common areas of knowledge unnecessarily confuses the issue. While either might be able to explain the action to the jury, liability is based on compliance with standards of practice of fellow professionals. Thus a nurse is being judged in comparison to other nurses, not physicians. Allowing individuals from another profession to testify tends to divert attention from evaluating the professional by compliance with his own professional standards. This distinction becomes critically important when a question of nursing judgment is being evaluated. Since liability is established by reference to what constitutes competent nursing behavior, physician testimony is irrelevant. On the other hand, there is an obvious overlap between medicine and nursing and, in cases involving shared expertise, it could be proper for nurses or physicians to be permitted to be expert witnesses. The Georgia Supreme Court has upheld the right of a nurse to testify in a malpractice action against a physician on the question of the standard of care in keeping sterile a needle used to draw blood from a patient.[123]

Once it is recognized that nursing is a separate discipline and profession, it becomes clear that the key concern is how nurses have been trained to act. Only those familiar with this training can testify on that score. *Thompson v. United States*[124] supports this conclusion.

In *Thompson* the plaintiff, who complained of chest pains, was sent unattended to the laboratory for tests by a practical nurse.[125] The plaintiff fainted while standing in line and as a result of the fall, had to have a finger amputated. At trial the plaintiff claimed that a nurse should be held to the same standard of care as a physician. The court rejected this contention and, applying a Louisiana law, decided actions by nurses should be measured against standards of the nursing profession.[126] Thus, *Thompson* recognized that there are differences in the medical and nursing professions, and that competence in one profession does not necessarily indicate competence in the other. The court erred, however, in concluding that practical nurses should be judged by standards applicable to professional nurses. Practical nurses are licensed separately by the state[127] and have neither the educational background nor the legal authority to act in the same manner that registered nurses act. Several recent statutes also support the above reasoning and indicate that expert witnesses can come only from the defendant's profession. The relevant Arizona[128] statute provides that persons against whom malpractice claims are asserted should be measured against members of their own profession.

A more recent case with a similar holding is *Fein v. Permanente Medical Group*,[129] in which plaintiff alleged that a nurse practitioner had negligently failed to diagnose his heart attack. The trial court instructed the jury that the standard of care applicable to a nurse practitioner "'is that of a physician and surgeon . . . when the nurse practitioner is examining a patient or making a diagnosis'."[130] Noting that the relevant California statute included within its definition of the practice of nursing "observation of signs and symptoms of illness" and determining of whether such symptoms "exhibit abnormal characteristics," the court said diagnosis cannot be said, as a matter of law, to be a function reserved to a physician. The applicable standard of care, said the *Fein* court, is that of "a reasonably prudent nurse practitioner in conducting the examination and prescribing treatment in conjunction with her supervising physician."[131]

Two well-reasoned cases support the twin conclusions that nurses can serve as expert witnesses and that expert witnesses should be used to establish whether the applicable standard of nursing care has been met in a particular case. In *Wood v. Rowland*[132] the trial court had refused to permit a nurse to testify because the nurse had only practiced in one hospital. The Colorado appeals court concluded that the failure to permit the nurse to testify constituted reversible error. The court first concluded that the proper standard to use in determining whether a person is an expert is whether that person has superior knowledge on the subject under consideration that would prove helpful to the court and to a jury. The court noted that a nurse's education and experience are not common to the average layperson and that a nurse can qualify as an expert witness. The court then concluded that working in only one hospital did not affect a nurse's standing as an expert witness because it was the standard of professional nursing, and not hospital practice, that was the critical factor. It is hard to overstress the importance of or improve on the court's reasoning.

> What a hospital may require of its nurses has little, if anything, to do with the obligations that specialized training and experience may impose on nurses. . . . The practice of nursing is a highly regulated profession in this state and therefore the applicable standard of care is that of a reasonable professional.[133]

A proper corollary is that only experts competent to testify as to that standard of care are members of that highly regulated profession—nurses.

In *Fraijo v. Hartland Hospital*[134] a California appeals court upheld a trial court that had given the jury an instruction normally only given in medical malpractice actions. In *Fraijo* a woman was admitted to a hospital experiencing difficulty in breathing. The woman was asthmatic and her physician left an order for Demerol (meperidine hydrochloride) prn (*pro re nata*, as required or whenever necessary). The nurse administered Demerol and the woman subsequently died. The trial court instructed the jury:

> Where there is more than one recognized method of diagnosis or treatment, and no one of them is used exclusively and uniformly by all practitioners of good standing, a physician or *nurse* is not negligent if, in exercising their best judgment, they select one of the approved methods, which later turns out to be a wrong selection or one not favored by certain other practitioners[135] (emphasis added).

The plaintiff argued that the inclusion of nurses in the instruction was incorrect because nurses do not act independently. The appeals court rejected this argument by noting that, while there are varying levels of competence relating to education and experience, nurses are held to strict professional levels of competence. In this case the nurse was to administer Demerol prn. Implicit in that order, the court concluded, was the recognition that the nurse was to use the nurse's independent judgment of whether or not to administer Demerol. Thus, while administering Demerol might have been a factor in the patient's death, liability will only be found if evidence is produced that its administration violated acceptable nursing practice. That evidence can only be supplied by expert nurse testimony. Again, the logical next step to the court's analysis is that only nurses should be permitted to testify as experts on questions dealing with *nursing* diagnosis or treatment.

Several recent cases show the willingness of modern courts to accept the testimony of nurses as experts on acceptable nursing practice.[136] Regrettably, however, the courts also continue to accept the testimony of physicians on the same issue.[137]

The Locality Standard Rule and the Significance of Educational Differences.

One of the most criticized of the special rules for malpractice actions is the so-called *locality* rule. The locality rule measures the actions of the professional practitioner against the standards of those practitioners practicing in the same or a similar community, rather than against a national standard of practice. Improvements in communication and standardization of educational requirements for entry into the profession have eroded the need and justification for a strict locality rule.[138] Thus, many modern courts[139] as well as some state legislatures[140] have rejected it. Those states that still follow the locality rule in other professional and malpractice cases tend to use the rule for nursing malpractice actions as well. In the leading Louisiana case of *Norton v. Argounout*[141] a nurse was found liable for the death of an infant after she administered a drug to the child with a needle instead of orally. In affirming the finding of liability, the appellate court evaluated the nurse's actions by comparing them to nurses practicing in the same or a similar community.[142] Subsequent Louisiana cases have continued to use the locality standard in nursing malpractice actions.[143]

In contrast, the Supreme Court of Nevada rejected the locality rule and permitted a nurse who had practiced at hospitals in Pennsylvania and New Jersey to testify regarding the standard of care applicable to hospital nurses in Las Vegas. In *Wickliffe v. Sunrise Hospital*,[144] the court adopted a national standard of care for hospitals and reversed the trial court's ruling that had barred the out-of-state nurse from testifying. The court noted that:

> Nursing education and licensing is . . . standardized. Nurses are licensed after passing an examination in the state where they wish to work and a national examination. A licensed nurse in good standing in one state can practice in another without taking the second state's local examination.[145]

With the promulgation of standards of practice applicable to all nurses,[146] there is little justification for retention of the locality rule in nursing malpractice actions. The profession recognizes minimum levels of performance applicable to all nurses regardless of where the nurse is practicing. These standards are designed both to specify minimum levels of acceptable performance and to give the consumer a tool with which to evaluate the quality of nursing care he receives.[147] Retention of a locality rule would defeat both these goals. Whatever additional protection the locality rule is designed to give to professionals is not necessary, since the professionals themselves desire to be judged by universal standards. Because there is little justification in retaining the locality rule in nursing malpractice cases, it is necessary to determine which standards of practice should be selected and used. Minimum acceptable norms of behavior should not be measured by reference to a particular hospital's practice, but by reference to acceptable nursing practice. The rationale in *Wickliffe and Wood*[148] supports this conclusion.

Until recently courts seldom evaluated the quality of care provided by a nurse in reference to the nurse's educational background. Since nurses enter the profession through one of three different educational programs, and since the programs are not designed to provide the same training,[149] such an analysis seems appropriate in determining negligence. In *Northern Trust Co. v. Louis A. Weiss Memorial Hospital*,[150] the court implicitly adopted just such an approach. Plaintiff in *Northern Trust* brought a malpractice action against a hospital, a physician, and two nurses, alleging that their negligence in caring for a newborn baby had left the infant with severe brain damage. The jury found the hospital liable but absolved the individual defendants. On appeal, the defendant hospital argued that it could not be found negligent unless its employees were negligent. In particular, the hospital argued, a finding that Shirley Anderson, the nurse on duty in the nursery on the night the infant became seriously ill, had met the applicable standard of care must also absolve the hospital of negligence. But the court, noting that nurse Anderson had no special training in caring for newborn babies, disagreed:

> The jury reasonably could have found that Anderson had and applied the knowledge and used the care of a reasonably well-qualified nurse observing newborns, and that what was lacking was the supervision of a specially trained nurse. Nurse Anderson would have met the applicable standards of care by conscientiously charting the progress of the infants. The hospital alone is responsible for providing a nurse to supervise the nursery, and that supervising nurse must be specially trained so that she can appropriately judge when there is an emergency which warrants calling a doctor.[151]

Although plaintiff's expert witness had testified that Nurse Anderson did not meet the standard of care, the court said the witness had wrongly assumed that the applicable standard of care was that of a nurse specially trained to supervise a nursery. The jury, the *Northern Trust* court said, could reasonably have concluded that the standard of care applicable to nurse Anderson was "the care required of a competent nurse, without special training in care of newborns, working in a nursery under the supervision of a specially trained nurse."[152] Thus it appears clear that the court understood that nurses have different levels of training and skill, and that different standards are applicable to nurses with different levels of education.

Once the proposition is accepted that education is a factor in the negligence standard to be used, a court must evaluate each nurse's training in order to determine if he or she has breached any duty owed to the patient. Thus, since associate degree nurses are trained to perform routinized tasks,[153] failure to exercise independent judgment on the part of such a nurse should not violate any duty owed to any patient. The same patient could reasonably expect a different form of care, however, if treated by a baccalaureate or more highly educated nurse.[154] Courts, therefore, should evaluate the educational background of professional nurses in determining whether the nurse breached a duty owed to the claimant. As health care consumers become aware of these distinctions, they could well demand information on the training of the nurses who will be providing care.

The "Captain of the Ship" Doctrine

Another legal doctrine that has contributed to the delayed recognition of the professional status of nurses is the "captain of the ship" doctrine. This doctrine is usually applied to surgery, and holds the surgeon in charge of the operation responsible for the acts of all those who work with him during the operation.[155]

The early case of *Beadles v. Metakya*[156] demonstrates the application of this doctrine and suggests proper limitations on its use. In *Beadles* the surgeon in charge gave conflicting instructions to an orderly, who carried the instructions out without considering the result of such actions to the patient. The surgeon was held responsible for the resulting harm. Two factors in *Beadles* should be stressed. First, the surgeon gave specific instructions to the orderly, and it was these conflicting instructions that led to the patient's injury. Secondly, the instructions were given to a nonprofessional who did not have an independent base of professional knowledge to use in administering care to the patient. Thus, the physician's liability appears appropriately established.

A much more difficult problem is confronted with the modern surgical team. These teams, in performing increasingly complex surgical procedures, are composed of several different professionals, each of whom must apply his or her own professional skill if the procedure is to be successful. While each professional member of the team is working toward a common end result, the lead surgeon has neither the time nor expertise to direct specifically the performance of each person's assigned task. Perforce, the surgeon must rely on each team member. In this situation, the justification of one-man control and hence liability is increasingly difficult to maintain.[157]

Several cases reflect a movement away from the "captain of the ship" doctrine as applied to nurses. In *Miller v. Hood*[158] a midlevel Texas court refused to hold a physician responsible for injuries caused when a nurse incorrectly administered an injection to a patient. The court, noting that this was not an operating room situation, held that in the absence of the controlled circumstances of the operating room, the physician is not responsible when a treatment he has ordered for the patient is administered incorrectly by a nurse. The case thus recognizes that the "captain of the ship" doctrine is limited to operating room cases. Additionally, the case implied recognition of the independent professional nature of nursing outside the operating room. Under this view, nurses will be liable for their own actions and errors.

Although the captain of the ship doctrine retains vitality, there are cases that suggest that courts are reconsidering its applicability to modern medical situations, In *Sesselman v. Muhlenberg*[159] the appellate court reversed a trial court verdict in favor of a malpractice claimant. The plaintiff claimed she suffered tooth and mouth injuries as a result of the incorrect administration of anesthesia by a nurse anesthetist during childbirth. At trial the claimant offered the testimony of a physician expert witness who claimed that a physician is responsible for anything that goes wrong in the operating room. The court noted that the nurse anesthetist was an employee of the hospital and that the record did not indicate that the surgeon attempted to control the manner in which she carried out her professional duties. The court thus concluded that the physician was not responsible for injuries that resulted from the anesthetist's actions.[160]

Parker v. St. Paul Fire and Marine Insurance Company[161] is another case refusing to apply the captain of the ship doctrine to all operating room accidents. In *Parker*, the plaintiff was undergoing an emergency hysterectomy following the birth of her third child. During surgery, additional transfusions of blood were necessary. The operating room nurse took two units of blood for another patient and administered it to the plaintiff. The blood was matched incorrectly, was tagged with another patient's name and room number, but was nonetheless administered by the nurse to the plaintiff. Following the surgery, the plaintiff claimed to suffer numerous postoperative problems caused by the incorrect transfusion. The court refused to hold the surgeon liable for the negligence of the nurse, finding that the nurse was not under the direct control of the surgeon.[162] This finding restricts the "captain of the ship" doctrine to very limited situations in which the nurse is responding to a direct order of the surgeon. When the nurse is carrying out tasks necessary for the operation but the surgeon is relying on the nurse to perform those tasks on the basis of her own professional skill, the surgeon should be relieved of liability.

These cases, particularly *Parker*, correctly limit the "captain of the ship" doctrine. When a surgical team member responds to a direct order of the lead surgeon, it is proper to impose liability on that surgeon, since he or she is coordinating the efforts of all team members. On the other hand, when the various tasks of a complex surgical procedure are divided among team members, the other professionals, including professional nurses, should be independently liable for their actions.

NURSING MALPRACTICE LAW: SUGGESTIONS FOR THE FUTURE

Determination of Liability: The Use of Standards of Practice

Both the legal community and the health care consumer appear largely unaware of the changes in nursing and the potential legal implications of these changes. The increasingly independent basis of nursing practice,[163] the promulgation of nationwide standards of practice,[164] the identification of different nursing roles based on educational preparation,[165] and the movement toward a certification program[166] have all gone practically unnoticed. Thus, the public expects too little from nurses because it knows too little about them. The case law demonstrates that while many courts view nursing in its traditional dependent role and thus impose liability only in cases involving falls,[167] failure to carry out a physician's orders,[168] and neglect of a patient,[169] there are evolving changes that carry profound implications for nursing. These changes, while lagging behind the developments in nursing itself, show that courts will be more sophisticated in evaluating the adequacy of nursing care provided to patients. The following suggestions offer a framework for the development of a rational and reasonable method of evaluating the quality of nursing care.

To determine whether a nurse should be held liable for malpractice, three questions must be asked: First, what is the nature of the act at issue complained of? Second, what are the qualifications of the nurse who performed the act? Third, where was the care provided? In considering the first question, a court should first determine the nature of the act being questioned. If it is an act that relates to a nursing function requiring specialized knowledge, then it is appropriate to proceed to the next two questions in order to determine whether the nurse acted appropriately.

If liability is to attach because the nurse failed to conform to the expected standards of nursing practice, then only nurses should be competent to testify about the applicable standard, about the nursing implication of the act in question, and about the alleged failure of the nursing act to conform to the applicable nursing standard. A physician's expertise in medical practice should not qualify him or her as an expert in evaluating nursing practice; therefore, the practice of allowing physicians to testify as expert witnesses on the quality of nursing care[170] is inappropriate if liability is established by showing a violation of a nursing standard.

The second question required to formulate the appropriate standard of care focuses on the nurse's educational background and, if applicable, advanced certification. This second factor should be combined with the first in the following fashion: deviation from a standard of practice would establish liability for all nurses, but a nurse with more expertise would be expected to conduct his or her actions in accordance with that level of expertise. For the purposes of the following discussion, the term *technical nurse* will apply to all nonbaccalaureate degree nurses and the term *professional nurse* shall apply to all nurses with a baccalaureate or higher degree in nursing. Recognition of the educational differences among nurses will result in greater exposure to liability for professional nurses, since they have the background and ability to assume independent roles in the expansion of nursing practice.[171] The discussion of the educational programs above supports this conclusion.[172] The professional nurse will function in three settings, the technical nurse, primarily in one setting. Technical nurses will be found on general care floors of hospitals, while professional nurses will be found outside the hospitals, in specialty areas within hospitals, and on general care floors of hospitals.

The professional nurse treats clients on a one-to-one basis outside the hospital, evaluates the symptoms, and refers clients to other health care providers and direct services that prevent diseases.[173] In the hospital the professional nurse directs the general nursing care for the patient or provides specialty care for the patient. Technical nurses, on the other hand, perform basic care for patients under the supervision of a professional nurse or other health care provider.[174] Thus, while it is possible, indeed likely, that both technical and professional nurses will be found in the same setting, the law should not require them to react identically to the same medical problem. Failure of the technical nurse to exercise independent judgment in a given situation would not establish liability, since that nurse would not be expected to act independently. In fact, independent action might result in liability. In contrast, the same failure to exercise independent judgment on the part of the professional nurse could well establish liability.[175] The clinical nurse specialist offers another example of the necessity of a flexible standard of care based on educational background. The clinical nurse specialist has at least a master's degree in a clinical area of nursing practice. With this advanced preparation, the nurse has the ability to act in an even more independent manner than would the nurse with only a baccalaureate degree. It would be completely unrealistic to hold the nurse specialist only to the level of performance expected from a technical nurse.

The clear trend towards state recognition of advanced levels of licensure—at least 26 states and the District of Columbia now officially recognize advanced levels of nursing practice—poses significant potential for expanded liability for nurses.[176] Florida has one of the most complete statutory approaches to advanced licensure. Florida provides for certification of nursing specialists as nurse anesthetists or nurse midwives, as well as for certification of advanced registered nurse practitioners in five areas (family care and family planning, geriatrics, pediatrics, primary adult care, and psychiatric mental health)[177] with expanded areas of practice for each of these areas. For example, subject to the established protocol approved by the medical staff of the health care facility in which a midwife practices, a nurse-midwife may, among other things, perform superficial minor surgical procedures; order appropriate medications; order, initiate, and perform appropriate anesthetic procedures and manage a patient during labor and delivery to include amniotomy, episiotomy, and surgical repair. A clinical nurse specialist in psychiatric mental health may establish a behavioral problems diagnosis and make treatment recommendations. This kind of detailed legislative enactment underscores the increased level of independent nursing practice of advanced practitioners. Legislating to this degree of detail poses the risk that future changes in the nature of nursing practice may require repeated legislative updating, resulting in increased opportunity for other health care providers to limit the areas of permissible nursing practice. Nevertheless, it is a clear indication that all nurses are not the same and should not and will not be judged by the same standards.

These expanded areas of practice imply that nurses so licensed should be held to a higher standard of care than nurses without such advanced licensure. Furthermore, to the extent advanced licensed nurses perform in a more independent manner and deal with increasingly complicated medical problems, it is reasonable to expect that their actions will receive increased judicial scrutiny.

Differentiation of a standard of care based on educational preparation or advanced certification has one additional component. In order to prove deviance from a professional norm, the expert witness will have to have an educational background at least equal to that of the nurse whose act is subject to review. Thus, if liability is to be established in an independent area of practice, a technical nurse would not be competent to testify on whether a professional nurse acted in accord with professional norms.

In summary, all nurses must act in accordance with the national standards of practice. A court focusing on a nurse's allegedly negligent act must determine if the act called for a dependent response or an independent judgment. If independent action was called for, the educational background and, if applicable, the advanced certification of the nurse must be considered in order to determine if the act was unreasonable. Nursing science has progressed to the point that nursing experts can evaluate the professional nurse's act and determine if that act meets acceptable nursing standards.

The third consideration, the setting in which the care is provided, has been alluded to above. Certain institutions, particularly hospitals, will use graduates from different programs with different skills.[178] This should not present any serious analytical difficulty, however, since these institutions are designed to provide a wide range of services. The hospital should be designed and staffed so that nurses' skills are effectively utilized. For instance, those patients who require hospitalization, but whose illnesses are well defined and predictable, can be cared for adequately by technical nurses.[179] On the other hand, there will be patients whose illnesses are either undefined or unpredictable. Individuals in critical care or specialty units might be in this category. Those patients require closer attention, and their conditions might change dramatically in a very short period of time, requiring quick response by the attending nurse. Since professional nurses have the education to respond to such situations,[180] they should be utilized in this area. The Illinois Court of Appeals employed this approach in holding a hospital liable for improper staffing of a nursery in *Northern Trust*.[181] Although the nurse on duty was found to have acted properly, the hospital was found to have "negligently '[f]ailed to provide registered professional nurses with special training in the care of the newborn supervising the care of [the injured infant] at all times'."[182]

Individuals in a hospital, therefore, will receive different nursing care depending on their condition. The classification system described above, while idealized, does provide for a cost-effective delivery of health care. At first it may seem inequitable, since some patients (those most critically or unpredictably ill) will receive different nursing care than other patients in the same institution at the same time. This apparent inequity is justified and indeed consonant with current medical practice. Traditionally, those individuals deemed most ill have received the most attention. This description projects the delivery of nursing care into the current system to ensure that those individuals most in need of independent nursing care receive that care.

Although the above discussion has focused on nursing care in an institutional setting, nurses are currently practicing in many different areas. A development has included nurses going into private practice.[183] While professional nurses are prepared to assume this role with some additional training,[184] current experience indicates that most frequently it is nurses with master's degrees or higher who are in private practice.

With the three elements outlined above, it is now possible to describe a framework for determining how a possible nursing malpractice problem should be approached. If the act in question occurred in a hospital, it is necessary to determine if the patient was provided with appropriate nursing care. This involves a review of the classification of the patient. If the patient was receiving routinized care because the illness indicated such care was appropriate, then technical nursing practice would be the appropriate measure of whether adequate care was theoretically provided. If, however, the patient needed professional nursing care and was provided only with technical nursing care, the institution might well be liable for failing to provide that greater care. Such potential liability should affect hiring and staffing decisions by hospital administrators.

If the patient was provided initially with the appropriate level of nursing care, the inquiry should focus on the nurse and the act in question. At this point, the nurse's educational background would suggest the degree of skill expected of the nurse. The various professional standards would indicate whether the act in question met, or failed to meet, minimal standards of professional performance. Expert witnesses would evaluate the act in terms of these standards and in terms of the educational preparation of the nurse.

If the nurse is in private practice, the initial inquiry is virtually unnecessary. There is no need to determine if the plaintiff was appropriately classified, since the plaintiff will have selected the nurse to provide the care in question. Instead, attention will focus on whether the individual nurse had the education and experience to practice independently and, if so, whether the nurse was negligent in providing the care that is being questioned.

Implications of a Higher Standard of Care

Adoption of the suggestions above will result in nurses being held to a higher standard of care and will result in increased malpractice judgments against nurses. With the hue and cry about increasing numbers of medical malpractice actions, can such a result be justified? Not only can the result be justified, but it can also produce benefits for nurses themselves.

One of the major reasons that nursing has received inadequate attention is the public's lack of understanding about what it should expect from nurses. The adoption of advanced certification by the states, and the development of an analytical framework for differentiating what nurses from different backgrounds are prepared to do, could largely eliminate the source of this confusion. A more realistic standard of care becomes an absolute necessity as nurses assume independent roles. As the independent roles become understood and utilized, nurses should be held accountable for their actions.

Adoption of a more realistic standard of care can be justified on two grounds. First, the increased educational level of nurses indicates a growing sophistication of knowledge that allows nurses to function in an increasingly independent manner. With the increase of health care costs and with nurses offering an alternative to total physician delivery of health care that can lower these costs, the public benefits from nursing's ability to assume a more responsible role in health care. With this more responsible role it seems appropriate to recognize the underlying expertise of the nursing profession and to allow the profession to use its expertise to determine what is satisfactory nursing behavior.

The concern with allowing any profession to set its own standards is that the profession will act in a manner of self-interest and the individual consumer will thereby be harmed. It is precisely this concern, however, that provides the second justification for allowing nursing to set its own standards. The nursing profession has been quick to recognize the needs of the health care consumer. Nursing has moved to include lay representatives on its various state boards of nursing,[185] has stressed the right of consumers to participate and control decisions about their own care, and has adopted and published national standards of practice that consumers can use in measuring the quality of nursing care received. All of these factors reflect a keen sensitivity to public needs and suggest that the nursing profession is ready to live up to the responsibility that accompanies the privilege of helping to define the appropriate standard of liability. By permitting nursing to establish the appropriate standard of liability, the trend toward more independent nursing action will be reinforced.

Allowing the nursing profession the right to define its own standard of liability will produce a further result. If nurses are hospital employees, the hospital will be liable for acts of nursing malpractice under the concept of *respondeat superior*. Once hospitals recognize that their potential liability has expanded and that nursing standards are one of the major sources for defining the extent of potential liability, the hospitals will, out of economic self-interest, accord nurses a greater say in the allocation of resources in order to limit their potential exposure.

In allocating resources, rationally run institutions will ensure that perceived critical needs are met before considering less critical needs. Currently, since nurses are held to a low standard of care, there is no great external pressure on hospitals to upgrade this care. If hospitals faced significant financial liability because they provided either insufficient numbers of nurses or inadequate nursing care, there would be reasons to upgrade nursing care. If liability attached because nursing standards established by nurses were violated, hospitals by necessity would have to consult with nurses in order to ensure that they provide satisfactory nursing care. Further, if nursing standards indicated that with x number of patients there must be y number of nurses, and that certain kinds of patients required professional rather than technical nursing care, hospitals would be under pressure to ensure that floors were not understaffed and that professional nursing care was available. This will not only give nurses more power and status in the health care system, but also will enable them to lobby for changes that will benefit the health care consumer.

NOTES

1. See, e.g., Curran & Moseley, *The Malpractice Experience of Health Maintenance Organizations*, 70 NW. L. Rev. 69 (1975); King, *In Search of a Standard of Care for the Medical Profession*: The "accepted practice" formula, 28 Vand. L. Rev. 1213 (1975); *The Symposium: Medical Malpractice*, 1975 Duke L.H. 1 (1975).

2. CAL. BUS. & PROF. CODE § 2725.1 (repealed, effective July 1, 1983, by its own terms); UTAH CODE ANN. § 58-31-4 (repealed by Laws 1985, ch 54, § 3, effective July 1, 1985).

3. For a general discussion of traditional nursing malpractice case law, see Pavalon & Robin, *Damage Suits Based on Nursing Malpractice*, 57 Ill. B. J. 282 (1968); Note, *Hospital Nurses and Tort Liability*, 18 Clev.-Mar. L. Rev. 53 (1968). These articles, however, do not relate current changes in the nursing profession to possible changes in nursing malpractice laws.

4. See, e.g., Morris, *Negligent Nurse: The Physician and the Hospital*, 33 Bay L. Rev. 109 (1981); Walker, Nursing 1980, New Responsibility, New Liability, 16 Trial 45 (1980); Note, Critical care nurses: A case for legal recognition of the growing responsibilities and accountability in the nursing profession, 11 J. Contemp. L. 240 (1984). Note, *The Use of Nurses as Expert Witnesses*, 19 Hous. L. Rev. 555 (1982).

5. *Washington State Nurses Association v. Board of Medical Examiners*, 95 Wash. 2d 117, 605 P.2d 1269 (1980). In this case the Washington Supreme Court upheld a regulation permitting physician's assistants to issue prescriptions for medication and write medical orders for patient care. In supporting this regulation, doctors had argued that physician's assistant are the agents of their supervising physicians and not independent practitioners. The court contrasted physician's assistants with nurses noting: "Nurses, for example, are independently authorized to perform many different functions and they are directly accountable to the patient for the quality of their services. In contrast, the use of physician assistants (*sic*) is closely regulated under the statutes to assure that they do not exercise independent authority."

6. L. Flanagan, *One Strong Voice* 10 (1976) (hereinafter cited as Flanagan).

7. Id. at 11.

8. Id. at 13.

9. Id.

10. Id. at 16.

11. Id. at 17, 20. Interestingly, up to this point physicians had been in the forefront in pushing for improvements in the quality of nurse training. This early role of the medical community in the development and improvement of nursing had continuing influences later when nursing began to assert its autonomy. See note 46 infra and accompanying text.

12. Flanagan, supra note 6, at 27.

13. Shannon, "Our First Licensing Laws," 73 Am. J. Nurs. 1327 (1975).

14. Id. The constitutionality of state licensure laws was upheld in *Dent. v. West Virginia*, 129 U.S. 114 (1888).

15. See, e.g., WIS. STAT. ANN § 441.11(4).

16. See, e.g., COL. REV. STAT. § 12–38–103.(10).

17. See, e.g., N.Y. EDUC. LAW § 6901.

18. Id.

19. California, Louisiana (where physicians are ex-officio members only), and Mississippi. CALIF. BUS. & PROF. CODE § 19.2702; LA. REV. STAT. ANN. § 37:914; MISS. CODE ANN. § 73–15–9. In 1984, a fourth state, Tennessee, dropped in statutory requirement that a physician be a member of that state's board of nursing.

20. Since these laws were passed prior to the Nineteenth Amendment, it was necessary to find and use powerful allies. The New York experience indicates the successful implementation of this strategy. The New York nurses received support from members of the State Board of Regents, Susan B. Anthony, and the New York Medical Society. In fact, the Medical Society permitted the nurses to use the services of its chief legal counsel. Shannon, supra note 13, at 1329.

21. Both movements developed during the same period of time—the last two decades—and both movements reflect a common theme—the improvement of nursing practice. These movements further underscore the emerging sense of professionalism in nursing.

22. Flanagan, supra note 6, at 651–53.

23. Two examples of these specialty organizations are the Nurses Association

of the American College of Obstetricians and Gynecologists (NAACOG) and the Ass'n of Operating Room Nurses (AORN).

24. Throughout this chapter the terms *client* and *consumer* are used interchangeably with the more traditional term *patient*. This reflects the change in nursing that stresses individual involvement in care and decisions concerning that care. Patient suggests a more passive role in receipt of care.

25. Flanagan, supra note 6, at 219. In its preface to the first published standard, the ANA stressed: "A profession must seek control of its practice in order to guarantee the quality of its service to the public." American Nurses Association, *Standards of Nursing Practice* (1973).

26. Schrader, *"ANA Changes Certification Program,"* 24 Association Operating Room Nurses J. 203 (1976).

27. Flanagan, supra note 6, at 219a.

28. American Nurses Association. Proceedings of the ANA 1966 Convention 45 (1966). For a summary of the debate that preceded the adoption of these changes, see id. at 37–45. The five specialty areas that were created are: (1) community health, (2) geriatrics, (3) maternal and child health, (4) medical-surgical, and (5) psychiatric-mental health.

29. Interview with Rosamond Gabrielson, Past President of the ANA, in Nashville, Tennessee, (Feb. 14, 1977).

30. Flanagan, supra note 6, at 223–25; see also M. Phaneuf and N. Lang, *Standards of Nursing Practice* 3–4 (1985).

31. This approach was adopted by a number of organizations in the medical-surgical specialty area. Thus emergency room coronary care, and other groups participated in the formulation of the medical-surgical standards. Id. at 226.

32. See, e.g., Nurses Association of the American College of Obstetricians and Gynecologists, Obstetric, Gynecological and Neonatal Nursing Functions and Standards (1974) (hereinafter cited as NAACOG).

33. Interview with Dr. Ingeborg Mauksch, Professor of Nursing and Director of the Robert Wood Johnson Foundation Project, Vanderbilt University, Nashville, TN (Jan. 22, 1977).

34. See, e.g., American Nurses Ass'n, Standards of Medical-Surgical Nursing Practice (1974).

35. Id. at 2.

36. Id.

37. See, e.g., American Nurses Association, *Standards of Psychiatric and Mental Health Nursing Practice* (1982); *Standards of School Nursing Practice* (1983); *Standards of Practice for the Prenatal Nurse Specialist* (1984); *Nursing Practice in Correctional Facilities* (1985); *Community Health Nursing Practice* (1986).

38. See note 32 supra and accompanying text.

39. NAACOG, supra note 32, at 16–17.

40. Nurses Association of the American College of Obstetricians and Gynecologists, *Standards for Obstetric, Gynecological and Neonatal Nursing* 20–21 (3d ed. 1986).

41. Flanagan, supra note 6, at 231–234.

42. Id. at 234.

43. Id. at 234–35.

44. American Nurse, February 1976, at 18, col. 3.

45. *ANA and NAACOG Announce Joint Certification in Maternal, Gynecologic, and Neonatal Nursing.* 4 J. Obs. Gyn, Neonatal Nurs. 58 (1975).

46. Letter from Dr. Robert Frazier to Fellows of the American Academy of Pediatrics (Jan. 16, 1974). This letter provoked a letter in response from the ANA. This response letter provides further details of the controversy between the ANA and the American Academy of Pediatrics. Letter from Dr. Eileen Jacobi to Pediatric Nurse Practitioners and Fellows of the American Academy of Pediatrics (Jan. 29, 1974).

47. See Nat'l League for Nurses. *Credentialing in Nursing: Design for a Workshop* (1980).

48. CAL. BUS. 7 PROF. CODE § 2835.5 (West).

49. FLA. STAT. § 464.012.

50. N.H. REV. STAT. § 326–B:10.

51. MICH. STAT. ANN. § 14.15 (17210).

52. N.M. STAT. ANN. § 61–3–3(H).

53. OKLA. STAT. title. 59, § 567.3(4).

54. UTAH CODE ANN. § 58–31–9.1.

55. These jurisdictions are Arkansas, Colorado, Connecticut, Delaware, District of Columbia, Idaho, Indiana, Kansas, Kentucky, Massachusetts, Minnesota, Montana, Nebraska, North Carolina, Oregon, Rhode Island, South Dakota, Tennessee, Virginia and Washington. These provisions can be found as follows: ARK. STAT. ANN. § 17–86–303; COLO. STAT. § 12–38–103(1); CONN. GEN. STAT. ANN § 20–87a(b); DEL. CODE ANN. Tit. 24 § 1902(d); D.C. CODE § 2–3306.1 et. seq.; IND. CODE ANN. § 25–23–1–1(b); IDAHO CODE § 54–1402(d); KAN. STAT. ANN. § 65–1113(g); KY. REV. STAT. ANN. § 314.042; MASS. ANN. LAWS ch. 112, § 80E; MINN. STAT. ANN. § 148.235; MONT. CODE ANN. § 37–8–202(s); NEB. REV. STAT. § 71–1704 et seq.; N.C. GEN. STAT. § 90–18.2; OR. REV. STAT. § 678.375; R.I. GEN. LAWS § 5–34–35 et seq.; S.D. CODIFIED LAWS ANN. § 39–9A; TENN. CODE ANN. § 63–7–123; VA. CODE ANN. § 54.1–2957; and WASH. REV. CODE ANN. § 18.88.175.

56. American Nurses Association, *Standards for Nursing Education* 17 (1975).

57. Id. at 23.

58. Graduate education in nursing also is expanding. In 1988 there were approximately 125,000 registered nurses with master's degrees and 5,600 with doctoral degrees. Health Resources and Services Administration, Public Health Service, *1988 National Sample Survey of Registered Nurses.*

59. 196 Neb. 681, 244 N.W.2d 683 (1976).

60. For licensure the relevant Nebraska statute required that the applicant:

(1) Be of good moral character
(2) Have completed high school
(3) Have graduated from a professional school of nursing approved by the State

The applicant met these qualifications. 196 Neb. at 683, 244 N.W.2d at 686.

61. The state board of nursing was empowered to deny licenses if an applicant was guilty of unprofessional conduct. NEB. REV. STAT. § 71-1,132.29.

62. Specifically, the board found that the applicant did not recheck the temperature of a 7-month old infant who was admitted to the hospital with a reported temperature of 105°F and further failed to notify the physician of the infant's condition. 196 Neb. at 684, 244 N.W.2d at 686.

63. Id.

64. Most states have granted their state boards of nursing power to deny or revoke licenses in a fashion similar to the Nebraska statute and decisions. See, e.g., COLO. REV. STAT. § 12-38-117. WYO. STAT. ANN. § 33-21-146.

65. Id. Indeed, two recent cases indicate that boards are exercising oversight. In *Leib v. Bd. of Examiners*, 177 Conn. 78, 411 A.2d 42 (1979), the Connecticut Supreme Court upheld a decision of that state's Board of Nursing to revoke the license of a nurse who admitted that she used Demerol that she charted that she had given to a patient. The court stated, "It is to be presumed that the members of the defendant board . . . are qualified to pass upon questions of professional conduct and competence." In *Lunsford v. Bd. Nurs. Ex.*, 648 S.W. 2d 391 (Tex. App. Dist. 1983) the court upheld a one-year suspension imposed on a nurse who breached a duty of care to a patient. The court concluded that the duty arose out of the nurse-patient relationship.

66. Letter from Sharon R. Lunn, M.S., R.N., Senior Staff Specialist/Education Services, American Nurses Association (June 5, 1991).

67. Twelve states currently have mandatory continuing education for relicensing of nurses: California, Colorado, Florida, Iowa, Kansas, Kentucky, Louisiana, Massachusetts, Minnesota, Nebraska, Nevada, and New Mexico. Three states have adopted a continuing education requirement but have not begun implementation: Alabama, Ohio, and Texas. Id. Eight additional jurisdictions have specific continuing education requirements that pertain to particular groups of nurses, such as nurses who have not been employed in nursing for several years or nurses in specialized areas of practice. These jurisdictions are: Alaska, Delaware, District of Columbia, Idaho, Mississippi, New Hampshire, New York, and Oregon. In Michigan, legislation has been enacted that authorizes the Board of Nursing to impose a mandatory continuing education requirement at any time. Id.

68. Hislop and Vallor, *Continuing Education Revisited* 1976 Supervisor Nurse 36.

69. See, e.g., ALASKA STAT. § 09.55.560; ARIZ. REV. STAT. 12-561, CAL. CIV. PROC. CODE § 340.5.

70. See, e.g., CONN. GEN. STAT. ANN. § 52-584.

71. See, e.g., ME. REV. STAT. tit. 14 § 753 N.H. REV. STAT. ANN. ch. 508:4.

72. See, e.g., *Wright v. Central Du Page Hospital Ass'n*, Ill. 2d 313, 347 N.E.2d 736 (1978). The Illinois statute was found fatally defective on three grounds: First, a $500,000 limitation on the maximum recovery for medical malpractice

actions was found too arbitrary and special interest legislation in violation of the Illinois constitution. Secondly, the three-member medical malpractice review panel (consisting of a judge, an attorney, and a physician) had been empowered to make findings of fact and conclusions of law and the court found this was a restriction of the right to a jury trial guaranteed by the Illinois constitution. Finally, a statutory requirement of prior hearing and approval before an increase on medical malpractice insurance policy premiums was also found to be a special interest legislation.

In *Oregon Medical Ass'n v. Rawls*, 557 P.2d 664 (Or. 1976), a portion of the new Oregon malpractice statute was found unconstitutional. The statute attempted to deprive physicians and hospitals of the common law right to indemnity. The courts found that this violated an Oregon constitutional provision that required the legislature to provide a substitute remedy when it abolished a common law remedy. This provision was then severed from the rest of the statute.

73. For a well-documented, if somewhat dated, study of the interpretation of malpractice statute of limitations problems, see Lillich, *The Malpractice Statute of Limitations in New York and Other Jurisdictions*, 47 Cornell L.Q. 359 (1962).

74. 176 Ohio St. 370, 199 N.E.2d 878 (1964); Anot., 8 A.L.R.3d 1331 (1965).

75. The *Richardson* holding was followed in *Kambas v. St. Joseph's Mercy Hosp.*, 389 Mich. 249, 205 N.W.2d 431 (1973), and *Cordial v. Grimm*, 346 N.E.2d 266 (Ind. 976). Both of these decisions appear to have been rendered moot by recent legislative enactments. See IND. CODE ANN. § 16-9.5-1-1, 9.5-3-1; MICH. STAT. ANN. § 27A.5838.

76. 176 Ohio St. at 372, 199 N.E.2d at 380. In 1984, three justices of the Rhode Island Supreme Court quoted this statement with approval. *Vigue v. John E. Fogarty Memorial Hosp.* 481 A.2d 1, 6 (R.I. 1984).

77. *ANA Board Approves a Definition of Nursing Practice*, 55 Am. J. Nurs. 1974.

78. Interview with Rosomond Gabrielson, 1974 past president of the ANA.

79. See notes 16–18 supra and accompanying text.

80. 227 App. Div. 66, 236 N.Y.S. 641 (1929).

81. Mandatory licensure envisions a scheme in which everyone practicing nursing for compensation must be licensed by the state. See D'Amico, *Nursing Practice Acts Revisions*, 22 Ass'n Operating Room Nurses J. 105 (1975).

82. Id.

83. 11 Appl Div.2d 801, 205 N.Y.S.2d 152 (1960).

84. 83 Ohio L. Abs. 28 (C. P. Franklin County 1960).

85. In *Davis*, in order to determine if nurses were professionals, the court reviewed the nursing licensure statute. The court noted that the statute repeatedly referred to nurses as professionals and reasoned that this indicated that the legislature intended nurses to be treated as professionals. Id. at 18.

86. 69 Ohio St. 2d 471, 433 N.E. 20 162 (1982). See also *Holman v. Grandview Hospital & Medical Center*, 37 Ohio App.3d 151, 524 N.E.2d 903 (1987).

87. 65 N.Y.2d 65, 479 N.E.2d 230 (1985).

88. Id. at 71, 479 N.E.2d at 234.

89. Id. (quoting 1 Louisell & Williams, *Medical Malpractice*, § 16A.01, at 16A–2).

90. Id.

91. Id.

92. NEB. REV. STAT. § 25–208 end 222. Section 25–207 sets a four-year statute of limitations for simple negligence actions.

93. NEB. REV. STAT. § 71–1, 132.05.

94. HAWAII REV. STAT. § 657–7.3; MICH. STAT. ANN. § 27A.5838.

95. W. Prosser, *The Law of Torts* 164 (4th ed. 1971) [hereinafter cited as Prosser]. Prosser suggests that this is permitted either because the physician has impliedly represented that he will follow customary medical methods and thus should be judged in accordance with those methods or because of the respect the legal community has for a fellow profession and the reluctance to establish liability based on uneducated judgments. Id. at 165.

96. Id.

97. McCoid, *The Care Required of Medical Practitioners*, 12 Vand. L. Rev. 549 (1959).

98. Id. This rationale is applicable to this study of nurses and nursing malpractice. As described above, nurses are receiving the education to act in a more independent manner, see note 92 supra and accompanying text, and licensing laws are being changed to permit nurses legally to act in this more independent manner.

99. For an excellent discussion of the validity of letting the medical profession set its own standard of care, see King, supra note 1.

100. Prosser, supra note 95, at 164.

101. Thus, the older cases should be studied and analyzed in terms of both the state of nursing practice and the nature of the nursing act. Findings of liability based on dependent nursing acts, while historically accurate, should not be used to preclude the current necessity of expert nursing testimony to prove liability under an expanded standard of care.

102. 175 Ohio St. 503, 196 N.E.2d 592 (1964).

103. Id. at 505, 508, 196 N.E.2d at 594, 598.

104. Both *Hawkes and Richardson*, see notes 70–72 supra and accompanying text, were decided in the same year by the Ohio Supreme Court. Taken together, both opinions indicate that the Ohio court was not sympathetic to the claim that nursing was a profession.

105. 175 Ohio St. at 506, 196 N.E.2d at 595.

106. Id. at 508, 196 N.E.2d at 598.

107. See note 100 supra and accompanying text.

108. 22 Ohio App. 2d 119, 258 N.E.2d 611 (1969).

109. 31 Ohio App. 2d 118, 286 N.E.2d 308 (1972).

110. Id. at 123, 286 N.E.2d at 313.

111. Id. at 127, 286 N.E.2d at 317. Further, the dissent questioned the factual

conclusion of the court in *Jones* that an ordinary juror could determine negligence without the aid of expert testimony.

112. 45 Wis. 2d 147, 172 N.W.2d 427 (1969).

113. 262 S.E. 2d 865 (N.C. App. 1980).

114. 173 N.J. Super. 566, 414 A.2d 1350 (1980).

115. 215 KAN. 14, 523 P.2d 320 (1974).

116. There was testimony at trial that on the night in question the nurse and the plaintiff had argued about the nurse's alleged lack of concern about the plaintiff's condition. In addition, while the nurse in fact delivered the baby, the hospital records indicated that a physician delivered the baby. Since the experts had relied on the hospital records, the demonstrated inaccuracy of the records undermined the value of the expert testimony. 215 Kan. at 20–21, 523 P.2d at 326–37.

117. Id. at 19, 523 P.2d at 325.

118. Id.

119. 6 Kans. App 2d 910, 636 P.2d 215 (1981).

120. Id. at 920, 636 P.2d at 224.

121. This example is used for illustrative purposes only and is not intended to reflect or define the areas of competence of each profession.

122. The logical extension of allowing physicians to testify and to evaluate a nurse's action in those areas of shared expertise would be to allow nurses to testify as expert witnesses in an action against a physician in those same areas. Interview with Dr. Mauksch, supra note 33.

123. 246 Ga. 401, 271 S.E.2d 832 (1980). See also, Note, *The Use of Nurses as Expert Witnesses*, 19 Hous. L. Rev. 555 (1982). On the other hand, the expert witness must have specialized knowledge on the technical issue being considered. Thus, in *Fountain v. Cobb Genl. Hosp.*, 167 Ga. App. 36, 306 S.E.2d 37 (1983), the court did not permit a nurse to qualify as an expert witness because there was nothing in the record to demonstrate the nurse was an expert on the administration of anesthesia or on when an epidural catheter should be removed.

124. 368 F. Supp. 466 (W.D. La. 1973).

125. It should be noted that the defendant was not a registered nurse and therefore did not have the level of education or training that would qualify her for professional status. Thus, while the discussion in the case is helpful for the general concepts developed, the analysis would be more satisfactory if it were limited to professional nurses. The court's apparent confusion and its implied suggestion that all nurses are the same reflects judicial confusion about the current status of nursing.

126. 368 F. Suppl. at 468.

127. See, e.g. LA. REV. SAT. ANN. tit. 37 § 961.

128. ARIZ. REV. STAT. § 12–563.

129. 38 Cal.3d 137, 211 Cal. Rptr. 368, 695 P.2d 665 (1985).

130. Id. at 149, 211 Cal. Rptr. at 376, 695 P.2d at 673 (quoting the trial court's instructions to the jury).

131. Id. at 150–51, 211 Cal. Rptr. at 377, 695 P.2d at 674.

132. 592 P.2d 1332 (Ct. App. Colo. 1978).

133. 592 P.2d at 1334.

134. 99 Cal. App.3d 331, 160 Cal. Rptr. 246 (1979).

135. 99 Cal. App.3d at 333, 160 Ca. Rptr. at 251 n.8.

136. See e.g., *Koeniguer v. Eckrich*, 422 N.W.2d 600 (S.D. 1988); *Wickliffe v. Sunrise Hospital*, 706 P.2d 1383 (Nev. 1985).

137. See, e.g., *Cowan v. Doering*, 111 N.J. 451, 545 A.2d 159 (1988); *Northern Trust Co. v. Louis A. Wiss Memorial Hospital*, 143 Ill. App.3d 479, 493 N.E.2d 6 (1986); *Wickliffe v. Sunrise Hospital*, 706 P.2d 1383 (1985).

138. Prosser, supra note 95, at 164.

139. See, e.g., *Washington v. Washington Hospital Center*, 579 A.2d 177 (D.C. App. 1990); *Wickliffe v. Sunrise Hospital*, 706 P.2d 1383 (Nev. 1985); *Landeros v. Flood*, 17 Ca. 3d 399, 551 P.2d 389, 131 Cal. Rptr. 69 (1976); *Speed v. State*, 240 N.W.2d 901 (Iowa 1976).

140. See, e.g., N.H. REV. STAT. ANN. § 519.A-7.

141. 144 So.2d 249 (La. App. 1962).

142. Id at 251.

143. *Novak v. Texada, Miller, Masterson and Davis Clinic*, 514 So.2d 524 (La. App. 3 Cir. 1987).

144. 706 P.2d 1383 (Nev. 1985).

145. Id. at 1387.

146. See notes 24–40 supra and accompanying text.

147. See notes 24–25 supra and accompanying text.

148. See notes 132–33, 144–45 supra and accompanying text.

149. See notes 56–58 supra and accompanying text.

150. 143 Ill. App.3d 479, 493 N.E.2d 6 (1986).

151. Id. at 485–86, 493 N.E.2d at 10. For a discussion of the significance of the court's holding that a hospital may be liable for failure to provide properly trained nursing staff, see text following note 184 infra.

152. Id. at 493–94, 483 N.E.2d at 16.

153. See note 57 supra and accompanying text.

154. See note 58 supra and accompanying text.

155. S. Willig, *The Nurses' Guide to the Law* 59 (1970).

156. 135 Colo. 366, 311 P.2d 711 (1957).

157. I. Murchison & T. Nichols, *Legal Foundation of Nursing Practice* 245 (1970).

158. 536 S.W.2d 278 (Tex. Civ. App. 1976). Texas courts do, however, apply the captain of the ship doctrine in operating room cases. In *Ramone v. Mani*, 535 S.W.2d 654 (Tex. Civ. App. 1975), the court restated the Texas rule that "an operating surgeon may be held liable for the negligence of an assisting nurse in the general employment of the hospital when the alleged acts of negligence are done while the nurse is under the direct control or supervision of the surgeon." Id. at 655.

159. 124 N.J. Super. 285, 306 A.2d 474 (Super. Ct. App. Div. 1973).

160. Id. at 290, 306 A.2d at 476.

161. 336 So.2d 725 (La. App. 1976).

162. Id. at 734–35.

163. See note 18 supra and accompanying text.

164. See notes 27–40 supra and accompanying text.

165. See notes 56–58 supra and accompanying text.

166. See notes 41–55 supra and accompanying text.

167. See note 112 supra and accompanying text

168. See notes 109–110 supra and accompanying text.

169. See notes 80 and 115 supra and accompanying text.

170. See note 118 supra and accompanying text. But see note 123 supra and accompanying text if the issue involves an area of shared expertise.

171. Southern Regional Education Board, *Nursing Curriculum Project: Summary Recommendations* (1976). (hereinafter cited as SREB).

172. See notes 56–58 supra and accompanying text.

173. SREB supra note 171 at 9.

174. Tertiary care is provided to clients whose illnesses are rare or complex and who require specialized nursing care. Tertiary care usually is association with large medical centers and may include experimentation. SREB, supra note 171 at 9.

175. It is necessary to distinguish two bases of liability—failing to exercise professional judgment in the first instance, and exercising faulty professional judgment. This discussion focuses primarily on the duty of the professional nurse to exercise her professional judgment. It is that failure that suggests liability. Determining liability if the nurse does not exercise professional judgment but does so in a faulty manner should be subject to the "school of thought" exception that recognizes that there may be different schools of thought on how to treat a particular disease and that if a professional follows one of these schools of thought, liability cannot attach simply because other professionals would have followed other schools of thought. See Prosser, supra note 95 at 163.

176. See notes 48–55 supra and accompanying text.

177. FLA. STAT. ANN. § 464.012.

178. See notes 56–58 supra and accompanying text.

179. Yura, *A Climate to Foster Utilization of the Nursing Process, in Providing a Climate for Utilization of Nursing Personnel* 11 (1975), at 23.

180. See notes 173–174 supra and accompanying text.

181. See notes 150–152 supra and accompanying text.

182. 143 Ill. App.3d 479, 485, 493 N.E.2d 6, 10 (1986) (quoting the trial court's instructions to the jury).

183. Alford & Jensen, *Reflections on Private Practice*, 76 Am. J. Nurs. 1966 (1976).

184. See note 173 supra and accompanying text.

185. See, e.g., NEV. REV. STAT. § 632.030. A review of all 50 states supports the conclusion that a majority of states include laypersons on their state board of nursing.

Chapter **13**

THIRD-PARTY REIMBURSEMENT FOR SERVICES OF NURSES IN ADVANCED PRACTICE: OBTAINING PAYMENT FOR YOUR SERVICES

Pamela Mittelstadt

T HE recognition and direct payment of nursing services by third-party payers is critical to the practice of nursing and has been a long-term goal of the profession. The direct reimbursement of nurses for their services, in particular nurses in advanced practice, in seen as a major factor in their ability to practice (Caraher, 1988). Recently there have been significant gains in the achievement of third-party reimbursement for the services of nurses in advanced practice. Changes in federal and state laws have increased the reimbursement of these services by public and private payers. This chapter will review the reimbursement authority nurses in advanced practice have under federal programs, state programs, and in private insurance plans. The discussion will focus primarily on nurses in advanced practice—nurse practitioners, clinical nurse specialists, nurse-midwives, and certified registered nurse anesthetists.

THE THIRD PARTY REIMBURSEMENT SYSTEM

Third-Party Payers

The well-established system of health insurance provided by both the public and private sector in this country has put the consumer in a unique position when purchasing health care—a position that is very different than in purchasing other consumer goods and services. The consumer purchasing health care from providers frequently does not make direct out-of-pocket payments for these services. When direct or out-of-pocket payments are made, they are usually for only a small percent of the total cost of the service. This situation occurs as a result of the health insurance system, whereby services are paid for by third-party payers that are the financial intermediaries between consumers and providers. The type of services covered and the level of payment are specific to the policy plan of the third party payer (LaBar, 1986).

There are three major categories of third-party payers: private health insurance companies, public government sponsored programs designed for specific groups of beneficiaries, and independent plans. The private health insurance industry has both nonprofit and for-profit companies and in 1989 accounted for the payment of 33 percent of national health care expenditures (Levit & Lazenby, 1991).

Blue Cross and Blue Shield is an example of a nonprofit insurance plan that is tax-exempt and is directed by a board representing the hospitals, medical profession, and the public in a particular region. (There is one known instance of a nurse serving on a regional board of directors.) These regional plans are coordinated through a central organization. Each regional plan usually represents a state and functions in a noncompetitive manner with other regional plans. Blue Cross was assisted in its development by the American Hospital Association to help assure payment of individuals' hospital bills. Blue Shield plans were originally developed by local medical associations to assist in the payment of physicians' services.

Commercial insurance companies, such as Aetna, are for-profit and pay taxes. These insurers frequently provide other types of insurance, such as life insurance (LaBar, 1986).

Independent plans are private insurance plans, such as self-insured employer plans, union plans, health maintenance organizations, and preferred provider organizations (LaBar, 1985). Health maintenance organizations (HMOs) offer comprehensive health care services to their members for a fixed periodic payment. Preferred provider organizations (PPOs) are groups of providers, such as physicians and hospitals, who contract to give services on a fee-for-service basis, usually for a discount to a specific group of beneficiaries. Self-insured employer plans are arranged by the employer and the employer assumes the financial risk. These plans may be administrated by an insurance company (American Nurses Association [ANA], 1991). Union plans make health insurance available to their members (Health Insurance Association of America [HIAA], 1990).

Government sponsored programs in 1989 accounted for 42% of health care expenditures. (Besides private insurance, other sources of payment for health care were out-of-pocket, at 21%, and private sources, at 4%.) The two largest government programs are Medicare and Medicaid. In 1989 Medicare and Medicaid paid one-fourth of the national health care bill. Both programs were established in 1965 by amendments to the Social Security Act (Levit & Lazenby, 1991).

Medicare is a health insurance program that provides hospital and medical insurance protection to those persons aged 65 and older, disabled persons under age 65 who receive cash benefits under Social Security or Railroad Retirement programs, and people of all ages with chronic kidney disease. It is financed by employer and employee contributions through payroll taxes and beneficiaries' copayments and premiums. The program is administered by a federal agency, the Health Care Financing Administration (HCFA) of the Department of Health and Human Services (HIAA, 1990).

Medicaid is a jointly funded federal-state program of medical assistance for certain low-income individuals and families. The program is administered by each state according to federal requirements that stipulate basic services covered and eligible individuals. States may choose to expand services and population served (HIAA, 1990).

Other public programs are the Civilian Health and Medical Program of the Uniformed Services (CHAMPUS) and the Federal Employees Health Benefit Program (FEHBP). CHAMPUS provides medical benefits to about 8 million specified military personnel and their families, who are unable to use government medical facilities. REHBP is a voluntary program that provides health insurance for about four million federal employees and their dependents (HIAA, 1990).

Importance of Third-Party Reimbursement for Nurses

Since 1948, the American Nurses Association (ANA) has pressed for the recognition of third-party payment for nursing services in prepaid health insurance plans (ANA, 1977). The achievement of this recognition has many significant effects on the profession of nursing and on the delivery of health care. The direct payment of nursing services promotes the following:

1. Improved access to health care, especially for the vulnerable groups of the elderly, poor, disabled, minorities, and those living in underserved areas, such as rural areas (Harrington, 1991).
2. Increased recruitment and retention of nurses by becoming a profession that receives adequate compensation and direct payment for its services (Harrington, 1991).
3. Improved recognition of nursing as a profession (Hogue, 1989).
4. Increased practice and full utilization of nurses as the providers of health care services (Pulcini, 1984).
5. Recognition of nurses as independent providers and increased autonomy and authority to act for patients' benefits (Hoffman & Fonteyn, 1988).
6. Increased ability to practice without the limit of the employer/employee relationship.
7. Increased consumer access to qualified health care providers (LaBar, 1986).
8. Empowered nurses' roles in the health care system (Mittelstadt, 1991).

Barriers to Obtaining Third-Party Reimbursement

Despite the efforts of the professional nursing community and studies that have documented the quality of nursing services (Office of Technology Assessment, 1986), the direct payment of nursing services by third-party payers has not been fully achieved. There have been many well-recognized barriers to the obtainment of reimbursement that have slowed the process.

One major barrier has been the opposition of organized medicine. Organized medicine has lobbied against federal and state legislation that would allow the direct reimbursement of nursing services, and against the revisions in state nurse practice acts to allow nurses to practice in the expanded role. Another barrier has been the rapid rise in health care costs and the massive federal budget. Members of Congress and the executive branch have been reluctant to increase reimbursement for nurses because of a fear that an increase in the number of providers will increase the costs of health care. There is also the fear

TABLE 13.1   Federal Reimbursement of Nurses in Advanced Practice

	Nurse Providers			
	Nurse Practitioner	Certified Nurse-Midwife	Certified Registered Nurse Anesthetiot	Clinical Nurse Specialist
Federal Programs				
MEDICARE				
Part A	No	No	No	No
Part B	Yes[1]	Yes	Yes	Yes[2]
MEDICAID	Yes[3]	Yes	State discretion	State discretion
CHAMPUS*	Yes	Yes	Yes	Yes[4]
FEHB**	Yes	Yes	Yes	Yes

[1]Limited to nursing facilities and rural areas.
[2]Limited to rural areas.
[3]Limited to Pediatric NPs and Family NPs.
[4]Limited to certified psychiatric nurse specialists.
*Civilian Health and Medical Program of Uniformed Services.
**Federal Employee Health Benefit Program.
Source: American Nurses Association (1992).

of third-party payers that the reimbursement of nursing services will lead to the reimbursement of other providers, followed by an increase in costs. Yet another impediment to the achievement of reimbursement is the lack of knowledge the public has of the extent of the care that can be provided by nurses. Consumer demand for access to nursing services would have a powerful effect on achieving direct payment for services.

LEGISLATION MANDATING THIRD-PARTY REIMBURSEMENT FOR NURSES

Federal Government-Sponsored Programs

The services of nurses in advanced practice are reimbursed under four federal programs: Medicare, Medicaid, FEHBP, and CHAMPUS. Table 13-1 shows the coverage of those services by category of nurses and program.

Medicare

Medicare consists of two parts: Part A, for hospitalization insurance, and Part B, a voluntary supplementary medical insurance. Under Part A, nursing services are covered as part of the payment received by hospitals for inpatient stays. Medicare Part B coverage includes physician services, treatment for end-stage renal disease, durable medical equipment, hospital outpatient services, and laboratory services and rural health clinics (Health Care Financing Administration [HCFA], 1988).

Medicare Part B covers nursing services in eight areas:

1. The services of nurses, who are employees of physicians, are reimbursed by Medicare under the "incident to" provision. This provision states that services that are furnished as an incident to a physician's professional service, are commonly furnished in physicians' offices, and are commonly either rendered without charge or included in physicians' bills will be reimbursed and payment will go to the physician. The service must be furnished as an integral, although incidental, part of the physician's personal and professional services in the course of diagnosing or treating any injury or illness. In addition, the service delivered by the physician's employee must be delivered under the physician's direct supervision. Supervision in the office setting means the physician must be present on site, but not necessarily in the same room. (HCFA, 1991).

An incident to service delivered by a nurse practitioner is one that is related to the clinical reason for the patient seeing the physician. For example, the physician conducts a comprehensive assessment for possible hypertension. On the return visit the patient sees the nurse practitioner for follow-up and assessment of blood pressure, nutrition, and medications. This visit to the nurse practitioner would be an "incident to" visit. The claim submitted for Medicare payment would indicate the employing physician's provider number and the payment would be at the physician's rate.

Medicare regional carriers have interpreted differently the coverage of services under this provision, which leads to much confusion. Some carriers determine "incident to" services to mean the administration of medications or treatments. Others interpret the provision more broadly to include physical assessments.

2. Nurse practitioner (NP) services are covered when provided in rural health clinics. In 1977 (Public Law 95–210) Congress authorized reimbursement for any medical service typically furnished by a physician in an office or as a home visit, whether performed by a physician, NP, or physician's assistant in a rural health clinic. The intent of the legisla-

tion was to improve access to care in rural areas. This provision is also included under Medicaid. The payment is to the clinic and not directly to the NP. Services must be periodically reviewed by a physician (Wriston, 1981).

3. NP services are covered in Medicare health maintenance organizations (HMOs) and competitive medical plans (CMP). The payment goes directly to the HMO in the form of a prepaid, capitated payment for each enrolled beneficiary (Michels, 1990).

4. In 1986 Congress (Public Law 99–509) authorized direct reimbursement to certified registered nurse anesthetists (CRNAs) to be effective in 1988. In 1990 Congress (Public Law 101–508) authorized the payment rates to differ depending on whether they are medically directed or nonmedically directed. By 1996 payment rates for nonmedically directed CRNAs will be the same as payment rates for anesthesiologists for the same service.

5. The services of certified nurse midwives (CNMs) were covered in 1987 (Public Law 100–203). The payment goes directly to the CNM and is at the rate of 65% of the prevailing charge that would be recognized if the service had been performed by a physician. No supervision by any other health professional is required. However, in states where supervision is required, that requirement must be met (Michels, 1990). Although only approximately 50 births per year occur to mothers who are Medicare beneficiaries, Medicare reimbursement was sought by the CNMs because Medicare usually determines payment policy for other third party payers.

6. Community Nursing Organization (CNO) demonstration projects were authorized by Congress in 1987 (Public Law 100–203). A CNO allows the nurse to coordinate and establish the plan of care for Medicare beneficiaries in need of postacute health care services, such as home health. Payment to the CNO is a prepaid, capitated monthly fee per CNO enrollee. In return, the CNO is at risk to provide all the postacute care services that may be needed by the enrollee and are required by Medicare. Minimum services include nursing care, physical, occupational, or speech therapy, social services, home health care, and durable medical equipment. The CNO may offer additional services, such as health promotion and disease prevention services, for a small monthly premium paid by the enrollee.

7. Nurse practitioners received reimbursement authority for services provided to residents of nursing facilities in 1989 (Public Law 101–239). The enactment of this provision occurred at a time when Congress was concerned about improving the care of nursing home residents. Payment for the NP services are made to the employer of the NP. The NP must be an employee or have a contractual relationship with the indi-

vidual or facility who submits the claim and excludes the ability of a group of NPs to act as the employer. The NP must work in collaboration with a physician. Payment is made on assignment and will not exceed 85% of the prevailing charge rate. The services are performed by a member of a team who can be an NP, physician, or physician assistant, and the provision allows for up to 1.5 visits per month per resident.

8. Nurse practitioner and clinical nurse specialist (CNS) services were covered in 1990 (Public Law 101–508) if the service is provided in a rural area. The intent of this provision was to improve access to primary care in rural areas. This provision allows for the direct reimbursement of NPs and CNSs working in collaboration with a physician. The services covered are those that NPs and CNSs are legally authorized to provide according to state law and are covered by the Medicare program, including mental health services. The payment level is 85% of the prevailing charge for services provided in outpatient settings and 75% for services provided on an inpatient basis.

Medicaid

Because the Medicaid program is administered by the states, all states have the ability to pay for the services delivered by nurses and some states have chosen to pay for the services of some nurses in advanced practice. (See Table 13-2 for a list of those states and categories of nurses with Medicaid reimbursement authority.) However, not all states have chosen to cover the services of nurses in advanced practice, and Congress has taken the opportunity to mandate the coverage of certain nurse practitioners in order to increase access to care in certain areas or for certain vulnerable populations. Those federal mandates are as follows:

1. Under the Rural Health Clinics Act, NP services are covered in rural clinics.
2. Private duty nursing is a mandatory service of the Medicaid program. The payment goes to the employer of the nurse.
3. Certified nurse-midwife services are also a covered mandatory service. The provision was enacted by Congress in 1980 (Public Law 96–499). Payment goes directly to the CNM and supervision requirements are dependent on state law.
4. In 1989 Congress enacted mandatory coverage of certified pediatric nurse practitioner (PNP) and certified family nurse practitioner (FNP) services because of concern for the high rate of infant mortality (Public Law 101–239). Under this provision PNPs and FNPs are paid directly for their services and need not be under the supervision of or

TABLE 13.2   Medicaid Reimbursement of Nurses in Advanced Practice by State

States	NP*	CNS	CNM*	CRNA**
AL			x	x
AK			x	
AZ			x	x
AR	x		x	x
CA	x		x	x
CO	x		x	x
CT			x	
DE			x	
DC	x		x	
FL	x	x	x	x
GA			x	
HI	x		x	
ID	x		x	
IL			x	x
IN			x	
IA			x	x
KS	x	x	x	x
KY	x		x	x
LA	x		x	x
ME			x	
MD	x		x	x
MA	x		x	
MI			x	
MN	x	x	x	x
MS	x		x	x
MO	x		x	x
MT	x		x	x
NE			x	x
NV	x		x	x
NH	x			
NJ	x	x	x	
NM	x		x	x
NY	x		x	
NC	x		x	
ND			x	
OH			x	x
OK			x	x
OR	x		x	x
PA	x		x	

(continued)

TABLE 13.2 (*continued*)

States	Nurses in Advanced Practice			
	NP*	CNS	CNM*	CRNA**
RI			X	
SC			X	X
SD	X		X	X
TN			X	X
TX	X	X	X	X
UT			X	
VT			X	
VA			X	
WA	X		X	
WV	X		X	X
WI	X	X	X	X
WY			X	X

*All states by federal mandate must cover the services of certified nurse midwives and pediatric nurse practitioners and family nurse practitioners.
NP = nurse practitioner
CNS = clinical nurse specialist
CNM = certified nurse-midwife
CRNA = certified nurse anesthetist
Source: From American Nurses Association, Division of Governmental Affairs, 1992.

associated with a physician or other health care provider. Services covered are those which are covered by the Medicaid program and those which the PNPs and FNPs are legally authorized to perform in accordance with State law or State regulations. Some states, such as New York and Wisconsin, have chosen to expand the provision to all NPs.

Federal Employee Health Benefit Plan

This health insurance plan for federal employees has been affected by two federal changes in the law mandating the coverage of nursing services.

1. In 1985 Congress mandated that the services of nonphysician providers, including registered nurses, be covered in all federal health plans in medically underserved areas. This provision would cover the services of all nurses in advanced practice.
2. The services of NPs, CNSs, and CNMs were covered by a Congressional mandate (Public Law 101–509) in 1990. Under this provision, insurance carriers for federal employee plans must make payment directly to these providers if their services are a covered service under

the plan. For example, if the service, such as immunization, is a covered service, then the provider would receive payment. This provision does not require collaboration with or supervision by any other health care practitioner.

Civilian Health and Medical Program of the Uniformed Service (CHAMPUS)

Nurses in advanced practice have limited coverage under this program.

1. The services of certified nurse midwives were covered in 1979 (Public Law 95–457). The provision provides for direct payment and does not require physician supervision.
2. The services of certified nurse practitioners and certified psychiatric nurse specialists were covered in 1982 (Public Law 97–114) and, as in the case of the CNMs, physician supervision is not required.

Private Health Insurance Programs

Increased reimbursement under federal programs, especially Medicare, has had a significant effect on the coverage of the services of nurses in privately sponsored health insurance programs, such as Blue Cross and Blue Shield plans and Aetna plans. In fact, health policy analysts see Medicare as the trend setter for all health policy plans. In addition, changes in state health insurance laws and individual nurses' negotiations with private plans have also increased third-party reimbursement of nursing services.

A large proportion of the health care dollar spent on personal health care is reimbursed by private health insurers, as compared to the proportion spent by federal and state government plans. In 1988 private insurance plans, including Blue Cross and Blue Shield plans, spent $312.4 billion (57.8%) out of a total of $539.9 billion on medical and health care services, including research and medical facility construction. The federal and state government share was $227.5 billion. Of those who have some kind of health insurance, 86% are covered by private plans (HIAA, 1990). Thus, the largest share of third-party reimbursed health care is financed by the private sector.

Many nurses in advanced practice submit claims and are reimbursed for their services, even though an insurance policy does not explicitly include the coverage of nursing services. According to a survey conducted by the Blue Cross/Blue Shield (1988), of 69 plans, over 60% paid for the services of NPs and CNMs. However, data is not available on the number of private plans that reimburse claims for the services of nurses.

Changes in State Health Insurance Laws

Beginning in the late 1970s, state legislatures began to mandate the coverage of nursing services in health insurance plans (See Table 13-3.) Since 1977, 35 states have passed laws requiring the coverage of services delivered by nurses, certified nurse midwives, nurse practitioners, certified registered nurse anesthetists, and psychiatric nurses (Blue Cross/Blue Shield Association, 1990).

State health insurance laws vary according to three factors: (1) insurers affected, (2) providers affected, and (3) reimbursable services (La-Bar, 1985).

Insurers Affected

State health insurance laws affect two types of insurers: nonprofit and commercial or for-profit insurers. Most laws affect all types of insurance policies, such as individual and group policies, hospital and medical service plans, disability insurance contracts, self-insured employee welfare plans, and fraternal benefit society contracts. Some state laws will only affect nonprofit plans. In these states nurses have negotiated directly with commercial insurance companies to receive reimbursement.

Another variable affecting coverage is whether the law is a mandatory benefit law or a mandatory option law. Mandatory benefit laws are preferable because it requires the coverage of the nursing service, while mandatory option laws only require the insurer to offer nurse reimbursement as an option. In this case, nurses need to do extensive consumer education to inform subscribers of the option available.

Providers Affected

Not all nurse providers are affected when a state health insurance law is changed, as is seen in Table 13-3. The category of nurses affected by the law is determined by the lobbying of special interest groups, such as the certified registered nurse anesthetists, or the health care needs of the state. A state may need increased availability of prenatal care and would be inclined to change state health insurance laws to mandate coverage of nurse-midwifery services.

As of September, 1990, 8 states require the coverage of the services of all registered nurses; 14 require the services of NPs to be covered; 24

TABLE 13.3   States Mandating Third-Party Coverage for Nurses by Year Enacted

States	All RNs	NPs	CNMs*	CRNAs**	Psychiatric Nurses
AL		x	x	x	
AK		x		x	
AZ		x		x	
AR					
CA			x		x
CO	x		x	x	x
CT		x	x		
DE		x		x	
FL			x		
GA					
HI					
ID					
IL					
IN					
IA	x				
KS		x		x	
KY					
LA					
ME					
MD		x	x	x	x
MA			x		x
MI					
MN		x	x	x	
MS		x	x	x	
MO			x		
MT		x	x	x	
NE					
NV		x	x		
NH		x			
NJ	x		x	x	
NM			x	x	
NY	x		x		
NC					
ND	x	x	x	x	x
OH			x		
OK					
OR		x	x		
PA		x	x	x	x
RI		x	x		
SC					

(continued)

TABLE 13.3 *(continued)*

States	All RNs	NPs	CNMs*	CRNAs**	Psychiatric Nurses
SD		x	x	x	
TN					
TX					
UT	x	x	x		x
VT					
VA					x
WA	x	x	x	x	x
WV	x	x	x	x	
WI					
WY					x
DC					

RN = registered nurse
NP = nurse practitioner
CNM = certified nurse midwife
CRNA = certified registered nurse anesthetist
*American College of Nurse-Midwives, 1992.
**American Association of Nurse Anesthetists, 1992.
Source: American Nurses Association, Governmental Affairs Division, 1992.

require coverage for nurse-midwives; 9 for certified registered nurse anesthetists; and 9 for psychiatric nurses (Blue Cross/Blue Shield, 1990). Some states will choose to change the law to affect most categories of nurse providers in a given year, such as Arizona, Mississippi, Montana, North Dakota, Pennsylvania, and Washington. Other states achieved the coverage of all nurse providers over several years. Maryland achieved coverage over a four-year period, while South Dakota changed the laws in a period of nine years. The state laws will also sometimes address additional requirements for the nurse provider, such as certification by a private certifying agency or national professional association.

Reimbursable Services

State health insurance laws also affect the services that can be reimbursed. Most laws will name the services of the nurse provider, such as the services provided by nurse-midwives. However, the law will allow for the reimbursement of all services within the lawful scope of practice of the nurse provider (LaBar, 1985). All legislation passed at this time includes language that limits the reimbursement of services to those covered in current health insurance plans within the state.

Implementation of Third-Party Reimbursement Legislation

The passage of a federal or state law is just the first step in a series of three steps for obtaining reimbursement. The development of rules and/or instructions for the implementation of the laws is the second step. These require careful monitoring and lobbying. Although the law will outline the scope of coverage, the federal or state agency is given the responsibility for defining the provider involved, the scope of services, and the conditions that must be met for reimbursement. The law may or may not identify an effective date. If none is mentioned then the law's implementation may be more difficult, requiring intensive lobbying.

The federal government's rulemaking process is quite cumbersome and in spite of an existing effective date, there may be a delay in the implementation. In many cases the federal agency will issue instructional guidelines to be followed until the rulemaking process is complete.

The rules for the implementation of a state health insurance law will most likely be written by a state health insurance commission. This will require the interested parties to meet with the commission to explain the practice of the nurse provider and her services and to affirm the interest in the implementation of this law. The implementation of state mandates for Medicaid services and state health insurance laws has been known to have taken several years due to the politics of health care and the public's unawareness of nurses as independent providers of health care.

The third step is the education of the nurse providers affected by the law. Nurses must be informed about the passage and implementation of reimbursement laws in order to utilize their authority. If nurses do not access these reimbursement provisions, the benefits of reimbursement will not be realized.

KEY REIMBURSEMENT ISSUES

Despite nursing's long history of interest in third-party reimbursement, several issues still remain. Which nursing services are reimbursed? Should the payment of all nursing services be direct? What is the level of payment for nursing services? What makes a nursing service cost-effective?

Reimbursable Services

Under most third-party insurance laws, only the services delivered by nurses that are already covered by an existing health plan or are considered to be a physician service are reimbursed. This excludes many of those services provided by nurses that are considered unique to the practice of nursing, such as health promotion services. The nursing profession can help move this discussion by identifying those services, showing how those services are provided in a cost-effective way, and identifying the costs of these services (LaBar, 1986).

Direct Payment

The issue of direct payment to nurses appears to be resolved when it comes to the payment of nurses in advanced practice. Direct payment gives nurses more control over their practice, eliminates unnecessary barriers, and reduces the costs of health care (McGrath, 1990; Pulcini, 1984). However, where a nurse is employed by an institution, such as a hospital, the issue has not been resolved. Identification of the cost of nurses' services has been seen as important to the control of nursing practice. The identification of nursing services in an institutional setting and the development of a common method to allocate costs has not been sufficiently developed for nurses to receive direct payment for their services in those settings.

Payment Level

The payment level for the services of nurses in advanced practice has received considerable attention lately with Congress's plan to reform payment to physicians under the Medicare program. Because of the increased rise in health care costs, and especially the costs of physician care, Congress mandated that a new system be in place by 1992 that will contain the rising costs of physician services. This action has particular importance to nurses in advanced practice because they are directly reimbursed under the Medicare program and also because this new policy change will affect the way other payers reimburse their services (Mittelstadt, 1991).

The new Medicare payment system for physicians' services, which is a national fee schedule dependent on a resource-based relative value scale, values similar services at the same rate regardless of the provider. For example, a similar service delivered by a neurologist and a family practitioner would be paid the same by Medicare. Several professional nursing organizations, including the American Nurses Association, have adapted that position to the payment of nurses' services and have stated that the value of a similar service should be the same, regardless of whether the service is provided by a nurse or a physician. The actual payment for the service delivered by the nurse may be less, depending on the other costs involved in the provision of the service, such as overhead costs and malpractice liability costs (ANA, 1990).

Some have argued that in a truly competitive market the service should be paid at the level of the lowest cost provider; nurses in many instances, would be that lowest cost provider. But this new Medicare payment system is not a competitive system but a regulatory one with the establishment of prices for services. The system also contains barriers that prevent nurses from effectively marketing their services to consumers (Pulcini, 1984). Others have stated that the payment of a similar service should be the same for both physician and nurse because to do otherwise would imply that the services of nurses were of lesser value than those of physicians. Nurses' clients would feel that they have received a second rate service (Harrington, 1991; Pulcini, 1984).

There exists also the option to continue paying for nurses in advanced practice at the current discounted rate because this will encourage facilities to hire nurses in advanced practice over physicians. Education costs are different for nurses and they should be paid less (McGrath, 1990). While nurses' salaries may also be less because they deliver less costly services, the economic incentive for health care practices or facilities to employ nurses rises as the reimbursement rate increases. A lower rate of reimbursement can act as a disincentive for employers to hire nurses with skills that could substitute for the physician service (Pulcini, 1984). The employers, such as nursing homes and hospitals, receive their payment from third-party payers.

The issue of payment level will be resolved in the Congress. A federal commission has presented its recommendations to Congress on this issue and professional nursing associations are working with the Congress to achieve an appropriate payment level (Physician Payment Review Commission Report to Congress, 1991).

Cost Effectiveness

The cost effectiveness of nursing has been used as an incentive for third-party payers to reimburse nurses. However, this concept has sometimes been misused. Nurses should not present themselves as cheaper providers, but rather as high-quality providers who can offer health promotion and disease prevention services and lower the costs of health care through their style of practice. Studies have shown that nursing services can reduce the utilization of hospitals, emergency rooms, and nursing homes and can reduce the costs of laboratory services and save physician time (Feldman & Ventura, 1987; Harrington, 1991; see also Freund, Chapter 3). Nurses' style of practice has also been shown to be cost-effective to the consumer through increased compliance to treatment (Office of Technology Assessment, 1986).

CONCLUSION

There have been significant changes in the reimbursement of nursing services by both public and private payers. More federal reimbursement has been mandated in the last two years than since the inception of Medicare and Medicaid, 25 years ago. Since 1986, 21 additional states have passed state health insurance laws to reimburse nursing services, bringing the total number of states with changes in health insurance laws to 35. This increased recognition of nursing by third-party payers has contributed to nursing's increased autonomy and to nursing's stronger role in the nation's health care system.

Barriers to practice still remain in the indirect payment of nursing services and the many conditions on reimbursement. Nursing needs to carefully monitor practice acts and prescriptive authority. These areas are frequently under attack by those who would like to limit nurses' ability to practice independently.

To improve the utilization of nurses, the services need to be clearly identified, and a price should be put on the delivery of those services. This would allow for the costing and direct payment of nursing services in institutional settings.

Another area that needs to be addressed is the education of the public on the provision of primary health care services by nurses. Until the public is aware of the expanded role of nursing, the complete utilization of nurses will not take place, and the real benefits to the public of increased access to health care and choice of health care providers will not be realized.

REFERENCES

American Nurses Association. (1977). *Reimbursement for nursing services: Position statement of the commissioner on economic and general welfare*. Kansas City, MO: Author.

American Nurses Association (1990, December 5). Testimony before the Physician Payment Review Commission.

American Nurses Association (1991a). *Third party payment for nurses. State issues*. Kansas City, MO: Author.

Blue Cross/Blue Shield Association. *1988 survey of 69 Blue Cross/Blue Shield plans*.

Caraher, M. T. (1988). The importance of third-party reimbursement for NPs. *Nurse Practitioner, 13*(4), 50, 52, 54.

Feldman, M. J., & Ventura, M. R. (1987). Studies of nurse practitioner effectiveness. *Nursing Research, 36*(5), 303–308.

Harrington, C. (1991). *Effects of nursing reimbursement rates on access to care for Medicare beneficiaries, particularly those who are underserved*. Unpublished manuscript.

Health Care Financing Administration (1988). *Medicare and Medicaid Data Book*. Washington, DC: U.S. Government Printing Office.

Health Care Financing Administration. (1991). *Medicare Carrier's Manual*. Washington, DC: U.S. Government Printing Office.

Health Insurance Association of America. *Source book of health insurance data: 1990*. Washington, DC: U.S. Government Printing Office.

Hoffman, S. E., & Fonteyn, M. E. (1988). Third party reimbursement for CNS consultation. *Nursing Economics, 6*(5), 245–247.

Hogue, E. E. (1989). Opportunities for nurses seeking third party reimbursement using existing mechanisms. *Pediatric Nursing, 15*(3), 279–280.

LaBar, C. (1985). Third-party reimbursement: Status of legislation. *Oncology Nursing Forum, 12*(6), 53–58.

LaBar, C. (1986). Third-party reimbursement for services of nurses. In M. D. Mezey & D.O.M. McGivern (Eds.), *Nurses, nurse-practitioners: The evolution of primary care*. (pp. 450–470). Boston: Little, Brown.

Levit, K. R., & Lazenby, H. C. (1991). National health care spending, 1989. *Health Affairs, 10*(1), 117–130.

McGrath, M. S. (1990). The cost-effectiveness of nurse practitioners. *Nurse Practitioner, 15*(7), 40–42.

Michels, K. (1990). ANA policy on reimbursement for nurses. Washington, DC: American Nurses Association.

Mittelstadt, P. (1991). Laws empower nurses as independent providers. *The American Nurse, 23*(1), 7.

Physician Payment Review Commission (1991). *Annual report*. Washington, DC.

Pulcini, J. (1984). Perspectives on level of reimbursement for nursing services. *Nursing Economics, 2*(2), 118–124.

U.S. Congress, Office of Technology Assessment. (1986). Nurse practitioners, physician assistants, and certified nurse-midwives: A policy analysis (Health Technology Case Study 37), OTA–HCS–37. Washington, DC: U.S. Government Printing Office.

Wriston, S. (1981). Nurse practitioner reimbursement. *Journal of Health Politics, Policy & Law, 6*(3), 444–462.

Chapter 14

POLITICS AND POLICY IN PRIMARY CARE

Pamela J. Maraldo

I N these days of ubiquitous cost containment, many health manpower authorities believe that it makes eminently good sense to use nurses as the mainstream primary care providers in our society (Davis, 1992; Garrard, Kane, Ratner, & Buchanan, 1991; Moccia, 1992; Office of Technology Assessment [OTA], 1986). Recent proposals to establish a national health plan have been criticized and often dismissed for their lack of attention to economic pressures and failure to include cost containment measures. In this regard, the merit of widespread use of nurses as primary care providers in a variety of delivery settings is often overlooked. Though the utilization of the nurse practitioner is not without political controversy, it has been shown to alleviate cost, quality, and access problems. Experience and more than a decade of data suggest that nursing manpower can be substituted for relatively expensive physician manpower without impairing the quality of care. Nurses over the last decade have provided access to primary care services in rural and urban shortage areas for populations who would not have otherwise received care. It has been shown time and again that nurses are effective providers of primary care for adults with acute and chronic illness, providing care consistent with patients' and families' biological and social needs (OTA, 1986).

It is an important time for nurses to assume more leadership in society. Health professionals and policymakers alike are becoming acutely aware of the serious problems we face in health care delivery. Indeed, the limits of our current system have become all too apparent (Califano, 1986; Davis, 1992; Hayward, Shapiro, Freeman, & Corey, 1988). Because nursing focuses on the total needs of the individual, consumers of health services would do well to begin to regard nurses as the mainstream primary care providers of the health care system.

It is now well established that an independent nurse provider is employable for half the price of a physician. The quality of care provided by a nurse practitioner, as measured by patient satisfaction and patient recovery, is rated equal to or higher than that provided by a physician (OTA, 1986; see also Freund, Chapter 3).

In studies of home and nursing home care of chronically ill elderly persons utilizing nurse practitioners, hospitalization frequency, and length of stay were markedly reduced when compared with similar populations receiving traditional care. Not surprisingly, nurse practitioners have been found to expand service, order fewer costly procedures, provide more health education, and show sensitivity to the needs of the entire family system (Garrard et al., 1991; Kane et al., 1989; Mezey, 1991; Riner, 1989).

Presently, many nurse practitioners are providing care to underserved populations and show promise for addressing many of society's unmet health needs. And indeed, in recent years policymakers have begun to make incremental changes in the Medicare program that will enable the potential of nurse practitioners to come to fruition. The Omnibus Reconciliation Act of 1989 was responsible for the reimbursement, under the Medicare program, of nurse practitioners in nursing homes (OBRA, 1989). It is estimated that the total reimbursement of these nurse providers under the Medicare program will substantially alleviate the shortage of primary care services in the long-term care area.

Another area where policymakers have considered the potential for nurse practitioners to provide basic health services has been in rural health areas through the country. In the 1990 Rural Health Services Act, sponsored by Senator Tom Daschle, nurse practitioners were reimbursed under Medicare because of the very pressing need for basic health care in rural areas (Rural Health Act, 1990).

The utilization of nurse practitioners has historically been met with strong resistance—especially if there is an oversupply of physicians—by the American Medical Association (AMA). For example, at the 1982 and 1990 annual meetings of the AMA, delegates voted to place a moratorium on supporting any further federal funding of these programs. Withdrawal of federal funding could have serious repercussions, placing formidable restrictions on the continued growth of the nurse practitioner movement and precluding access to care in many underserved areas.

In order to forecast nursing's place in the delivery of primary care in light of the changing health care system, it is helpful to examine federal policy as it applies to the development of nurse practitioners

Federal Policy
Preparation of Nurse Practitioners for Primary Care

When federal health manpower authorities refer to a nurse involved in the provision of primary care, they use the term *nurse practitioner*. Primary care in this context has two dimensions: (1) a person's first contact in any given episode of illness with the health care system that leads to a decision of what must be done to help resolve the problem; and (2) the responsibility for the continuum of care, that is, maintenance of health, evaluation and management of symptoms, and appropriate referrals (Department of Health, Education and Welfare, 1971).

From the outset, the nurse practitioner created considerable controversy in the nursing community, and initially there was a definite lack of acceptance of this new role on the part of nursing leadership. Many leaders in the profession maintained that nurses have always been involved in the business of delivering primary care, and resisted the idea of an expanded role because the expansion was thought to be into the realm of medical practice (Rogers, 1978). In such a context, nursing considered the nurse practitioner concept to be "other-defined," or an infringement on nursing's ability to chart its own destiny. After all, it was not nursing's idea, and was not, nurses claimed, developed according to nursing's standards, despite the fact that public and private recognition of nurses in the delivery of primary care virtually began anew with the innovation of the nurse practitioner role. The specific underpinnings of nursing's opposition will become apparent with a closer look at the birth of the nurse practitioner concept and the political forces in the health care field that impinged on the development. In the meantime, gradual acceptance of the concept by the nursing community has grown, and at present both the National League for Nursing (NLN) and the American Nurses Association (ANA) have developed definitions of the nurse practitioner and position statements regarding their usage. Today there is very little opposition among nurses to the nurse practitioner role.

SUPPORT FOR NURSE PRACTITIONERS

Following successful evaluation of the first nurse practitioner demonstration program, the federal government eventually invested close to $100 million developing the practitioner role. Precise figures are not possible because of the wide range of federal bureaus and foundations that provided support for these programs. The Health Resources Administration, the National Center for Health Services Research, and the Department of Labor all funded nurse practitioner programs. Beginning in 1969 with a request by then Secretary of the Department of Health, Education, and Welfare (DHEW) Elliot Richardson, who asked a group of leaders in health care to examine and report on the potential of these new practitioners, the movement gained visibility and expanded rapidly. This landmark report, *Extending the Scope of Nursing Practice*, concluded that enlarging the role of the nurse was absolutely essential to providing equal access to health services to all citizens:

> Without a doubt, the nursing profession can and must occupy a larger and more effective place in the delivery of health services for the American people. . . . A basic problem is that many nurses are not practicing at their highest potential nor receiving training and experience that would enable them to extend the scope of their practice and thereby extend the availability of health services. (DHEW, 1971)

Beginning in the early 1970s, the federal government became seriously interested in the potential benefits of preparing new health practitioners. In his annual health message in 1971, President Richard M. Nixon recognized the value of nurse practitioners in increasing the availability of primary care services. Congress demonstrated a similar attitude by providing a 3-year authorization for the training of certain types of nurse practitioners in the Nurse Training Act of 1967 and in the Comprehensive Health Manpower Act of 1971.

Nurse Training Act

Continuing Congressional concern with the issue of the availability of primary care services and reliance on the nurse practitioner as a partial solution to the problem is reflected in four pieces of legislation. The Nurse Training Act of 1975 established new authorities for special projects for nurse practitioners and also provided traineeships for individuals in nurse practitioner programs. The Health Professions Educational Assistance Act of 1976, as amended by the Health Services Extension

Act of 1977, authorized traineeships for nurses who resided in health manpower shortage areas and who promised to practice in those areas when they completed their practitioner training.

In 1978, during the Carter administration, the Nurse Training act of 1975, a 3-year authorization, expired. Because of ever-mounting concern with inflation, particularly in the health field, the administration took the position that the country had an adequate number of nurses and cut federal funding for nursing education in every area—except for nurse practitioner programs and special project grants. Congress, on the other hand, acting on the belief that there was a persistent nursing shortage, extended the legislation for 2 consecutive years, and Congressional action overrode a Presidential veto.

Thus, nurse practitioner programs remained the government's "fair-haired children" and have continued to hold great promise for meeting primary care health needs in underserved areas.

The federal programs authorized by the Nurse Training Act constitute by far the most important group, in expenditure, of all funding programs for nurse practitioners in the past decade. There are, however, some very sizable federal programs besides the nurse training authorizations that have directly or indirectly supported nurse practitioner programs in primary care, such as those of the Department of Defense, the Department of Labor, the Bureau of Health Resources Development, and the National Center for Health Services Research and Development.

It is crucial to note that since the mid-1960s, when the federal government determined that providing access to primary health service was a major priority, there have been a number of approaches other than nurse practitioner programs employed to rectify the situation.

Other Federal Programs

Six federal programs outside the realm of nursing were directed at affecting the supply of primary care services: practice-agreement-loan-for-giveness programs for medical students; rural preceptorships for medical students; increasing the number of family practitioners; increasing the number of physicians; the National Health Service Corps; and the training of physician's assistants. Five additional programs were launched to reduce barriers to access: Medicare, Medicaid, Neighborhood Health Centers, Children and Youth Projects, and Health Maintenance Organizations.

These programs had considerable bearing on the development of nursing's role in primary care for the important reason that they were geared to attracting physicians to practice in underserved areas. Beginning with the National Health Service Corps in 1970, federal programs have placed their highest dollar and otherwise stated health manpower priority on encouraging physicians to enter primary care specialties. Before the enactment of the Comprehensive Health Manpower Act in 1971, the federal government had already spent more than $1.9 billion to increase the supply of physicians. At the time when awareness of the lack of access to health care in underserved areas began, federal authorities reasoned that if the government trained enough physicians, they would eventually *have* to locate in underserved areas to practice because metropolitan and suburban areas would be glutted with an oversupply. Health policy observers such as Ginzberg (1989, 1990), however, learned that there is no way to get physicians to practice in an underserved area if they do not choose to live there.

The first major federal effort to remedy the problem of access to health services in underserved areas was directed exclusively toward the maldistribution of physicians by diverting them to rural areas to practice. The National Health Service Corps was established for this purpose by the Emergency Health Personnel Act 1970. Its original purpose was to "improve the delivery of health services to persons living in communities and areas of the U.S. where health personnel and services are inadequate to meet the needs of residents of such communities and areas."

At first, enrollment in the Corps took place on a voluntary basis, and the Corps' presence in a community was intended to last long enough to get a physician established in a community. The Corps was later expanded in size and directly tied to obligated service due to the lack of care in so many areas. Nurses entered its ranks in 1976, after strenuous lobbying efforts on the part of the nursing profession and an acute awareness that severe manpower shortages still remained.

In 1971 the federal government enacted the Comprehensive Health Manpower Act, which also acknowledged the necessity of encouraging redistribution efforts. Over $12 million was authorized for the specific purpose of attracting physicians to practice in rural underserved areas in the form of rural preceptorship programs. These programs operated on the assumption that medical students exposed to rural locations during training would choose to locate in these areas upon graduation. In addition, this legislation authorized another $20 million for family practitioner programs, encouraging physicians to go into primary care.

In total, the federal government has invested $1 billion in relatively unsuccessful efforts to encourage primary care physician practice in underserved areas. Federal authorities always turned to physicians first to resolve the maldistribution and access problems in the health care system; nurses were an afterthought. Many nursing leaders believe that the expansion of the primary care effort in medicine was an error (Robert Wood Johnson Foundation, 1978).

REIMBURSEMENT FOR PRIMARY CARE

While the question inevitably arises as to which political factors motivated the government to invest millions of dollars in an enterprise that would expand the role of nurses in the health care system, it is apparent that the expansion of nursing's "turf" was probably very much an unintended consequence of the federal government's support for nurse practitioner programs. Most federal authorities state that the main reason for the creation of the nurse practitioner was quite simply the provision of a substitute for a physician where none had existed. Illustrating this intention, the 1971 Nurse Training Act, the first federal program to fund the nurse practitioner program, states:

> The nursing special project authorities have made great contributions to improvement in nursing training. This program would be continued. New emphasis would be given to programs for training of pediatric nurse practitioners, nurse midwives, and family health practitioners. Few programs have as much potential for increasing the availability of health care as those who prepare nurses to perform tasks which heretofore have been performed only by physicians. (p. 468)

During the legislative session, conducted by Chairman Paul Rogers, in which the Nurse Training act of 1971 was introduced, Congressman Neal Smith if Iowa stated:

> Now Mr. Chairman, it is nice to hope that the bill that was passed just a few minutes ago to help educate physicians will provide enough doctors so that everybody can have a specialist for every ailment they have, but I do not believe it is going to happen. The only way we will have adequate medical service in this country is to delegate some of the doctors' responsibility to the nurses. And that is the reason I think this is an important bill. (p. 498)

Many other accounts substantiate the idea that nurse practitioner programs were developed to alleviate physician shortages. Federal experts reasoned that by allowing nurses to perform specific medical functions previously reserved for the physician, the problem of maldistribution of medical manpower could be addressed (First Report, 1977; Miller, 1978; Second Report, 1979). Because physicians are attracted to specific practice opportunities in the metropolitan areas, medical shortages are created in rural areas, small towns, and inner cities. In addition, the concentration of physicians in certain specialties created shortages of personnel, particularly in general and family medicine. Nurse practitioners were thus seen as a mechanism for increasing access to primary care in those areas where there was an existing need for medical care. In addition, the use of nurse practitioners for certain tasks was viewed as a way to free physicians' time for the provision of more intensive care, thereby extending the scope of their services. As nurse practitioners can be trained less expensively than physicians, it was also assumed that cost savings would result (DHEW, 1971).

The federal government, however, has been somewhat reluctant to deploy nurse practitioners as primary care providers. In no instance is this ambivalence more in evidence than in federal legislation authorizing reimbursement for nurse practitioners. Historically, federal policy has placed nurse practitioners in an untenable position in their ability to deliver primary care services. This double bind is excruciatingly apparent when one examines the reimbursement potential for nurse practitioners in the two largest federal programs, Medicare and Medicaid.

Medicare and Medicaid

Medicare and Medicaid were both authorized in 1965 under Title XVIII of the Social Security Act. Medicare is a nationwide program that provides health insurance protection to most individuals aged 65 and over, to persons under 65 who have been entitled for a period of 24 months to Social Security or railroad retirement benefits because they are disabled, and to certain workers and their dependents who need kidney transplantation or dialysis.

The Medicaid program is a federal-state matching program providing medical assistance for low-income persons who are aged, blind, disabled, or members of families with dependent children.

These programs together constitute the nation's largest single source of third-party payment for health services. At its outset, the Social Security Administration (SSA), the federal agency which administers these programs, did not allow reimbursement for services performed by nurse practitioners. The provision in the law that would govern reimbursement for nurse practitioners is the following section (1961 [2] [A] of Title XVIII) of the Social Security Act:

(1) the term "medical and other health services" means any of the following items of services. . .
(2) services and supplies (including drugs and biologicals which cannot,

as determined in accordance with regulations, be self-administered) furnished as an incident to a physician's professional service, of kinds which are commonly furnished in physician's offices and are commonly either rendered without charge or included in the physician's bills.

The Social Security Administration interpreted this provision to mean that nurse practitioner services were not eligible for reimbursement unless they were provided under the personal and immediate supervision of a physician and were services normally delegated by physicians. This interpretation of "normally delegated" did not recognize that nurse practitioners are trained to perform delegated tasks of diagnosis and treatment and that many states in fact authorize delegation of these tasks. As a result, nurse practitioners employed in private practice cannot be reimbursed for services provided to medicare beneficiaries. Similarly, federally funded health centers who utilize nurse practitioners as primary providers functioning under written protocols cannot be reimbursed.

This created a fundamental contradiction in federal policy. Although two government agencies have heartily promoted the training and development of nurse practitioners and looked to them as a potential solution of the problem of providing access to underserved populations, a third has stated that statutory authority does not allow payment for their services.

If the federal government had made a serious and wholehearted commitment to promoting the utilization of nurse practitioners in primary care, a cogent, systematic policy to accomplish this goal could have been implemented within the Medicare and Medicaid programs. In such a case the Social Security Act might have been amended at the federal level to allow payment for the services of nurse practitioners. Furthermore, federal officials could have worked with the states to develop legislation clearly defining the role of nurse practitioners and providing the necessary legal framework for them to carry out the duties for which they have been trained. While the federal government has no legal jurisdiction over state Medicaid laws or nurse practice acts, it could have worked to create an atmosphere that allowed these professionals to practice as they were prepared to practice. Federal input could have required states to devise uniform policies and definitions for nurse practitioners and recognized nurse practitioner services as more than incidental. In short, while the federal government could have been instrumental in establishing Medicare-Medicaid reimbursement for nurse practitioners, it continued to press forward with a health manpower policy that was severely hampered by its inherent contradictions (Miller, 1978).

In early 1977, the tide began to shift somewhat. As a result of a pressing need to increase access to health care for underserved populations, in addition to the fundamental contradiction perceived in federal health manpower and reimbursement policy, Congress finally began to initiate legislation to change Medicare reimbursement. A series of bills introduced in January 1977 proposed to amend Title XVIII of the Social Security Act to authorize payment for services provided by *physician extenders*, regardless of practice setting or geographical location. Later bills proposed added coverage for staff in community mental health centers, or authorized payment under state Medicaid programs. The discussion accompanying these bills centered in the problem of increasing access by encouraging nurse practitioner utilization while still containing costs.

At that time, the stated barrier to effecting the change that would permit nurse practitioner reimbursement was the federal contention that there were no empirical data available to measure the impact of a change in reimbursement policy. The more pressing reasons, however, are reflected in reports of the National Center for Health Services Research (1977; Roy, 1977) which estimated at the time that the policy change would increase Medicare outlays by roughly $4 million. Washington perceived that reimbursing nurse practitioners would constitute an "add-on" to rapidly escalating Medicare costs. On the one hand, federal policymakers sought to utilize nurse practitioners to increase access to health services for the poor and underserved; on the other, they claimed that reimbursement to nurse practitioners would be costly, driving up already skyrocketing costs. In short, nurses were caught in the middle of the federal dilemma. Nursing lobbyists were once again placed in an untenable situation; after being targeted as a potential federal solution to provide needed access to health care, nurses met with a great deal of resistance when they attempted to lobby for reimbursement policies that would make this goal possible.

Rural Health Clinics Act

At the same time, Congress was very concerned with the growing problem of fraud and abuse under both Medicaid and Medicare. Many members of Congress feared that nurse practitioner reimbursement could lead to more fraudulent practices in clinics that would now be staffed with nonphysician providers.

Congress reached a compromise solution, deciding to introduce proposals that would permit the reimbursement for Rural Health Clinics' services. These were defined to include nurse practitioner-physician's assistant services provided with or without a physician onsite. The final enactment of the Rural Health Clinics Act that passed both Houses of Congress on November 30, 1977, was a landmark victory for the nursing community. This bill amended Titles XVIII and XIX of the Social Security Act to provide payment for Rural health Clinics' services and directed the Secretary of the DHEW, through demonstration projects, to provide reimbursement for nurse practitioner-physician's assistant services in clinics in urban underserved areas. Major features of the bill include provision for reimbursement under Medicare at 80% of reasonable cost; and provision for reimbursement under Medicaid at 100% of reasonable cost.

The intent of Congress in enacting the Rural Health Clinics legislation appeared to be cautious movement into reimbursement for nurse practitioners. Indeed, the passage of this bill was a major step in this direction. Yet, because payment is still restricted to those nurse practitioner services authorized under state legislation, change has occurred on a limited basis, and in some cases has been impossible to effect.

Even after the federal government attempted through the Rural Health Clinics' services legislation to provide nurses with the tools needed to deliver health services to underserved populations, many state laws, bolstered by the strong political standing of state medical societies, still prohibit the legal functioning of any such entity as the nurse practitioner. A 1980 report published by the Texas Rural Health Field Services Program serves as a poignant illustration of this dilemma (Miller, 1978). The signing into law of Public Law 95-120, the Rural Health Clinics Act, was reported to have led to the following series of events because of restricted implementation of the act in Texas:

1. Formation of a Senate subcommittee which conducted four public hearings because of concern that state laws did not permit full implementation of Public Law 95-210;
2. A request for and the issuance of an attorney general's opinion as to whether certain services may be provided by a nurse practitioner acting under indirect physician supervision;
3. The introduction of Senate and House bills to resolve problems inherent within the issue of accepting standing orders (written sets of instructions designed for patient populations which delineate the health care to be provided);
4. Legislative interim charges to study the implications of the attorney general's opinion H-1295 on the use of protocols and standing orders in the provision of health services.

Most importantly, these actions led to the attorney general's opinion stating that the common practice of a nurse providing medications to patients through protocols and general standing orders was generally illegal. The Medical Practice Act, Physician's Assistant Rules and Regulations, the Nurse Practice Act, Guidelines for Advanced Nurse Practitioners, and the three pharmacy laws were examined in relationship to the legal usage of protocols and standing orders. The legal briefs were submitted to the attorney general and it was determined that:

1. Generally, a physician must have prescribed a medication for each *individual* patient prior to the provision of the medication.
2. In relationship to the provision of medication, a standing order is an unlawful method of prescribing.
3. There remains legal uncertainty as to the definitions of a medical act and a nursing act and when and where these acts overlap.
4. There is confusion as to the extent to which medical acts are legally delegable to a nurse and the type and degree of physician supervision required.
5. The legal status of nurses performing medical acts utilizing written protocols and/or standing orders is unclear.
6. However, standing orders which illegally delegate the provision of prescription medications are a vital tool used in all components of the health care delivery system in Texas.

Since the Rural Health Clinics Act specifically requires that the activities of the physician assistant and/or nurse practitioner shall be "consistent with the provision of state and local laws relative to the practice, performance and delivery of health services." only those clinics staffed with a *physician physically* present when the clinic was providing services were considered eligible for certification as a Rural Health Clinic in Texas. Consequently, the implementation of Public Law 95–210 in Texas was greatly retarded. The report concludes with a number of recommended legislative and administrative changes needed to *legally* continue the present level of health and medical care services in Texas (Miller, 1978).

FEDERAL FINANCING AND HEALTH CARE CURRENT PERSPECTIVES

Now, after several years and the expenditure of millions of dollars in federal funds, the initiative to involve nurses equipped with minimal medical skills has produced some 15,000 to 20,000 nurse practitioners throughout the nation with the potential to provide the primary care services they have been prepared to provide. It seems reasonable to expect the federal government to stand behind its commitment, and offer some leadership in the appropriate utilization of the nurse provider, especially in light of the serious national shortages of nursing resources. The Secretary's Commission on the Nursing shortage discovered in 1988 that the cause of the nursing shortage was not in the inadequate numbers of nurses but the inappropriate, inefficient utilization of registered nurses (Secretary's Commission, 1988). It is generally agreed that rational planning would be far more effective than policy constructed on a piecemeal basis in response to periodic, critical shortages.

It is the case, however, in any democratic, pluralistic society that policy in health matters is determined by a cadre of special interest groups, consumers, congressional representatives, and bureaucrats, each believing in a different path to follow. Many times, health professionals act on their belief that government is encroaching on their territory with the coercion of the federal dollar. From the government's perspective, the professions have not lived up to their original charge of providing quality care at affordable prices. The democratic process is designed to be and is responsive to the shifting pressures and priorities of a diversified public. Despite the fact that government has often been a helpful prime mover in manpower activities, federal decisions are not always made by employees of freestanding agencies. Policies are not fashioned in a political vacuum, but rather are an outgrowth of the legislative process which involves a whole array of special interest groups pressing for their own policies, standards, and controls.

During times of economic hardship, however, even the most powerful special interests must take a back seat to urgent, budget-driven considerations. The dramatically rising costs in health care have created a situation which has eliminated unilateral physician control in the health field because of the pressing need to decrease costs. Christopher Press, contributor to *Modern Health Care* (1991) has eloquently expressed the circumstances of this shift:

> Prospective payment—whether diagnosis-related groups, direct contracting or per diems—unmasked [the role of the physician]. Since it capped payment, it converted physician activity from revenue-generating (customer) to expense generating (margin eroding or margin-creating: a producer).

Thus, as a result of prospective payment, decisionmaking power in health care has shifted from traditional providers of care, physicians and hospitals, to purchasers of care, or those who pay the bills. Consumers or agents of consumers in the form of employers, insurers, and the Federal government are clearly in charge of health care spending.

Furthermore, physician fees have been the subject of close congressional scrutiny in a very nervous budget conscious environment (Hagland, 1991; Inglehart, 1991; Lee & Ginsburg, 1991). As physician fees continued to rise at an 18% annualized rate, even after economy-wide inflation had cooled to a modest 4–5% annualized rate, Congress decided to take the bull by the horns.

As a result, the Omnibus Budget Reconciliation Act of 1989 (OBRA 89) mandated that the Commission conduct a study of the impact that nonphysician providers have on cost of care. OBRA (1990) went further, authorizing Medicaid reimbursement for nursing services in two key areas: nurse practitioners and clinical specialists conducting required periodic visits to nursing facility residents, and nurse providers offering primary care and other services in designated rural health clinics.

In a cost-conscious climate of this nature, other providers, especially nurses, have indeed become more prominent in the decision making that determines health care policy. Since sentiment has been unanimous among policymakers that health care spending must be brought under control, nurses have found renewed receptivity among policy makers as well as the public at large for the expansion of nurses' roles.

In the 1980s, because of the state of the economy and the strong popular mandate from the American people to lower inflation and to cut down on government spending, resources allocated to the health field become more and more scarce. Because of the federal government's budget deficit woes, however, the states have been unable to expect any substantial assistance in addressing the health needs of the poor. Most states have severe financial problems and, unlike the Federal government, they can't borrow money indefinitely to pay for their share of the Medicaid cost. Medicaid spending rose to $68.5 billion nationwide in 1991, an 18% jump from the previous year. The states paid 44% or $29.7 billion of the bill. In 1981, the government paid for over 50% of the entire national cost for health care, spending over $275 billion. This figure becomes more meaningful if one considers that only a little more than three decades ago, in 1960, the nation spent $27 billion for health care. In 1990 we spent $671 billion on health care—twice the amount spent eight years ago—the government portion of that was approximately $360 billion.

Ushered in by popular mandate in 1980 to reduce economywide inflation, the Reagan administration took far-reaching actions in the health field in its drive to curtail health spending. The Omnibus Reconciliation Act of 1981, decreased federal spending by $36 billion, including $2.3

billion from the Medicare and Medicaid budgets. Every Reagan budget proposal since 1983 proposed cuts in health and social welfare programs, including Medicare, Medicaid, and other areas such as health manpower, nurse training, and public health programs. The 1985 budget proposal totally eliminated federal funding for nursing education.

The Bush administration similarly sought to keep the lid on health spending by introducing legislation measures to share hospital payments under Medicare and placing a moratorium on capital expenditures for hospitals under the Medicare program.

COST-BENEFIT RATIO OF NURSE PRACTITIONER PROVIDERS

In the midst of the strong desire to bring down health spending, many policy makers believe that utilizing nurses as primary care providers could result in a large savings for the health care system. Yet, as every administration since President Richard M. Nixon's has approached the question of cost control in the health field, the use of nurse practitioners in the delivery of primary care has been conspicuously absent as a viable policy option. Dr. Richard Rubin, Assistant Secretary for Planning and Evaluation in the Reagan administration, acknowledged this possibility, but no systematic attempts were made to include nurses in policy discussions regarding lowering health care costs. For a long time no administration had ever, on a dollar-for-dollar basis, seriously considered utilizing nurse providers in the mainstream of primary care as a cost-effective public policy initiative. In spite of the potential cost savings that could be realized by the system, it was a long time before nurse practitioners were taken seriously as a cost-savings option in the entire system. They were used, instead, to provide access to health care for certain groups and segments of the population that physicians did not choose to take care of. Promotion of the nurse practitioner as a low-cost option for the mainstream of society, a provider that consumers could visit and relate to as they did to the old family GP, has only recently been seriously considered.

This oversight is especially unsettling since the American public has always been receptive to using nurse providers and concerned enough about the problems of health care to welcome new measures to alleviate the situation. Although the executive branch has been reluctant to proceed in promoting the nurse practitioner role, Congress has shown interest. For instance, Senator Thomas A. Daschle (D-South Dakota) introduced two bills in 1990 to support primary nursing. Senator Daschle's bill to provide federal incentives for school-based, nurse-operated clinics ultimately did not succeed, but set an important precedent for planners looking at new alternatives in the nation's communities; his bill to allow direct reimbursement for rural-based nurse practitioners was approved by Congress and signed into law. In addition, other members of Congress such as Rep. Mary Rose Aakar (D-Ohio) have included nursing reimbursement language in their health reform packages.

Many benefits would accrue from the widespread use of nurse providers in primary, preventive, and emergency care. In very incisive economic terms, physicians, who are highly trained in expensive specialized and subspecialized care, do not constitute the best mix of human capital to serve the health care marketplace. Physicians are often poorly suited to provide primary care. A *New York Times* survey of the health care-consuming public taken in March 1982 demonstrated that many individuals in this country have started to think along similar lines. Surveyors asked a representative sample of adults throughout the United States how they would feel about seeing a nurse instead of a physician for primary care services if it would lower health care costs. Six out of ten said they would be very willing to see a nurse if it would lower their health care expenses.

A multitude of studies have been published regarding the ability of nurse practitioners to simultaneously lower the cost of care, improve access, and possibly even raise health status levels. As early as the 1970s, studies reported that nurse practitioners had greater success than physicians at lowering the diastolic blood pressure of hypertensive patients and in lowering the blood glucose levels of diabetics (Runyon, 1975). A Miami clinic staffed with nurse practitioners proved more cost-effective than an on-call physician (Hauri, 1979).

Despite the documented potential of nurse practitioners to generate significant savings in the health field, a number of reports sponsored by various government agencies have been pessimistic about the future of the nurse practitioner as a primary care provider. The political powers that dominate the health care system are the key to understanding the implicit message in these reports. One major reason stated for the lack of enthusiasm regarding the utilization of nurses in primary care is the projected oversupply of physicians by 1990. The Graduate Medical Education National Advisory Committee report (known as the GMENAC report) published in 1980 documented that there will be 145,000 physicians in excess of the number that will be needed by the year 2000 (Tarlov, 1980).

GMENAC (Tarlov, 1980) concluded that nurse practitioners, physician's assistants, and nurse-midwives make positive contributions to the health care system when working in close alliance with physicians. The Committee supported the practice of *nonphysician providers,* even though they did not endorse the concept of independent practice for these providers, and stated that nonphysician providers enhance patient access to services, decrease costs, and provide a broader range of services. The report even acknowledges that certain consumers prefer the nonphysician provider. Yet, it goes on to urge caution:

> A public policy dilemma occurs in an era of physician surplus because we do not know how simultaneously to preserve or extend the nonmedical services of nonphysician providers without simultaneously extending their contribution to the medical surplus. . . . Extensive research is needed to determine the relative efficacy of medical services provided by nonphysicians and physicians. (p. 34)

The report goes on to recommend that until such research is completed, "the number of nurse practitioners, physicians assistants and nurse midwives should remain stable at their present numbers" (p. 43). These recommendations appear to contradict earlier statements in the report, which espoused the cost benefits of utilizing nonphysician providers in primary care.

In contrast to GMENAC's final recommendation, tempered with what the Committee apparently considered to be the political realities of the system, Dr. Claire Fagin, Dean of the School of Nursing at the University of Pennsylvania, who served on the Secretary's Task Force on Competition, advocated that a very different direction be taken in utilizing nurse practitioners in the development of health policy. After enumerating several studies that document the cost benefit of using nurses for the delivery of primary care, she stated:

> From the standpoint of opening the system, the studies cited earlier (in this article) have shown that nurses are cost-effective providers of a wide variety of primary care services. Not only are their direct costs lower than those of physician providers but the cost of ancillary services is greatly reduced when nurses are the primary carers. These cost benefits must be made accessible to consumers by new state and federal legislation. Barriers must be eliminated which prevent direct access to nurses for ambulatory health services for children and teenagers, prenatal and postnatal care, nursing-determined home care, and care of the elderly. (Fagin, 1972, p. 59)

A report published by the Office of Technology Assessment (OTA, 1986) cites the benefits that accrue from the utilization of nurse practitioners. Summarizing the findings of the numerous studies of physician extender performance in a variety of practice settings, the report cites the conclusion of the Congressional Budget Office:

> Physician extenders have performed as well as physicians with respect to patient outcome, proper diagnosis, management of "indicator" medical conditions (an indicator condition according to Spitzer is a distinct clinical entity occurring frequently in primary care, with an outcome that can be affected favorably or adversely by choice of treatment), frequency of patient hospitalization, number of drug prescriptions, documentation of medical findings and patient satisfaction. (OTA, 1986, p. 78)

The report also cites the results of a study that concluded that between 75% and 80% of adult primary care services and up to 90% of pediatric primary care services could be delegated to physician extenders (OTA, 1986). The purpose of Record et al.'s study (1980) was to estimate different combinations of physicians and physician extenders that could produce given levels of primary care services. Cost estimates associated with the various configurations revealed potential cost savings of $0.5 billion to over $100 billion in cases with higher physician extender participation. This amounted to 19% to 49% of total primary care provider costs.

In spite of the plethora of studies and reports that the OTA Report (1986) enumerates specifying the cost benefits of utilizing nurses in primary care, it concludes, that "the use of nurse practitioners and physicians [sic] assistants results in productivity gains and cost reductions. Yet, their future participation in medical care delivery is uncertain" (p. 84).

The Report urges caution:

> In evaluating the role of physician extenders, it is insufficient to assess their cost effectiveness without also looking at who gains from the savings. Are the financial benefits of lower training and employment costs to be shared with the public or reaped only by providers? (p. 86)

and it concludes:

> With the existing structure of health services financing and delivery and the recent vast expansion in physician supply, the number of NPs engaged in independent practice should be expected to remain very small. If any change in current practice patterns were to occur, it might entail efforts by NPs to move from institutional settings into physician private practices where ultimate authority would remain with the physician. With the growing supply of physicians, however, such employment opportunities for NPs may in fact diminish in the next decade. (p. 93)

In 1983 the Institute of Medicine (IOM) published a report of a 2-year study on nursing and nursing education which documents the benefits of utilizing nurse practitioners in the health care system: "Studies have demonstrated that qualified nurse practitioners provide primary health care services of an equal quality at less than one-half of the cost of primary care physicians" (IOM, 1983, p. 56). The study cites a paper prepared for the Select Panel for the Promotion of Child Health (1981), in which it is suggested that by involving nurse practitioners in reimbursement schemes and further supporting their role as primary care providers, health care could be rendered at a more reasonable cost. Like the GMENAC (Tarlov, 1980) and OTA (1986) reports, however, the IOM study does not, in the final analysis, issue a favorable forecast for the future utilization of nurse practitioners in the health system:

> Raising the supply of nurse practitioners, it is often argued, would reduce the volume of unmet needs occasioned by the shortage of medical and generalized nurse providers. However, in the face of present legal and reimbursement constraints, theoretical arguments supporting greater numbers of nurse practitioners will not necessarily increase their supply. (IOM, 1983, p. 87)

Despite the economic evidence supporting greater utilization of nurses in primary care, the federal reports cited do not see this as a viable policy direction. The seeming contradictions in these reports can be traced to the political landscape of the health care system, the undertones reflecting physician control or influence over most health care spending in the United States. As Enthoven (1980) expresses it: "Even though it may not appear so on an organization chart, physicians are the primary decision makers in the health care system" (p. 28). It is from this position of power and control that physicians as a group have erected political and legal barriers to the practice of nurses as primary care providers.

Goodman (1980) gives the following historical account of organized medicine's actions with regard to the utilization of physician extenders: "In December 1970 the AMA's House of Delegates recommended that state medical practice acts be amended to remove any barriers to the increased delegation of tasks to allied health personnel by physicians" (p. 47). As more and more states began to follow this recommendation, however, the concern of organized medicine began to grow. In its December 1971 meeting, the AMA's House of Delegates recommended that new legislation be written so that the physician extender "will not supplant the doctor in the sphere of decision-making required to establish a diagnosis and plan therapy" (p. 1). Goodman (1980) reasons that the view that only the physician should make diagnoses and plan therapy was motivated by a desire to supplement, not substitute for, physician services.

Dolan (1980) also addresses the issue of physician dominance of the health care system and speculates as to medicine's "broad susceptibility" to antitrust attack. He states:

> In order to maintain its hegemony, the medical profession has discouraged its members from cooperating with these [nonphysician providers] competing groups. History reveals that the [medical] profession is willing to go beyond mere dissuasion to prevent cooperative arrangements. It should be repeated that it is the patients of these insurgent providers who are the actual targets of these actions. Here, as in other areas we have seen, the medical establishment seeks to crush the competing providers in order to force their patients back into mainstream medicine." (p. 682)-

COMPETITION AND HEALTH CARE ECONOMICS

The future success of utilizing nurses in primary care to contain costs will undoubtedly and inevitably depend on nursing's ability to challenge the formidable political power of organized medicine at state and national levels. Fagin (1982) has expressed this situation in no uncertain terms: "It should be clear that proposals for direct reimbursement for nurse providers who substitute for physicians imply head-on competition with them for the health care dollar" (p. 56). Certainly, physicians realize nurse practitioners are potential rivals, as evidenced by resolutions (mentioned previously), passed by the AMA House of Delegates calling for ceased funding for midlevel practitioners (Goodman, 1980).

Debate on the subject of utilizing nurses in the primary care area promises to become more strident as policymakers increasingly consider injecting competition into the health care system to contain costs. The competition concept was introduced into health policy discussions as part of the general mandate to reduce inflation and government intrusion. Because of the still prominent public concern over the high cost of health care, competition discussions are continuing into the health policy dialogue of the 1990s, as discussions of national health insurance have in past decades.

Several competition proposals were introduced during the 96th and 97th sessions of the U.S. Congress by various lawmakers who believe that prices for health services should be managed by the fluctuations of the free market, in the same way other commodities are managed. More recently many in Congress and in the executive branch have commented that it is an error of assumption that health care is unique. They explain that, until recently, health care had been considered a sort of spiritual or social or collective good, and not thought of as an economic good. Therefore, policymakers in the past have believed that health care has to be thought about, treated, regulated, and managed by society in a unique way that departs from the way in which markets normally handle other economic goods. Those who view health care as a commodity criticize this philosophy and are convinced that the health care marketplace should be competitive (Enthoven, 1993).

The competition proposals being considered to date are all aimed at the freemarket philosophy. In addition, these options are geared to providing greater incentives for consumers to select low-cost options. Generally speaking, all embody the same major concepts noted below. These common denominators are geared to reforming the health care system to render it more competitive (Enthoven, 1993).

Tax Reform to Establish Fixed Dollar Subsidies

All the health care options that have been introduced call for changes in the tax laws to provide financial incentives to increase consumer awareness of costs. Currently, tax laws allow consumers to purchase health benefits for employees; and the employee essentially receives income in the form of health benefits without paying income tax on these benefits. This income tax exemption would only be maintained under the competition proposals if employees purchased lower-cost plans that would be limited to a certain maximum dollar amount. If an employee chooses to purchase a plan over that limit, it would be up to him or her to pay for it. If the employee chose a lower-cost option, he would receive a rebate. The idea is that the amount of financial help (tax break) a consumer might receive toward the purchase of a health plan should be only up to a fixed dollar amount. Persons choosing more costly coverage would have to pay the extra cost themselves.

Periodic Multiple Choice

Each consumer of health services would periodically "be able to choose among several "qualified" health plans." (Plans would become "qualified" by meeting government standards.)

Same Standards Would Apply to All Competing Insurances

Each health care plan would be subject to the same rules and premium-setting standards. These rules would include a federally mandated minimum set of benefits that would be offered to everyone irrespective of type of place of employment (Bergthold, 1993).

Consumer Cost Sharing

Through the use of substantial deductibles and co-insurance, consumers would become more aware of physician fees and hospital charges.

The overall theory of the competition approach pulls these various concepts together in the following way: The limited dollar amount (set by the government) that employers will be allowed to spend to purchase tax-free health plans on behalf of employees will pressure insurers to reconfigure plans congruent with a set of minimum benefits for that limited amount. Insurers, in turn will make demands on the delivery system to render health care services for the limited tax-free dollar amount. In a world of health care competition, insurance companies and health care agencies are likely to feel a great deal of economic pressure; and thus find it in their interests to seek out cost-saving options in order to attract more customers and compete with other health care institutions.

A system that places a high premium on the low-cost options would be likely to find the prospect of utilizing nurse providers in the primary care arena very attractive. Since insurers, who are the major purchasers of health care, will be seeking the most economical mix of health services to include in their plans, many policymakers believe that opportunities for nurse providers could expand considerably in a world of competition. Fagin (1981) expressed this opinion in a keynote address to the American Academy of Nursing: "The present push toward competition in health delivery system should be seized as an opportunity to lobby for legitimizing nursing's role and realizing its potential."

Resolution of contradictions in health policy at national, state, and local levels will only be possible when nurses grow in their understanding of the uses of political power, thus enabling them to engage in more active participation in the development of health policies.

NURSING AND THE POLITICAL PROCESS

Many authors have written about the need for nurses to become more active participants in the political process. Nursing is inevitably becoming more and more shaped by political decisions. Political participation is the most effective way to communicate the needs and desires of a and interests. Perhaps the greatest detriment to nursing resulting from the profession's lack of political participation are the restrictive reimbursement practices that directly limit nursing practice and indirectly prohibit individuals from receiving nursing care.

Although little research has been done on the political participation of nurses, Archer and Goehner (1981) reported the results of a study on the level of political participation of 1086 nursing service administrators. The participation rate of these administrators was very comparable to U.S. citizenry at large, representing mostly voting acts, which require little expenditure of time and energy. The comparability of the political participation of these nursing administrators with the general public is diminished when the educational level of the nurses in the study is taken into account. Sixty-eight percent of the nurses tested had master's degrees and higher, which is far from representative of the general population of the United States. Archer reports that she deliberately selected a group of highly educated nurses, believing that they would be more politically active. She subsequently had intended to ask questions about various political strategies they employed. The subjects were not, however, sufficiently active to warrant further exploration.

Any professional group desiring to have an impact on policy formulation in government must strive for political consensus and cohesion. The potential to shape health manpower policy and to promote nursing's role in primary care in the future will undoubtedly depend on nurses participating in the political arena in much greater numbers than has previously been the case. In addition, the strength of politically active nurses will depend on their greater willingness to seek compromise solutions in their own professional ranks in order to obtain greater unity and consensus. Obtaining a voice in policymaking is dependent on a group's ability to join together to elect its own leaders, who will in turn represent the group's collective interests.

Historically, there has been great disagreement and little cohesion among nurses regarding issues affecting nurses in primary care. Some supporters of the nurse practitioner movement have not objected to the government policy of utilizing nurse practitioners in areas where there is a physician shortage. Others have objected to the nurse practitioner concept from its inception, on the grounds that these nurses were actually practicing as physician substitutes. In an *American Journal of Nursing* article on reimbursement, Griffith (1982) addresses this issue:

> We need to break out of our theoretical isolation and examine how our professional language relates to the reality of the reimbursement system. For example, many nurses oppose having their services viewed as being substitutive for reimbursable physician services; they argue that the ser-

vices provided by nurses are unique. Philosophically and in practice, they may be right, but pragmatically, a preoccupation with the unique is counterproductive in today's legislative arena. (p. 409)

The issue of whether the nurse practitioner should practice independently or with physician supervision is also a source of great controversy. In 13 states nurses now have prescription and diagnostic privileges, and as a result, large numbers of nurses are now practicing independently throughout the nation. On the national level, groups representing over a million nurses endorsed *Nursing's Agenda for Health Care Reform*, (NLN, 1991) a proposed national health plan that explicitly calls for direct reimbursement for nurse practitioners and nurse-midwives. The future success of nurses in primary care will depend on whether we can devise a strategy for implementation that can:

- *Address organized medicine* on the issue of primary care nursing. A recent public opinion survey by Peter Hart Associates (1989) offers a blueprint for advancing nursing's agenda beyond medicine's traditional opposition. The Hart poll suggests that the public trusts nurses more than any other provider in the system and would like to see some of the reforms highlighted in nursing's agenda—including the increased usage of nurse practitioners. This is a position of strength from which nurses must be willing to move forward.
- *Build alliances with the business community*, whose health costs have soared to untenable levels in the past few years. The business community is demanding change and will be key to the successful enactment of any major change in health care,
- *Develop a groundswell of support* within the nursing community as well as among the general public. Health care of the future will be driven increasingly by consumer demand for quality care at a reasonable cost. No longer willing to approve of health policies and interventions on the word of the "experts" alone, consumers are coming of age politically and demanding that their perspective be counted along with the experts. Nurses should form strategic alliances with consumers to advance this vision.

In some parts of the nation nurses have worked to develop unity and have, indeed, used political strategies effectively to make significant legislative and political gains. In Maryland, for example, Marilyn Goldwater, a nurse delegate to the Maryland State Legislature, succeeded in organizing nursing's ranks to obtain third-party reimbursement (Goldwater, 1982). This effort began in 1977 and ended with the 1982 enactment of legislation that permits nurses to receive third-party payments. The pertinent phrase in the legislative language of the law is as follows; "Any insurance policy issued in accordance with this section may not require that, as a condition for the payment of benefits, the nurse midwife (nurse practitioner) must be employed by a physician or must act pursuant to a physician's orders" (Goldwater, 1982, p. 413).

Initially, the state medical society was successful in convincing the Maryland House of Delegates that direct physician supervision must be added to the proposal as an amendment. Goldwater, however, immediately directed her efforts to the state Senate and persuaded them to remove the provision mandating physician supervision. Ultimately, a compromise provision was included stating, in effect, that insurance companies *may* offer the services of nurse practitioners in their benefit packages, but are not *mandated* by law to do so. Health policy observers in Maryland are unsure of the extent to which the amendment will affect the implementation of the bill—but in any event, the legislation marks a major breakthrough in the nursing profession's struggle for autonomy and independence. Goldwater and her colleagues were astute enough to know that legislative gains in a pluralistic society are always incremental, and that an all-or-nothing approach that is unreceptive to compromise is counterproductive.

Another striking instance of nursing's progress in the political arena culminated in the appointment, in 1984, of Dr. Carolyne Davis to the position of Administrator of the Health Care Financing Administration, the agency having jurisdiction over the Medicare and Medicaid budgets. Dr. Davis is well known for her outstanding contributions in nursing and health care administration, but one of the key factors in her appointment was the leadership she provided in organizing the nurses in her Michigan congressional campaign district to reelect Representative Carl Pursell. Dr. Davis held several meeting at her home for nurses who wished to become active in the campaign. These meetings included a wide range of campaign activities, such as writing letters, developing brochures, and making phone calls and personal contacts as needed. Dr. Davis recruited nurses from all kinds of nursing organizations and different educational levels. In addition, she arranged speaking engagements for the Congressman before the nursing community in his district to elicit nursing support for his re-election. On these occasions, Congressman Pursell had an excellent opportunity to tell the nursing community how he would represent their interests. For every meeting Dr. Davis prepared a clear agenda to keep the group's unity of purpose in sharp focus and prevent them from slipping off into divisive tangents.

These examples of legislative gains for nurses illustrate that in the political process, gaining power and effectiveness depends mostly on participation in electoral politics. This means active involvement in some aspect of elections, with the ultimate goal the establishment of a voting bloc: a sizable segment of the voting population known to represent a special interest. In an election, a voting bloc will cast votes and campaign in favor of legislators that support their special interest group. When a large segment of votes is at stake, legislators understand that if they are to be elected, they must listen very carefully to the group's concerns. If the group has been instrumental in a legislator's election, she or he will listen all the more carefully. The ultimate aim for any group is to get its own representatives elected to the legislature so that they can be assured of a large degree of responsiveness to their opinions and goals.

CONCLUSIONS

The prospect of nurses functioning in the primary care arena would undoubtedly constitute a major step forward, not only for the consumer of health services, but for the nursing profession. Nursing's struggle for autonomy will become little more than an academic exercise if the profession does not acquire a greater degree of financial independence.

Decisionmaking in public policy is inextricably tied to a political environment that determines the allocation of resources in society. Control of health care resources—in large part financial resources—is essential if nursing is to have a voice in deciding how the health care system is to be run. If nurses wish to have a decisionmaking role in directing health policy in the primary care arena, some control of the health care dollar is essential. The future of nursing in the delivery of primary care services will indeed require financial independence. Achievement of financial independence, in turn, requires major political participation efforts on the part of the nursing community. Because of the requirement in most states that professional nurses function under the supervision of a physician, state nurse practice acts will have to be reshaped to allow nurses the necessary freedom to render competitive, cost-effective primary care services. Restrictive reimbursement practices that prohibit individuals from procuring necessary primary care services must be altered to allow nurses to receive third-party payment. Major revisions will be needed in state nurse practice acts and federal legislation to remove restrictions and allow nurses to deliver health services to the consumer public as independent providers. The first step in this undertaking must be political action; it is not only nursing's right but its moral obligation to learn the business of trading-off, negotiating, and compromising in the political arena.

REFERENCES

American Medical Association House of Delegates. (December 1971). *Essentials of an approved education program for the assistant to the primary care physician. 1.* Washington, DC: American Medical Association Press.

Archer, S., & Goehner, P. (1981). Acquiring political clout: Guidelines for nurse administrators. *Journal of Nursing Administration, 8,* 49–55.

Bergthold, L.A. (1993). Benefit design choices under managed competition. *Health Affairs, 12,* 99–109.

Califano, J. (1986). *America's health care revolution.* New York: Simon & Schuster.

Davis, C. (1992). New leaders needed. *Nursing and Health Care, 13,* 3.

Department of Health, Education and Welfare. (1971). *Extending the scope of nursing practice: A report of the Secretary's committee to study extended roles for nurses* (Publication No. HSM 73–2037). Washington, DC: U.S. Government Printing Office.

Department of Health, Education and Welfare [DHEW]. (1977). *First report to the Congress: Report of the Secretary of Health, Education, and Welfare on the supply and distribution of and requirements for nurses as required by Section 951, Nurse Training Act of 1975, Title IX, Public Law 94–63.* Washington, DC: Department of Health, Education and Welfare.

Department of Health, Education and Welfare [DHEW]. (1979). *Second report to the Congress: Nurse Training Act of 1975.* (Revised). Washington, DC: DHEW.

Dolan, A. K. (1980). Antitrust law and physician dominance of other health practitioners. *Journal of Health Politics, Policy, and Law, 4,* 675–690.

Emerging Health Personnel Act. (1970). PL 92–685. 84 Stat 868. Washington, DC: U.S. Superintendent of Documents.

Enthoven, A. C. (1993). The history and principles of managed competition. *Health Affairs, 12,* 24–48.

Fagin, C. M. (1981, September 21). *Nursing's pivotal role in achieving competition in health care.* Keynote address, American Academy of Nursing, Washington, DC.

Fagin, C. M. (1982). Nursing as an alternative to high-cost care. *American Journal of Nursing, 82,* 56–60.

Garrard, J., Kane, R., Ratner, E., & Buchanan, J. (1991). The impact of nurse practitioners on the care of nursing home residents. In P. Katz, R. Kane, & M. Mezey (Eds.), *Advances in long-term care: Vol. 1* (pp. 169–185). New York: Springer Publishing Co.

Ginzberg, E. (1989). Physician supply in the year 2000. *Health Affairs, 8*(2), 84–90.

Ginzberg, E. (1990). *The medical transfer: Physicians, politicians and the public.* Cambridge, MA: Harvard University Press.

Goldwater, M. (1982). From a legislator: View on third-party reimbursement for nurses. *American Journal of Nursing, 82,* 411–414.

Goodman, J. C. (1980). *The regulation of medical care: Is the price too high?* San Francisco: Cato Institute.

Griffith, H. M. (1982). Strategies for direct third-party reimbursement for nurses. *American Journal of Nursing, 82,* 408–411.

Hagland, M. M. (1991). The RBRNS and hospitals: The physician payment revolution on our doorstep. *Hospitals, 65*(4), 24–27.

Hauri, C. M., Morris, C., & Kein, L. (1979). Cost effective primary care. *The Nurse Practitioner, 4,* 54.

Hart, P. (1989). *Survey of attitudes toward health care and nurses.* New York: National League for Nursing.

Hayward, R., Shapiro, M., Freeman, H., & Corey, C. (1988). Inequities in health care services among insured Americans: Do working-age adults have less access to medical care than the elderly? *New England Journal of Medicine, 318,* 1507–1512.

Inglehart, J. K. (1991). The struggle over physician-payment reforms. *New England Journal of Medicine, 325*(11), 823–828.

Institute of Medicine [IOM] (1983). *Nursing and nursing education: Public policies and private actions.* Washington, DC: National Academy Press.

Kane, R., Garrard, J., Skay, C., Radosevich, D., Buchanon, J., McDermott, S., Arnold, S., & Kepferle, I.. (1989). Effect of a geriatric nurse practitioner on the process and outcomes of nursing home care. *American Journal of Public Health, 79,* 1271–1277.

Lee, P. R., & Ginsberg, P. B. (1991). The trials of Medicare physician payment reform. *Journal of the American Medical Association, 266*(11), 1562–1565.

Mezey, M., & Lynaugh, J. (1991). Teaching nursing home program. A lesson in quality. *Geriatric Nursing, 12*(2), 76–77.

Miller, H. C. (1978). *Review and analysis of state legislation and reimbursement practices of physicians' assistants and nurse practitioners* (Executive Summary, Report No. HRA 230-77-0011). Washington, DC: U.S. Department of Health and Human Services, National Center for Health Sciences Research.

Moccia, P. (1992). In 1992: A nurse in every school. *Nursing and Health Care, 13,* 14–18.

National Center for Health Services Research. (1977). *Financing and reimbursement of graduate medical education.* Rockville, MD: U.S. DHEW.

Nurse Training Act of 1971. (PL 92-158). 85 Stat. 465. Washington, DC: U.S. Government Printing Office.

Nursing's agenda for health care reform. (1991). New York: Author. National League for Nursing.

Office of Technology Assessment. (1986). *Nurse practitioners, physician assistants, and certified nurse-midwives: A policy analysis* (Health Technology Case Study 37), OTA-HCS-37. Washington, DC: U.S. Government Printing Office.

Omnibus Budget Reconciliation Act of 1981. (PL 97-35, 95 Stat. 35). Washington, DC: U.S. Government Printing Office.

Omnibus Budget Reconciliation Act of 1989. (OBRA: Publication 101-239) 103 Stat. 2 106. Washington, DC: U.S. Government Printing Office.

Omnibus Reconciliation Act of 1990. (OBRA PL 101-50F). 104 Stat. 1388. Washington, DC: U.S. Government Printing Office.

Press, L. (1991). Patients, not physicians, are hospitals' customers. *Modern Healthcare*, 21(25), 30.

Record, J. C., McCally, M., Schweitzer, S. D., Blomquist, Z. M., & Berger, B. D. (1980). New health professionals after a decade and a half: Delegation, productivity, and costs of primary care. *Journal of Health Politics, Policy, and Law*, 5, 470–497.

Reinhold, R. (1982). Majority in survey on health care are open to changes to cut cost. *New York Times*, March 29, 1 3.

Riner, M. (1989). Expanding services: The role of the community health nurse and the advanced nurse practitioner. *Journal of Community Health Nursing*, 6, 223–240.

Robert Wood Johnson Foundation. (1978). First Annual Symposium.

Rogers, M. E. (1978). Legislative and licensing problems in health care. *Nursing Administration*, 2, 71–78.

Roy, W. (1971). *Effects of the payment mechanism on health care delivery system*. Hyattsville, MD: National Center for Health Services Research.

Runyon, J. W. (1975). The Memphis chronic disease program: Comparisons in outcome and the nurse's extended role. *Journal of the American Medical Association*, 231, 264–267.

Rural Health Clinics Act of 1983. U.S. Code 42 Section 254g.

Select Panel for the Promotion of Child Health. (1981). *Better health for our children: A national strategy. Vol. 1*, Report to Congress and the Secretary of Health and Human Services. Washington, DC: U.S. Government Printing Office.

Social Security Act. (1988). U.S. Code 42 Section 1395ec–1399.

Smith, N. (1971). *Hearings before the subcommittee on public health and environment of the committee on interstate and foreign commerce*. House of Representatives 92nd Congress, 1st session HR 4156. Washington, DC: U.S. Government Printing Office.

Tarlov, A. (1980). *Report of the Graduate Medical Education National Advisory Committee to the Secretary*. Washington, DC: U.S. Department of Health and Human Services, Public Health Service, Health Resources Administration.

INDEX

Springer Publishing Company

AN ADDICTIONS CURRICULUM
For Nurses and Other Helping Professionals: Volumes I and II

Elizabeth M. Burns, RN, PhD, FAAN,
Arlene Thompson, RN, PhD, and
Janet K. Ciccone, MA, APR, Editors

These two volumes present a comprehensive model program for teaching nurses about alcohol and drug addiction. It is specifically designed to be integrated into existing nursing courses, but can also be taught as a separate course. Both classroom and hands-on clinical learning are covered. Volume I is designed for undergraduates and includes a special section on training faculty. Volume II is for graduate and advanced-level students.

Volume I: Basic Knowledge and Practice

Contents: Foreword, *H. Werley* • Guide to Using The Addicitons Curriculum • Introduction to Alcohol and Other Drug Use, Abuse, and Dependence: A Focus on Education and Prevention, *A. Thompson* • The Psychosocial Effects of Chemical Abuse and Dependence, *C. Bininger* • Chemical Dependence: Assessment and Prevention of Medical Complications, *C.A. Baker* • Clinical Experiences with Treatment of Chemical Dependence (Tertiary Dependence), *A. Thompson and C. Bininger* • Professional, Legal, and Ethical Issues: An Integrative Seminar, *C. Bininger and A. Thompson* • Faculty and Staff Development: Chemical Dependence and Nursing Education, *A. Thompson & B. Melragon*

288pp   0-8261-8190-2   *softcover*

Volume II: Advanced Knowledge and Practice

Contents: Foreword, *H. Werley* • Introduction: Concept and Content • Health Promotion and Risk Reduction for Use and Misuse of Alcohol and Other Psychoactive Drugs, *M. E. Wewers* • Central Nervous System Effects of Psychoactive Drugs, *E.M. Burns and J.D. Wagner* • Chemical Dependence Issues of School-Age Youth and Adolescents, *E.M. Menke* • Interventions with Families Experiencing Chemical Dependence, *J.A. Clement* • Older Adults and Alcohol, Psychoactive Drugs, and Over-the-Counter Drugs: Misuse, Abuse, and Dependence, *J.S. Stevenson* • Central Nervous System Effects of Psychoactive Drugs: A Review, *E.M. Burns*

392pp   0-8261-8191-0   *softcover*

536 Broadway, New York, NY 10012-3955 • (212) 431-4370 • Fax (212) 941-7842

Springer Publishing Company

THEORY-DIRECTED NURSING PRACTICE

Shirley M. Ziegler, PhD, RN, Editor

The book first describes and then illustrates the use of critical thinking in moving from theory to the actual steps of the nursing process. Client cases are presented, and competing theories that might be used to direct nursing process are briefly introduced. Finally, one theory is selected for illustration for each case. The volume covers a range of theorists not found in other texts, including Aguilera, Messick, Bandura, Beck, Bowen, Erickson, Lazarus, Lewin, and Thomas.

Contents:

280pp   0-8261-7630-5   hardcover

536 Broadway, New York, NY 10012-3955 • (212) 431-4370 • Fax (212) 941-7842